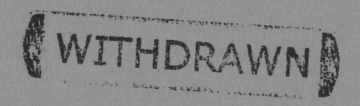

*Books for the Millions*

# *Books*
# *for the*
# *Millions*

A HISTORY OF THE MEN
WHOSE METHODS AND MACHINES
PACKAGED THE PRINTED WORD

## Frank E. Comparato

THE STACKPOLE COMPANY, *Harrisburg, Pennsylvania*

"ROWS OF TYPE, AND NOTHING MORE": Linotype Caslon and Janson faces offset printed two thirty-twomos up on #60 antique stock. Composition and manufacture by The Book Press, Brattleboro; jacket printed by Algen Press Corp., New York; design and layout by the author, Beverly Hills.

"THINGS THAT STEAM CAN STAMP AND FOLD": Machine forwarded and sewn eight sheets on by Smyth No. 12 machines; cased in and pressed on Smyth equipment. Canfield colortext endleaf, Interlaken bookcloth, Lustrofoil gold.

Library of Congress Catalog Card No. 71–162441

Standard Book Number 8117–0263–4

*Printed in the United States of America*

TO *My Mother*

who taught me what
books are all about

# ACKNOWLEDGMENTS

My profound thanks are due to the following people who generously granted interviews or furnished historical materials; many of them have personally participated in bindery development or are descendants of the principals of this history.

Mr. Charles Aaron, Cameron Machine Company
Mr. Charles E. Brainard, The Smyth Manufacturing Company
Mr. Oscar Bredenberg, Champlain, New York
Mr. Victor Bredenberg, Windsor, Connecticut
Mr. Joseph Coviello, Easton, Pennsylvania
Mr. Joseph A. Daley, East Setauket, New York
Mr. Walter G. Evans, Old Windsor, England
Mr. S. G. Gervase, John F. Cuneo Company
Mr. T. Blair Hawkes, Easton, Pennsylvania
Mr. Wolcott M. Heyl, Philadelphia, Pennsylvania
Mr. Paul E. Kleineberg, Easton, Pennsylvania
Miss Marian Lawson, London, England
Miss Rotha G. Matthews, East Orange, New Jersey
Mr. Theodore Meier, Martini Bookbinding Machinery Company
Miss Fay Margolis, F. M. Charlton Company
Mrs. James Moore, Croton Falls, New York
Mr. W. Pertuch, The Franklin Institute, Philadelphia
Mr. George W. Prentiss, Holyoke, Massachusetts
Mr. Allan Ramsey, Thomas Nelson & Sons, Ltd.
Dr. Joseph W. Rogers, Arlington, Virginia
Mr. Lynn B. Tipson, The Sheridan Company
Mr. John T. Zurlo, The Sheridan Company

My thanks are also offered to the following firms which generously supplied descriptive material on current bindery equipment:

Cameron Machine Company, Dover, New Jersey
The Crawley Book Machinery Company, Newport, Kentucky
E. C. Fuller Company, New York
Geliot-Hurner-Ewen, Ltd., London
MGD Graphic Systems, Inc., New York
Schuler Sales and Service Company, Bergenfield, New Jersey
The Sheridan Company, Easton, Pennsylvania
The Smyth Manufacturing Company, Bloomfield, Connecticut

Particular appreciation goes to Mr. Paul D. Doebler, Editor of *Book Production Industry*, for permission to quote extensively from that journal and its predecessors, *Book Industry, Book Production, Bookbinding and Book Production,* and *Bookbinding*. Similar acknowledgment of heavy use is made to *Publishers' Weekly* and *Inland Printer/American Lithographer*. Notice must also be made of the American Type Founders' collection at the Library Service Library, Columbia University, for many unique 19th-century materials in typography and bookmaking.

F.E.C.

# CONTENTS

# Introduction:

# The Books of Old

ONE DAY IN 1887 AN IRATE BIBLIOPHILE WROTE A SHARP LETTER TO THE editor of a book-trade journal, concluding in desperation, "To execute artistic bookbinding through the aid of machinery is almost as impossible as to paint a fine picture by the same means." By the use of the word "almost," this distinguished gentleman—the great Robert Hoe—left the book industry one chance to improve matters, for he might have known by then (he was himself instrumentally involved) that the ubiquitous machine would encroach everywhere.

The developments which forced this and similar observations upon distraught lovers of books, both in Europe and the United States, and the validity of their allegations, unfold in one frenetic century. That someone might perform the improbable task is not surprising of itself in today's world of contradiction and reversal. We smile understandingly at Arnett's 1837 appraisal of the industry: "To what greater perfection bookbinding may come it would be hazardous to give an opinion, seeing that now it appears scarcely capable of progressing much further. . . ." Yet, almost a century later when mechanization unsuspected by Arnett was not only accomplished but a matter of routine, it was criticized anew with absolute scorn by still unappreciative bibliophiles: "there is the cheap and nasty novel of to-day," said A. Edward Newton, who seemed to hold the manufacturer accountable for literary quality as well, ". . . written on a typewriter, printed and bound by machinery, sold by the hundreds of thousands, and forgotten as soon as read."

There was, however, in those one hundred years more than mere contradiction and irony. There were problems and inadequacies of traditional bookmaking and selling; inspiration and persistence among publishers and binders who saw those shortcomings; and trials, frustrations, and successes among machinery makers who tried to remedy them. Thus bookmaking efforts span three distinct industries, all striving with some dignity to identify themselves with a single distinguished product: the book.

As an entity the book quietly owes its integrity to its binding. Arnett's treatise on bookbinding defined this subject as the "Art of arranging the pages of a book in proper order, and confining them there by means of thread, glue, paste, pasteboard and leather." These are still the essentials of it (although changing rapidly); they encompass in addition the scope of labor and operations which, for all practical purposes, insure that the printed words so encapsulated do endure the ravages of time and moderate use. William Matthews, acknowledged "the greatest binder of America—indeed, the only great binder of America" called such work (the *forwarding*—sewing, shaping the spine, making and attaching the cover) the true domain of the bookbinder; the remainder (the *finishing*—decorative work upon the cover) would always be superficial, and serve to protect the book only by making the shell artificially precious. Yet, exterior excellence had been the classic—if distorted—viewpoint of fine bookwork even before the invention of printing.

With the greater dissemination of books in the middle ages, binding treatment became increasingly formalized. Leather clearly was paramount as a covering material because of its ample supply, its suitability as a hinge, and its receptivity to attractive finishes and hand tooling. Goatskin was available in morocco, levant, or niger finishes; seal and pigskin were also good for bookwork; calfskin as calf or russia and sheepskin as skiver or roan wore poorly and were considered cheap materials. Leather was decorated either by "blind" (unpigmented) hammering called *cuir bouillé* (French, "dressed leather") or blind cutting called *cuir ciselé* ("chiseled or carved"), to obtain designs in relief, or by stamping with metal dies, alone or in combinations, blind or with gold leaf. The inside cover or lining (French *doublé*, "doublure") was often decorated like the outside, as French collectors disdained a sudden change from heavily ornamented cover to plain endsheet. Such handwork, more or less costly and ornate, enjoyed several major periods of excellence:

(1) Aldine or Early Italian (early 16th century): named after the printer Aldus Manutius who employed Venetian bookbinders; characterized by vestiges of arabic design ("arabesques"), interlaced cablework, and sunken almond-shaped panels.

(2) Maioli or Later Italian (mid 16th century): named after French collector Thomas Maioli (or Mahieu), secretary to Catherine de Medici; characterized by rich floral borders with center panel containing book title.

(3) Grolier (mid 16th century): named after bibliophile Jean Grolier de Servières (1479–1565), Treasurer-General of France, who designed many of his own bindings; characterized by interlaced bands in outer borders, title in center panel.

(4) Eve/Fanfare (late 16th, early 17th century): named after French father and son Nicolas and Clovis Eve, Royal Binders 1579–1634 (successively); characterized by all-over patterns of small stamps. Fanfare, actually named when the style was rediscovered (p 35), is characterized by diapered geometric compartments, rectangular or oval, each heavily decorated.

(5) Le Gascon/Du Seuil (17th century): "Le Gascon" vaguely identifies a group of unknown French binders whose work is characterized by very delicate *pointillé* (dotted-line) designs. The work of Augustin Du Seuil (1673–1746), French Royal Binder, is characterized by wide *dentélle* (lace-like) borders and lavish doublures.

(6) Jansenist (late 17th century): A French style using only blind linework; very severely conservative.

(7) Derome/Padeloup (18th century): "Nicolas the younger" with his exquisite *dentélle* borders is acknowledged master of the prolific Derome family of binders. Antoine-Michel Padeloup (1685–1758) worked for Madame Pompadour; his work is characterized by a style similar to the Deromes, and also by "mosaic" (inlaid colored leathers) bindings.

(8) Harleian (18th century): named after Robert Lord Harley, first Earl of Oxford, who bequeathed his library to Oxford University; characterized by lozenge-shaped designs with borders done by fillet (cylindrical tool rolling a continuous engraved pattern).

Fine binding is regally defined—for a single book as well as a complete library—as the clothing of a work according to its character, its merit, or its destination. As an art it served most persuasively to furnish a cultured gentleman with a large collection of esthetically compatible books, suited to the owner's taste and pocketbook. Noblemen of the 17th and 18th centuries had so established the status of such libraries the collector of even modest means a century later felt compelled to follow. In an early United States the eroding factors of shortages in workmen and materials, the democratization of scholarship, and the impatient pioneer temperament scarcely mitigated the enthusiasm for a good-looking library. Well beyond the 1850's the paperback was properly deemed suitable, as in France, only for later definitive binding in morocco. Anything else was quite unacceptable:

"Muslin binding, so much in vogue [an American newspaper reflected in 1867], has nothing to defend it. It is paltry, perishable, and at the same time expensive, and as every different work is bound in an independent style and of an independent size, it is far from suitable for libraries. A row of books in faded, many-colored muslin covers, variously gilded, and no two volumes alike in height, presents a motley and distasteful confusion. . . ."[1]

As late as the turn of the century muslin or buckram (considered today the best available covering material) was to bibliophiles still a coarse, cheap expedient.

To avoid the chromatic disharmony of unrelated bindings, the role of color and decoration under the doubtful umbra of new perceptual sciences was never more firm. For those affluent but unwitting collectors who furnished their binders no specific instructions (one, according to Zaehnsdorf, was so unacquainted with the craft he brought in a book one day for binding and professed to wait for it), schemes were formulated for the logical development of a coordinated book collection. Dark blue was recommended for serious works; light blue was "distinctly feminine"; purple for religion; gray was "effacing, relentless"; white "bespeaks candor and truth"; various reds described the passions of man while greens reflected life and growth.

These general guidelines gave way to others, seriously proffered with considerably less subtlety. Botany must have a floral design "made to grow from a stem"; political economy was "antagonistic" to decoration but natural history may be quite ornate; Chaucer called for flowers, Shakespeare for a spear, and Spenser for a lion. But why? said T. J. Cobden-Sanderson, who in the 1890's found the state of custom bookbinding so deplorable he wanted to start a guild to set some sensible rules. But the color codifiers would not stop: a decade later binders were advised to observe "scientific" tests establishing the power of colors: ruby red (passion, energy), scarlet (force, triumph), vermillion (bitterness, cruelty), yellow-green (hope, bounty), blue-green (richness, sonority), lemon-yellow (cheer, activity), and so on.

Fine binding, nevertheless, as with fine art in general, is recognized as paying absolutely no heed to cost, whereas its industrial brother pays it all due attention. Where the cult of fine binders and collectors overwhelmingly devoted themselves to preservation of sumptuous books (without necessarily reading them), the industrial bookmaker worked for the impecunious mass reader who owns, reads, and treasures his literature, such as it is, sometimes with as much pleasure as the collector. In the fine binding the beauty had been in the materials and the care; in the commercial binding it is in economical and speedy production. The book and its appearance has always meant many things to different people but the communicative power of its contents has seldom been disputed.

It is generally acknowledged that Gutenberg intended specifically to reproduce books when he developed moveable type and printing press. The book (from Anglo-Saxon *boc*, beech, referring to the inner bark used as a writing surface), since Gutenberg's time acclaimed "the noblest form of printing," has never been suitably defined except to describe the materials from which it is made. Until the beginning of the industrial revolution, nevertheless, the scarcity of books had not only inflated their own value, it created an awe and appreciation for literature and education which still endures. An army of bibliophiles soon hoarded much of what tomes were not chained to church and monastery lecterns. Their profound—if rabid—respect for the printed word largely motivated the care exercised on bindings; for this historians must sometimes be thankful, as many ancient pages— ordinarily ephemera—have survived today only because their covers were too precious to destroy.

John Pleger, who himself contributed significantly to the industrialization of bookwork, paradoxically seemed to regret the collapse of such old values. In 1924 he wrote:

"Could the craftsmen of the sixteenth to the nineteenth centuries see the present decadence of the bookbinding art, which in their time was on a par with painting and sculpture, they would view with horror its prostitution, and the lowering of the standard may be largely attributed to the lethargy of the bookbinders in permitting without protest the selection of men who have no knowledge of binding material, and are unable to distinguish between genuine and imitation leathers, to determine the styles of binding. . . ."[2]

Although the French, and, as we shall see, isolated groups in London and New York, all under extraordinary circumstances, shared Pleger's —and Hoe's—concern, it was a difficult position to maintain. Nostalgic confusion seems built into this often quoted 19th-century verse:

"Not as ours the books of old—
Things that steam can stamp and fold;
Not as ours the books of yore—
Rows of type, and nothing more."[3]

Pleger's enlightened contemporaries in the 1920's had quite another view. As a century of books tumbled from the industrial binderies for a hungry reading public, perceptive bookmen—beginning with Charles Knight—had lauded them not as prized possessions to be locked up, but as mediums of information and entertainment to be distributed as widely as possible. If we are to do justice to the author, we must admit that his tome, however handsome, is not an end in itself. "Type, stitching and paper," are not the book, said Cornelius Mathews, whose 1842 plea was for international copyright: ". . . When you buy a book you do not buy the whole body of its thoughts in their entire breadth and construction, to be yours in fee simple for all uses . . . but simply the usufruct of the book as a reader. . . ." "When we hold it in our hands," said Robert Escarpit, a modern commentator, "all we hold is the paper: the *book* is elsewhere. . . ."

Similarly, books are indeed perishable, if literature is not. Francis Meynell's expostulation must almost daily be repeated to those who would make indestructible books:

"A book is planned to be read, not to be examined through a microscope, not even to be held close up to the eye for the detection of possible minute imperfections. A stained-vellum binding for which I was lately responsible won a very hearty general approval. Then a critic said to me 'But will the colour hold? Have you tried putting it out in the sun?' To which my answer was, 'No, nor in a hot bath nor a dish of porridge.' "[4]

Meynell, in his own way, had eccentricities of course: he favored buckram as an "almost noble cloth" (just two decades after fine binders were still condemning it), although for economy he recommended a canvas spine and paper sides. "[A] label should be on the spine only," he added, "not on the side (the proper place for a book is on its shelf or in the hand, being read). . . ."

A 1927 French publication revealed the modern art viewpoint:

"A book is physically perfect when it is pleasant to read, delightful to look at; when, in short, the transitions from reading to contemplation to reading are very easy and correspond to the imperceptible changes of visual adaptation. Then the blacks and whites are at rest in relation one to the other, the eye moves about without effort in its well-arranged domain, appraises its ensemble and details, and is sensitively aware that the ideal conditions for its proper functioning are present. . . ."[5]

It is no oversight that this gallic definition of book excellence does not include any requirements for the binding.

In the manufacture of books for the millions, utility, not magnificence, is the criterion—and it is a special utility based on quantity. The more important a work of literature is, the more bold a publisher can be in manufacturing it with some taste and individuality. Price is secondary. But in the scramble to appease popular literary tastes, competition is keen and lure and price are foremost considerations. Industrialization has shown the publisher, like every other manufacturer, that economies are effected as quantities increase—provided, of course, that all operations are indeed mechanized. But a spiraling factor is also at work: the larger the quantity, the more acute are the manufacturing costs—and often, the smaller the profit for all.

Thus the small, selective publishers have made little contribution to the industrialization of the book, except to set up classic standards of design and workmanship. Sifting through many manuscripts for a few best sellers, they don't economize foremost and they don't cater to a mass market; their success so revolves around the prestige of their authors they pay only token notice to manufacturing. Many such publishing empires have come and gone, unfortunately, like fiery rockets, for publishing entrepreneurship at its theatrical best goes by no business rules that less gifted practitioners can follow.

The more commercial publishers, however, directing their efforts to the mass reader, did not only foment a revolution in reading by the ambitious scope of their sales concepts. Necessarily, they also sought from their printers and binders the concessions—in speed and quality, to be sure—that would give them, cheaply, books for the millions. Few publishers of stature have been unfamiliar with printing and binding technology—a surprising number of them in fact having practiced at one of those trades before turning to the nobler pursuit of literature.

So the history of mechanized bookmaking follows the course of the most popular type of package. The popular or general "trade" book is the novel which, ironically, if not itself a product of the Industrial Revolution, certainly has paralleled it since the decline of poetry. Michael Sadleir has established the novel's position in bookmaking:

"[The novel has always] been constructed with a keener eye for economy and utility and with less thought of eccentricity, elegance or embellishment than any other *genre* of published work; so that in a structural sense it occupies a sort of central position in the scale of book-building possibilities and probably represents at any one period the norm of practical and cheap design."[6]

The more ambitious or successful a publisher is with a cheap series, the more influential is his pressure on binders to develop cheaper and faster processes; only with this compelling drive have binders them-

selves succeeded in getting machinery manufacturers to furnish greater
and greater automation. Joseph Rogers, in his pioneering 1941 work
on bindery industrialization, seemed reasonably satisfied with the situation in America:

> "For the general purpose of the publishing trade and the requirements
> of the average book buyer, the usual edition binding is an eminently
> satisfactory article, sturdily though mechanically manufactured and
> pleasantly, often beautifully designed. . . ."[7]

Rogers himself had noticed that the product he was describing was
currently fashioned quite without technological advances since the
beginning of the century. New processes, especially since World War
II, have only recently engendered new concepts in book construction.
Rogers in a 1969 observation indicates a librarian's disappointment over
the new trends: "Whether we like perfect bindings or not, their use in
the twentieth century has clearly made a tremendous contribution to
the mass distribution of books. . . ."

With the paperback a physical success, nevertheless, publishers are
contemplating—if not today actually presenting—much original fiction
in paper covers. This development obliges us to track the paperback
rather than the hard-cover book as the "norm" of future popular
publishing. And as the modern buyer is a reader, not a collector,
styles and methods of construction must still pragmatically suit a
book's purpose.

"In the design of books intended to be read (not all books are),"
said Ruari McLean, "nothing must come between author and reader."
McLean furnishes modern guidelines by which the book, hard-cover
or paperback, can be appraised:

> "The main thing one looks for in judging a commercially produced
> book is whether it serves, with some *élan*, distinction or grace, the
> purpose for which it was designed. The materials, whether rich or
> humble, should be at least honest, and should not pretend to be some-
> thing else. They should be right for the manufacturing processes
> used. . . . The whole book should feel pleasant in the hands and be
> harmonious in all its parts. . . ."[8]

Whether the modern commercially made book can indeed serve its
public honestly is, after a century and a half of bindery industrialization—the first half of which, as Hoe remarked, a failure—still seriously
contested, even with what publishers believe to be their best work.

Judges of the American Institute of Graphic Arts' "50 Books of the
Year" shows have, since 1923, excruciatingly selected annual examples
of outstanding American bookmaking. Their professional experience
in the graphic arts usually makes them caustic, and over the years their

comments—when they cared to utter them—were seldom enthusiastic about the quality of book manufacture: "below standards . . ." (1950); "regrets . . ." (1955); no comment (1960, 1965). Recent juror remarks have not changed:

> "The outer cases and bindings were felt to be the weakest single feature of concept and manufacture. The books did not open easily, nor was the stamping of cases imaginatively, or even adequately done. . . . [1968]"

And again,

> "With few exceptions, the design, production and printing were undistinguished, uninspired, and uneven. Is this mediocrity born of assembly-line design, economics, lack of sensibility, apathy? [1969] "

Frequent indictments of the physical appearance of the book—the "best" annual examples—are serious indeed. We should like to be able to say that, today, with reading in jeopardy from several quarters, we can make a good book by machine, for at least we know at last how to make a good binding.

The binding of a book, whether ornate or utilitarian, must perform its function of keeping the pages together. In French the word for bookbinding (*relieur*) refers to the collecting of "quires" and repositioning them for use; in Italian (*legatore*) it describes directly the "connecting" of sheets by tying; in German (*einband*) it is the joining of many sheets into one. "Sewing is the foundation of good binding," said the R. R. Donnelley Company in 1928, advertising its hand bindery. Of all the operations in bookmaking, "confining [pages] by means of thread" was the only practical method for centuries. Although hidden, the sewing played a part in all but one of Williamson's requirements for a good binding: "the ability to hold the text pages together and to protect them, to open flat, to endure in use and storage, and to withstand both climate and time." Done by hand for almost a thousand years, sewing became the most critical modern impediment to mass production of any proportions.

Two schemes to by-pass the sewing of books were quickly attempted as demand for the printed word threatened to exceed the supply. The simple wire stitcher invented by Heyl, Averell, and others, was one; the intriguing "threadless" rubber binding was another. The speed with which both were widely embraced, despite obvious imperfections, indicates the severity of the situation. And both were just as promptly dismissed: sewing with wire was "an abomination to all persons of a rightly-constituted and well-balanced mind," said a librarian in 1892. "Nor do I look upon Hancock's patent for india-rubber binding as one which need be taken notice of by a serious person. . . ." Something better was urgently needed—and at that time already finding its way into the shops.

The invention of the book-sewing machine was an unassuming, unheralded novelty from several points of view: although it promptly removed the most serious obstacle to book mechanization, it was also one of the first bindery machines of more than simply labor-reducing value—of more than incidental importance to the finished product. It did not merely duplicate with deft mechanisms what delicate fingers could do; it produced a simultaneous sequence of multiple stitches in many ways far superior to hand work. Unlike earlier bindery machines, it proved that bookwork need not remain a handicraft. At the same time it was for the bindery the last crucial machine—of truly great complexity—to be invented by an individual with independent resources. After it, the evolution of book mechanization became the routine work of research and design staffs, almost lost to public and trade acknowledgment alike.

Unfortunately, perhaps, even machine sewing became a bottleneck; a still simpler method of connecting sheets was sought—and found. The science of mechanics had, with the sewer, delivered all of which it was capable—self-operating needles infinitely faster, more uniform, and cheaper than ever so many feminine fingers. But now, with the prospect of adhesive binding, it was a problem for the science of chemistry—a quick dip into an adhesive solution whose tenacious molecules, again, proved faster, more uniform, and cheaper than ever so many mechanical stitches. All the while, in both cases, utility and cost were factors, as were author satisfaction and public acceptance, sometimes hostile, sometimes devoid of understanding, in a confusing literary marketplace.

The realm of commercial binding today is divided into four main branches: (1) stationery and blank book work, (2) periodical and pamphlet work, (3) library and job work, (4) edition or publisher's work. To the last category—the manufacture of identical books in quantity, using automatic machinery to produce "cased-in" hardbound books—must be added the binding of paperbacks, or softcovered books. For the history of edition work, however, important precedents established by the other branches of binding must not be overlooked. The library or custom binder cannot be slighted, although his work actually predates the invention of printing (stamped letters on bindings executed between 1436–1440 in Nuremberg may actually have inspired Gutenberg). The pamphlet and periodical binders, with far more advanced machinery for the production of magazines, have given direction and impetus to the mechanization of the book. The edition binder today finds himself occupying a middle ground between the publisher and the manufacturer of bindery machinery—the latter constituting an extraordinarily secluded domain three times removed from the pressures of the book-buying general public.

In the vast American machinery world the makers of bookbinding equipment play a small part indeed. Where publishers may easily develop unlimited sales (for the right books, to be sure), binders may similarly enjoy increased edition or commercial work as reading flourishes; the bindery equipment manufacturer, however, caters to a fairly small market. As recently as 1958 the US Department of Commerce, canvassing American bindery firms with 50 or more employees, found the following limited quantities of machinery on hand:

| folding machines | 1989 | McCain, Singer side sewers | 148 |
| paper cutters | 3465 | Singer saddle sewers | 179 |
| board cutters | 222 | case-making machines | 259 |
| three-knife trimmers | 400 | casing-in machines | 185 |
| Smyth sewing machines | 761 | adhesive binders | 96[10] |

Since 1958 the number of US book manufacturing establishments has hovered around 750 shops. It is easy, therefore, to appreciate that, in what is at best a very modest scale of mass production, much bindery equipment today is still custom built to order. Larger machinery houses were quick to develop world-wide distributorships to find adequate markets—still confined largely to small areas where literacy is high. For the handful of such manufacturers, however, technological diversity and corporate mergers find them still relatively insecure as publishers—their ultimate patrons—turn increasingly to various nonbook communications media.

For the first 100 years of its industrialization, the trade bindery had only a few tinkerers and mechanics to thank for its equipment. What a proud, independent group these mechanicians were, with grease on their hands, often poorly educated but with a spark of genius about how mechanical motion could perform useful work. Almost always considered "before their time" in a very conservative area—as with hand sewing, book construction itself had changed little in a thousand years—they knew neglect and resistance. Somehow they drove themselves far beyond what the industry would pay them for their talent. Perhaps because books—precious literature—were involved, they had few reservations about the sanctity of their work.

It is possible to protest that Heyl, Smyth, Bredenberg, Juengst, and others, as inventors and mechanics, have made little contribution to the esthetics of bookwork, being neither graphic artists nor bibliophiles.

Indeed, the unrelated diversity of their inventions would substantiate this attitude; a British writer in 1959 was puzzled to note that Smyth had eight patents registered in England, one of them a device to open petcocks on gas mains. Heyl and Juengst similarly had many non-bindery interests. Yet, to call these men only tinkerers would be to deny to Ottmar Mergenthaler, too, an equivalent place in the history of typography, for he was also an inventor of broad interest: few are aware that his second greatest invention was a machine for fabricating wooden grape and fruit baskets.

False and incomplete accounts of bindery industrialization, however humorous, must of course be set aright, like one biographical dictionary which in 1914 credited Smyth only for his veneer and toothpick inventions and his adjustable mitre box. Another as recent as 1938 is legendary stuff:

> "According to the information I am able to gather, the earliest sewing machine was invented by a David Smythe [sic], who hailed from Ireland and came to London with his project; but finding little financial assistance, emigrated to America, and was there engaged as an engineer, making book sewing machines. About sixty years ago (1878) he founded the Smythe Manufacturing Company and toured England and the Continent, installing these machines. . . ."[11]

(Smyth had been brought to the United States at the age of two.) Even today myth-making goes on: Daniel Melcher has frequently been credited with the belt-press concept, although Basil Blackwell may more properly claim that honor (p 319).

Of Heyl, Juengst, and Bredenberg, less is known. Henry R. Heyl has never before been clearly associated with the history of bookbinding, his contribution now established. Like Smyth, Juengst is better known by equipment in the shop that bears his name but which evokes no human visage. Juengst almost knew public fame: one of his bookbinding devices was hailed "as wonderful a machine as the Linotype" by a "well-known printer," but the latter's preferred anonymity made for a timid nomination.

Upon examining the mechanical excellence of several American publications, a Briton in 1939 unexpectedly complimented all four inventors for exactly what they themselves would have considered the merits of their work. Commending accurate folding, stitching, and trimming in staggering circulations up to 3 million (as represented by *Saturday Evening Post* and *Collier's*), and multiple thread-stitched flexible square-back binding in quality periodicals (particularly *Fortune*, until 1949), James Shand said:

> "We should do well to recognize that the country which evolved the linotype, the monotype, the newspaper rotary, the multiple-station

feeder-stitcher, the three-knife continuous trimmer, is now evolving a production technique ["quality" mass production] for periodicals without equal in any other part of the world. . . . We have much to learn. . . ."[12]

Shand could not comment on adhesive binding, which had just begun to gain momentum when the war interfered. Indeed, the imperfect "perfect" binding had few champions on either side of the Atlantic in its first five decades. Like other ephemera and short fads, it has had fewer historians. With the emergence of successful adhesives, however, it is now possible to record the development of a process now acknowledged to be more than transitory.

Many other inventors and inventive binders, of course, are also part of the story, some similarly quite unknown today for their technological contributions—even among book manufacturing people. Although a few of them were perhaps even more gifted than the four principal inventors presented here (Luther Crowell, Louis Goddu, and Talbot Dexter, for example, together tallied well over 500 patents), they must necessarily stand somewhat to the side in a history that attempts to confine itself to Arnett's simple bookbinding definition. Nevertheless, those binderies and publishing firms whose operations have had some special impact on the physical book or the method of its construction are also represented, although, again, peripheral areas, like paper- and board-making, foil- and cloth-making, and many auxiliary bindery operations, cannot be covered.

If the American way of life can be said to rely on American intelligence and ingenuity, it must rest therefore all the more soundly on American education and books. Thus the work of bookmaking pioneers—in the bindery and in the machine shop—assumes a fuller, more valuable position both in United States history and in the progress of world graphic arts and communications. "The Industrial Revolution," said Kenneth Day, "was largely borne on the back of the printing trade, which provided the necessary means of transition from street ballads to manuals of instruction. . . ." The assembly of masses of literature into usable form—the protection of that literature in durable covers—is not an incidental aspect.

Invention, the craft of those individuals obsessed by mechanical motion, today enjoys precious little attention now that the darker hours of the Industrial Revolution have passed. Yet not so long ago inventors had status:

"The world owes as much to inventors as to statesmen or warriors. To them the United States is the greatest debtor, so much have they advanced American manufactures. Their labor-saving machinery does work that it would take millions of men using hand implements to perform. In this century the debt will be piled still higher, for inventors never rest."[13]

So had C. H. Duell, US Commissioner of Patents in 1900, proclaimed a new century of development, hopefully as fruitful as the old.

The contemporary bookmaker, however, still finds himself somewhat perplexed by industrialization. He is far from being a confident master of his equipment. The earliest pieces, once angrily controversial but now a century old, seem unworthy of his attention: "Backers of the roller type," said *Bookbinding* in 1953, "are manually operated and few therefore regard them as machines, frequently neglecting to oil them properly. . . ." Edward J. Triebe, responsible for important progress at Kingsport Press, warned that the future bindery would not permit "the abusing of machine bearings and delicate moving parts with accumulated gobs of dried glues and paste, richly flecked with tobacco juice. . . ." But the latest equipment is equally misunderstood: it has been observed that new paper cutters deliver only half their capacity, apparently because of "inability of operators to understand the new control devices."

More and more, unfortunately, the bindery worker is asked less and less to exercise either judgment or taste in the performance of his machine-tending duties. The bindery of the future (p 330) may be nothing more than a single multi-purpose machine spewing out books by the millions for readers by the millions. That is, alas, the nature of mass production.

But the bookbinding world today approaches the threshold of a far more exciting era than automation of machinery dictates. Although publishers have savored for themselves some of the genuinely reward-ing and commercially critical decisions about the esthetics and the construction of their books (salesmanship is the essence of publishing —plus a touch of the missionary), the bindery need not relegate itself to slave status. As graphic arts operations rely increasingly on the chemistry of photography and adhesive-bonding, and the physics of electrostatic printing and electronic heat forming and drying, the age of simple mechanical invention for the bindery undoubtedly is at an end. But inventors never rest, even now. The modern binder must master these techniques—and dozens of others to come—for they will be faster, cheaper, and better than anything available today for manufacturing books by the millions.[14]

["Imagine yourself in a huge barn-like edifice of a couple of acres, spanned by immense arches, like the ribs of some leviathan ship, . . . and this building, crowded and crammed with incipient displays of goods and machinery—everything that grows and is made—and a thousand men actually at work, in their shirt-sleeves, putting the said goods and machinery in order—all with a noise, movement, and variety as if a good-sized city was in process of being built. In the middle of this, to an audience of perhaps two or three thousand people, with a fringe on the outside of five or six hundred partially-hushed workmen, carpenters, machinists, and the like, with saws, wrenches, or hammers in their hands, Walt Whitman, last Thursday, gave his already celebrated poem before the American Institute. . . ."]

*Part I*

# THE EUROPEAN TRADITION
# IN BOOKMAKING

*"After all, not to create only, or found only*
*But to bring, perhaps from afar, what is already founded,*
*To give it our own identity, average, limitless, free;*
*To fill the gross, the torpid bulk with vital religious fire;*
*Not to repel or destroy, so much as to accept, fuse, rehabilitate;*
*To obey, as well as command—to follow, more than to lead;*
*These are the lessons of our New World;*
*—While how little the New, after all—how much the Old, Old*
  *World!"*

[Walt Whitman]

# 1 *France:*

# *La Reliure Belle*

THE WORLD OF BOOKS AND BOOKMAKING IS NORMALLY A QUIET
one, dignified by its long association with literature and the arts—all
the more so in France, a country for centuries responsible for sophisticated literature and modish styles. But the fury of the French Revolution respected no sheltered microcosm. Although that crisis occurred
over 50 years before the Industrial Revolution touched the French
book bindery, its repercussions have had almost more lasting effect on
the shape of books in the French library, public or private, than technology's promise of inexpensive reading for the common man. In 19th-
century France there was no common man; interest in books was
nothing less than passionate.

Influential in so many sociological aspects, the French Revolution
was no less drastic in its attitudes toward the book arts. Although the
vandalism of books and the destruction of libraries was specifically
prohibited by the governing Convention (1792–1795) in a paper
ordering all to "respect the signs of feudalism, the armorials, the
escutcheons which ornament the books and writings having art, history, and instructional interest," uncontrollable citizens nevertheless

spent their wrath on the sumptuous libraries of the nobility. The very suggestion of luxury was distasteful; gilded armorial bearings and royal decorations were stripped off many books. Precious wide margins were trimmed without mercy as not only superfluous but inconvenient —page margins for which collectors a century later would gladly have paid handsomely. It was unfashionable even to possess a well bound book: one purchaser, unable to find a cheap edition, accepted a rich binding, broke its back, and had a brochure made of it. Among other effects of the Reign of Terror was the binding of several books in human skin. It was not a time of rational tastes.

French bookbinders, having devoted themselves entirely to the lavish requirements of the rich and titled, had perhaps wisely emigrated along with their patrons. In England they resumed their practice, almost anonymously, still surrounded by bibliophiles, some of whom now found it necessary to earn a living. The Comte de Caumont established himself as a binder; Vicomte Gautbier de Brécy was librarian to a wealthy Englishman; Comte de Clermont-Lodève became a bookseller. Many others resorted to coloring prints and book illustrations (p 53). More pointedly, that there were few outstanding binders left in France at the turn of the century is indicated by Arnett who noted wryly that the best French binding was being done in London.

In another directive the Convention decreed that papermakers would no longer use the fleur de lis or armorials as watermarks, and that printers and binders would no longer use them either. In the National Libraries bindings were to carry only the initials "RF" (Republic of France) and the symbols for liberty and equality. Thus books became violently "democratic" just as the new political doctrines housed in them became violently Jacobin. Imitation morocco replaced genuine leather, and the backs of books, of cheap sheep or calf skin, displayed the bookbinder's "arsenal"—the phrygian cap of liberty, squares and triangles of "equality," tripods, Roman fasces, and other devices of classic republicanism.

The disintegration and scattering of French bookmaking operations during the revolution was almost as calamitous to the routine dissemination of newly printed materials. The continuing hostility of France between 1800–1815, the uncertainty of overseas empires, and general unrest at home could only affect bookwork adversely. To their delight, Belgian printers and binders found great profit in the confusion for almost half a century, and Frenchmen like Balzac himself entertained the wildest schemes for making and selling literature. Only the strongest tradition could provide any continuity to the preservation of the book trades.

With public interest in styles and designs dormant, patrons scarce and impecunious, and materials in poor quality, binders bravely carried on. Pre-revolutionary book ornamentation in France, the 18th-century "lace" decoration very much like the wrought-iron balconies and chiseled bronze furniture of that earlier period, managed to persist until 1810. Under the Directory (1795–1799) the decorative arts had been transformed dramatically into classic forms which would remain for another decade. The "Empire" style of about 1804 took for its repertoire the motifs of Greece and Rome—with impetus from Napoleon's expedition to North Africa adding lyres and vases, obelisks and sphinxes, griffins and palm trees. The eagles and stars of the Emperor's arms also appeared frequently. Deville saw some value in the eclecticism: "If the heaping of gold toolwork was not a personal style, it was at least a new manner." Beraldi (p 34) also called the Empire a very original period.

The Restoration (1814–1848) was not similarly a period of intense activity, however, since the wealth of former times, alas, could not be reinstated with the monarchy. Bourgeois society was too poor, too practical, and too timorous to provide ample business for quality binders. The books of this period were solidly made, of good materials, but often heavily and unexpressively decorated. According to Marius Michel, gilding "fell into the hands" of German workers (Muller, Koehler, Germain, Ihrig, Kleinhaus, Vogel) who enjoyed some reputation in spite of mediocrity; Simier, binder to the king, and the Germans all ornamented coldly in the gothic style of the 16th century. On official volumes they routinely replaced Napoleon's arms with the fleur de lis, but most royal work, on the whole, was termed ugly.

The 1820–1840 period found some novelty in what is called the *à la cathedral* binding, that is, draftsman-like renderings of castle and church architecture. Revived interest in gothic and later in other monumental remnants—the hallmarks of Romanticism—had been promoted by an inundation of landscape and "churchscape" prints reproduced by the still new lithographic process. For this treatment binders demanded of an architect an entire façade, complete with rose windows, gargoyles, pinnacles, and arcatures. Toward the end of the Restoration the cathedral bindings fell into disfavor, although other archeological influences persisted until 1870.

The normal binding of the 1830's was mediocre, according to Beraldi. He particularly disliked a half-bound style with flat back, covered with large contorted stampings, called Louis-Philippe *rocaille* ("rockery") after its pebbly appearance. The half-binding, and the temporary binding, however, as we shall see, were actually the first signs of relaxation in the bibliophile's rigid insistence on beautiful designs and lasting materials. Substitutes for the full leather binding began to shake the foundations of book production unchanged since medieval times. They paved the way to "industrial" binding in France.

Alexis P. Bradel, a German, was a nephew of Derome and carried on in France between 1772–1809. He developed a temporary binding without forwarding, a style naturally called *à la Bradel*. Much like the later board case of machine-made books, the temporary binding was a convenient way to preserve newly printed signatures immediately after printing. Several months later the pages would be tested by placing a slip of unsized paper over one of them, and rubbing with thumbnail or bone folder: if no impression were transferred to the scrap, the signatures were likely to withstand the heavy beating necessary for a proper binding.

About 30 years after Bradel the binder François A. D. Lesné also explored the "temporary" binding. Calling himself the "Poet-Binder" for his poems eulogizing the art (1827), Lesné elicited from the British bibliophile Thomas F. Dibdin the sarcastic hope that his bindings were more durable than his rhymes. Lesné retaliated with more poetry—"A Letter to Thouvenin":

> ". . . You know that Dibdin occupies himself with missives;
> He knows a hundred ways to disgorge invectives.
> In London and Paris they recognize his jeers;
> We are not the only object of his sneers. . . .
> Nay, all the gold of Dibdin cannot debase us;
> He can rant and rail, but never disgrace us."[1]

Lesné developed an improved temporary soft-cover binding of plain calf. In an official announcement at the Exposition of 1834, which awarded him a bronze medal for his "conservative boarding," Lesné explained:

> "The principal purpose of this binding is to facilitate the usage of books newly printed, since bibliophiles, wishing to have good bindings, properly are not to have them bound at least for a year after their printing. Its principal merit is to conserve the book intact until the definitive binding."[2]

Lesné's binding consisted of front and back boards sewed to a linen strip, without pasting. The sheets were usually uncut. They could be undone without damage to the book ("something which never happens in *à la Bradel* bindings," said Lesné) since it contained no glue and no sawcuts for sunken cords. The process was applicable to albums, commercial registers, and brochures, according to its creator, and in order not to deceive the public books so bound would always bear the blind-stamped inscription, "Exposition de 1834. Cartonnages conservateurs de Lesné." His description, however, does not divulge what holds the pages to the linen backing, but an American process which later "infringed" on Lesné's provides a clue: in the "Workman System" (Workman Manufacturing Company, Chicago) "a double sewing on cloth boards joins between them all the sheets of the volume." (Charles Workman's and other methods at the end of the century offered finished, permanent bindings—usually for libraries— in exactly the style the French tolerated only for ephemera.) Although Bradel and Lesné possessed the noblest of intentions, they must be credited, willy nilly, with the initial French impetus leading to the acceptance of change—however minor—in the construction of books.[3]

While the Restoration, therefore, was undistinguished in design, it was, nevertheless, the era in which hand bookbinders began to separate themselves—with disdain—from the new and growing field of commercial work. In the perpetual tug-of-war between utility and beauty, the middle decades of the 19th century would become years of pragmatic experimentation. Beraldi, ever the champion of fine binding, wrote of the Restoration: "There was binding of the first class, in spite of the custom called '*grecquer*' [sawing across the spine to provide notches for the cords—named only in confused respect for the discoveries of Herculaneum and Pompeii] and the intrusion of the stamping press and engraved plate." Beraldi claimed that 1838 marked the end of decoration by stamped dies in the shops of the deluxe binders. "It was henceforth impossible to practice, side by side, the binding of bibliophiles and that of publishers; the deliberate work and the rapid work; the hand work and the machine." With collectors' work considerably more lucrative than publishers', the choice for some must have been agonizing.

French bookbinders had begun as early as 1818 to experiment with the engraved plate which they supposed would produce stampings as handsome as hand-tooled work, and yet as quickly as type could produce pages of printing. Even the better binders, like Thouvenin, were interested in it, but they found themselves hampered by a lack of direction and, most of all, a lack of the necessary tools.

Emile Bosquet, himself an accomplished binder, described in detail the work involved in producing a stamped gilt binding before 1838. The plates were of engraved copper, sometimes mounted singly, but often composed of several diverse pieces. The plates (dies) were glued to boards 10–15 millimeters thick, and heated on a heavy sheet of iron over a charcoal fire. When hot, they were placed by hand ("taking care not to burn the fingers") on the book cover which was in position on a wooden press and already dusted with graphite. The press, a "standing" press also used in the shop to apply pressure to newly bound books as their glue dried, had a large wood screw, turned by hand with a long iron bar. Depending on the area of the plate, one, sometimes two, men were required to obtain the necessary impression. "When, at the end of a twelve hour day, one had succeeded in gilding 70–75 copies, tracings, glaires, and impressions in gold, not counting certain inevitable retakes, in a perfect state of things, one had worked well!" The system obviously left much to be desired.

Yet at this time the stamping press was the only machine in the bindery. Along with a number of vises, there was still the hand-held plough knife for cutting; the guillotine cutter in France did not appear until 1844 (p 27), and was not generally available for another decade. With the plough books already in their covers could only be trimmed one at a time (so-called "in-board" work); with the guillotine several books not yet in boards or cases ("out-of-board") would be trimmed simultaneously. The bindery shop in 1835, it was said, was as rudimentary as the printer's before the 1803 Stanhope Press. Manual labor was not only inefficient, but it was making the book inaccessible to the great mass of public readers. The production of books, in a word, was not keeping up with the demand.

Indifferently educated, the French public nevertheless began to enjoy graphic art through the spontaneity and humor of a wave of social and political caricaturists. Lithographed or engraved on wood, their daily commentaries soon stimulated interest in other reading materials. Charles Philipon's *La Caricature* (begun 1830) and *Le Charivari* (1832)—of which Balzac was editor—created world-wide demand for the sophisticated graphic humor and social observations best demonstrated by Daumier, who in his lifetime executed some 4000 lithographs, many for Philipon.

Léon Curmer founded his publishing firm in 1834 and quickly used the wood engraving in books and serialized publications. Doré almost single-handedly developed the illustrated book into a permanent genre with his engravings of scenes from the bible and classic literature. So successful were such endeavors that the French today still prefer illustrated books, with almost complete disregard for accompanying text. But on the heels of picture books came sensational authors like Balzac, Chateaubriand, Constant, Dumas, Gautier, Hugo, Mérimée, Monnier, Sand, Stendahl, whose popularity quickly taxed all efforts to publish quickly and cheaply. It was time for bringing the world of bookmaking out of its dark ages of laborious handwork, time-consuming procedures, and expensive individual bindings. Only the machine could eliminate all three extravagances at once.

The industrialization of French bookbinding can be told almost in its entirety by following the life of a single binder: Jean Engel. Born 1811 in Württemberg, Germany, Engel came to Paris at the age of 21. After apprenticeship in several firms he established his own business, all the while becoming one of those extremely inventive persons, always able to find a quicker or better way to get things done; a genius, in fact, at mechanization.

In 1842 Engel bought from Cope & Sherwin, London, their new gilding press, called the Imperial Arming Press (p 46). Actually only a modified iron printing press, it had in principle long been used in France for the coining of money. In the bindery, however, an engraved plate was mounted on the press before a bin repeatedly filled with red-hot rivets. It handled only small plates, but the Imperial rendered useful service by reducing the amount of pressure required of the operator. Later on the availability of illuminating gas made the heating of the plates less troublesome.

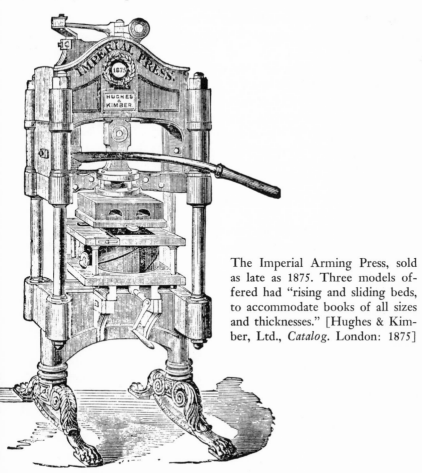

The Imperial Arming Press, sold as late as 1875. Three models offered had "rising and sliding beds, to accommodate books of all sizes and thicknesses." [Hughes & Kimber, Ltd., *Catalog*. London: 1875]

## TRADITIONAL BOOKWORK SHEET SIZES[4]

| *Sheet Dimensions* | | | | *Sections and Formats Obtained, in Inches*[a] | | | | |
|---|---|---|---|---|---|---|---|---|
| *French Name* | *Decimeters* | *Inches* | *English Name* | *Folio 1 fold, 4 pp* | *Quarto 2 folds, 8 pp* | *Octavo 3 folds, 16 pp* | *Twelvmo or Duodecimo 4 folds, 24 pp* | *Sixteenmo 4 folds, 32 pp* |
| Ecu | 40 × 52[b] | 15 × 20[b] | Crown[d] | 15 × 10[c] | 7½ × 10 | 7½ × 5 | | |
| Coquille<br>Carré | 44 × 56<br>45 × 56 | 17½ × 22½ | Demy[d] | 17½ × 11¼ | 8¾ × 11¼ | 8¾ × 5⅝ | 7½ × 4¼ | 5⅝ × 4⅜ |
| Cavalier | | 18 × 23 | Medium[d] | 18 × 11½ | 9 × 11½ | 9 × 5¾ | 7¾ × 4½ | 5¾ × 4½ |
| Raisin | 50 × 65 | 20 × 25 | Royal[d] | 20 × 12½ | 10 × 12½ | 10 × 6¼ | 8¼ × 5 | 6¼ × 5 |
| Jésus | 55 × 72 | 21½ × 28½ | Super | 21½ × 14¼ | 10¾ × 14¼ | 10¾ × 7⅛ | | |
| Columbier<br>Grand Jésus | 56 × 76 | 22 × 30 | Imperial[d] | 22 × 15 | 11 × 15 | 11 × 7½ | 10 × 5½ | 7½ × 5½ |
| Grand Aigle | 75 × 106 | 29¾ × 41¾<br>26¾ × 40 | Double Elephant | | | | | |

a. Untrimmed dimensions; after trimming width is about ⅛ inch less, length about ¼ inch less.

b. French nominal sizes do not always correspond to conventional British sizes; American 19th-century dimensions also vary slightly from the British.

c. British practice in giving page size is to state bound (spine) dimension first; American practice usually gives smaller dimension first, without reference to binding edge.

d. Common sizes; when formats were given without specifying sheet names, the medium sheet was usually meant.

In 1854 Engel had his arming press modified with parts from London, replacing the iron hand bar with a heavy flying weight controlled by a winch arrangement. The complete device, called by the French a *balancier à genouillère* (literally, "knee [toggle] -joint balancing press"), was later improved by Engel himself, who, by 1863 had annexed a machine shop to his establishment. His were the only presses in France that permitted goffering (blind embossing on cloth), gold-stamping, and printing in color automatically and without removing the work to a special press.

Engel had made for Lenègre, another commercial binder, the first rolling machine in 1847, to replace beating by hand. "This was an enormous progress [although] we have always remained partial to hand beating for precious books," Bosquet commented, daringly complimenting the device without offending his bibliophilic friends. ". . . However, certain papers, above all those of wood pulp, smooth better by machine than by heavy hammer," he added. Engel was also responsible for the first glueing vise, made for him in 1853 by Van de Weghe, a student of the engineer Bernard Steinmetz. Engel first used the roller-backer exhibited by Sanborn (p 110) at the Paris Exposition of 1855. He is said to have divulged this discovery to Mâme & Fils, as he was known to share many of his developments; it may be supposed that Mâme at Tours had not seen the Sanborn demonstration, but more likely Engel's endorsement meant not that the machine existed, but that it really worked. Van de Weghe later made an improved version of the rounding and backing machine which was commercially successful. He also constructed, from Engel's plans, a *machine à grecquer*.

In France the paper-cutting machine was invented by Guillaume Massiquot, an itinerant bindery mechanic who developed the idea in 1844 while recuperating from an illness. This prestigious act won him membership in several professional organizations; indeed, such a concept seemed so personally unique, so audacious, at least to French etymologists, *massiquot* has become the generic name for all paper cutters. Yet the massiquot apparently was more concept than reality: a decade passed before Engel obtained a machine cutter—and not Massiquot's.

The house of Poirer, Paris engineers and machinists, exhibited at the 1855 show a cutting machine appropriate to bindery needs, and Engel was first to acquire it. With medals from 1839, 1844, 1849, 1851, and 1855 expositions, Poirer by 1864 offered a family of hand paper- and board-cutters whose capacities accommodated the extraordinarily named French paper sizes (named after their watermarks): *coquille* ("shell"), *raisin* ("grape"), *Jésus, columbier* ("dovecote"), *grand Aigle* ("large eagle"), and others (see table). A year later Boildieu, another engineer in Paris, offered "continuous movement" cutters, hand- or steam-powered; by 1874 he offered cutters, standing presses, embossers, and stabbing machines for the entire French binding and brochure trade. Engel nevertheless had Van de Weghe make several cutters for him especially for trimming glued and sewed volumes, machines still not then available commercially.

In 1863 Engel built a vast new Paris shop where he installed the first steam engine in France devoted to bindery work. He soon added hydraulic presses which gave him tremendous capacity for the increased volume of work. In 1866 he had constructed the first circular cutter for binder's board, and, at the same time, a beveling machine; these were quickly copied by mechanics for other shops. Engel went on to devise a doubly strong embosser which, Bosquet claimed, brought the stamping press up to the standards of 1900. By the end of the 1880's the Engel bindery employed 800 workers.

Engel was named a jury member at the Expositions of 1878 and 1889 and received the cross of the Legion of Honor in 1891. He taught bindery subjects at a vocational school for the last six years of his life, and died, age 81, in 1892—ironically crushed by an alpine avalanche while vacationing for his health. Jean Engel's whole life was unselfishly devoted to the improvement of bindery production in France, although few booklovers would have known to thank him for it.

W. O. Hickok's book-sawing machine, about 1856, for cutting notches in the spines of books to house the cords. Adjustable blades (just visible on table top) were held in position by set screws. [Nicholson]

Another binder pioneering in commercial work was Charles Magnier, who shortly after a period with Lenègre organized a thriving shop (1853) employing both hand and machine processes. He had, among others, machines by Steinmetz, Van de Weghe, and Janiot, the last a newly established printing and bindery machine supplier ("one can always see one of these machines functioning at my shop," Janiot advertised). As with Engel, however, Magnier's equipment was made mostly under his own specifications; it was reported that he spent 12,000 francs ($2400) developing a stamping press which was scrapped without ever having been used. To illustrate his interest in the continuation of his hand shop, Magnier kept 6 specialists all year round in hand cutting alone; and 12 gilders (of whom 4 performed only the most exquisite work). As of 1894, however, he employed 400— and as many as 500 during gift-giving seasons—in a very lucrative commercial bindery as well. Magnier was a difficult, meticulous master: with a glance around the shop he spotted faults in workmanship that he would not tolerate. Thus Bosquet said of Magnier, "While he made cheap commercial bindings, he never made *camelotes* ["trash"], that is, what binders call a badly made book. He could always sign his name without hesitation, to a book leaving his premises."

After mid-century, in addition to Engel and Magnier, were Lenègre, known for good work, especially albums, and Lesort. But overshadowing these few edition binders—whose output consisted mainly of small publishers' works in paper covers—were a few giant publishers whose own manufacturing facilities became models of industrialization.

In 1833 25-year old Alfred Mâme became head of the Tours publishing house already well established by his father in 1796. He worked at expanding the diversified businesses of publishing, printing, binding, and papermaking, until, with 800 workers in almost 5 acres of shops, he all but monopolized liturgies and prayer books, in addition to much general work. By this time (1890) the firm had engines totalling 120 horsepower and was manufacturing 8000 bound books a day, scrupulously maintaining three admirable principles: (1) publish only what was pure and moral; (2) retain beauty and fine finish; (3) retail all volumes inexpensively. Many wondered how he managed to produce a quality book for 32 centimes—6 cents. From this gigantic enterprise, in typical paternal fashion, Mâme offered his workers a profit-sharing plan, a cooperative bakery, and free schools for their children. His own passion had been horticulture: his gardens were so beautiful and remarkable that invading German troops in 1870 were reportedly ordered not to touch a single flower.

The house of Hachette & Company, Paris, grew even larger than Mâme. Louis C. F. Hachette, bureaucratically denied a license to teach, in 1822 opened a bookshop instead. This led almost inevitably to the formation of a publishing house in 1826, when he was 26. Concentrating on texts, manuals, and dictionaries, and adding general titles —railway literature, for which he had the principal terminal concessions—from about 1852 on, Hachette did well in the public arena. (One of the earliest titles in the "Bibliothèque des Chemins de fer [Railway Library]" was deLamartine, *Gutenberg: Inventeur de l'imprimerie* (1853, 50 centimes).

The prestige of scholarly publishing persisted, however, based as it was on monumental projects: beginning in 1842 he issued Bouillet, *Dictionnaire universel d'histoire et de géographie*, then *Atlas universel d'histoire et de géographie* and *Dictionnaire universel des sciences, des lettres et des arts*. By 1876 the firm had published 12 such encyclopedic works, with 5 more on press and 3 in preparation. Company aims (the founder had died in 1864) were noble:

Adams' hydraulic standing press, about 1856. Other manufacturers had similar presses at this time, including inclined models exclusively for smashing (and bundling for compact storage) book signatures after folding. [Nicholson]

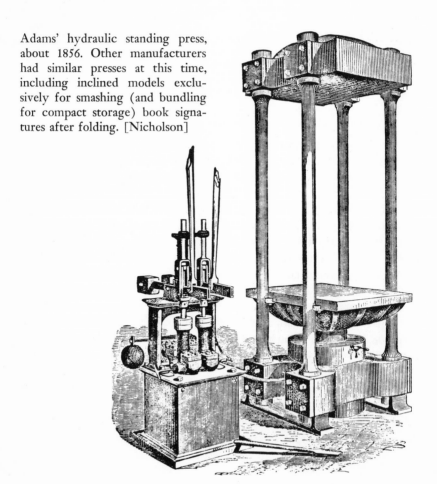

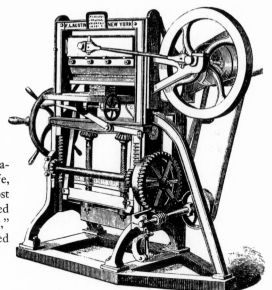

Frederick J. Austin's "Cutting Machine, No. 1, Oscillating Knife, Patented," about 1861. Uppermost wheel with long crank furnished "oscillation." Built for "fine work," this guillotine cutter was endorsed by William Matthews. [Austin]

"It has been seen that our ambition is to bring instruction within the reach of the humblest classes, and of the least exercised of intelligences, as well as to offer greater resources to higher and more cultivated minds, to second the aspirations of the learned, whose end is to attain for the recompense of their labours the pinnacle of Science."[5]

At that time, furthermore, Hachette had published a total of 4000 titles, and continued to function ambitiously as wholesalers and retailers as well as publishers and manufacturers.

Hachette composition, printing, and binding shops nearby employed 250 hands in 1877. Georges Hachette, Louis' son, recommended the installation of rotary presses a decade later, but they did not materialize until after World War I. The firm nevertheless considered itself very progressive; it certainly grew and prospered. On its centennial the company had 6620 employees in a world-wide organization, and a sizable manufacturing plant—just before it was sold in 1936 to Brodart & Taupin (p 85).

Around so enterprising a firm many delightful publishing ventures revolved. George H. Putnam in 1869 visited "the great warerooms of Hachette, the Harper of France," finding tons of cheap, popular books in immense piles, as well as "those famous folios which Doré has illustrated with that magician's pencil which he wields"; he tarried only long enough to secure an invitation to Doré's studio.

So the book world in France had, with Mâme and Hachette, grown almost miraculously out of the chaos of the beginning of the century.

Conditions in 1862 were still hectic and shifting: at the International Exposition of that year the jurors were unable to judge any relative progress in the art of binding, as no binder on display had previously exhibited in 1851. The situation was "better" in 1874, and by the Exposition of 1889, among dozens of publishers, many indicated their stability by the degree to which they had become specialists:

Hachette, in educational as well as general works
Mâme, general works, strong in liturgical publishing
Lenègre, Engel, Magnier, busy with industrial work
Jeener, Cornu-Gille, both for fine prayer books
Champs, Meunier, excellent half bindings
Noulhac, known for jansenist doublures

The second half of the 19th century continued hectically for commercial book design and production. There was a time for imitation ("We call 1860 the age of the copy," said Beraldi) and a time for originality. There were unbelievable production records (2.5 million bound volumes per year) and unbelievable prices for collector's items. Bibliomania had—if Beraldi's 1838 date had not—truly separated binders into two camps. At first, however, all wanted to share the work.

In their initial attempts to compete with the deluxe work of the hand binder, the commercial binders experienced several problems in their conversion from hand to machine. Foremost was the desire to imitate handwork—a fault deplored by Beraldi. The earliest plate designers had tried to apply Empire and gothic styles to commercial bindings; their versions of *à la cathedral* and flamboyant rose designs were termed "clumsy" by Lejard, and Beraldi had already condemned them: "Nothing so horrible was ever seen again!" Finding the contemporary patterns too intricate, they had to resort to simpler renaissance styles.

Yet these edition binders paid well for their dies, in order to get special designers and renowned artists to execute them. Grandeville and Gavarni, both prolific graphic artists and caricaturists, did some. But Beraldi says that after 1845 commercial binding became a peculiar art, not resembling anything, having its own style and masters. The desire to imitate had lasted about 25 years, but did not endure.

Some publishers, like Janet, Curmer, and Mâme, solved their design problems simply, by ordering an extra drawing from the illustrator for use on the board covers. For children's books they used charming and naive pictures done in chromolithography. Carried to excess, however, color work was another treatment which Beraldi criticized as a binding: "It owes its design not to binding but to a chrome image. The pride of these binders is to have their presses print the most colors possible. At eight colors they hold their heads up high; at twelve they don't even acknowledge the King as a cousin. . . . The epitome is to have someone mistake a book for a chromolithograph! And that's the trouble."

Early dies were executed by the engraver Haarhaus, who made a specialty of binders' work. Haarhaus was followed by Auguste Souze, whose establishment, founded in 1857, also performed the stamping, working in gold on colored papers at first. Toward the 1870's it offered both gold and black work, and around the 1880's was handling inks of several colors. Souze retired in 1892 whereupon his place was taken by his son Paul through the turn of the century. The Souze shop produced nearly all the dies of French publishers—thousands upon thousands of them.

The most ostentatious designs naturally became the most conspicuous gifts. The Paris correspondent for *American Publishers' Circular* found the 1863 Christmas a great trial:

". . . during this season of holiday books a book-lover is constantly in a state of high nervous irritation [since] you cannot get a book well bound from the first of December to the first of February; all the bookbinders are busy with gift books. The shops look like confectioners' shops, for the external appearance of the gift book closely resembles the outside of those paper boxes in which Bordeaux distributes her dried plums. . . . It is revolting to stand in shops and hear the comments made upon these garish books. Few people know what a book is, fewer people still can read books. . . ."[6]

Worse, said the report, 19th-century consumers who spent liberally for liquor and cosmetics would not pay adequately for decent books, however bound.

Another problem for shopkeepers and commercial binders alike is suggested by a question of Beraldi's, referring to a cheap 30-centime binding: "Do you know why the ornamentation was placed near the center of the book, leaving the edges bare? It was because one places his hands at the edges, and the hands turned the copper 'gilding' to red. It was very judicious, but it was still necessary to reckon with the consumer who complained, 'There isn't enough gold for the price!' "

Beraldi recognized what he considered the "special" purpose of the modern commercial binder—to bind more books, quickly and cheaply. He categorized contemporary binding designs into three groups: (1) regular ornamentation, symmetrical, architectural, approaching the bibliophile's taste; (2) a vignette; an illustration in gold (a scene from the book transported to the cover); (3) emblematic ornamentation, non-symmetrical, free in style. "We could add a fourth," he wrote, "unfortunately too frequent: that of the scribbler who, having no idea of the composition of ornamentation, renders crude accumulations on his plates, to the opprobrium of machine binding." He also noted, humorously, that stampings could also be classified by publisher, some of whom had "*never* had a plate made with taste." Nevertheless, Beraldi concluded, "Toward 1880 industrial binding, in spite of its errors, had absolute liberty with which to play, and showed itself frankly new, frankly nineteenth-century." Charged with esthetic meaning, Beraldi's statement was far from true technologically.

Suddenly, however, the public seemed unwilling to press for more and better commercially bound books. The average Frenchman possibly had less to spend on cloth and cardboard than British and American readers. For the fine hand-bound book, on the other hand, the rabid collectors had never slackened their pace. The years 1870–1885 were times of frenetic bibliomania, although—tiring quickly of new mechanically made books and designs—bibliophiles delved into the works of earlier centuries for inspiration, ordering their binders to recreate the former styles, which they did slavishly, coldly, although perfectly in forwarding and gilding. "It's not a binding—it's an opera foyer!" exclaimed Henri Beraldi in mock horror at an over-decorated work; his more honest attitude was quite the opposite: "Have the courage to place 40 francs of binding on a 3.75 franc book," he urged. "It is the only way to have a library that is not mundane. . . ." On still another occasion he topped himself: "Bind, bind sumptuously—without counting cost!" Beraldi's opinionated but exhaustive histories of 19th-century engravers (12 volumes) and bookbinding (4 volumes) were unashamedly bibliomaniacal. Others, of course, had a wide range of indiscriminate tastes. "Bibliomania in France is responsible for much that is disastrously eccentric and decadent," wrote Sarah T. Prideaux in 1906. Among hand binders the counterbalancing tradition of excellence hung on slender threads.[7]

The house of Gruel & Engelmann was a uniquely long-lived repository of the best binder's art. Paul Gruel had married his master's daughter and was taken into partnership in 1825. When he died in 1846 his second wife ran the shop and soon married a printer, Jean Engelmann, whose family had introduced lithography into France. When Engelmann died in 1875 she carried on with her two sons, Léon Gruel and Edmund Engelmann, turning out exquisite art books and ecclesiastical pieces. In their small shop (4 *doreurs* [gilders, finishers], 3 coverers, 3 women folders, 1 girl to lay on the gold, 4 general workers, and 2 overseers, in the 1880's), they managed also to teach Marius Michel, Thibaron (nephew of Thouvenin), Chambolle (who succeeded Duru), and other craftsmen. The shop, "a paradise of cleanliness and order," said a visitor, did contain a rolling machine, but it was seldom used. Gruel's reputation, while well founded, soon exceeded his output, and one American correspondent felt it necessary to warn fellow bibliophiles that "a book signed Gruel will have been made by half-a-dozen anonymous workmen. . . ."

Like Gruel, younger binders took the reins of leadership away from the industrialists. But Trautz and Marius Michel, unlike Gruel, maintained the admiration of bibliophiles through their rare combination of high quality and artistic originality—despite their small yield. Whereas Thouvenin, for example, had bound about 3000 volumes per year, Trautz did 300, and Marius Michel not more than 200.

A German, George Trautz traveled through France, finally taking a job with the binder Kleinhaus in Paris. In 1831 Thouvenin had showed Kleinhaus a rare 1613 book he had just rebound for collector Charles Nodier (who, when he later received it, named the binding style—actually as old as the book itself—after its title, *Les fanfares et corvés abbadesques*). This volume so impressed young Trautz he spent Sundays without pay to perfect himself as a gilder. He went on to work (until 1840) for the binder Antoine Bauzonnet, married Bauzonnet's partner's daughter, and in this approved manner became a member of the firm. When Bauzonnet retired in 1848 Trautz succeeded him, calling the firm "Trautz-Bauzonnet." Because of his great care and workmanship, Trautz in 1869 received the Legion of Honor —the first bookbinder to do so—although his work was still almost unknown even to collectors. Quickly, however, his skill was sought by the new cult of bibliophiles—Baron Rothschild was a special patron —and was almost unmatched in all France. He died in 1879, leaving no children to carry on.

Marius Michel (actually christened Jean Michel) between 1839 and 1848 gilded impeccably for Gruel. He then opened a shop for gilding only, before starting his own firm in 1874 which, upon his death in 1890 was continued by his son Henri Marius Michel. Working diligently—and by copiously chronicling the art of bookmaking—through the years of intense bibliomania in France, Marius Michel fostered and enjoyed a delirious climate of appreciation for beautiful books. Striving to share this atmosphere were the houses of Duru (founded 1834), Pierre M. Lortic (rival of Trautz, recipient of the Legion of Honor in 1878), Emil Mercier (successor to François Cuzin), and Charles Meunier (once apprenticed to Marius Michel), all of whom produced very creditable work.

After the death of Trautz, however, his rabid collectors, skeptical that anyone could replace him, seemed to tolerate—if only for an instant in the history of collecting—the "worst" of French bookwork.

This was the commercial *cartonnage,* or simple cased-in board binding inspired by its successful introduction in England 40 years before (p 45). This late treatment in the 1870's was the sole heir in France of a purely industrial book technology: it was probably the only kind of work the French produced without some handwork.

The cased-in book was first manufactured by E. Carayon, who called himself "the most warped of binders" because his entry into the profession was a circuitous one: soldier, painter, decorator, then binder. Carayon's *à la Bradel* work was provisional at first, but later considered quite durable; Sarah Prideaux found his bindings "the only really comfortable form of binding" to come from France. Beraldi compliments him in unusually glowing terms for his exquisite neatness, elegance, freshness with which he handled materials, and taste in papers and cloths. Carayon did *à la Bradel* moroccos, full- and half-calf work, white vellum, and, of course, all kinds of paper-covered bindings. His display at the Book Exposition of 1894 was said to be the smartest at the show.

The binder Lemardeley was also mentioned at this time for *cartonnages* of notable quality.

Half-bindings at the end of the century were being done in flat back (no rounding of the spine) 1830 style, and were popular because of the growing price of full leather. Generally the half binding had leather back and outer corners, its sides being cloth, marbled or colored paper, or parchment; a variant, the Roxburghe binding (proffered by a British club of bibliophiles founded 1812 and named to honor collector John Kerr, Duke of Roxburghe) simply dispensed with the leather corners. Beraldi, however, would not concede to inflation: "The half binding is only an expedient," he railed, "—bind, bind in full!" The half binding, however, very carefully done, cost 20 francs ($4.00), the price Thouvenin once charged for a full binding.

Among bibliophiles, of course, expense was not at all a consideration. Although a French binder had once reportedly said to a customer, "Sir, I will not dishonor myself by binding a modern book," there was not surprisingly a diminishing store of ancient treasures to refurbish. Since bibliophiles had already seized for rebinding all the old books they could get their hands on, some publishers, like Léon Conquet, Quantin, and Testaud, began to produce entirely new books with lavish attention. Making a deliberate program of this, the *Société des amis des livres* ("Society of Friends of Books") started in 1874 as an organization to encourage contemporary artists to work with the book as a medium. Its aims were:

"to publish books, with or without illustration, which by their typographic execution, or by their artistic selection, shall be an encouragement to painters and to engravers as well as a motive of emulation to French printers, [and] to create a friendly feeling among all bibliophiles by means of frequent reunions. . . ."[8]

Its fifty members included Beraldi, writer Octave Uzanne, founder in 1889 with 160 others of the *Société des bibliophiles contemporains* ("Society of Contemporary Bibliophiles"), historian Henri Houssaye, writer August Laugel, judge Eugène Paillet, and other important critics, for whom artists and authors in unison collaborated to produce some unusual books.

Carrying such commissioned work to its ultimate destination—a complete art form—Ambrose Vollard, a picture dealer, in 1900 published the first of his sumptuous art books, Verlaine, *Parallèlement*, illustrated by Pierre Bonnard; this was followed by others executed by Picasso, Roualt, Chagall. Called *livres de peintre*, these limited editions were illustrated by the artist's own hand, and issued unbound. French collectors, however, welcomed anew the opportunity of binding such objets d'art in a style worthy of their contents. By thus furnishing bibliophiles a new and respectable vein of raw material for extraordinary bindings, Vollard suddenly became the greatest patron of 20th-century book art.

Henry Kahnweiler, a German banker, also opened a Paris gallery in 1907, and published art books done by his friends. Through Vollard and Kahnweiler the tradition of modern illustrated books is firmly established in France, even today, and a direct influence on art books everywhere, like Kessler's Cranach Presse (p 83) in Germany, and Albert Skira in Switzerland. Other publishers in France no longer lacked either the direction nor the tools to do technically outstanding work—of this nonmechanical genre—and had finally managed to maintain a dignified posture despite their indifference to truly commercial work. None of them, consequently, were able—or cared to—dissuade the French public from venerating the sumptuously bound book.

The new business of bookselling required publishers to popularize books, although they wisely continued to devote themselves to educational and instructional materials, for which the need was most critical. Writing in 1894, Bosquet admitted "The book, such as it is, can only gain in attraction if it is convenably dressed, that is, a cover for it convenient and easy to use, and which, for the greatest number, attracts attention." With this comparatively modern sales tenet the French publishing industry would seem to have anticipated its technological future if its role in disseminating literature was to be realized. A few publishers did manage to "produce the cheapest possible, a sole end being to place [books] in the hands of all," but these unrecognized public benefactors in France were a special minority (p 92).

Bosquet was among the first (and the few) to deplore the twenty or thirty year lapse in French bindery industrialization—very easy to compare against English and American progress. Bosquet's history of contemporary French commercial bookwork was so unusual that Léon Gruel, when solicited, was genuinely overwhelmed: "A preface! You ask me for a preface, my dear author . . . !" Gruel's contribution duly cautioned hand binders they would have to learn the new techniques quickly, but he was of the old generation himself, perhaps not fully aware either as to what esthetic and craftsmanship concessions were necessary. Bosquet, scarcely satisfied merely to warn his countrymen, complained rather bitingly:

> "Our mechanics and builders don't appear interested in making ma-
> chines for binders, and don't seem to appreciate their needs. If, as in
> England and Germany, they acquaint themselves with our good prac-
> tices (they don't lack the opportunity to do so in Paris) in order to
> serve as a guide and indicate to them the requirements of our trade;
> if they would make for binderies what printing houses have made and
> make daily for themselves, without doubt our trade would hold first
> place, and would not be forced to buy from foreigners."[9]

It was almost as if no one but Bosquet had noticed there was more to binding than hand-made books.

The rounder-backer had come late to France, as had the folding machine—despite an 1850 patent by French press manufacturer A. Marinoni and one by nearby Martini (p 196). These indispensable items, and others, had indeed been introduced by foreigners. The French development of machine stamping fell into quicksands of design and pulled down with it any great public appreciation for the cased-in book. *L'Imprimerie*, the French journal of printing and kindred trades (founded 1863), had long warned that *"Ça s'est toujours fait comme ça!* [We've always done it that way!"] would be fatal to France. But warnings without implementations were worth little.

The question of bookbinding education was an important factor. In England, America, and Germany, said Bosquet, the effort to learn bookwork was prodigious; industrial schools appeared all over. (This contention was more exaggerated than truthful; bookbinding has al-ways appeared to be more an in-house training than a formal sub-ject). The Paris *Ecole Estienne* taught graphic arts and bookbinding; Engel's class there had 30 students meeting 3 nights a week. But France had only one major *Ecole du livre*, featuring a three-year course in bookbinding, half in practical work and half liberal arts. Yet binders themselves seemed to encourage formal education; apprentice systems, although difficult to arrange, continued, and the more prominent binders managed to publish on the subject. Marius Michel had written several definitive works, and Gruel, as binder-publisher, had issued a monumental *Manuel historique et bibliographie de l'amateur de reliures.* Bosquet concluded with a plaintive cry, "France can not, *must* not let itself be surpassed."

By the end of the 19th century, however, the great nation of bibliophiles was indeed behind England and America in technological development. Cundall noted that around the world cloth about 1880 had superseded the temporary paper cover, although France was again repetitiously excepted, using, "for durable cheap bindings [nothing less than] levant morocco." Seventy years later Steinberg still had to distinguish between two camps: "With the exception of France, the cased book, provided by the publisher, has conquered the whole world." Neither Cundall nor Steinberg had really bothered to justify the situation for France.

The fact is that France never gave up its love for fine bindings as had England and America. Frenchmen refused to value the literary work of the author above the quality of the package in which it was housed. Binding was a national art: a book simply was not finished until it was well bound. Although the term stands for the trade in general, *reliure* in France refers first and foremost to the binding of books by hand. (For machine work *cartonnage* is used.)

Such a century of biblio-superiority was crushing to the English book trade. In 1880 Wheatley asked, "Why does binding flourish more in France than in England?" He admired the countless collectors in France possessing small cabinets of well-bound books. "It has been remarked," he continued, jealously, "that in spite of our boasted culture, few houses of well-to-do persons contain any handsome books" —an observation Harrison would glumly make 40 years later. For the British the situation was frustrating, forced to concede to the French "the merit of the invention of the modern arabesque," and another highly ornamented illuminated binding design (which Brassington claimed had to be smuggled into Great Britain), with others as well— indorsing, doublure, and 19th century styles among them.

France could not seem to adjust to machine-made books, and England could not do exquisite work; they seemed ironically unable to help each other. Upon a visit to the 1889 Paris Book Exhibition a British binder discovered that of 2700 workers in the French capital only 45 belonged to the union. "As far as I was able to see and learn," he added, after visiting the firms of Marius Michel, Gruel, and Engel, "some of our London shops are far better off for the newest improvements in machinery than any in Paris. . . . some were very badly off in this respect." Shortly thereafter a French binding official, sent to

London, arriving almost without warning and speaking little English, was turned away from Zaehnsdorf's door—and Zaehnsdorf was reputedly receptive to such professional visits.

The French are still more proud of their design achievements than their industrial progress. The French paper binding of today, the *livre broché,* is still constructed with later hand binding in mind. Called "French sewing," the thread jumps from first to second signature during the center third of its travel, and second to third signature in the next pass, and so on—with the chief advantage of being readily pulled apart without injury for the definitive binding.

Wheatley concluded his history of binding as a fine art appropriately: "The French consider binding as a national art, and believe that they long ago distanced, and still excel, all other nations." France would not know for many decades the folly of such narcissism.[10]

# 2 England:

## The Book Beautiful

As in France, bookbinders in England at the end of the 18th century practiced their subtle, literary art for the nobility and rich. Cultured work, however, was not always a sinecure: King George III, an avid book collector who enjoyed visiting his private Buckingham House bindery, in 1786 magnanimously granted his shop a reduction from 14 to 13 hours per day—although commercial workers in London were dismissed for asking the same. As in France, too, such socioeconomic inequalities would not long remain stifled, especially as the industrial revolution made men all the more aware of unsatisfactory labor conditions. The older generation of binders, however, had remained aloof from such troublesome commercial environmental problems—but with only diminishing success.

Most conspicuous and colorful of the 18th century hand binders was hard-working, humble—reputedly "tipsy"—Roger Payne, whose work from about 1770 on was of peculiarly delicate style. Unlike other master binders who employed workmen to sew, forward, finish, or gild, Payne did all these operations himself. Sarah T. Prideaux, herself a binder, considered Payne's books well stitched and headbanded, but found his leather joint (the groove between spine and cover) clumsy and his endpapers, usually purple or buff, clashing with his leathers. Payne died in 1797, leaving only a small, unimportant following of displaced Germans: Hering, Kalthoeber, Staggemeier, and Walther among them.

Charles Lewis, whose work the great antiquarian Bernard Quaritch (p 57) deemed elegant and classic but lacking in vitality, and Francis Bedford followed Payne. Bedford, after an apprenticeship, long worked for Charles Lewis, and when he died, carried on the business with Lewis' widow. W. T. Morrell acquired the shop in 1861 boasting, as late as 1891, that he used absolutely no machinery. Bedford had left to form the firm of (John) Clarke & Bedford, becoming, according to Quaritch, "the best English bookbinder of modern times." Plagued with rheumatic gout for many years, Bedford died in 1883.

Conspicuous for his efforts to "improve" hand bindery technology was James Hayday, who began his shop in 1833. With "Bagster's Renowned Binding" (the original yapp treatment—limp leather overlapping the boards to protect the edges of pages, named after a London bookseller) common on bibles, Hayday had learned to make books open flat by simply sewing "all along" with fine silk thread. He was recommended by the publisher Pickering but, gradually unable to compete with cheaper binders, sold his shop in 1861 to William Mansell.

British "artist-bookbinders" were in fact so eclipsed by the French, as we have seen, in new designs and technical excellence, their contributions to the industry went almost unnoticed. Hering had revived a stamped calf binding unsuccessful for lack of power to emboss sharply; Bedford specialized in tree-marbled calf (stain allowed to trickle down the sides of a finished binding, usually resulting in a dendritic effect); other English binders "introduced" painted book edges, velvet and silk covers (techniques originating in the 15th and 16th centuries), and an "Etruscan" style of binding. But these novelties had only declining influence on England's taste for fine books. Bindery people, it seemed, were preoccupied—for several decades—in other areas of the trade, labor problems foremost.

British master commercial bookbinders had formed an association in 1794 to stabilize prices and reduce working hours (from 13 per day) during growing inflationary and political turmoil. Almost 200 journeymen and 100 master binders were working in London, earning—for a 66-hour week—15 to 20 shillings (about $2.50). Women were engaged for folding and sewing at 9 shillings, although during slack periods many, especially the more unskilled, went unemployed for months. Nevertheless, despite a financial crisis in 1797 the commercial bookbinding fraternity remained prosperous throughout the long Napoleonic War years. One binder later recollected this era:

> "The war [with France] was then in full operation; above six hundred government ships were afloat and the dockyards in full activity, and to supply all these with account books, stationery and printed orders, the quantity of work done for the Admiralty was immense. Then, as to the leather binders, there existed at that time a great branch of the trade of which scarcely a vestige now [1845] remains. I allude to the exportation of books to America, which indeed was very great. America, in fact, relied for the whole of her standard literature entirely from Britain, and even Bibles and Prayer Books were exported from Scotland in great quantities."[1]

Until the 1820's in England, as in France too, the printed book reached the public in loose sheets, or at best in "boards" loosely stitched and covered in simple brown paper, often without any exterior labeling—definitely meant to be rebound. Bindings in "extra boards" were folded and sewn on 3 cords, but not trimmed; with patterned endpapers and printed labels they cost slightly more. For dictionaries, classic works, and schoolbooks, however, some publishers offered stamped bindings in roan (hide of Scottish sheep) and other cheap leathers; often, too, a jobber in sheets, the "novel-distributor," gambled on binding small quantities of fiction for sale to the new circulating libraries. But these were exceptions. Since the per copy cost of hand binding far exceeded that of composition and presswork, impecunious publishers were understandably reluctant to bind copies they had not yet sold; there was no discount for hand binding in quantity, and no point tying up capital and time in speculative bindery work.

The book wholesaler, like the publisher, left the commissioning of bindings to his own customers, the booksellers, so that they (or the individual buyer) could choose style and materials according to taste and pocketbook. As long as the possession of books remained the delight of wealthy collectors the custom seemed sure to endure. "The expense and responsibility of binding," wrote John Carter in 1935, "in fact, was passed on right down the line: and if the alternative of leather or wrappers [paper cover] had remained, as it largely has in France, there seems no reason why the publishers of England (or America) should ever have undertaken edition binding at all." But rich bibliophiles were vanishing everywhere, and other economic factors were at work driving the binders to find book buyers of more modest inclinations.

After the conclusion of the Napoleonic Wars England was in a calamitous economic slump. Industry and commerce lay exhausted;

exports and imports were disorganized; for the book trades old patrons were gone, and new ones, if found, were not rich. Competition was keen: the association efforts at stability and decent working conditions were soon forgotten. To face these new times and their new problems, new methods and materials were needed. They were scarcely obvious, at first.

Since the 1770's, English binders had recognized woven flax canvas as a suitable book covering material: because it resisted the penetration of glue (which made other loosely woven fabrics unsatisfactory for binding) it handled much like leather. Schoolbooks and other heavily used tomes were often bound in buff or brown canvas until the turn of the century, but alongside leather they scarcely had elegance or appeal commensurate with their cheapness and durability. They proved only that cloth was a practical material, nothing more.

William Pickering, apprenticed to a publisher and bookseller at 14, was only 24 in 1820 when he started his own business: with £1000 he plunged into the hectic arena of cheap novels, reprints, and classics, knowing, perhaps, that he would need vitally to call attention to his new wares. Although he would later help revive sound interest in Caslon's typefaces (p 60), for his initial tour de force, the "Diamond Classics" (named for their 4½-point "diamond" size text type, 16 lines to the inch), novelty, not legibility, was the selling feature: the books would be read "with great discomfort under a magnifying glass," and were, according to Pickering himself, "the smallest edition of the classics ever published." Shopping about for an equally startling cover material, Pickering found a book of guitar music, hand-bound by R. E. Lawson from scraps of curtain fabric, just what he wanted. For the "extra board" portion of the Diamond Classics Pickering furnished a quantity of red calico to his binder, Archibald Leighton.

One of 23 children of a bookbinder who came to London in 1764, Archibald Leighton, Jr., with his mother ran his father's shop (as Leighton & Son) after his father's death. Some time in 1821 Leighton covered two books, Baxter, *Poetical Fragments*, and a Dante work, both in Pickering's series, to the publisher's specifications. The Diamond Classics, in cloth, with tiny printed paper labels, thus went to market in what Pickering called a "neater mode," although he did not apparently so advertise them with confidence until 1825. "Cloth binding," wrote Carter in 1932 after exhaustive research, "slipped into the world unheralded by the smallest trumpeting of a blurb writer . . . and seems to have made its way against an inertia, which must almost have been a prejudice, in the trade and therefore presumably in the public."

Such a practical and inexpensive covering material, nevertheless, was a grand asset to Leighton in the rough depression binding market. He had experimented to find that, when stiffened with starch, cloth could be as workable and durable as canvas. Cheap cotton fabrics, commonly imported to London via Manchester, were recommended to him, and he dyed, stiffened, and patterned small (15-inch) rolls in his own shop. Leighton had begun to goffer (from the French *gaufrer*, to impress with a honeycomb pattern), using embossing techniques then common for paper, while other binders employed engraved cylinders which imparted a low-relief design. For British book buyers accustomed to the "delectable" decorations of earlier hand binders, the stamped cloth binding was only tolerably acceptable. Leighton nevertheless could barely process it fast enough: he then approached Thomas Hughes, a cloth manufacturer, who soon supplied him with quantities of calico in one-yard widths surfaced with dyed starch and embossed to resemble leather. As stocks of commercial binding cloth became reliable, however, Leighton and other binders stopped treating it themselves.

Within a few years, thanks to Leighton and Pickering, the cloth binding—although done by hand with materials that took 50 years to become fully perfected—was soon appreciated nearly everywhere as reasonably attractive and pleasant to the touch. And it was uniquely British: the French called it *la toile anglaise,* and the Germans, *Englisches Einband.* A bookbinding manual tells how the hand-made cloth case was formed:

"Cloth boarding, now so extensively adopted [wrote John Hannett in the 1848 edition of his 1835 work], offers nothing new for remark in the early operations, except that the covers are put on the boards with glue, as paste would tend to destroy the gloss on the cloth, by the damp striking through it. Where a great number of one work (which on first publication is generally the case) are executed at one time, it is usual to prepare the covers before placing them on the volume, by cutting the boards to the proper size with the plough, and covering them with cloth. A piece of stiff paste-board, of the width of the back, must be placed between the boards, which should be at a distance from each other equal to the breadth of the back and the allowance for the joints. This board must also be covered with the cloth at the head and tail, and when the case is applied to the volume, will form an open back. This mode is called CASE-WORK, and executed as follows:—Back the volume, and cut off the bands or slips [frayed cord ends] on which it has been sewn; then place it in the cover by pasting the guards (small slips of paper), left over the end-papers, which answers the purpose of lacing [anchoring the slips to the boards]. . . ."[2]

By 1832 Leighton was not only embossing cloth with die-stamped patterns, but was stamping (or blocking) cloth in gold leaf, having discarded the printed paper label he had found necessary at first. Because the case was separately made and decorated, any amount of embellishment upon it was possible, subject only to the limitations of the pressure required to impress the pattern. The press for this kind of work was already available: the arming press had for a long time catered to the special stamping (with brass plates) of family monograms and insignias on finished books destined for fine libraries. About 1832 Cope & Sherwin, London printing press manufacturers, developed their Imperial Press, an improved iron press using a powerful fulcrum and wedge system instead of the simple vertical screw. Improved further with a toggle joint (p 116), the device became known as "The Rock" for its power, and before 1843 had a jet of gas incorporated with it to heat the dies—years before Engel in France continued to use hot rivets. The great pressure of such presses so hardened the cloth as well as the boards that many examples were in "perfect condition" at the end of the century, and often still durable and sharp today.

The Imperial Arming Press was quickly put to work for edition (multiple-quantity) bindings. Alexander Bain, another British binder, had in 1828 already contrived a special adjustable frame for four corner blocks and one center piece, so as to expand the five-element decoration to any size book; for this he received the Society of Arts' silver Isis Medal and £5. For the publisher John Murray, Leighton first gold-stamped a multiple-volume edition of Byron's life and works (1832): volumes 1 and 2 had pasted paper labels, the remainder was completely stamped.

But Leighton & Son went further still to establish the methodology of edition bookwork by machine. Although Archibald, 57 years old, died in 1841, his son Robert continued pioneering in the use of steam power for all operations. He put to work Starr's new backing and trimming machines (p 109). He was first to use aluminum and black and colored inks on cloth, examples of which were exhibited—although commended only obliquely by official notice—at the London Exposition of 1851: item No. 158 of Class 17, "Paper, Printing, and Bookbinding," was:

"Leighton, Jane and Rob. Harp Alley, Shoe Lane.—Specimens of bookbinding by machinery, each book being ornamented at a blow by an engraved die. Designs by Luke Limner [Archibald's nephew]."[3]

Among his customers, in addition to Pickering and Murray, were the publishers Colburn (who may have preceded Pickering with a title issued in 1818—but possibly bound much later—done in purple glazed calico with slightly ribbed surface), Tilt, Knight, Moon, Boys & Graves, and others who began to approach a new reading public

The London book bindery of Westley & Clark, about 1843. Each worker performed all forwarding operations on a single volume. Aside from standing presses (*left*) and embossing press (*far left*), no machinery is used. Man in center foreground is planing with a hand plough. [Dodd, *Days at the Factories*]

through series of cheap works. Surviving today as Leighton-Straker Bookbinding Company, the long-lived book manufactory has seen a colossal industry grow from its ideas. Robert Leighton, its present director, was knighted in 1946.

The introduction of cloth had proved at least an acceptable substitute for leather, and unlike leather, which yielded only 3 or 4 covers per skin with considerable waste, offered more economical and systematic cuttings in prelude to multiple piece-work preparation of books. And piece-work—the repetition of small bindery operations, successively until completion—made mechanization possible. Under such increasingly technical conditions the responsibility—although not the esthetics—of binding sheets into books quickly reverted to the publisher, where it has since remained.

Josiah Westley, a London binder, introduced large-scale piece-work between 1804 and 1817 with a contract to bind a £300,000 project, Rees' *Cyclopedia* (39 volumes, 1802–1820). By 1843 the firm, now

Westley & Clark, maintained a 6-story factory employing between 250 and 300 hands. In a number of specialty rooms workers toiled together doing piece-work on a given edition. The "Pinnock room," for example, "is mainly devoted to sewing and covering little 9 penny books, Pinnock's Catechisms," wrote George Dodd in 1843, "of which the sale is so large and uninterrupted, that sewing and covering proceed continuously." Storage of materials and operation of heavy equipment, like their 3 embossing machines and millboard cutters, remained on lower floors, again in clearly defined rooms. The "cloth-cylinder room," Dodd continued, "contains two machines for imparting to cloth the diamond or granulated or speckled appearance usually presented by books in cloth boards,—an appearance which nearly hides the rectangular interlacings of the warp and weft threads. . . ."

With more aggressive piece-work pay systems and large volumes of repetitious work almost unsuspected a few decades before, small, isolated machines gradually appeared. The hand-cranked standing press, modernized by hydraulic action in 1823, saved three-quarters of the time required to bring books to their desired compactness ("Hydraulic Presses, for Book Pressing, to any dimensions," Cope advertised, that year.) Shops that did not "modernize," however slowly, would suffer; a half dozen large shops, like Westley's with at least 40–60 workers, soon wiped away many smaller ones. Two shifts were often scheduled: night workmen with lighted candles stuck in spare book presses would, after 10 hours on the job, sometimes fall asleep among paper shavings on the floor—often to resume their work at dawn. Using a few such hand-operated devices, a large plant could in days bind 3000 demy octavo books of 800 pages in full morocco with raised bands—liberally ornamented with gold on spine and front—each of 150,000 signatures hammered and sewn by hand.

Hand beating the sheets of a book, necessary after printing on dampened paper (which left ripples on every page), took a 14-pound hammer and was laborious enough to cause hernia—strangely serious in a supposedly artistic profession. To William Burn the process cried for improvement. William and James F. Burn were two of 12 sons of Thomas Burn who had started a commercial bindery in 1781. Capturing a coveted bible contract with the British and Foreign Bible Society in 1804, the shop prospered. About 1827 William developed a rolling press which a Royal Society of Arts committee, in awarding him a medal, described with simple admiration: "The press consists of two iron cylinders about a foot in diameter, . . . and put in motion by the power of one man, or of two if convenient, applied to one or two cranked handles." The delegation watched a boy, sitting in front, gather sheets into packets and place them into the machine on a tin tray. A bible, passing through the rollers, was flattened in a minute—twenty minutes' work by hand. Within three years all large shops would use it, but not without considerable resistance.

Nearly 500 journeymen bookbinders rose en masse against the rolling machine in 1830, calling—delicately, for bible work was sacrosanct—upon their employers to discard it. These were fearful years for labor against the march of industrialization, but the rolling press (like other machines in the final analysis) was really the binder's friend. The irate journeymen in London grew to 3600 in 1861 and still left enough work for 4000 bindery "females." The rolling press performed in a day what the hand beater had done in a week, and more pragmatic observers simply wondered how any but a few London shops would ever have the volume of work it demanded. They would soon see for themselves.

The rolling press was not the only contribution of Burn & Son. In 1843 the firm lost its bible contract and turned desperately to general edition binding. Bohn's "Standard Library" (p 57) was welcomed; soon George Routledge, John Murray, Smith, Elder, and Chapman & Hall also became customers. In 1851 The Macmillan Company, through a Burn relative working in Macmillan's Cambridge bookstore, became so close—and substantial—a business relationship it still continues intimately. Burn & Son had nevertheless suffered its doldrums but was now alive to plan and grow: James R. Burn (James F.'s son) was taken into the business in 1857. Foregoing the customary bindery apprenticeship, young Burn had consequently few of the traditional workers' prohibitions. He objected to the extravagant embossings then in fashion and proudly introduced a "plain" washed cloth style—with gold stamping only on spine, simple front border and single decorative spot in front center. But James dreamed even more boldly: he visualized steam-powered machinery in the shop, and in 1863 persuaded his father to try it.

By 1885 Burn & Son, fully mechanized and machine-powered, would turn out 80,000 books per week on an appreciable variety of devices: 1 folding machine, 23 sewing machines (11 Brehmer wire stitchers and 12 Smyth thread sewers—an extraordinary investment and testimonial for two new machines), 9 guillotine cutters, 2 smashing machines, 4 circular trimmers, 10 backing machines, 7 hydraulic presses, 11 hand blocking presses, and over 30 other hand- and power-operated pieces. John B. Mercer (whose first task was to inventory the machinery), a Burn nephew, invented the first British gathering machine (1897), and in 1900 developed a book trimmer. In the 1920's once again the firm ambitiously planned drastic bindery changes—ultramodern pilot models were long concealed under tarpaulins—but depression and mechanical difficulties brought no result. So binders, forced literally to develop their own equipment and dictate their own progress, often sustained heavy expenses for the privilege. James Burn & Company further automated its Esher plant in 1958 (p 281) with the latest commercially available equipment, and so continues today.

The Great Exhibition of 1851, at the Crystal Palace, London, was with almost supernatural perspicacity the showplace of world industry, with the graphic arts themselves a compelling example of progress. The catalog alone (p 225), selling for 1 shilling, weighed ¾ pound and could scarcely have been attempted had not steam presses and machine-made paper been newly available. At the show all the conventional forms of printing were featured, including brilliant new chromolithography. Also exhibited were folding machines: hand-fed at 500–1000 signatures per hour, they were not as popular—or necessary—as the marvelous envelope-making machines.

With the 1839 introduction of penny postage all of England had need of vast quantities of envelopes. The envelope-making machine was invented by Edwin Hill and Warren de la Rue and manufactured by Thomas de la Rue & Company, stationers whose process for embossing paper had inspired Leighton's solution for cloth. It took a stack of diamond-shaped paper, folded over three of the triangular tabs, gluing their edges together as a pocket, and gummed the fourth tab as a flap. "India-rubber fingers" gently pushed the finished envelope aside, 60 times a minute. Messrs. Waterlow & Sons' rival machine, despite "an ingenious application of atmospheric pressure" (suction

The rolling machine, invented about 1827 to replace hand beating of sheets which, said *Penny Magazine,* "in most cases, render[s] them perfectly illegible, by transferring the ink of one page to the opposite." The pressure of the rolling press was adjustable. [*Penny Magazine's Monthly Supplement,* December 1833]

instead of manual feeding), made only 30–35 envelopes per minute. De la Rue's fingers and Waterlow's feeding nevertheless were adjudged among the "prettiest novelties of the machine age" at the Exposition. They were essentially the first multiple-action (folding, glueing, gumming) bindery devices to demonstrate that manual dexterity could indeed be imitated successfully.

The judges at the Crystal Palace had not failed to notice the intrusion of machinery into the book bindery, proudly emphasizing the advantages of even the simplest equipment:

"Modern bookbinding is now carried on on a scale of such magnitude as the binders of former times could scarcely have foreseen. The production of books greatly exceeds that of any former period and has caused the application of so much machinery to bookbinding that it may fairly be said to have become a manufacturing business. . . . Mr. Burn of Hatton Garden first introduced the rolling machine; the iron printing press of Hopkinson [Sherwin's later partner] and others were altered to form arming presses. . . . Wilson cutting machines which superseded the plough; the cutting tables with shears . . . all indispensable to large binding establishments. . . . Binding in cloth boards is carried on with such rapidity by houses like the Remnants, the Leightons, the Westleys, and others that 1,000 volumes can be put in cloth, gilt, in *six hours,* provided the covers be previously got ready, and this [case-making] can be done in less than two days!"[4]

The invasion of binding machinery became a trial to many proud hand binders. James and George (Jr.) Kitcat took over their father's bindery in 1821, and although they did not approve of cloth—or of machinery either—for bookwork, their shop nevertheless prospered: they corralled the lucrative Lloyd's of London annual *Register of Shipping* (which Kitcat still binds, almost continuously since 1834), and the business of other publishers—George Routledge, John Cassell, Chapman & Hall, Batsford, Frederick Warne (a brother-in-law of Routledge). As they planned a new factory, they could not escape industry's progress; their deliberations against buying early equipment left them free to select anew. Where steam had been inefficient, there was now gas. By the 1880's an enlightened Kitcat confessed Smyth's book-sewing machines to be "the greatest labour-savers the industry has yet seen," finding that one sewer could turn out as much as 6 girls by hand, and better in quality. A modern G. & J. Kitcat continues today: himself an inventor—the "transmatic" cellophane book jacket and "steamset" binding (p 312)—Lewis Kitcat in 1958 admitted that Britain had "missed the boat" when Americans almost single-handedly "mechanised" the bindery, but he happily found the result to be better books, not at all the "cheap and nasty" products they once had been.

Charles Knight, with both the sincerity of an intrepid humanitarian and the eagerness of an impulsive publisher, was a dominant figure in both these worlds when the bindery industrial revolution began. He, like the Exposition judges, saw the benefits of cloth and machinery almost immediately, and (unlike them) perceived the greater necessity of communicating his keen enthusiasm to a public familiar only with the excesses of industrialization. He considered the rolling machine "the greatest blessing ever conferred upon bookbinders," for it did not merely throw men out of work, it released them from drudgery to find skilled jobs at better wages. He might also have praised it for initiating mechanization into the shops, an example of which progress he itemized in an 1856 popular tract (with apologies to the Exposition judges):

> "We have rolling-machines to make the book solid; cutting machines, to supersede the hand-labour of the little instrument called a plough; embossing machines, to produce elaborate raised patterns on leather or cloth; embossing presses, to give the gilt ornament and lettering. These contrivances, and other similar inventions, have not only cheapened books, but have enabled the publisher to give them a permanent instead of a temporary cover, ornamental as well as useful."[5]

Knight had realistically defined exactly the entire British contribution to bookbinding mechanization (almost everything thereafter was to be American in origin). From then on, however, British "mechanicians" had not simply abandoned—witlessly—a promising mechanical trend: the state of bookbinding industrialization had already outdistanced all expectations. One economic truth nevertheless became paramount: British publishers would have to demonstrate an extraordinary ability to sell great numbers of mechanically made books if the equipment were to justify its expense and the commercial binders were to find themselves on sound footing. (Many straddled the fence between hand and machine work for decades.) But publishers of all description were indeed already hard at work exploiting the fruits of several graphic arts developments which in all their ramifications would soon find the cased-in cloth binding capping a period of truly monumental publishing activity.[6]

"Sheer stark ugliness prevailed everywhere," wrote Philip James, referring to the introduction of the railroads and other industrial developments. But beginning with Thomas Bewick, British book artists, by their love of nature, literary approach, and romantic temper—an enduring "English tradition"—created a beautiful printed microcosm for those not quite ready to read voraciously.

Bewick, a country engraver, was first to think of using the end of his boxwood blocks to obtain gentle tones and great detail from the close grain of the wood. His delicate "white lines" have made his works forever precious. George Nicol, bookseller to George III, displayed some of Bewick's prints, but the king refused to believe they were done on wood until he was shown the blocks. Thomas Carlyle said of Bewick, "Not a great man at all; but a very true of his sort, a well completed and a very *enviable*—living there in communion with the skies and woods and brooks, not here in ditto with the London fogs, the roaring witchmongeries, and railway yellings and howlings." Bewick's pupils were few, and fewer still were the shops among fogs, mongeries, and railway depots which a dolorous wood engraving business could support—at first.

George Cruikshank illustrated the first English translation of Grimm, *German Popular Stories* (1823–1826), bringing new life and imagination into books via the woodcut. But of more importance to the masses, Knight's *Penny Magazine* (begun 1832) suddenly brought Cruikshank, Doyle, Leech, Tenniel, and other artists to the public with delightfully illustrated articles. Similarly, *Saturday Magazine* (1832), *Punch* (1841), and *The Illustrated London News* (1842) all quickly gave wood engraving an astonishing new impetus—the engravers suddenly required five or six apprentices to help get the work out. The public was beginning to read.

Capable of many more impressions than the woodcut, the steel engraving went into keepsakes, annuals, and souvenirs, and for overlooking the ugliness of industrial living, it excelled in spontaneity for graphic humor. Rudolf Ackermann, a German coach designer, opened his "Repository of the Arts" in the Strand, and engaged celebrated caricaturists, among them Hogarth, Gilray, and Rowlandson, to issue a stream of social and political aquatints, printed copies of which were colored by teams of children or French immigrés—both of whom worked with delicacy and sensitivity despite the repetitiousness of their chore. Periodically Ackermann put accumulations of these engravings and etchings into book form, creating a new genre of popular "parlour" or gift picture books, very carefully executed in printing and binding.

Through these years the art of graphic illustration whetted the mass appetite; George Baxter with his "prints for the millions" furnished them for decades, although the finest illustration work, as we have seen, passed to the French who made it distinctly their own, as a book art for collectors. Although the arts connected with more serious literature might also in England (as they had in France) have become pleasure and past-time for rich book collectors, there were many who thought it should not be so.

British publishers and booksellers, unlike their French and German

counterparts who organized and specialized among themselves, preferred instead to rely highly on their individual and personal methods
of salesmanship. Their business thrived on general or "trade" books—
for the masses. In the brisk intellectual climate of London there was
much scurrying and public-house dickering to land a coveted manuscript. So much business was conducted at the convenient Chapter
Coffee House that books on which several publishers—up to 10 or 12—
jointly pooled their interests were called "chapter" books. Few of the
London publishers had printing or binding works of their own, nor
any organization for distribution. They turned out ten or twelve books
a year (for a total, around 1838, of 1500 new titles annually), cut
manufacturing costs to the bone, allowed irregular discounts, and
personally journeyed from city to town persuading booksellers,
drapers, and other merchants to take a few copies from their traveling
stocks.

The traditional home of British publishing was the neighborhood of
St. Paul's Churchyard, Ave-Maria Lane, and Paternoster Row, around
which binderies, publishers, and book shops clustered:

> "Paternoster Row is by no means an attractive place externally [said
> a traveler's guide in the 1830's]. It is a narrow dark street, or rather a
> sort of lane, and is about two hundred yards in length. The houses on
> either side have a dingy and gloomy appearance; and the atmosphere
> is close and heavy. Owing to the height of the houses, the narrowness
> of the street—for there is barely room for two carts to pass in it—
> and the fact of there being no thoroughfare in a direct line at the
> western end, a breath of wind is a luxury very rarely enjoyed in that
> locality."[7]

Although books themselves had only sporadic "publication days" on
which street activity might be lively, one day each month, usually the
last, was heralded as "magazine day." Within hours all the London
periodicals—about 240 titles—were distributed by jobbers and out in
the book shops for sale. On that occasion journal contributors appeared on the Row to see if their copy had been used, and authors
converged to read the magazine reviews of their books. The periodicals, increasingly illustrated, as we have seen, brought a great new
public to book publishers' doorsteps. George H. Putnam revisited the
bustling publishing community in 1869:

> "The new and elegant premises of the Longmans, and the newer and
> handsome palace of the rising Nelsons are both lost in the narrow lane,
> where booksellers most do congregate—Paternoster Row. . . . Baldwin,
> Moxon, Tilt, the elder Bohn [Henry G., whom Putnam called "the
> Napoleon of remainders"], Pickering, and others, have passed off the

stage. . . . But the newer men who have risen up to fame and fortune in this responsible vocation are rapidly eclipsing the old fogies in the magnitude and activity if not respectability of their operations. Of these, Routledge, Warne, Strahan, Macmillan, and Low & Marston, are the most notable. . . ."[8]

It was clear to Putnam—and true for almost a century to come—that publishing in England was still conducted by a group of highly gifted entrepreneurs.

Paternoster Row and its environs were destroyed by incendiary bombs, particularly on the night of 29–30 December 1940; some 20 million volumes were "blitzed" into smoke and ashes along with dozens of venerable binderies and publishing offices. From their gloomy but revered headquarters, nevertheless, British publishers never ceased to furnish great gales of literary and graphic "freshness" to stir the stifling air of Paternoster Row. Some had begun as early as the 18th century.

Although a bookseller, John Bell, had successfully issued a cheap 109-volume series between 1776 and 1792, and another, John Cooke, had issued weekly poetry and prose from the 1790's in cheap book form, their efforts were understandably small, and directed mainly to upper-class readers. For the impecunious who could not buy books, circulating libraries began in the mid 1700's, reaching a well-developed state in 1791 with William Lane (proprietor of the Minerva Press), who sold shopkeepers complete packages of books for a circulating library to be run as a sideline.

Throughout the first half of the 19th century, consequently, reading societies and circulating libraries grew in all the major cities, as did mechanics' institutes and other educational organizations. The Society for the Diffusion of Useful Knowledge and other publishers of pamphlets and tracts more than any other force cultivated reading habits among thousands who had only learned the rudiments of reading in schools only indifferently operated. And they succeeded in establishing a demand: "Books, which at the beginning of the century had been a luxury," Knight wrote, "had now become a necessity."

Knight himself had undertaken several publishing ventures to offer cheap popular instruction and entertainment, both under the auspices of the Society for the Diffusion of Useful Knowledge (*Penny Magazine, Penny Cyclopedia*), and also under his own imprint. To appeal to illiterate factory hands—using hawkers with a subscription scheme—he produced the "Picture Museum of Animated Literature," "Pictorial Sunday Book," and "Pictorial Gallery of Arts," as much surprised as his critics at their immediate success.

In 1844 Knight launched an original series of "Weekly Volumes," pocket-sized books (approximately 3 x 5½ inches) costing 1 shilling in paper, 18 pence in cloth (for example, Vol. LXVII, *Capital and Labour; including the Results of Machinery*, 250 pages, 1845), scrupulously paying royalties on all copyrighted material. Although some titles ran to 10–20,000 copies, the public was not especially fond of educational nonfiction, and most ran to only 5000. By 1847, however, he was running two monthly series as well, one a biographical series on authors which reached 300 issues, and another on England, "The Land We Live In." A printing juror at the 1855 Paris Exposition, Knight regretted that—since by some discrepancy British book printers did not participate in either the English (1851) or French (1855) shows—British books, although "numerous, cheap, neatly printed," got little international notice. He judged them, nevertheless, best. Other British publishers, without Knight's capacity for social enlightenment and bookwork chauvinism, apparently had absented themselves from public scrutiny more by indifference than by accident.

Economic conditions and trade customs were both at work keeping the prices of British books high. To individual entrepreneurs accustomed to issue small, tidy editions, necessarily costly, "The very notion of cheap books stank in the nostrils," wrote Knight, who determined to change it all. The legitimate book trade permitted retailers to buy from wholesalers only on regulated conditions; individuals could bypass the retailer only with difficulty. Despite these circumstances, one "restless and audacious" publisher in Scotland, Archibald Constable, dreamed in 1826 of starting a cheap "Miscellany" ("Series") of new books. "I have now settled my outline of operations," he told Sir Walter Scott, "—a three-shilling or half-crown volume every month, which must and shall sell, not by thousands or tens of thousands, but by hundreds of thousands—ay, by millions!" Although Scott approved, Paternoster Row, maintaining 12 and 14 shilling octavos and 2-guinea quartos, sneered—and rightly so—for there were not then in England any millions of readers. Constable's vision collapsed in bankruptcy.

But the cheap series in fact became a new, exciting mania throughout literary England. They became the medium in which a gigantic British publishing profession—engineered by numbers of remarkable publishing individuals—flourished. John Murray started his "Family Library" in 1829. Pickering's "Aldine Poet" series totalled 53 volumes between 1830–1844. Colburn & Bentley entered with their "Standard Novels" (1831) and then their "National Library"; Henry Colburn was known as the "prince of puffers" for his aggressive and incessant use (and misuse) of reviews, promotion, and advertising to sell books.

David Bogue began a nonfiction "European Library" (1845) which Henry G. Bohn acquired and enlarged into a well-received "Standard Library" (1846); Bohn spoke five languages in the pursuit of manuscripts throughout Europe for his other scientific, antiquarian, and classical series—and taught Bernard Quaritch to become "king of booksellers." George Bell began as a bookseller in 1838, but after a series of annotated classics he (with a partner) purchased Bohn's libraries and kept them going until 1872. Sims & McIntyre (Belfast) had the "Irish Parlour Library" (1846) and for children (accustomed only to the crude chap book—a sheet of paper folded octavo—cheaply printed and hawked by street "chapmen") Sir Henry Cole inaugurated the "Home Treasury" series, whose pleasant artwork revived the whole domain of juvenile literature. But this was just the beginning.

For a restlessly mobile public now growing accustomed to the iron horse, George Routledge started his "Railway Library" (1849), capitalizing on passengers who, with enforced leisure, would want to read voraciously. Routledge, who had commenced in business 1843, introduced Fenimore Cooper and *Uncle Tom's Cabin* to England, the latter so successful, he claimed at his retirement dinner, it was common to see it being read by all six passengers in a single railway compartment. The Routledge firm ultimately ran the Railway Library to 1300 titles, and also published the "Universal Library." Messrs. Longmans simultaneously issued "Traveller's Library."

To distribute this wave of popular reading material, Charles E. Mudie organized a lending library in 1842, charging a 1 guinea ($5.00) annual fee for membership. He employed eight vans for speedy delivery to rural as well as city customers, making his unique subscription service attractive to middle-class readers and intellectuals alike. "Mudie's Select Library" became so successful through extensive advertising he dictated—by what books he would carry—much of British taste for romantic literature. The Mudie bindery, begun in 1864 to repair damaged books, developed into a profitable subsidiary: 76 workers specialized in "Mudie calf" alone.

For travelers William H. Smith promptly began to open "quality" railway station bookstalls in 1848 to distribute the myriad 12mo and 16mo series, with titles selling between 6 and 18 pence. His task was urgent: a London *Times* reporter—watching passengers for hours reading French trash (the works of Eugène Sue, for example)—undertook to examine all the wares in the more unenlightened municipal stations, finding much junk. "It was a painful and a humiliating inspection," he wrote in 1851, and concluded with an incidental observation: "Ladies—we beg their pardon for revealing the singular fact—are not great purchasers of good books at the station." The Smith stalls—700 of them by 1905, decorated with posters, efficient and pleasant, soon drove the lewd stuff out of the terminals. In 1852 Smith dropped Mudie's circulating library to start his own, called "Yellow-backs." At first, so as to mollify other publishers who might think a distributor had no business publishing, Smith used Chapman & Hall's imprint on his new series, but this precaution became quite unnecessary. On the contrary, it was, according to Richard Altick, the start of the "most inspired publishing invention of the era," in which most of them participated.

The yellowbacks, hundreds of inexpensive—vulgar—novels, with covers containing an illustration in blue or green and black ink on yellow enameled paper (nicknamed "mustard plasters") pushed serious reading matter out of sight. "But," said an observer, "as only a few select souls can read a serious book to much purpose in a railway train, there is an apology for railway literature." Sold for 1 or 2 shillings, the 4⅛- x 6⅝-inch yellowbacks flourished between 1855 and 1870, bridging a shortage in the supply of cloth from cotton denied to England by both the Crimean and American Civil Wars. Yellowbacks actually continued until the 1890's, their covers becoming the fore-runner of later book jackets (p 263). Chapman & Hall, Routledge, and Smith, Elder (publishers of *Pall Mall Gazette, Cornhill* magazine, and later, the great *Dictionary of National Biography*) also issued yellowbacks, but W. H. Smith, not wishing to remain in publishing, shortly discontinued his revolutionary series.

John Carter found in the cloth-bound "railway libraries," as the cheap series were called, generically, "a very respectable standard of tasteful workmanship," although the earliest of them had small type and narrow margins—cheaply produced in every sense. The poorest series, of course, both in design and content, quickly perished. Knight, with participatory pride, tried to explain the paradox: "The cheapness consisted in the employment of the best writers to produce books of original merit at a price that was essentially low, by comparison with the ordinary rate at which books for the few were sold. . . ." With more candor elsewhere, however, he admitted that the "single volumes, printed in small type on indifferent paper, and sold mostly at a shilling —are almost wholly devoted to novels, English or American." They were, in the words of another publisher struck by the irony of mass production, "marvels of cheapness and elegance." But this—popular content in cheap format—was exactly what the new reading audience wanted.

Literary critics, however, could find little praise for the new literature, despite its popularity. The chief form of the novel was the "triple decker," a long—"infernally padded"—gothic romance divided into 3 (occasionally 4) cliff-hanging installments, each separately bound and selling for 31s 6d the set. Like most cheap fiction, they were unimportant, "mawkish and unnatural," devoured mostly by women. But unlike the early circulating and institutional libraries, which offered works fully a generation old, the new cheap series contained the newest and best that was then being written or translated from other languages.

Issued at first in calf, boards, or sheets, popular fiction was avidly "read to death" by the new urban middle class. Its "stabilisation" in cloth occurred about 1859, according to Carter, who also, with British collector and authority Michael Sadleir, considered the novel in publishers' original bindings the normal product of the commercial binder. Carter traced five developmental periods for clothwork: (1) origins and primitive style, 182?–1831; (2) struggle for recognition, 1832–1840; (3) establishment of supremacy, 1841–1855; (4) expansion of fabric range, 1856–1870; (5) variations on the technically perfect product, 1871–1900. Blind arabesques for poetry (about 1837), pictorial stampings for novels (about 1840), new cloth patterns—wavy, bead, bubble, pebble, herringbone (between 1856–65) were almost as gaudy as French deluxe books during the gift season.

The British publisher and his binder had become so confident with these progressive theatrics they—and their public—had all but forgotten the original leather binding, once so unimpeachable. Bernard Quaritch in 1889 complained:

> "The reading public is wholly ignorant of what is meant by 'bookbinding.' It is one of the industrial arts, capable of high and splendid cultivation, and absolutely indispensable for the preservation of the literary monuments of former ages. Most men who have handled and used books are aware of the necessity of such a mode of protecting them; but, ordinarily, the work of the binder is not supposed [by the public today] to be anything more elegant or enduring than the mere temporary covering bestowed by the publisher upon his printed wares. . . ."[9]

The three-decker continued supreme through the 1860's and '70's, thanks nevertheless to the still prosperous circulating libraries: with a modest subscription it took many times that fee to read the whole continuing episode. With the perfection of ink-stamping techniques during the same time, "the technical equipment of the bookbinder was virtually complete," according to Sadleir (whose wonderful library of gothic romances—a priceless specimen collection of period bindings—was deposited at the University of Virginia by another avid collector, Robert K. Black). At one busy bindery a *Bookbinder* reporter was shown a book's case which required 13 blockings, the colors "very deftly blended." It is possible that binders and public alike still disliked the texture of the cloth.

Finally, however, in the 1890's the public, consisting more of book buyers than borrowers, began to insist on getting the three segments inside one cheaper cover, resulting in a large, plainly bound tome selling for 6 shillings. Such a book was George Moore's *A Mummer's Wife*, published deliberately in one volume to challenge Mudie's demand for triple-deckers. It worked. "Thus [with heavy gilt stamping and sometimes patterned edges all around] in an orgy of magnilo-quence—preposterous but pathetic," wrote Sadleir, "—the three-decker plunged to extinction."

By the 1890's, of course, if the trade book's literary qualifications had improved, its physical state was still open to criticism. "The average novel," wrote designer Ruari McLean, "was not actively ugly; it was negative. It was produced, not in bad taste, but in no taste at all." With emphasis on utility (electrotyped, an edition could last 30–40 years), design had been left to manufacturers. Along with ugliness, cheapness prevailed: even Pickering's Aldine Classics, 5 shillings in 1830–1844, were 1½ in 1870—but most books were so poorly made and fragile they had no chance of lasting. A few pub-lishers, at least, noticed the deplorable state of bookmaking and would try to combine beauty, economy, and durability—almost an act of prestidigitation. There were few precedents.

English bookmaking, by the 1880's "as dead as cold mutton" and facing depression times a decade later, was well on the road to ex-haustion after the manias of cheap series and penny novels, much as it had found itself after the Napoleonic Wars. A handful of small publishers, actually functioning more like the private presses to come, managed to turn out a trickle of high-quality keepsakes and chap books. In 1844 William Pickering had persuaded the Chiswick Press, Charles Whittingham's fine establishment (dating to 1789), to order a recasting of the long neglected original Caslon types for his edition of Juvenal's *Satires* and a few other selected titles. Pickering's taste for typography was as keen as his sense of publishing; his Aldine Poets, his editions of Milton and other classics, and his prayer books earned among bibliophiles the simple commendation, "a Pickering edition." Edward Moxon also published well-designed books and parlour albums, but to Pickering, along with his development of the cloth binding, go all accolades for maintaining the thread of fine bookwork. The thread, happily, was not lost.

Eighteen year old Joseph M. Dent came to London in 1867 to work for a small bookbinder, and shortly developed his own thriving busi-ness. But on New Year's Eve, 1888, Dent's shop burned to the ground, and all was gone. Dent toured Europe with his family to forget the loss —and began to think of publishing. Reprint work had recently appealed to him as a way to provide himself with quantities of sheets for deluxe binding as profitable gift work. Within a year of the fire, Dent, whom bookman Frank Swinnerton (once a Dent employee) characterized as a disagreeable boss, a violent temper, and a bad speller, promptly began publishing "The Temple Library" and later, "The Temple Classics" (1896). The former series got welcome praise, recorded with careless modesty by Dent in his memoirs: " 'The best piece of book-making he had ever seen for many a year,' said the great book seller Quaritch, or words to that effect." Like Pickering, Dent entered publishing via cheap reprints, and in so doing improved the mechanical construction of books everywhere.

To put good literature into even more homes, Dent launched his 1-shilling "Everyman's Library" with 50 titles in 1906, precariously authorizing giant printings of 10,000 to 30,000 to keep unit costs down. Bravely he issued in this series Grote, *History of Greece* in 12 volumes, and Hakluyt, *Voyages*, in 8. But so overwhelming was the public's response Dent quickly outgrew his London facilities, and moved his plant to Letchworth, Hertfordshire, an idealistic garden community where his workers might escape some of the usual evils of factory-town living. Dent's audacious plans paid off—and he was long commended for books "cheap as well as beautiful," a feat attributable perhaps more to his intimate knowledge of printing and binding methods than to a compulsion for art reform.

But publishers are seldom so shallow: Basil Blackwell, whose Oxford bookshop is today reputedly the largest in the world, in the first (1932) of several Dent Memorial Lectures expressed his admiration— possibly of Dent himself—for the traditional London publisher: "One lobe of his brain must be devoted to literature, scholarship, art; the other to adroit bargaining. . . ." As discoverer of literary merit and anticipator of reading tastes, the publisher, said Blackwell, carried author, printer, papermaker, binder, and book-seller hanging on his judgment. Author J. B. Priestley flattered Dent's academic influence: "Everyman's Library," he said, "has probably done more for education than some of our universities." Dent's success nevertheless became one of the most conspicuous triumphs of machine bookwork, and the series—still going strong—almost contains the 1000 titles he originally visualized. But not all readers and bookmen cared for the mechanical solution of what they deemed an art problem.[10]

After hectic decades of industrial speed and ugliness, it seems natural a counterforce should develop. An "archenemy of the modern machine" materialized in the life and work of William Morris, architect, poet, painter, interior decorator. Always an insatiable and cultured worker striving to achieve the social dignity of man, he soon added calligrapher, type designer, and printer to his many skills. No branch of art escaped the impact of his genius.

When he attended a lantern-slide lecture by artist (Sir) Emery Walker in 1888 at a London arts and crafts exhibit, Morris began to visualize his own printing shop as an opportunity to practice his esthetic dreams. Although he detested Bodoni's work as cold and mechanical (". . . the sweltering hideousness of the Bodoni letter, the most illegible type that was ever cut, with its preposterous thick and thins . . ."), his plunge into medieval letter forms was just as pervasive as the Italian's experimentation with modern typography and enameled paper. Morris' contention that a book ought to be well designed, was, of course, valid: "In fact," he wrote, "a book, printed or written, has a tendency to be a beautiful object, and that we of this age should generally produce ugly books, shows, I fear, something like malice prepense—a determination to put our eyes in our pockets wherever we can." Morris had indeed caught publishers, printers, and binders alike at their lowest moment.

From the very start of his Kelmscott Press in 1891 Morris made magnificent books for a small audience of educated collectors. Stressing "utility and beauty," his productions contained—exuded—all the rubricator's and typographer's devices long forgotten by common English readers. He combined woodcut and type into a perfect marriage. Unlike many contemporary experimenters with the printed word, Morris was financially successful—although more respected in America and Germany than England—and gave considerable impetus to the appreciation of books.

Morris' intention was to treat the book as an integrated whole—type, paper, margins, artwork, binding—much in keeping with the medieval scribes (and the earliest printers counterfeiting them), who singly produced manuscripts of great beauty. And so the Kelmscott books in their papers, the colors of their inks, the impression of their types, betray immensely the feeling of craftsmanship and achievement. The Kelmscott *Chaucer* (1896) took 1 year and 9 months to print: it contained in addition to 87 pictures by artist Edward Burne-Jones (who once claimed books were of no use except "to prop up models in difficult positions"), a full-page woodcut title, and numerous frames, borders, and initial words designed by Morris himself.

But Morris' beautiful typefaces, designed, cast, and set to evoke images of medieval calligraphy and illumination, of necessity contained neo-medieval eccentricities which impeded the modern appreciation of a book's editorial content. Morris was not beyond changing the copy to improve his word spacing—a refuge other compositors could not seek. And sensible bookmen could not fully praise the net effect: "When a book becomes decorative at the expense of its readability," wrote Daniel B. Updike, "it ceases to be a book and becomes a decoration, and has then no *raison d'etre* as a book." Aside from a very select public charmed by the freshness of his approach (ironically, only the rich could afford what Morris—an active socialist —proudly offered as a humble laborer), others found his books affected, faddish, and utterly unreadable. Nevertheless, in the development of an art form and as a moving force, the sublime idiosyncrasies could be tolerated: "During the greater part [of the 19th century]," wrote bibliophile Holbrook Jackson, "a well-designed book was so rare that self-consciousness in the early days of the revival was inevitable and even excusable."

And revival it was. Timed providentially with the upsurge of a new young reading public with money and leisure, renewed interest in the graphic arts was sparked by Morris' writings and work. Herbert P. Horne restored forgotten Scotch typefaces in his art nouveau magazine, *The Century Guild Hobby Horse* (begun 1886), printed at Chiswick Press. *The Hobby Horse* (wherein each contributor had "free reign") played a crucial role in the arts and crafts movement; even Morris contributed to it and claimed it had inspired his Kelmscott Press. Horne went on to design several typefaces himself, one of which was cut especially for Chatto & Windus—a firm, according to Ruari McLean, with the longest unbroken record for excellence in book design. Charles Ricketts, with his Vale Press in London, turned out superb printing, designing some typefaces, and decorating a number of fine books. He produced *The Dial*, a sumptuous literary quarterly much like *Yellow Book* (p 69). Andrew Tuer's Leadenhall Press also did outstanding work. C. H. St. John Hornby, later a senior partner of W. H. Smith (now growing stationers and booksellers), founded his Ashendene Press in 1894. More than the relaxation of a business man, Ashendene gave Eric Gill one of his first lettering assignments, and endured until 1935.

A new generation refused to slacken the pace. The Curwen Press (begun 1863) was revived in 1917 by Harold Curwen, a grandson of the founder, a student of Edward Johnston (p 65), and a perfectionist—working only in Caslon for discipline. Some publishers could be both commendable and commercial: William Heinemann paid careful attention to design, as did Jonathan Cape, who maintained an elegant style through World War II despite shortages which made other publishers' books look like "remainder biscuits." R. & R. Clark and T. & A. Constable, both in Edinburgh, were also two commercial presses long known for excellent printing. By the turn of the century, obviously, the arts and crafts movement had cultivated a hearty appetite for fine presswork that would not easily dissipate. For the binding arts Morris' influence was devious, perhaps, but no less revolutionary.

Thomas J. Cobden-Sanderson, long an accomplished and practicing corporation lawyer, strangely felt the influence of Morris' "arts and crafts" revival. Morris' wife recommended that "C-S" (as he was known to friends) learn bookbinding, since it was the only remaining art form her husband had not attempted. In 1883 after studying six months under the master binder Roger de Coverly (first lesson: pulling a book to pieces; refolding; collating), C-S quickly applied himself. His first work, a book of poems, he gave to his wife; the second, Marx, *Le Capital*, he gave to Morris—both gifts artistically and intellectually accepted with profound admiration.

Cobden-Sanderson was at first (like Morris) considered a "gentleman amateur" by an unfriendly, uncomprehending trade—the slip of a tool was a blemish to them, but a mark of "individualism" to him. "We need hardly say," *Bookbinder* commented in 1888, "that we cannot assent to this new doctrine." Nevertheless, a year later when Bernard Quaritch praised him for fine work "in flat contradiction to the *précieuseté* of his theories," the journal deigned to interview him. "On an average," said C-S, not beyond a commercial plug, "I work five or six hours a day—doing all the work, the rough (if there is any) and the smooth, with the assistance of my wife who sews, and sews admirably, and always from 'end to end' and 'round the bands.'" His work was frequently on display, and he began to win wide recognition.

Soon Cobden-Sanderson turned out such fresh and perfect work he was credited with establishing a "ninth" style of binding—really only a renewed affirmation of traditional craftsmanship—as collectors counted the principal masters of old. The French government bought two of his bindings, the only foreigner so honored during his lifetime. In 1893 Morris invited C-S to move close to his shop in Hammersmith so as to work together; with a small "company" of four fellow workers the Doves "Bindery" (an "American" word apparently new to C-S) thus began in a little "slum" by the Thames. Among the many girls he engaged for their instruction—training three at a time for a 500-guinea fee, Chicagoan Emily Preston in 1902 described her infatuation with the shop. Employees were from the working class, except the sewer, "a girl who has seen better days, and has to work," all so capable that C-S "raises them" in his eyes to his own level. She found Mrs. Cobden-Sanderson (with little time now for sewing) a violent socialist, wearing "aesthetic" gowns to reform meetings.

Although C-S too no longer did any work personally, he approached near-philosophic heights in his task, with more than a trace of legalism in his quest:

> "The ideal book or book beautiful, is a composite thing made up of many parts, and may be made beautiful by the beauty of each of its parts; its contents, material, writing or printing, illumination or illustration, and binding; of each of its parts in subordination to the whole which collectively they constitute: or it may be made beautiful by the beauty of one or more of its parts, all the other parts subordinating or even effacing themselves that the one or the other may be supreme, each in turn being capable of playing this supreme part, and each in its own peculiar and characteristic way."[11]

Bookseller Thomas Bain sold many of C-S' books with little effort and warm personal encouragement (upon Morris' death Bain bought *Le Capital* at auction and presented it to Mrs. Cobden-Sanderson). By 1896 C-S was independent enough to disregard customers' instructions to bind in certain colors or in matching style: he worked, a trade journal reported with a touch of sarcasm, "only by inspiration." Cobden-Sanderson nevertheless had become as much a commercial success as life-time craftsmen.

In partnership with Emery Walker, C-S, 60 years old in 1900, formed the Doves Press, assuming a special typographic challenge to correct Morris' humanist leanings: "The whole duty of Typography," he wrote, "is to communicate to the imagination, without loss by the way, the thought or image intended to be conveyed by the Author. . . ." He demonstrated that printing with plain type, well set, and good margins and paper, could be noble work. The Doves Press Bible (5 volumes, 1903–1905) has been called "the triumph of perfect austerity." His books were never illustrated, although most had decorative colored initials by Graily Hewitt or Edward Johnston— whose *Writing & Illuminating & Lettering* (1906, Pitman), now so compact and disorganized, was considered the "best handbook ever written for any craft." To Walker's utter dismay, C-S in 1916 decided he had solved all his typographic problems, and methodically began throwing the precious Doves Press matrices and types nightly into the Thames. Partnership notwithstanding, C-S felt he owed Walker nothing: "Finally," he wrote to Sydney Cockerell, "if E. W. [sic] launched the Kelmscott Press did not I launch E. W.? It was I who invited him to give that first lecture at the Arts and Crafts Exhibition in 1888!" A "small, insignificant-looking man," husband of a "militant suffragette," Cobden-Sanderson had styled himself "a visionary and a fanatic," rationalizing to some extent conduct indeed unbecoming a barrister.

The Doves Press Bible, the Ashendene Press edition of Dante (*Divina Commedia*, 3 volumes: *Inferno, Purgatorio, Paradiso*, 1902–1905), and the Kelmscott *Chaucer* became classically "three ideal books of modern typography," since they were superb pieces from the three most ideal revival presses. But Cobden-Sanderson, having first become a master binder quite independent of his press record, single-handedly by his design and execution of inspiring works taught a new generation of binders to carry on. Douglas Cockerell, C-S' first apprentice, for many years operated the London hand bindery of W. H. Smith: "Books for binding can be handed in at any of Messrs. W. H. Smith & Sons Railway Bookstalls or branches . . . ," could not have been more accommodating to commuting booklovers of modest means. Cockerell, with his son Sydney (as Douglas Cockerell & Son), performed fine bookbinding as did his pupils Francis Sangorski and George Sutcliffe, who started their own shop in 1901. The revival gave young binders the opportunity to bask in honorable, lucrative work—and the boldness to fight mediocrity however they saw it. Zaehnsdorf and Chivers especially railed against bad sewing (p 200); Riviére and de Coverly were harder workers if somewhat less vociferous.

Robert Riviére was apprenticed to a bookseller in Bath, 1829, but became a binder in London in 1840—so good he bound a special 1000-copy edition of the 1851 Exposition catalog for presentation to "all the crowned heads in the world," but who, according to Quaritch, had a "wrong-headed elaborateness." Having only two daughters, Riviére took a son-in-law into the business, nevertheless renaming the shop Robert Riviére & Son in 1881. (Riviére was also Cobden-Sanderson's uncle.) The firm did excellent hand work for libraries and private collectors around the world.

Roger de Coverly was apprenticed to Zaehnsdorf until 1851, at which time he worked for J. & J. Leighton. In 1863 he apprehensively opened his own shop and almost to his own surprise got an order from Basil M. Pickering, William's son, himself a bookseller and publisher, who further provided de Coverly encouragement later when times were rough. William Morris also gave him work and recommended him to friends—like Cobden-Sanderson. A *Bookbinder* reporter found de Coverly proud of C-S as a pupil, "although Mr. Sanderson has developed one or two fads of which his former teacher greatly disapproves." An amateur musician, music collector, and founder of madrigal societies, de Coverly also complained of bad sewing, without having time, apparently, to offer a solution. "Upon one subject he feels strongly:" *Bookbinder* reported, "his opinion is that a certain machine [Brehmer?] used in some cloth shops for sewing cannot be too strongly condemned. It sews with thread or cotton, which rips the sheet up in the fold at the back for a short distance both at top and bottom, and thus wounds the book in its most vital part. . . ." Never before, at any rate, had there been so much interest over the technical state of bookbinding; never again would all parties in bookwork ignore the smallest element of design or quality.

Morris, Ricketts, and Cobden-Sanderson had succeeded, above all, in getting commercial publishers to reexamine their own output of books. They took the design of the binding out of the manufacturer's shop at last. Ended was the practice wherein a finisher simply labeled the spine and used a stock plate on the front; ended too was the use of an illustration borrowed from the text, duplicated for the cover. But it was a slow exercise of responsibility; bibliophile Brander Matthews persisted in finding publisher's bindings "mostly ill-bound from haste and greed, from ignorance and reckless disregard of art." It was almost always a matter of full gold stamping.

Through the 1860's, '70's, and '80's, books continued to boast heavy ink and gold embellishments which left scarcely a blank square inch on front or spine. So much real gold went into covers that binders even in those bountiful times refused to discard the waste: in each shop a "rubbing off" chest, a large wood bin topped with a grill on which book cases were hand rubbed to remove excess gold (called "skewings") was carted twice a year to a refinery, its contents exchanged for a gold bar. Librarian George A. Stephen took the trouble to categorize stampings: purely decorative, symbolic, heraldic, and pictorial. "The aim of the artist in producing a decorative design," he said, naively, "is simply to cover the available space in a dignified and beautiful manner."

But others—particularly the artists themselves—described pressures more compelling than dignity and beauty. One of them, Charles E. Dawson, in 1908 dismissed authors as totally incapable of a suitable—salable—cover idea, and regarded publishers as "old Rip van Winkles of Paternoster Row" who also lacked any artistic perception: "the formidable imprint of Messrs. So and So & Co., Ltd. really stands for a very ordinary middle-aged gentleman with the education of a grocer, and the outlook on life of a bookstall clerk." This man seemed hardly the individual Blackwell found to be carrying five ancillary industries on his shoulders! Dawson recommended 4 colors as the limit for the cover of an ordinary novel (with cost becoming the "bug-bear" of the bindery), although the designer who could simulate 4 with only 2 stampings could win a publisher's affection and "an occasional lunch." As to subject matter for both cloth and paper covers, Dawson revealed that the highest reaction—in circulation and sales—came with "the pretty woman, full length or head." *Bookbinder*, after years of praise for the fine (stylized) binding, found itself now advocating: "The artist must subjugate himself to his client"; he must furnish a design "striking enough to call a person from one side of the street to the other to look at it. . . ." The demands of commercial bookwork (even as we know them today) had turned the publisher's noble aims into the salesman's raucous pitch.

John Leighton, under the name Luke Limner, produced many elaborate book covers and drawing-room albums mostly for the Leighton bindery, 1840–1880. Gustav Doré contributed many designs through mid-century. Edmund Evans—who originated the yellowback—set up a wood engraving business specializing in impeccable color work; for Randolph Caldecott (honored by an award founded by Frederic G. Melcher for outstanding children's art) and Kate Greenaway he sometimes used 8 to 10 colors, his inks scrupulously matching the artist's colors. The delicate Evans-produced picture books foreshadowed a revolt against "machine-art" similar to the objections against "machine-books."

Walter Crane had designed some of Routledge's yellowbacks, and went on to a series of children's "Picture Books" printed by Evans; along with his love of medieval illuminated manuscripts, and like Morris' own control over an entire project, his "crane" insignia on art work by the 1890's similarly stood for complete control over chapter opening, title page, and binding. Crane became president of an arts and crafts exhibition group for whom, as its spokesman, he was obliged, apparently, to criticize much of the machine bookwork he had designed (p 84). Other artists like Charles Ricketts, William Nicholson, Laurence Housman, A. A. Turbayne, and Arthur Rackham also found themselves welcoming book assignments, sometimes with mixed feelings. A sweeping reform on a higher, "aesthetic" level soon brought Victorian ambivalences to a confrontation with "modern" times.

J. M. Dent had been introduced to Aubrey Beardsley by a mutual bookseller friend, Frederick H. Evans, and with extraordinary daring to match the extraordinary confrontation of two unlikely coworkers, commissioned Beardsley, then a 19-year-old insurance clerk, to illustrate an edition of Malory, *Morte d'Arthur* (2 volumes issued in monthly installments, 1893–1894). The publisher—whose forte was binding economy—thereby started a new art era. From his *Morte d'Arthur* work—over 350 illustrations—Beardsley quickly learned to

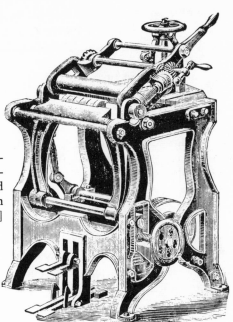

American hand rounding and backing machine at height of its development, about 1890. A rounded and backed book may be seen clamped in the vise. [Lockwood]

apply the fashionable Japanese black and white technique to book illustration. In a prim London of the 1890's he horrified society with subtle and ingenious delineations, often with a few undulating lines, of the human torso. Within 8 years (until his death in 1898), working in a candle-lit room hung with black velvet, Beardsley tossed off over 1000 sketches, frontispieces, title pages, endpapers, covers, and posters. Such unusual circumstances and outpourings gave unusual direction to all commercial bookwork.

The publisher John Lane employed Beardsley for his *Yellow Book*, a hard-bound literary quarterly, which for a tiring reading public needed startling approaches for survival. To attract a purchaser from across the street the book's covers used a brilliant yellow with thick black lines—much like the old mustard plasters and like lurid French novels then in vogue. For *Yellow Book* Beardsley did something "startling, mordant, bitter or freshly beautiful" in every issue, the first four of which were so in demand they were reprinted several times. When Lane was forced to dismiss Beardsley (because of Oscar Wilde's scandals) the fifth issue was scrapped, and subsequent ones were dull. The Beardsley touch nevertheless rescued bookwork from intolerably busy bindings by diverting public interest to the outer jacket. The integral book itself recaptured its dignity and beauty at last.

Neither William Morris nor all of England, however, had yet seen the heights to which industrialization would become possible; as far as the bindery was concerned, Morris' protestations were eloquent but premature. As in France, the binderies were last to witness technological improvements. Many shop "inventions" were simply specific, temporary solutions to difficult jobs, neither acknowledged nor publicized. Those discoveries deemed valuable were patented in a wild display of trade exclusivity: Robert Peck's bindery had "photergon" stamping; Messrs. Birdsall & Son had a "Stronghold" (leather spine) case and a "Bibliofortis" (double sewn) binding. Bagster, Riviére, Chivers, and the others all had their specialties which were, in the last analysis, nothing more than shortcuts to limited production methods, almost incapable of enlargement to industry-wide production.

Some important bindery equipment in England was unrecognized as such, and never patented. As in France, the guillotine, the roller-backer, and the embosser replaced the most taxing manual operations: they were protested on the grounds that labor-saving devices put men out of work (the very measure of their success), but teleologically they were bound to endure. Single-operation devices, they were neither too sophisticated, hand- or steam-operated, to make the transition to fuller mass production: the cutter, for example, was appropriate for a single cut, 10 consecutive cuts, or continuous use. Nor were they prohibitive in cost for the smallest shops to acquire.

Because of the many small publishers in England, however, binders usually found themselves happy to cop many short, non-standard jobs not really suitable for machinery capable of continuous, mass-produced

Paper and book trimmer, about 1890. Once clamped, one or a stack of unbound books was in position for trimming on three sides. [Lockwood]

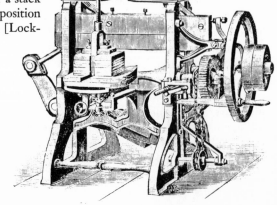

output. "We send nothing out," said an official of William Collins, Sons & Company, London, for whom specialization was unknown, "if it pays other people to do it, it will pay us." Although a folding machine (Brown's) had been patented in 1850, the economy of hand labor was not displaced for decades; although a case-making machine (Nichol's) had been invented in 1855, even the largest binders did not obtain one until the 1890's—from America. The book and commercial binderies, with so many individual—hand—processes at first kept up with the increasing speed of the pressroom generally only by hiring more and more manual workers, mostly women. With the adoption of the 8-hour work day in the bookbinding trades (1890), other solutions presented themselves: reducing costs (replacing genuine gold with colored inks or imitation foils), and, inevitably, acceding to more standardization—and machinery.

A nipping machine (replacing the rolling press) was introduced to British shops in 1882, utilizing a mechanical "pounding" action to compress (smash) books. It was a "second generation" solution for the original beating hammer. But in a forest of machinery it was hard to distinguish claims and promises from what was truly practical and lasting. A master binder lamented:

"... The compulsory education of the masses has enormously increased the call for cheap books. ... The development of the business by steam machinery, coupled with competition, has tended considerably to cheapen the binding. We are constantly putting our hands into our pockets to buy a new machine of one kind or another, and no sooner do we get one than some improvement is introduced, which either renders necessary a new machine or an expensive alteration or addition to the old one. ..."[12]

Suddenly, in the 1890's an invasion of fast, intricate, American machinery punctuated such worries, and hit England hard: the Smyth book sewing machine (1882), the Sheridan case-maker (1897), the Dexter folder (1898), the Crawley rounder and backer (1900). Some binders boasted that English work—with American machinery—was better and cheaper than France's or Germany's, although they criticized the latter mercilessly (p 79), one suspects, purely to stifle its ominously growing competition. What one publisher, Nelson, could do with quantities of such yankee equipment was far beyond traditional English entrepreneurship (p 273). At any rate, the British publisher and binder had, with unique self-confidence, demonstrated to the world throughout the latter half of the 19th century that the masses, capable of phenomenal reading appetites, wanted cheap books of all description and, said a thankful British newspaper, they could have them "serviceably and beautifully bound at the same price which the Frenchman pays for yellow-paper covers." Without the gigantic reading market any amount of ingenious new machinery—American or other—would have been just so much iron.

The entrance of machinery into bookmaking trades had not really jeopardized the craft of bookbinding; that much was plainly admitted by all. Machines had, instead, engendered a new industry altogether, from typecasting to case-making, with the manufacture of books, by the end of the 19th century, almost fully mechanized. The graphic arts industry was expanding, the book-buying public appreciated new efficiency and low prices. *Studio*, long an astute witness and commentator on European art tastes and trends, had perceived in 1899 the necessity of machine work:

> "For the popularizing of literature means that bookbinding, as an art and handicraft, has long since ceased to keep pace with the demand for books. To place them within the reach of average purses was inevitably to bring machine-production to the bookseller's aid. Either the whole world of literature was to remain closed to nine out of ten of the community, or the fine handicraft of bookbinding must be supplanted for all ordinary purposes by low-priced machine-made covers. For a century or so the English public accepted the latter alternative...."[13]

With penetrating uneasiness, however, *Studio*'s dedication to the arts forced it to conclude with the dilemma no one had yet been able to resolve: "Must all machine-work, under all circumstances, be hopelessly vulgar and commonplace?"

Not even Cobden-Sanderson, acknowledged master of his craft, cared to approach that question, although, ever the idealist, he was at least open-minded. After an 1889 bookbinding lecture illustrated by "oxyhydrogen light" he concluded: "I see in the immediate future, it is true, no new school to carry on the great traditions of the past, yet I am prepared to admit that the unexpected may happen...."[14]

# 3 Germany:

## Die Schone Borse

NAPOLEON I OF FRANCE, WITH AN IMPERIAL ARMY HUNGRY WITH visions of glory and plunder, fought at Leipzig, Saxony, yet another battle (October 1813) for the aggrandizement of an empire. Germans of wealth and culture were not unaware of French appetites. Whole libraries were frantically dispersed by families and religious institutions to avoid their falling into Napoleon's hands. Auctioneering of books was actually going on in Leipzig, traditionally the German publishing center, as French guns boomed outside the town. Although the "Battle of the Nations" was a defeat for the emperor, the German population found itself rendered destitute by the conflict and its aftermath. Rudolf Ackermann put aside his Strand shop caricatures to start a relief fund, so persuasive even the British Parliament contributed. Leipzig providently survived and returned compulsively to bookmaking.

After the Napoleonic Wars, nevertheless, publishing and book-manufacturing activities throughout central Europe were slow in developing. Some 38 states of the German Confederation each maintained a degree of sovereignty, and ever fearing some form of trespass, kept myopic legal eyes on boundaries and protective tariffs. Largely because of this political structure, for example, there was (until 1901) no uniform copyright law governing book printings. In Prussia, if the author's contract did not specify the quantity of an edition, the publisher might reprint (without alteration) as often as he cared to; in Saxony, however, the first printing usually could not exceed 1000 copies; in Baden the quantity was unlimited but reprints were prohibited.

Bookbinding too suffered from neglect and lack of direction; craftsmen without exchange of ideas and examples worked clumsily with wretched taste. German books were conventionally issued by their publishers, as in France, in paper covers, but unlike the French, the Germans made no pretense of later rebinding. The books were stitched only sufficiently to hold together. "In Germany," said a disappointed 19th century traveler, "all the books are in sheets and all the beds without." Although something like the lending library had been known as early as 1800 in Germany, there was little stimulation for the book arts or its trade.

Ironically, however, intellectual activity in Germany had never been stronger. In its heritage was the very invention of printing, the birthplace of Protestant thought, and the cradle of much scientific progress. These were the bountiful years of Beethoven, Goethe, Schiller, Kant, Hegel, the Humboldts; these were the fervent years of pan-Germanic folklore and ethnic research. The success of the works of gifted authors such as these seemed certain of finding suitable publication and manufacture, but distribution among the dozens of semi-independent states of the Confederation was blocked by almost insurmountable legal restrictions. Dissemination was for Germany the one serious problem it faced alone, and its solution, in retrospect, was uniquely German.

In 1825 an unusual organization for book distribution in Germany took shape at Leipzig. Booksellers there had long assembled daily in Richter's Coffee House (much like the Chapter Inn of London) to settle trade matters, and began to exercise some authority there. Called *Börsenverein der deutschen Buchhändler* ("Exchange Association of German Bookmen") or *Die Börse*, it soon handled business disputes, copyright problems, and allied issues throughout the German-speaking world. In 1865 the membership consisted of 668 book publishers, 121 engraving and music publishers, 2047 book sellers, and 167 print and music sellers. With a traditional love for organization, the Borse by the 1880's perfected a price control system, and functioned from 1842 on as a clearing house between publisher and bookseller, especially for single, hard-to-find titles (the most elusive of sales). Daily—or oftener—each bookseller throughout Germany would send his agent in Leipzig a quantity of orders which were forwarded to the Borse for sorting and delivery to publishers. In one year alone (1887) the Borse handled 24 million orders. It was to be the most comprehensive book trade organization ever formed. Membership—and training—were very strict.

For booksellers the German organization prescribed the tutelage of employees with care. A young man had to serve a 2 to 4 year bookstore apprenticeship before becoming a junior clerk; after many years as a senior clerk he might—with luck and capital—become a partner or start his own shop. Leipzig also had a School of Bookselling for more orthodox instruction. The professional bookseller proudly considered himself a good judge and a "servant" of literature: he sold magazines only grudgingly and would seldom consent to handle stationery.

Instrumental to the promotion of business activity in the German book world were a large number of periodicals devoted to bookmaking. Among two dozen of them the most influential—"the soul of the German book trade"—was the *Börsenblatt*, founded 1834 by the *verein*. A 9x12-inch publication of 20–24 pages, it appeared three times a week (daily during the book fairs) with various communications, complaints, selling suggestions, and lists of books published. Frederick Leypoldt, who on continental visits reported German activities to his New York book friends, eventually became first editor of *Publishers' Weekly* (a replacement in 1872 of *American Publishers' Circular & Literary Gazette*), a trade publication not surprisingly still similar in content.

In 1836 the Borse built a magnificent headquarters in Leipzig where its members could transact all manner of business. To meet old and new friends, to buy or sell sheets or books, and to settle their accounts, bookpeople came to town yearly "the fourth Tuesday after Easter," during which time the town gave itself heartily to a book trade fair. On the following Sunday, to discuss the state of the industry, the Borse held its general meeting, so important and commanding that absentees were obliged to pay a fine unless they could give "full and sufficient excuse" for their delinquency. A lavish headquarters was built anew in 1888 on property donated by the city, which in 1965 celebrated its 800th anniversary, still pledging continued faith and dedication in its heritage of book production.

To conclude the fair festivities it was the custom of the Leipzig Clerks' Association to give the book trade a grand official supper. Old and young, employer and employee, buyer and seller—all mixed with rare *gemütlichkeit* and respect for the venerable establishment. "The presence of so many men eminent for talent, genius, learning, or business ability," said an American observer in 1857, "incites the ambition of the younger members of the trade, and arouses their emulation to trade in their footsteps. . . ." A few days later all travelers vacated Leipzig to resume their business at home.

For one machinery manufacturer this flourishing German publishing business meant unprecedented success. Johann Gottfried Karl Krause, born 1823 a farmer's son, apprenticed himself to a locksmith and later worked at an engine factory. In 1855 he opened a small repair shop in Leipzig, soon adding a foundry, and by 1877 had a considerable manufactory of his own. Taking as his motto, "The best patent is good workmanship," Karl "Papa" Krause, virtually a self-made book-binding engineer, turned out cutting machines, three- and four-sided cutters, and steam-powered rounding and backing machines, "it having become notorious," said an 1899 Krause salesman, "that the powerful pressure necessary for an operator to apply to the foot treadle of the ordinary backing machine is remarkably detrimental to the physical well being of 'backers'. . . ." (Ironically, Germany, with most of continental Europe and England, usually rounded their books but did not back them.) Krause furnished gold stamping and inking presses in over 25 different sizes, and equipment for printers, boxmakers, and papermakers as well.

With 700 workers in the 1890's, Krause, despite the high quality of his merchandise, suffered unjustly along with the reputation of

Some German bindery equipment in the 1890's, mostly of Krause manufacture. From left to right, rotary board cutter, paper cutter, finishing stove (combination glue pot and finishing tool heater), stamping press. [Brockhaus' *Konversations-Lexikon*, 14th Ed.]

his country among foreigners. Messrs. Kampe & Company, London, sole British agents for Krause, found "enormous" prejudice against imported machinery. "Made in Germany" was often not a compliment, but the Germans were boasting of it, said a bewildered *Bookbinder*. ("Printed in Germany" was also becoming a common intrusion into England, said the journal, with that required phrase printed "low down on the sheets, so that after they are folded and sewn the guillotine cuts it off.") In 1893 nevertheless Krause was honored by a visit of King Albert of Saxony who named him *Kommerzienrat* ("Commercial Councilor") in recognition of his worldwide reputation. He died in 1902.

Henry Biagosch had joined the firm as a salesman and married Krause's daughter in 1881 to become a partner. He assumed personally the difficult development of overseas sales, bringing to the problem rare talent and acumen. When a fire destroyed half the factory in 1903, Biagosch laid off none of his 1000 men, and had a new plant going again in 15 months. Through the 1920's, as Director of Engineering, he made frequent trips to the United States to keep his factory—now with 4000 employees—humming with work. Like many paternal organizations, the giant Krause establishment offered library, canteen, widow's fund, and other fringe benefits. Thanks largely to Krause, Germany furnished much of the bookbinding equipment for Europe,

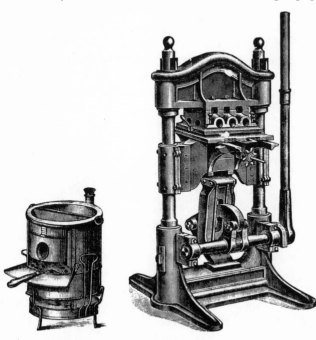

India, and other territories American salesmen had not managed to penetrate. So strong was this tradition that even after World War II, despite its location behind the Iron Curtain, the original factory continues to get large machinery orders. The Krause management, however, with neither tools nor capital, in 1945 relocated in Western Germany where ten years later it celebrated the centennial of Krause-Biagosch Gmbh, Bielefeld, which continues today.[1]

For the bookbinding industry of Germany, however, success was not so prompt or lasting. The period from about 1850 to 1900 was excruciatingly difficult. After conspicuous neglect of the art of bookbinding almost since the days of Gutenberg himself, German visitors to the Expositions of 1862 and 1867 were amazed to see the quality work of French and English binders. Their recoil prompted some action: new technical magazines, *Die Illustrirte Zeitung für Buchbinderei*, *Monatsschrift für Buchbinderei*, and *Buchgewerbeblatt Monatsschrifte* among them, began to offer binders a medium for communication, but their work still lacked direction.

Since German publishers continued to issue their titles in impermanent paper covers, binders were left to fend for themselves to drum up business. German "commissioners" (wholesale booksellers) came to their rescue by buying a portion of a publisher's edition in flat sheets, and commissioning the small but hopeful commercial binderies to execute deluxe hard-bound editions for the gift trade. Such wholesalers were F. Volckmar, L. Staackman, and K. F. Koehler. Gustav Fritzsche, founding his bindery in 1864, managed to avoid the wholesalers by turning out his own editions tastefully and inexpensively. Fritzsche/Ludwig, Berlin, is the 1932 merger of Adolph Ludwig's (1889) shop with Fritzsche's; in 1955 its new streamlined plants in Berlin and Darmstat totalled 600 hands, making it the largest German book bindery today.

Following the Franco-Prussian War several new "wholesale" binders started: F. A. Barthel, whose business soon kept 11 wire stitchers in constant operation; Paul Schambach, specializing in albums; H. Fikentscher's Steam Book Bindery; Moritz Göhre; A. Köllner; Adolf Bube; and Hübel & Denck's Steam Bookbindery, specializing in export work; Gebrüder Hoffmann; and M. Baumbach & Company. They worked long and hard to restore some reputation to German bookmaking efforts, but the principal stimulus was still foreign.

Wherever they appeared, German books never failed to elicit comment. The ordinary German book, said Updike, was simply bad—cheap and pretentious; "unmatched in impudence anywhere," said another critic. "Made in Germany," wrote Temple Scott, meant "a badly printed book, a book with poor paper and ugly binding, and a book with no taste or with bad taste applied to its making." Even Russia, he said, did better. The British, already proud of Morris' revival, were particularly persistent critics: "the great mass of the bound work of Germany (not cloth, but half-bound and whole-bound commercial bindings)," wrote *Bookbinder*, "is the most miserable trash, '*rubbish*,' to quote Herr Adam."

Master German bookbinder Paul Adam had vainly attempted to silence critics of German bookbinding. "The German buys many books but does not bind them," he admitted, sarcastically. "The French and English buy books, have them splendidly bound, but do not read them. . . ." Ludwig Nieper, Director of the Royal Academy of Graphic Arts, Leipzig, also fought the foreign "aesthetic" movement, refusing in 1887 to acknowledge either typography or good presswork as an art. Edition binders too would take no foreign nonsense: ". . . we in Germany are accustomed to being on our guard concerning American bookbinding machinery," said one. "We have had enough of the Smyth thread sewing machines, which, after having to be sent back three times as useless, were on the fourth trial found to be suited for only one class of work. . . ." But there was no use fighting any longer, for the worst was confirmed everywhere.

By the 1890's even Germans deplored the situation. *Die Illustrirte Zeitung für Buchbinderei* admitted that the "decline of the bookbinding trade in Germany is a well-established fact." Educated Germans weren't buying books with esthetic—or even literary—discrimination; they accepted common paper covers, and considered half-linen to be almost "deluxe" treatment. *Monatsschrift für Buchbinderei* in 1892 ceased publication altogether, perhaps from embarrassment. The official German handbook at "Bugra '14" (p 82) candidly recalled these years as "the era of the fraudulent concerns and shoddy undertakings"—publishing ostentatiously got up for the long popular "blood-and thunder" literature. Despite German prosperity through increased industrialization, printers and binders, without feeling, expected their machinery to do all the work—both the fabrication and the incidental design.

When asked why his covers were so loaded with ornamentation, one binder explained that most German leathers were so poor it was best to hide them with heavy gilding. Brander Matthews, American author and bibliophile, was not amused: he too found German work dull, pretentious, and "violently polychromatic," condemning the 8 to 10 colors often employed on a binding. (Matthew's own *Bookbindings Old and New*, ironically, was not above reproach: ". . . charming in subject matter and full of wise suggestions," said *American Bookmaker*, "[it] represents about the worst that can be done in the way of bookbinding. . . .") But a chorus of bibliophiles put a final end to German professional intentions. An 1894 exhibition committee at the Grolier Club in New York also deplored the meaningless ornamentation and heavy design, concluding in desperation, "In whatever direction the genius of Germany reaches its pinnacle, it must be confessed that it is not in the way of commercial bookbinding."

But there was little hope elsewhere on the continent; the state of bookwork in Germany was really no worse than the rest of Europe. In Belgium the *contrefaçon* ("counterfeit"—clandestine printing between 1815–1852 of pirated French works by cheap reprint houses) was conspicuous among printers who did not make bookwork a specialty, and, under strong French influence, produced only paper-covered books anyway. In Holland Jan van Krimpen later executed some classic book designs and bindings; more generally, however, big, heavy books were the style—even ephemera were cased in—prompting someone to wonder if the Dutch ever read in bed.

At an 1889 Paris binding exhibit a reporter found Russian work "ungainly, even ugly"; Italy showed "cloth work of a very mediocre character." (Italian bookwork, despite Bodoni, was to be quite undistinguished almost until the 1930's, when the Milan publisher Arnoldo Mondadori established his own large manufactory at Verona.) "In the Spanish Department," the reporter concluded, "there are two or three exhibits that are sufficient to make one wonder what on earth they are there for, and that is all." Again, at the 1893 Chicago World's Fair, binding prizes were confined to London and Paris. "Italy, Denmark, Norway, Sweden, Bohemia, Russia, Spain, and Mexico, none of these have the slightest chance of honours in an international competition . . . they do not know how to do it [bookbinding]."

Otto Zahn, like Leypoldt, also straddled the old and new German bookmaking worlds. Born 1856 and apprenticed to a German binder, Zahn began traveling around the world only to settle in Memphis, Tennessee, in 1884. With prodigious energy he executed scores of superb bindings, some in the difficult *cuir ciselé* technique he preferred to call "Lederschnitt." He described the American book world for *Die Illustrirte Zeitung für Buchbinderei*, and for his midwest audience he translated copiously from the German journals. Understandably sympathetic to Germany's problems throughout the century, Zahn

Side elevation of Tanner 1862 folding and stitching machine (p 196), marketed in Europe through the 1880's. Blade (D) descends to make first of three right-angle folds; gear mechanism at upper right thrusts two hooked needles through folded section which return pulling thread with them. [US Patent]

# J. H. Tanner.
## Mach. for Folding & Stitching Paper.

N.º 36428.           Patented Sept. 9. 1862.

Fig. 2.

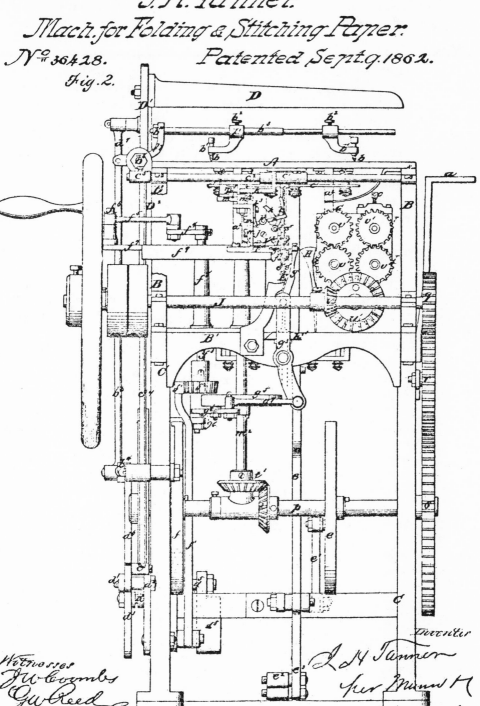

Witnesses
J. W. Coombs
G. W. Reed

Inventor
J. H. Tanner
per Munn &
attorneys

attributed them largely to "diffusion of the finer workmen throughout the numerous petty principalities," a lingering condition (the Confederation had actually ended 1866) removed only at the greatest cost—war.

France became the common cause against which all of Germany finally united. When Napoleon had a Nuremberg publisher-bookseller shot in 1806 for distributing hostile pamphlets, he was both toasted—facetiously—by authors as a "friend" of literature, and condemned—with growing antigallism—by the Borse, which in 1863 voted to erect a monument to the unfortunate victim. After the 1870–1871 Franco-Prussian War even emperors returned for a time to peaceful pursuits; Wilhelm I's court binders, Georg (a student of Zaehnsdorf) and Wilhelm Collin, had the best shop in Berlin; the monarch's great-grandson Crown Prince Friedrich Wilhelm, in the royal tradition that every king learn a trade, chose bookbinding. Despite the annoying commercial incursions of British and American machinery, a 20th-century Germany was ready to demonstrate to the world its appreciation of the graphic arts by the grandest book fair ever.

The International Exhibition for the Book Industry and the Graphic Arts ("Bugra") at Leipzig was to celebrate the 150th anniversary of the Royal Academy of Graphic Arts, in October 1914. It was majestically announced in several languages and received enthusiastically throughout Europe. In the United States it touched off the hasty but fortuitous creation of The American Institute of Graphic Arts (AIGA)—from remnants of an earlier (1911) group of New York graphic artists—which tried desperately to furnish an American bookmaking display. War erupted a few weeks after the show opened; the Germans, it seemed, to add insult to injury, would salve their chagrin by confiscating all the international treasures sent for display. Riviére & Son, who with many exhibitors sent their finest specimens, would remain unaware for the duration that their books were hastily secreted in the cellar of the Leipzig museum. Although the foreign exhibits were later retrieved in excellent condition, the state of the German book industry after the war was less fortunate.

The economic collapse of Germany after the first world war was costly for its publishing and printing interests. Although the manufacturing facilities had not been damaged, many old 19th century firms were wiped out, as well as the new private presses, so promising.

The revival of fine printing in Germany had begun only after long, wistful observation of William Morris' and Cobden-Sanderson's work in England, although there were a few early signs. In 1894 *Pan*, a lavish German art and literary periodical, was founded in Berlin by a group of artists headed by Julius Meier. Four years later Alfred W. von

Heymel, an 18-year old millionaire, his cousin Rudolf A. Schröder, a 19-year old poet, and Otto J. Bierbaum founded *Die Insel* ("The Island"), also a cultural quarterly. Its third issue of 1900 was a milestone in German bookwork: Emil R. Weiss, then 25, discarded the popular *Jugend* style (an *art nouveau* form named for the magazine which employed it), bringing in some of his own freshness. The offices of this publication eventually became Insel Verlag [publishers, from *lager*, to stock (books)], the first German firm to specialize in fine work.

Insel had sought Emery Walker's typographic advice, and Walker recommended Johnston, Grailey Hewitt, and Eric Gill. Under the direction of Dr. Anton Kippenberg, these artists created a series of German classics (the "Grossherzog Willhelm Ernst" Edition) which was printed by Walker and bound by Douglas Cockerell. From 1912 on Insel Bücherei in 800 titles produced about 50 million little volumes in its first 50 years. Each was patterned after the original quarterly, constructed of delicately designed paper cases and pasted labels. Like Dent's operations in England, Insel proudly issued all the old classics beautifully and cheaply; many titles are still available today.

Others with some esthetic qualifications joined the new publishing movement. George Müller in 1903 founded a publishing house at Munich, specializing in belles-lettres. In five years he turned out 400 titles, many of them designed by Paul Renner and still much appreciated today by collectors. S. Fischer also produced well-designed books, many by Weiss (who also designed the Tempel Klassiker series). Ernst Rowholt, Leipzig, issued pretty poetry and special editions. Count Harry Kessler, who had contributed to *Pan* and had brought Walker and Cockerell to *Insel*, developed his own Cranach Presse, a "pinnacle of achievement," as was the Ernst Ludwig Presse, under Christian H. Kleukens, whose edition of Shakespeare, bound in orange morocco, was dedicated to Cobden-Sanderson.

Walter Tiemann, who had from 1903 taught at (and headed) the *Staatliche Akademie der Graphischen Künste* ("State Academy for the Graphic Arts"), Leipzig, and Karl Ernst Poeschel together in 1906—exactly 15 years after Morris—established the Janus-Presse, the first private press in Germany devoted to fine bookwork. Poeschel had studied typography in the United States (1898–1900), assimilated Morris' message, and at 26 returned in 1900 to his father's Leipzig printing shop. He soon both published and printed important works (including the prestigious 1914 Bugra catalog), and designed them well: 21 of 150 German "50 Books" between 1929 and 1931 were produced by him. Other private presses at last joined the effort to restore Germany's place in fine graphic arts.[2]

But the "arts and crafts" trail left by William Morris was quite another thing, differently interpreted in several countries before it would settle in Germany ready to reconcile the problem of art versus machinery. Morris' desire to "overthrow" the machine was convincing among societies that saw nothing but dirty fumes, child labor, maimed workers, and rich bosses come out of the factories. Even with legislation to regulate the exploitation of labor, artists—who lived close, in time and temperament, to hand craftsmanship—could still not fully endorse mass production. After designing hundreds of bindings himself for machine stamping, Walter Crane in 1911 expounded,

> "As to machinery, I do not deny that it has its uses or that wonderful (and sometimes fearful) things have been produced; the commercial output is prodigious, in fact, modern existence has come to depend upon machinery in nearly every direction, but the machines themselves remain as a rule far more wonderful things than the things they produce, and the less machinery has to do with art the better. . . ."

Only after another decade would anyone in England attempt a reconciliation.

Sir Francis Meynell boldly countered the British anti-machine movement when he organized the "Nonsuch Press" (1923) to produce beautiful and readable books moderately priced: "Our stock-in-trade has been the theory that mechanical means could be made to serve fine ends; that the machine in printing was a controllable tool." Conversely, although Douglas Cockerell admitted "the machine binding is the logical completion of the machine-printed book," he preferred not to concern himself with it; his own *Bookbinding, and the Care of Books,* said a critic, was badly machine-bound as Cockerell feared— it had "sacrificed strength and durability to appearance." But in Morris' name many more or less gifted artists continued to turn their backs on mechanical progress—some, however, even using machinery to fabricate "hand-crafted" goods.

In France, of course, there was no William Morris following, no revival whatsoever. The conventional hand methods for bibliophilist work continued, although the awards of "grand" gold medals, in the 1890's, to the Smyth book-sewing machine and the Elliott Steam Thread-Knot Stitching machine were lost in the craze for hand-made books. Pierre Legrain, a designer of women's fashions and jewelry, perforce turned to bookbinding in 1914, achieving some success by 1927 for his fresh design. He died two years later with almost no following. After World War I young binders had not returned to the shops, and French domination of the hand-bound trade was lost along with any hopes of commercial work.

During the years of phenomenal reading growth, the French had never observed the value of bindery industrialization. Recently a French expert, Fourney, still rationalized the necessity of bookmaking mechanization, explaining that its purpose was not to make great profit for the binder, but to reduce the cost of books. He credited Joseph Taupin, "one of our grand industrial binders," with installing high-speed equipment in the 1920's, and constantly persuading fellow binders to do likewise. In 1923 Taupin's edition bindery was acquired by Hachette (which had, three years before, bought the old printing house of Brodart). The combined Paris plant after World War II employed 700, and a suburban installation for pamphlet work had 300 hands. Today Brodart & Taupin, along with Engel Reliure Industrielle, are the two largest edition and trade binders in France.

Industrialization in France, nevertheless, is still a minor phenomenon. Casing in—with imported machinery—was unfortunately introduced just before World War II, with immediate losses and shortages in parts and materials. Brodart & Taupin had 20 Smyth case-makers in the 1950's, according to Smyth-Horne, making a half million books per week—"or virtually all the hard binding that is produced in France." The principal sewing machines in France are the Swiss Martini, the German Brehmer, and the American Smyth—of which the semi-automatic No. 12 was deemed "impeccable" for uniformity and speed. Polly Lada-Mocarski, a student of Cockerell and Wiemeler, nevertheless examined French cased-in books in 1966 and found them badly stamped and badly made of inferior materials. A 1961 US Department of Commerce report, noting that French wages had climbed 60 percent in 9 years, had predicted a great demand in France for high-speed automated bindery equipment. But no major bookbinding machinery is manufactured in France; in the modern world of bookmaking, France still waits and watches.

In the United States book esthetes followed Morris only momentarily, until they found their own solid footing. DeVinne, like the obdurate German director, also refused to recognize printing as an art. Updike was also against the machine—his *Printing Types: Their History, Forms, and Use* (2 volumes, Harvard University Press, 1922), entirely set by hand, does not cover machine composition. "To me," Updike wrote, "all machinery is like a hideous form of algebra. . . ." Yet his Merrymount Press shone for typographic excellence.

At East Aurora, New York, Elbert Hubbard, on the other hand, clung to Morris' questionable precepts and effected a debasement of the arts and crafts movement almost inevitable because of his puzzling success. After almost 40 years of itinerant selling and odd literary pursuits, Hubbard established the Roycroft Shop (named after 17th century English printers Samuel and Thomas Roycroft) about 1893. Hubbard had met Morris, and with equal thoroughness proceeded to direct the same kind of movement in the United States, featuring publishing, wood and leather crafts, lecturing, and hostelling. His *Little Journeys to the Homes of Good Men and Great* series, at first rejected by G. P. Putnam's, began in 1895 with "George Eliot," and ran to 170 titles, subsequently issued by a more contrite Putnam's as a periodical.

"Three hundred and ten people are on the payroll at the present writing," said Hubbard in 1909. "The principal work is printing, illuminating, and binding books. We also work at ornamental black-smithing, weaving, cabinet work, painting pictures, clay-modeling, and terra cotta. We issue three monthly publications, *The Philistine* [100,000 circulation—at one time up to 225,000], *Little Journeys* [70,000], and *The Fra* [50,000]." There were certainly strong par-allels with Morris, including a reassuring reverence for well-made books: "I found five hundred people in a book-factory in Chicago binding books," said Hubbard, "but not a bookbinder among them. They simply fed the books into hoppers and shot them out of chutes, and said they were bound." Hubbard had attracted Louis Kinder to East Aurora after a seven-year apprenticeship at Leipzig. Kinder, whose book of bindery formulas is still respected, taught bookbinding to dozens of Roycrofters and found time to bind books with tradi-tional care. "I have specimens of the work done by Riviére, Zahn, Cobden-Sanderson, Zahnsdorf, 'The Guild of Women Binders,' [sic] of London, and the 'Club Bindery' of New York;" said Hubbard, "and we surely are not ashamed to show Mr. Kinder's work in the same case. . . ."

Hubbard's books for the masses, however, were printed on rough paper with eccentric typography, and manufactured without any regard to "art canons," said George French. "Their de-luxe bindings," according to James M. Wells, "were of that extremely soft and cheap suede known in the trade as 'limp ooze'; in their pretentiousness and lack of taste they reflected their flamboyant creator, with his long locks, soft hat, and flowing tie." Many critics characterized Hubbard (who unfortunately perished with his wife in the 1915 *Lusitania* sinking) as a "pseudo-Morris." His chief crime, to all final appearances, was to indulge the poor their unreadable books as Morris had indulged the rich.

Apart from Hubbard, many other American and British individuals, particularly women whose emancipation lent considerable enthusiasm, found hand binding remarkably appropriate to their inclinations. Surprisingly enough, they were not only apt pupils, but good teachers, carrying Morris' love of impeccable craftsmanship and Cobden-Sanderson's enviable reputation down, in genealogical fashion, to contemporary times. Sarah T. Prideaux in 1894 advised women to work "experimentally," but not to enter the industry (then torn by depression, anti-suffragettism, and bitter campaigns for decent hours and wages). The London Ladies' Association of Bookbinders, however, insisted instead on the right to perform all operations in the bindery, and have earned by their vigilance places today for all women who want to work.

Dozens of girls, individually financed, had traveled to Europe to study with the masters. Emily Preston not only worked with Cobden-Sanderson, but also studied under Marius Michel and with Dumont, a French commercial binder whose artistic commandments included strict rules for placing the feet while standing at the workbench. ("Splendid machines, those French binders," observed the British, not without sarcasm.) In 1906 Preston became a leading organizer of the Guild of Women Book Workers, British workers whose bindings were frequently exhibited with deserved pride. Evelyn H. Nordhoff (daughter of editor Charles Nordhoff; she died only 34 years old), Ellen G. Starr, Elizabeth G. Marot, Alice Provost, and others followed. Edith Diehl took her bookbinding lessons from impeccable teachers: Nordhoff, Cobden-Sanderson, Cockerell, Sangorski & Sutcliffe, Mercier, and Dumont. In 1941 she stopped her binding work in order to write a two-volume *Bookbinding: Its Background and Technique,* the only modern major treatise on the subject. She died in 1953, aged 76.

In Germany and elsewhere throughout continental Europe (except France), Morris' effect was profound, his early designwork quickly admired. In Hungary a Budapest bookbinder named Josef Halfer, with enthusiasm for revival approaching Morris', in 1884 reduced the 17th and 18th century art of making marbled papers to its fundamentals. Heavy patterned paper had originally been devised by binders to hide the oil stains which inevitably emerged from their hand-lubricated leather bindings. Halfer's book, *Die Fortschritte der Marmorier Kunst* [*Progress in the Art of Marbling*], is still the most comprehensive on the subject. Although Halfer felt that marbling had "hardly reached the middle rung of the ladder of its development," it was—like Morris' work—artistically a dead end.

Morris' medieval typefaces, similarly, and his ponderous rubrications on every page became even more unpleasantly exaggerated by other pseudo-Morrises, but the vitality of the original movement was genuinely overwhelming. Rudolf Koch gave up the *Jugend* style to imitate Morris, so strongly influenced he insisted Morris was really a fellow German. British editor and artist Bernard H. Newdigate saw calligraphy everywhere at the 1914 Leipzig fair: through Anna Simon's translation Johnston's handbook had become even more popular in Germany than in England.

After the hard times of war and depression the arts and crafts concept became a compulsive refuge from reality. Will Ransom noted unsurpassed craftsmanship, "serious art," and "spirited interpretations" in German bookwork; others believed German persistence with hand composition (despite the success elsewhere of Linotype and Mono-type) permitted great diversity and experimentation—a welcome "un-bridled freedom" in the graphic arts. But such experiments had need of concentration in the hands of a "German" William Morris to make a unified force of it. The man with true *"Buchkunst* [book artistry]" had not yet appeared in Germany, said a 1911 journal, but he would come. This long awaited messiah turned out to be a designer of buildings.

Architect and writer Walter Gropius in May 1919 invited war-weary art students to the opening of a new German school with a simple inducement: "Let us create a new guild of craftsmen, without the class distinctions which raise an arrogant barrier between crafts-man and artist. . . ." Although Germany had always respected sound technical training, Gropius was not merely recommending traditional academic instruction, nor was he simply preaching Morris' arts and crafts movement. The machine had become a ponderous new factor in his philosophy.

Founded that year in the city of Weimar, *The Staatliches Bauhaus* [*Bauen*, to build, create] *in Weimar* began with a small devoted staff offering design, pottery, typography, weaving, and woodworking. Students came enthusiastically from around the world—some dressed in old war uniforms, some bearded, some barefoot—many so poor they had to work in the school craft shops to support themselves. In addition to having lost the war, Germany faced inflation, depression, and dejection; this seeming bankrupt environment worked a complete physical and psychological transformation in the spirit of the school.

All design instruction at the Bauhaus was predicated on the rather radical principle that the machine was worthy of the artist; that the gap between artist and mass-produced artifact could be bridged by "industrial design." Gropius, years later, said, "The Bauhaus believes the machine to be our modern medium of design and seeks to come to terms with it." Although Morris had failed to subvert the machine,

its terms were surprisingly generous: the machine needed no taming—
it was never really wild—for its benign nature is to make things
beautifully. "It may make ugly things beautifully, or beautiful things
beautifully," said Beatrice Warde, simply.

Typography was taught by Herbert Bayer, who ruthlessly discarded the rigid conventions of roman, italic, and German gothic
alphabets, launching an all-lowercase sanserif movement. With it he
established a special identity for the Bauhaus books he designed. Bayer,
who came to the United States in 1938, could not forget the decades
of gilding excesses at last displaced by the Bauhaus. "I have yet to
design a book with gold stamped effects;" he said at that time. "I
incline towards ink stamping on cloth or on paper over boards, and
I advocate the free employment of color to make life a little
gayer. . . ."

In the United States, curiously, one gifted designer proceeded along
lines strikingly similar to Bauhaus work. Merle Armitage in 1932
found time to create books by and about the artists and celebrities of
his long theatrical management career. Finding no suitable guidance
for contemporary book design, he launched a style of his own with
the credo, "the content of the book should govern the design. . . ."
"My attempt," he wrote, "has been to let the entire book be a decoration, not to decorate the book."

"Decoration," however, is not the word for what is in effect a very
poster-like theatrical presentation: his design for Danz, *Dynamic Dis-
sonance in Nature and the Arts* (1952, Farrar, Straus & Young), for
example, has a twelve-page "title page" in black and red on gray
stock, following bright yellow endpapers. One might say more
realistically than Beraldi, it is not a book, it's a stage setting!
(Armitage's early books, ironically, were all produced in Hollywood.)
Although far removed from Weimar, Armitage's style bears strong
resemblance to the Bauhaus approach to books. "Armitage has created
a new machine esthetic," said one of his critics. "Before him, the set
up of mechanized books (with negligible exceptions) has been so dull
that we had ceased to expect anything stimulating. . . ."

Armitage, whom designer Bruce Rogers called "the best of modern
book designers—by far," became art director of *Look* magazine after
World War II. He had come to grips with the machine, and won his
battle quite without Bauhaus doctrines. His advice to others (p 270)
would not be easy to follow.

Bookbinding courses had been contemplated at the Bauhaus, but
they did not materialize. Yet the electric surge and esthetic energy of
the school could not avoid spilling over into all graphic forms. Associated unofficially with the Bauhaus was the hand binder Ignatz

Wiemeler (1895–1952), whom Walter Tiemann had engaged at his Leipzig academy and where he began to earn a fine reputation. At Offenbach too Wiemeler taught alongside Rudolf Koch through 1921–1925. To Wiemeler (and other hand workers of his time) the influence of "modernism" was not rejected. Ironically discarded were instructions from a 19th-century German bindery journal: "Avoid straight lines which give a stiff and formal look; let everything appear careless but graceful, and group artistically." Book covers were now almost "machine-made" in concept—featuring straight lines, geometrical patterns, and precise (impersonal) workmanship. "Many of the results are weird," wrote Douglas McMurtrie in 1927, "but many of the designs show much promise. . . ." Wiemeler finished about 380 leather bindings, using Cobden-Sanderson's unadorned "elemental" style and his "zig-zag" endsheets (a tiny accordion fold in the flyleaf to prevent cover from pulling away from first signature). Despite acknowledged debts to Morris and Cobden-Sanderson, he produced successions of rigid, overall geometrical designs described variously as "lean elegance," "studied austerity," and "severe artistic discipline." By 1937 Wiemeler was recognized as Europe's greatest living hand binder.

Aside from his designs, however, Wiemeler approached the physical construction of books with more humanist feeling than the machine age would seem to permit. His tenets may indeed have excluded him from true Bauhaus society. "Craftsmanship, as we see it," he said in 1933, "today has nothing in common in its aims with those of modern industry, and industry exerts its influence in too many ways on even the best-protected relics of craftsmanship [for the craftsman] to be able to remain without fear." Like Cobden-Sanderson's, Wiemeler's female pupils idolized him despite ruthless criticism and occasional expressions of rage. His frequent advice, "use the finest materials you can get, and do the best work of which you are capable," became all the more poignant for himself when, after World War II, he had only the most miserable supplies and materials. Notable pupils of Wiemeler were Gerhard and Kathryn Gerlach.

For Wiemeler craftsmanship could also stand for progress in spite of the dilemmas of machinery. He examined Bradel's "open-back" binding which had "degenerated" to the common commercial case, and improved the lacing and ingenious reinforcements of back and hinge to give his books the strength of a good binding without the "steel-trap" snapping shut of some of them. Hugo Steiner-Prag, teaching at Leipzig's graphic arts academy from 1907 to 1933, noted that Wiemeler and his fellow binders, however, by their tenets anchored only lightly to the commercially ambitious Bauhaus, worked quite apart from the publishing industry as well. "Bookbinding generally lacks the strong bond of union with book-making as a whole . . . ," he said, with quite universal truth, "—which above all else distinguishes the art of hand-binding in Germany."

Indeed, commercial publishers, for their part, in the 1930's did not care for Bauhaus experimentation, which they viewed as radical departure from sound, traditional book techniques. They believed, furthermore, that although fully 60 percent of German publications were still in paper covers, the public wanted a sturdy binding for the remainder—neither a pamphlet like the French, nor a cheap case, like the British. They talked of half leather or good linen, at worst. But the new German government gave the industry no opportunity to test its theories.

Thanks to the political tyranny which the Germans had so righteously protested over a century before, the Bauhaus staff was forced to flee from its native land. The German government in 1933 proclaimed modern art to be "foul scum cast up on the surface of life in 1918," and brought the usefulness of the Bauhaus to an end. Gropius, Joseph Albers, Mies van der Rohe, Lyonel Feininger, Laszlo Moholy-Nagy—all came to the United States to carry on. Many unrelated but equally outspoken publishing and manufacturing firms—as well as their offending books—were confiscated.

With the impending holocaust of World War II the book and its environment was ended—perhaps never to recover its traditional European domination. When Allied aircraft bombed Berlin and Leipzig in the winter of 1943 Frederic G. Melcher's *Publishers' Weekly* editorial recalled,

"Leipzig was the publishing capital of the German-speaking world, and its annual book output probably exceeded that of London, Paris or New York. . . . It may be that we shall learn that the Börsenverein and Buchhändler Börse and other book trade halls have suffered along with the great wholesale establishment of Koehler and Volckmar or such famous publishing houses as Brockhaus, [specialists in incunabula, Karl W.] Hiersemann and Insel Verlag, and many of the hundred printing plants and binderies. . . ."[4]

(Sir Stanley Unwin, who immensely admired the German distribution system, describing it in early editions of *The Truth about Publishing*, subsequently confirmed that Leipzig publishing had indeed been totally disrupted by the war and its aftermath. With Leipzig behind the Iron Curtain, much world-wide book activity has transferred to Frankfurt, West Germany.)

Along with the Bauhaus group, another segment of German publishing was obliged to leave the country—certain paperback publishers who brought with them the germ of a force even more pervasive than Bauhaus pyrotechnics. The paperback was not simply a cheap book; it was becoming an institution in its own right.

Without a traditional love of fine books, the Germans had had no scruples about cheap paperback publishing; with smaller homes in the 20th century than their fathers, even rich Germans pragmatically preferred paperbacks to be read and thrown away. Like publishing piracy elsewhere, the Germans had not been beyond borrowing literary properties and reissuing them fast and cheaply. Ironically, the French themselves—more the victims of piracy than benefiters—had set some precedents for this kind of operation.

Honoré Balzac himself in 1826 began, like Archibald Constable, to print popular, compact editions of native classics, but they sold poorly, incurring many debts for their creator. Three years later he fled Paris to resume his more profitable writing, although he still dreamed of mechanically made paper, stereotypes, and other industrially inspired progress. Gervaise-Hélène Charpentier similarly began publishing in 1829, but found the Belgian *contrefaçon* so debilitating he struck upon the idea, borrowed from England, of condensing his fiction and producing it so quickly and cheaply in small (twelvmo) format his pirates would be unable to respond lucratively. This scheme became his "Bibliothèque [Library] Charpentier," in vivid yellow paper covers: first title being Savarin, *Physiologie du goût*. The idea became so successful Charpentier's name became associated with the format, although he also published many other works.

Jean-Baptiste Alexandre Paulin early recognized the need for inexpensive French literature, issuing subscription titles and publishing two popular magazines, *Le National* and *L'Illustration* (founded 1843), long successful. His cheap illustrated edition of Lesage, *Gil Blas de Santillane*, sold by subscription, was also well received enough to bring other pictorial fiction into the race. Pierre-Jules Hetzel started in 1857, running some of Jules Verne's 66 titles to 30,000 copies by subscription. Hetzel, Hachette, and others followed the familiar British patterns of publishing, although their books, selling from 50 centimes to 1 franc, were generally excellent in quality. The Germans could see the value of such schemes.

J. G. Göschen in 1817 began to publish cheap German classics and nonfiction. Karl J. Meyer—one of the first to issue books in series, the "Groschen Bibliothek Deutscher Klassiker" ("Penny German Classical Library")—started in 1826; in the following year he offered for sale four separate editions of the same book. Rousseau, Lessing, Herder, Goethe, and Schiller became popular reading, but by the

1830's the German book market was soon flooded with romantic trash—novels and horror tales—everywhere. In 1841 Karl Preskauer founded the *Berliner Volksbücherei* and the *Verein zur Verbreitung guter und wohlfeiler Volksschriften* ("Society for the Diffusion of Good and Inexpensive Popular Literature") in Zwickau. Other societies and organizations also rallied to provide cheap literature to a new continental mass-reading audience which, unlike smug Britain and France, was strangely polyglot.

At the age of 21 Christian Bernhard (later Baron) Tauchnitz founded a publishing firm in 1837, unique in that he resolved to pay adequately for the international—hence unprotected—literature he chose to publish. Capitalizing on the transportation and communication problems separating the German Confederation from the remainder of Europe, Tauchnitz in 1841 began to reprint in English the famous—but almost unknown—works of British and American authors. His first selection was Lytton, *Pelham*. Although he also published many other German works, including dictionaries, Tauchnitz concentrated on English literature for a vast Germanic English-reading public. "It is with feelings of high satisfaction and most sincere gratitude," Tauchnitz wrote in an 1860 preface, "that I beg leave to offer to the Public the five-hundredth volume [*Five Centuries of the English Language and Literature*, edited by himself] of my Collection . . . ," which by this time contained many yankee titles as well, as Tauchnitz considered both British and Americans his "Anglo-Saxon cousins." By 1937, the firm's centennial year, 5290 titles had been issued, all "a brilliant achievement [and] . . . marvels of careful proofreading."

> "I have always felt a positive sense of relief [said Victor Gollancz in 1937, himself vitally interested in mass reading (p 239)], when I have seen a row of Tauchnitz books [paper covers color-coded red (adventure), blue (love), green (travel), orange (humor), yellow (romance), gray (poetry and drama)] on my journeys abroad: for Tauchnitz publishing is, unlike most publishing, sane publishing. The varieties of titles, the paper covers (instead of the deadly serious cloth binding), above all the reasonable price—all these are in startling contrast to the nightmare publishing traditions which exist in more than one country. . . ."[5]

Tauchnitz is credited with beginning the paperback movement thriving today.

Reclam Verlag's operations were much like Meyer's and Tauchnitz's. Anton Philipp Reclam had established a bookstore in 1828, but soon went in more for general publishing—atlases, Shakespeare, fiction.

When in 1867 a new German copyright law threw works into the public domain 30 years after an author's death, Reclam's "Universal-Bibliothek" started, and ran to 8000 titles in 75 years. Goethe's *Faust* sold 300,000 by 1900; Schiller's *William Tell*, 619,000; Goethe's *Hermann and Dorothea* 490,000. In this cheap series of classics and current literature Shakespeare, Molière, Byron, Heine, sold very well too. Between 1912 and 1940 Reclam would succeed with paperbacks sold from vending machines, although this degree of mechanization failed elsewhere.

Other German publishers followed with extraordinarily fruitful series. Hendel had "Bibliothek der Gesamtliteratur des In- und Auslandes" ("Library of Complete Native and Foreign Literature"), from 1886 to 1930 running to 2573 titles; *"Meyer's Volksbücherei"* from 1886 to 1915 ran to 1698; *"Hesse's Volksbücherei"* from 1903 to 1920 ran to 1350. The German public seemed to be the most avaricious readers of all.

Popular publishers, as might be expected, best weathered the trials of World War I and the depression which followed. Notable survivors were, in addition to Tauchnitz and Reclam, C. H. Beck, Munich; Karl Baedeker, Leipzig (who started his famous guidebooks with "Coblenz" in 1829); Friedrich A. Brockhaus, Leipzig (developer of the great *Konversations-Lexikon* and a classic German dictionary issued 1796–1808, with 16 editions over the following 150 years); S. Fischer, Frankfurt; Herder, Freiburg. Ullstein, Berlin, was founded by Leopold Ullstein with four sons; Franz, a fifth, entered the house 1892 and modernized it drastically, making it "among the first to develop mass production, distribution, and sale of popular-priced books in Europe, which retailed at the equivalent of $1.00 a copy, cloth-bound." It is today the largest publishing house in Germany.

Gradually the scattered industry collected itself. The original 108 members of the Borse, publishers, wholesalers, and retailers, grew to about 5000 through the 1920's and '30's. More importantly, perhaps, new entrepreneurs, unwilling to cry over the past, found exciting new direction and impetus in the future, however unstable it seemed.

After World War I, as Tauchnitz began to lose some appeal with its traditional old format, others rushed in to fill the "vacuum." The Albatross Modern Continental Library was conceived as a paperback venture by John Holroyd-Reece, Kurt Enoch, and Max Christian Wegener. Together in Hamburg in 1932, they soon made Albatross an international operation: headquarters in Luxemburg, editing in Paris, sales and promotion in Hamburg, printing at first in Italy, then Leipzig. The series, meant to be cheap but of good quality, soon reached 400 titles; the books, designed mostly by Enoch, were typographically attractive. Sales rights (in the English language) precluded distribution in England and the United States, thus giving the series little competition in its territories. In 1935 Albatross took over the Tauchnitz editions of English and American authors, although the German government compelled Tauchnitz to continue a similar series. Albatross headquarters escaped successively to Paris, England, and Sweden, while Enoch himself came to the United States, where he continued to make contributions to the paperback industry (p 245).

The countries of continental Europe continue today to publish paperbacks in great numbers: France with its livre broché for later rebinding, but also with modern series like "Livre de Poche" ("Pocket Books"), "Que sais-Je?" ("What do I know [about . . .]"), "Classiques Larousse," and "Collections Marabout"—and also "blitz books" (paperbacks issued within a week or two to capitalize on topical events). One French firm, Imprimerie Bussière, claims to be the largest paperback manufacturer in France—producing 125,000–150,000 daily. Italy enjoys a new but uncertain boom in *Tascabili* ("pocketed [books]") started with Mondadori's 1965 "Oscar" series. Germany continues with its many classic series and still small but growing preference for cloth covers. "Our binding tradition is at a cross-roads," said a German binder in 1957. "You in America are nearing complete mechanization while we still cling to the old traditions of individual craftsmanship in which the worker knows every detail in the construction of the finished book. Before long your mechanization problems will be ours. . . ."[6]

["His manner was at first sight coldly quiet, but you soon felt a magnetism and felt stirred. His great figure was clothed in gray, with white vest, no necktie, and his beard was unshorn as ever. His voice is magnificent, and is to be mentioned with Nature's oceans and the music of forests and hills. . . ."]

*Part II*

# THE INDUSTRIALIZATION
# OF THE AMERICAN BINDERY

"*As she* [a single muse, originally, custodian of poetry, music, and science, persuaded to vacate Parnassus for America], *the illustrious Emigré, (having, it is true, in her day, . . . journey'd considerable) Making directly for this rendezvous—vigorously clearing a path for herself—striding through the confusion, By thud of machinery and shrill steam-whistle undismay'd, Bluff'd not a bit by drain-pipe, gasometers, artificial fertilizers, Smiling and pleased, with palpable intent to stay, She's here, installed. . . .*"

[Walt Whitman]

# 4 *Publishing Heritage*

## *and the Wire Stitcher*

IT IS UNDERSTANDABLE THAT LITTLE "ARTISTIC" BINDING WAS DONE in the United States during its pre-Revolutionary War days, so strong was the orientation toward England for fine materials and workmanship. Yet by 1800 all important binding materials were locally manufactured: The Shryock Brothers founded their paperboard "Papyrus" mill in 1790 at Downington, Pennsylvania, and began to make board by machine in 1831. Fandango Mills, Milburn, and William B. Davey, Bloomfield, soon turned out binder's board from their New Jersey shops: made originally from tarred hemp, rope, yarn, cotton, or linen rags, the best board today continues to be fabricated with almost the original manual operations.

Elijah Upton in Boston began manufacturing glue from 1808 on (p 232). Gold leaf (1 ounce of gold yielded 200 square feet, $\frac{1}{280,000}$th of an inch thick) newly beaten in 1820 by John Hastings & Company, Pennsylvania—still in business—was first applied to cloth about 1832, "laid on" in sheets by batteries of girls to be "welded" there by the heat and pressure of the stamping press. To bring these many supplies and materials to binders throughout the struggling young country, wholesalers rallied to their task with efficiency and dispatch. Henry A. Gane, a Boston bookbinder, gave up his trade in 1846 to become a supplier (becoming Gane Brothers & Lane, Inc., in 1882); Louis DeJonge & Company (with brother Julius) also started 1846. Cloth merchants, used machinery dealers, and hundreds of lesser traders found their place eventually in a structure scarcely evidencing such growth at first.

American publishers who were not simply importers of British books (and there were many who could furnish complete libraries, entirely imported from England, to American colleges and individuals) followed the European custom of issuing locally printed books in plain boards so that "each purchaser might have his book bound to please himself, after the fashion of the times." But as labor and materials in America grew more expensive, "protective" tariffs became necessary to prevent entry of cheap materials; although "yankee" bibliophiles and some edition booksellers might still send their sheets to England for definitive binding, the routine work was forced to remain in the country. But American binders would handle it with growing competence.

Most binding work, such as it was, occupied a small place in the output of commercial printers, usually individual craftsmen often functioning as their own compositor, printer, binder, publisher, and bookseller—relying on wife and children to help in the shop. For them the apprentice system furnished welcome—and reliable—manpower at small expense, as an early contract demonstrates:

> "This indenture, made this 23rd day of February A.D. 1832 by and between Silas Andrus of Hartford of the one party, and Edward Day of Hartford of the other part, Witnesseth:—That the said Edward Day in consideration of the covenants and agreements hereinafter expressed [the apprentice shall do no damage, waste nothing, not marry, gamble, drink, or frequent play-houses; the master will furnish meat, drink, and lodging], doth by these presents, as Guardian of Edward T. Day, a minor, under the age of twenty-one years, with his free and voluntary consent, put and bind the said E. T. Day an apprentice to the said Silas Andrus to learn the art, trade or mystery of Book Binding and with him the said Silas Andrus of Hartford after the manner of an apprentice, to serve from and after the date of these presents, until he shall arrive at the age of twenty-one years, fully to be completed and ended, which will be on the 13th day of May A.D. 1838; during which term, the said apprentice his said master shall faithfully serve, his secrets keep, and his lawful commands every where gladly obey. . . ."[1]

Often, too, the printer-publisher solicited subscriptions (agreements from prospective customers to pay in advance for a forthcoming work) to remain solvent. But yankee craftsmen had the ingenuity and drive to move quickly into a more ambitious commercial climate no less erudite and artistic.

American publishers, functioning largely as booksellers at first, had already gravitated to the larger metropolitan areas, some before the 19th century. Business was lively even without money: where the scope of a bookshop was limited, bartering with unbound sheets and auctioneering of books was popular, to be taken by distant binders whose markets were beyond the range of stage coach and (ice-bound) river boats.

In Boston these literary arrangements found a happy community at Corn Hill, called "Booksellers' Row." Scholars and lawyers rubbed elbows with editors and pressmen in the old bookstalls, and considered it a privilege to do so:

> "O Messrs. Little, Brown & Company, and Messrs. Ticknor & Fields [said an 1859 booklover], though I rarely purchase anything of you, . . . as I am fond of descanting on books and reading, . . . I hope you will kindly tolerate my visits to your stores, and be pleased to have me examine your many beautiful and valuable books. . . ."[2]

In Boston were situated, besides Ticknor & Fields (founded 1832), and Little, Brown & Company (1837), Ginn & Company (1867), Estes & Lauriat (1872), and Houghton Mifflin, the last-named demonstrating the unusual production-oriented dilemma of manufacturer-turned-publisher.

The small Riverside Press, begun 1849, moved in 1852 to Cambridge, Massachusetts, where proprietor Henry O. Houghton (1823–1895) printed for Little, Brown, Ticknor & Fields (which Houghton bought in 1889), and other publishers. He looked forward, however, to clothing his own signatures with, in his words, "a binding whether of purple, crimson, green or brown, as plain & simple as the dress of a Quaker maiden." In 1863 he contracted to make dictionaries for G. & C. Merriam. Completely without a bindery, Houghton had boldly undertaken to print and bind, in quantity, the largest single volume up to its time in America. He quickly found men in Europe laboring for one-third the wages paid in the United States; he saw at first hand how books for which he charged 60¢ were manufactured for 21¢ in England— and became a firm supporter of tariffs and the US copyright manufacturing clause. In 1864 he brought 12 journeymen binders from England, leased a nearby shop for them, and was binding dictionaries that very year.

Houghton soon gave unremitting attention to the complete book production process, and by 1871 had over 300 workers doing fine bookwork and, shortly, other remarkable jobs (pp 142, 176). Ever alert to the latest machinery and developments, Houghton somehow also found time for a term as mayor of Cambridge, 1872. "He was a man of strong views and firm methods," said *Publishers' Weekly* with mixed feelings.

In 1889 Riverside Press' 100-horsepower steam engine operated all equipment, of which the bindery had 10 folders, 7 thread sewers, 4 wire stitchers, and 2 wire sewers. The more important work, however, was still folded and sewn by 30 to 40 women, for whom the firm installed a cheerful "private apartment" for off-time relaxation. The entire manufactory, for that matter, was kept, against creeping depreciation, "as neat and tidy as a shaker sitting room," with a fire brigade, a workers' library, and an employee savings plan (money invested in the company was a subtle deterrent to labor troubles). A decade later the bindery with 700 hands prematurely boasted "all conveniences," although they had only added a rounder-backer and a case-maker; without their ubiquitous founder the managers had not been quick to buy other important machinery then available. The Charles River plant nevertheless began to earn medals and citations from 1867 on for outstanding bookwork. In the 1880's its product was superior to anything in Europe (Morris' Kelmscott Press did not begin until 1891). By 1900 the press—with Updike and Rogers—worked almost exclusively for Houghton Mifflin, formed in 1880 after several earlier publishing partnerships.

In Boston too the Benjamin Bradley Company was founded simultaneously with the utilization of cloth (1832), claiming to be first American binder using it. Joseph Rogers noted: "That the introduction of cloth, the casing process, and the machines [about to invade the bindery] should be followed so closely by the founding of edition binderies, points clearly to the fact that it was because of these innovations that edition binderies could be established." Bradley served, among others, D. Appleton & Company (until 1854), Ticknor & Fields, and

HENRY O. HOUGHTON

Ginn & Company, and later merged with publisher Thomas Y. Crowell in 1870; Crowell had worked at Bradley's shop. (Crowell itself is now a part of Dun & Bradstreet, a 1968 merger.)

In Philadelphia Mathew Carey had begun writing, selling, and publishing books and periodicals as early as 1785, becoming a champion of American protective tariffs and a pioneer in the formation of professional publishing associations whose aims were also to defend the struggling US industry. With other new American publishers, all lacking capital to risk on untried American authors, Carey reissued popular British works with neither permission from nor payment to original publishers. From this "piracy" (which, strictly, was not illegal) grew the practice among established houses of buying advance proofs or sheets from Paternoster Row, furnishing at least token sums, and agreeing (among themselves)—as "trade courtesy"—to honor the prior publishing of an author as privilege to all his works. Carey's son Henry carried the business into important medical publishing, and the firm, after several names, continues today as Lea & Febiger. The Carey dynasty, however, was soon eclipsed by the Lippincott organization, whose growth seemed scarcely in need of protection or piracy.

Joshua B. Lippincott began his august Philadelphia publishing house by combining several earlier ventures, the oldest, a bookstore, dating to 1792. With a "natural fondness" for books Lippincott, according to J. C. Derby, "possessed an intuitive taste for the elegant bindings which afterwards made his books so famous among booksellers." To manufacture a wide range of imposing works, like *The Dispensatory of the United States of America* (1833—26th edition 1967), *Lippincott's Pronouncing Gazetteer of the World* (1855), *Lippincott's Magazine* (begun 1868), *Lippincott's Pronouncing Dictionary of Biography and Mythology* (1870), and bibles and scientific titles in addition to general works, the firm would need substantial production facilities. It was entirely situated, after the Civil War, in a new five-story plant (said, vacuously, to be the "largest and most complete in the world"). Folding and sewing were done on the fifth floor, with the finishing department, identified by its "mighty glue-pot, steaming like a witch-broth," on the fourth. Along with a "mimic saw-mill" for cutting spine grooves, and a unique case-printing machine (probably a stamping press), the factory by 1887 had machinery for every operation (except sewing). In a newer building (1901) Lippincott people looked enthusiastically in 1967 toward a 200th anniversary: "This building now has five stories;" said Barton H. Lippincott; "by 1990, it will have 15 stories. . . . I think the old-fashioned book will still be very popular in 1990 or even 2000."

The Philadelphia house of Henry Altemus, publishers, dated to 1790.

Joseph Altemus, Henry's father, had already introduced new labor-saving machinery (his British "toggle" press for stamping was among the first in America) before 1851, when he died, and when the son took charge. Henry was similarly among the first to install a book trimmer, rounder-backer, and wire stitcher. His five-story plant, capable of manufacturing 5000 books a day in 1886, frequently had greater capacity than his own editorial offices (specializing in bible work) could command. Thus obliged to solicit additional work, Altemus in an 1858 advertisement reveals the appreciable inventory of materials and hardware necessary for commercial bookwork:

> "[Altemus & Company] respectfully invite the attention of the Trade to their unsurpassed facilities for Binding Books in every Style and in any Quantity. Their extra morocco, extra calf, and law sheep leathers, as also the various qualities, colors, and styles of muslin and silk cloths and velvets, rims, clasps, and decorations, are prepared under their own directions and expressly for their own use. They possess all the requisite Machinery; and their assortment of tools, side and back ornaments, stamps, etc. etc., in Elegance, Variety, and Extent, is unrivalled in this country. . . ."[3]

Claiming for a long time to be the oldest continuous edition bindery, John Clark's Sons, Philadelphia, was founded 1810 by Thomas Clark, whose son John left three sons to carry on. In 1812 leather was so scarce Clark's was already using cotton for bindings—predating both Leighton and Harper's—but the circumstances only suggest wartime contingency. In 1927 Clark's was sold to the McNamee Bookbinding Company, which had seven years before bought the New York bindery of T. Y. Crowell; James T. McNamee had been a foreman of Harper's bindery.

In New York were located the Methodist Book Concern (1789, moving from Philadelphia in 1804), Charles Wiley (1807), American Bible Society (1816), D. Appleton & Company (1825), American Tract Society (1825), John Wiley (1828), G. P. Putnam's Sons (loosely dating to 1829), A. S. Barnes (1838), Dodd, Mead (1839), Scribner's (1846), Van Nostrand (1848). These and many others settled spiritually, if not physically, in the inspiring shadow of the Franklin Square Harper enterprise; with both capital and literary volume—and virtually symphonic fraternal relations—the four Harper brothers demonstrated to the entire literary nation the best techniques of manuscript acquisition and book production.

James and John Harper in 1817 had formed a printing establishment which, after enlargement in 1833 with two additional brothers, J. Wesley and Fletcher, began to publish steadily. Even with James serving as mayor of New York (1844) the quartet divided its responsibilities

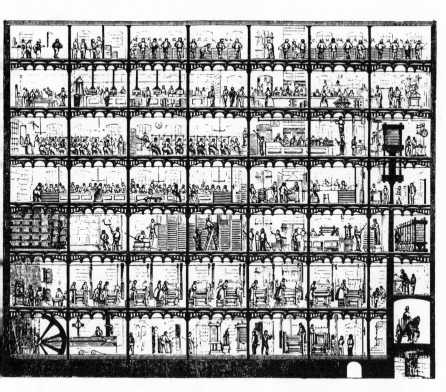

Harper & Brothers' Cliff Street, New York, manufactory, about 1855. The building featured fireproof wrought-iron columns and trusses recently designed by Peter Cooper, although the giant standing press (fourth floor) was not entrusted to their strength. Note the long banks of women sewing, folding (below sewers), and tending presses (first floor). [Abbott]

so capably it wrested from Henry Carey the domination of unblandished piracy of European works—and hence domination of US publishing. In one case they set, printed, and bound a volume in 21 hours to beat Carey to a waiting market. In 1827 Harper published—and manufactured—the first American cloth-bound book: Eaton, *Rome in the Nineteenth Century* (2 volumes), half purple cloth with paper sides, only five years after Leighton's introduction of fabric in England. Soon after (1831), Paulding, *The Dutchman's Fireside*, in Harper's "Library of Select Novels" was in full cloth, front and spine printed in black on light green muslin—today almost undecipherable, said Eugene Exman, a Harper biographer, and hard to read even when new; the same series, reissued in paperback, was manufactured at a loss only to counter the publishing of complete novels in the 1840's by the "mammoth" weekly newspapers with newly vacant press time (p 123). Books in series, nevertheless, like "Harper's Family Library" (begun 1830) were long popular and set great publishing trends.

In 1853 the Harper complex of 16 shops was destroyed (for the second time) by fire. Undaunted, the Harpers promptly decided to build the best plant in the country. Their organized layout (in a seven-floor building compositors set type and made electrotypes under bright top-floor skylights; paper stored—and dampened—in the basement was printed on the first floor, dried on the second, folded and gathered on the third, pressed, sawed, and sewn on the fourth, and bound on the fifth) was a veritable vertical assembly line. Resulting ease in handling materials permitted a large amount of female labor: at Harper's were 300 girls, 150 to gather and fold, 100 to sew, 30 to feed presses, and 12 to gild. Author Jacob Abbott visited the new plant in 1855 and found contentment everywhere: "Every visitor who sees these girls at their work [sewing] is struck with the extreme rapidity and dexterity of their movements, and with the healthy, and happy, and highly attractive appearance which they themselves and the scene of their labors exhibit. . . ." Light and clean, most bindery work—especially sewing—was always attractive to women. Harper's manpower requirements were indeed so large as to demand location in a large city, but there were other reasons too for staying there.

General publishers traditionally remained in the large cities (even in a modern age of urban decentralization) where they find essential the intellectual activity and commercial traffic on which they thrive. By 1865 New York developed a larger book trade than Boston and Philadelphia together, but it has never managed to extinguish the publishing flame in many such lesser communities. Although the largest publishers would retain their own manufacturing facilities until the end of the century (p 130), by the 1850's there were about 400 publishers in the United States—many of them functioning (by an early definition) only as distributors or salesmen for printers. But many too were without plants and clamoring for service. Their binders were close at hand.

Throughout the early years of industrial America, such as it was, the binder's hand tools were adequate to bind a book singly or by the dozen. As mechanical devices improved, however, and specialized bindery equipment became more and more expensive, it also became more and more limited in what it could do. Printing machinery, for example, could be used for most types of commercial or book work, but bookbinding equipment could only manufacture books. Edition book binders necessarily faced an expensive, self-excluding commitment by choosing such specialized work: they quickly settled close by, where publishers would be sure to find them.

Edward Walker and his two sons—trained by him—ran the New York Bindery to a state of near perfection in the 1850's. Their special delight were two embossing machines for stamping covers, made by Isaac Adams, Boston printing press manufacturers (p 116). Costing $1000 apiece and capable of up to 50 tons pressure, they were run and heated by steam to deliver 18 impressions per hour. With $15,000 worth of machinery, including some hydraulic standing presses, and between 60 and 100 employees, the New York Bindery could fabricate 800–1000 volumes a day. Sewing, that fussy, time-consuming operation, was no problem for Walker, for whom a "female" could sew two or three thousand sheets (4-page sections) daily. "So complete and ample are its appointments," the proud owner concluded, "that it is believed no similar establishment can boast superior facilities in this respect in the United States." Confidently he sent specimens of his work to the London Exposition of 1851, and continued in business until the end of the century.

Bookbinder Robert Rutter left Harper's—where he had won a gold watch for target shooting—to start his own shop in 1860. His son Horace L. joined in 1886. Robert is credited with developing, during World War I, a lustre stamping ink to match that of Germany's. In 1929 (14 years after his death) the firm merged with that of Thomas Russell, and Russell-Rutter itself in 1970 merged with the J. F. Tapley Company.

The J. F. Tapley Company (1850) had moved to New York from Springfield, Massachusetts. The firm once won a record order for 1 million bibles (still a specialty of the company), and is credited with inventing, among other devices, the concealed cloth joint, done originally as a reinforcement for the *Century Dictionary*. Jesse F. Tapley himself had been a prolific inventor. In 1887 Alfred C. Wessmann joined the company, and became its head from 1910 to 1924. During that time he designed a power lift truck, a building-in press truck, a nipping machine, and also developed standard terms and conditions by which binders and publishers now operate—one of his innovations was that printed sheets to be held for future binding would be folded and gathered, eliminating later waste and costly set-up times when the second portion was wanted. Wessmann was recognized as "one of the industry's most outstanding pioneers in new equipment and ideas to lessen bindery labor." The Tapley-Rutter Company, Moonachie, New Jersey, today uniquely survives, having assimilated three of the four binders considered in 1910 to have been the country's biggest: Tapley, Rutter, Russell, and Edwin S. Ives (p 310).

Other notable edition binders both capitalized on the introduction of machinery into the bindery and at the same time made significant contributions to the progress of industrialization: the Becktold Company, St. Louis (1872), W. B. Conkey, Chicago (1877), moving to Hammond, Indiana, in 1898, The Plimpton Press (p 189), Quinn & Boden, Inc., New Jersey, L. H. Jenkins, Inc., Virginia, [Charles A.] Braunworth & Company (p 149), H. Wolff Book Manufacturing Company (p 276), American Book Bindery (p 318), Edwin L. Hildreth & Company, Vermont, and Norwood Press, Massachusetts.

Industrial progress in America had kept up a pace almost as rapidly as in England, although it lacked leadership and direction: the acceptance of cloth in the late 1820's, for example, was more rapid and pervasive than in England, making publisher's bindings the rule by the 1830's, with the stamped case (although made by hand) welcome to almost all. There is no indication, however, that it would have started in America without British stimulus. Where there had been in England a market for costly books at the beginning of the 19th century, there was, as we have seen, a corresponding resistance by British publishers to mass-produce cheaply. In the United States, however, cheap production was a beginning necessity, and publishers could only promise better books in the future if the demand for them materialized. Edition bookmaking could scarcely improve from purer precepts.

Neither American publishers nor their binders, however, were ready to dismiss European guidance on taste or technical matters for the first half of the century. What France and England did must be right. Binders were already resigned to accept whatever instructions publishers gave them, although Walker, for one, expressed surprise, in an age of "highest cultivation of art" that bindings were reverting to "gorgeous designs" (à la cathedral and other romantic styles) of the gothic ages. James B. Nicholson, a New York binder, silenced such questions:

> "But, so long as the public remain unacquainted with [the cased-in cloth binding's] want of capability for use, and desire a mass of gold upon the sides,—so long, in fact, as there is a large class who desire books for mere show and not for use,—it will be in the interest of publishers to gratify them by furnishing cloth-gilt work."[4]

The American public was in fact delighted with profuse gilt work (so also was the French and British public), and, except for the occasional collector whose library was to be an interior decorating problem, there were few complaints beyond those who pragmatically wanted their pages trimmed all around, or those who subscribed to the European affectation that "the repeated slight interruptions [of cutting the bolts

—folds] heightened the pleasure of perusal." If anything, there was little time in America for contemplative perusal.[5]


We have seen how French binders, almost one by one, had to commission the special construction of machinery: with little persistence among binders the French machinery manufacturers camped elsewhere. In England inventions for the bindery were often dismissed as temporary expedients: a novelty, an adaptation, a modification—ideas seemed hardly worthy of exploitation. With this moderate impetus the British binders got only the equipment they fostered—that associated with the introduction of cloth and the rolling press (actually a vestigial device necessitated by the dampening of press sheets, a practice discontinued almost simultaneously with the spread of machine papers). Throughout Europe, nevertheless, the binder was so accustomed to respect the tradition of the well-made book he preached quality (and with labor surpluses could afford, economically, to practice it) to a public, as we have seen, poorly served for a long time.

America entertained no strong notions of tradition where labor was involved. Where all industries started anew simultaneously, the profundity and prestige of invention was sufficient to compel all mechanically inclined persons, knowledgeable or otherwise, to invent, to patent, to exploit. It was the national pastime for an entire century; the mental exercise for passing winter nights. In the printing and binding trades were excellent opportunities for the mechanical solution of repetitive chores like paper cutting and trimming, vises and presses for glueing, pressure devices for smoothing and compressing. They were recurring problems and sometimes were solved more than once.

The rolling press, for example, already at work for a decade in England despite its controversy, was developed anew in the United States. James Maxwell, a New York machinist, made a rolling press about 1840, possibly from descriptions by British immigrant binders. Charles Starr, a member of the "New-York Friendly Association of Master-Bookbinders" and superintendent of the American Bible Society bindery, displayed a rounder-backer at the 1851 London Exposition along with another device for trimming or finishing the backs of books, both "kept in operation during the Exhibition. . . ." Although Leighton had found it useful, as we have seen, such commercial attempts to introduce machinery—whether abroad or at home—required the dedication of a father for a child coupled with the persistence of a professional salesman. There were only a few such entrepreneurs even in the United States.

George H. Sanborn was one of the earliest bindery machinery

inventors equipped with commensurate salesmanship. While still at school and working part-time in a bindery, he and John Orr had invented a roller-type rounder and backer on which Orr reportedly took a patent in 1854. Sanborn, then 24, began to market the machine, sending the first ones to the 1855 Paris Exposition and to London, both cities awarding it a medal. But in his native land its reception was so cold, said *American Bookmaker*, Sanborn was "on one occasion compelled to jump from the window of a bindery in which he was endeavoring to introduce the machine, in order to save himself from violence." Workers feared—and rightly—that this machine, first to enter the shop, would upset the system of hand binding where each man performed all the functions on a single book until it was completed. This was essentially the complaint, unvoiced, of British binders to Burn's rolling press. Yet of many far more complicated devices to enter the bindery, the rounder-backer was consistently the most appreciated among old-timers who recalled the earlier conditions: Charles F. Kint, president of the John C. Winston Company and inventor of "Hercules," a patented textbook binding, called the roller-backer the greatest labor saving device of all.

Sanborn's appreciation of bindery conditions persuaded him of the utility of his machine—and in other devices for the bindery. With the Standard Machinery Company, a factory at Mystic River, Connecticut, once makers of cotton gins, steamboat boilers, and agricultural tools, Sanborn about 1860 enlarged the original 13-inch backer to 17½ inches. With John E. Coffin, Portland, Maine, he developed other spine-shaping machinery; he further produced a variety of guillotine cutters, circular saws, embossers, and smashers. In 1868 he transferred his sales headquarters from Boston to New York, offering by 1872 everything necessary to equip a modern shop, including the "Star" trimmer, an improvement on Hervey Law's automatic turntable book-edge cutter. Inventor of a churn and a freezer, railroad and glassmak-

GEORGE H. SANBORN

ing equipment, Sanborn with perception and ingenuity improved the mechanisms of the countless bindery tools and apparatuses he furnished to the trade; he died in 1881.

Sanborn's sons George E. and Hermann L. continued the business, being first to develop a case-smoothing machine (simply a bank of rollers to obviate the smoothing of hand-made cases with bone folders) which led to the 1893 Sheridan case-maker. In 1897 George H. Sanborn & Sons relinquished its interest in the Standard Machinery Company, although it continued to function as western agents for Standard, operating from Chicago. F. L. Montague & Company handled the eastern distribution of Standard's (Sanborn's) bindery line. In the uncertain book-machinery trade the relation between Sanborn salesmen and Standard manufacturers had been tenuous: each wanted some control over the other, but neither would yield to a single management with concerted objectives. At the Philadelphia Centennial they had separate booths: Sanborn displayed his steam-powered stabbing machine with revolving needles; Standard featured an automatic book trimmer. Both factions necessarily faced retrenchment in the greater competition which followed.

With scarcely less resistance, the folding machine next captured the binder's attention; again, overwhelming persistence was necessary. Folding machine patents had variously appeared in 1843, 1849, and 1853. The economics of labor, however, could at first barely support such novelties even if workable: early $600–$1000 machines could fold 1500 "octavo" sheets per hour (making three folds), yet an experienced hand folder doing only 500—but without high initial cost, set-up, or repairs—would be competitive for a long time to come. But try as they might, the girls were not always perfect. *American Publishers' Circular and Literary Gazette* criticized them in 1863:

"Publishers might much improve the appearance of books by having a little more attention paid to the folding of the sheets. Carelessness in this particular not infrequently spoils what would otherwise be a handsome volume. . . ."[5]

This smug European-oriented journal had scarcely considered that war raging in the south might, among other disruptions, be occupying the thoughts of bindery women in all the shops. But why indeed should the output of any repetitive task be at the mercy of distracted workers? Cyrus Chambers, Jr., had long thought otherwise.

Born 1833, Chambers at the age of 6 worked as a bobbin boy in a Philadelphia woolen mill operated by his father. His leisure, however, was spent in the mill's repair shop, where he constructed mechanical and electrical novelties. At 15 he built a brass steam engine, and a year

Steam-operated book folding machine, about 1871. Blade (in front of operator) descended to make first fold. Folded sections emerged in horizontal hopper below large gear. [Ringwalt]

later he made one of the smallest: weighing less than ½ ounce, the 150-part gold and silver machine, with cylinder diameter of 1⁄16 inch, ran at 3000 rpm. While studying dentistry under his brother Edwin he invented a saliva pump and other equipment. But dentistry was not for him.

After repeated failure, Chambers invented a steam-operated machine for folding newspapers, and one for bookwork, only to get little encouragement from publishers. He improved the equipment, however, assuring accurate folds by introducing register pins (similar to those on old hand presses) to hold the sheet in position, retracting during the descent of the folding blade. Chambers managed to sell one to the *Saturday Evening Post* (then a newspaper) and the *New York Tribune;* at about the same time (1856) he patented a new "quarto" book folder which he sold to Lippincott, and a "double-twelvmo" which, at Harper's, remained in use for 30 years. The prestige of these installations was enormous.

With Edwin, Chambers now formed a partnership to manufacture and market the folders. Despite a nagging eight-year patent infringement suit (which he won) and diversions into the manufacture of sewing machines and brick-making equipment, among other interests, Chambers improved his folders considerably, faced, as he was, with the trade epithet that these machines were "the invention of the devil," either working perfectly or exasperatingly without any precision whatsoever. When his brother died in 1875 Chambers managed the business alone although, as his eyesight failed, he gradually relaxed control—continuing, nevertheless, many folder, brick-making, and automotive and aircraft inventions all the while. One later Chambers machine was capable of folding a 16-page signature and an 8-page signature, inserting the 8 inside the 16, and pasting it down; another could feed, fold, staple, pack, and count 60 copies of *Ladies' Home Journal* (92 pages per issue) every minute (p 211). Chambers died in 1911; he had not only succeeded in manufacturing folders, his genius had sold the bindery world on steam-operated mechanization.

The Case, Lockwood & Brainard Company, Hartford (now Connecticut Printers, Inc.), had begun printing in 1836. It handled and sold 200,000 "cottage" bibles (2 volumes, royal octavo) and also for a time printed and bound Webster's unabridged dictionary. In the 1870's its entire third-floor edition bindery was turning out 354,000 books yearly, fed from the fourth-floor folding, gathering, and sewing room containing—a strong commitment—no less than six Chambers "patent" folders—all at work "under the supervision of a lady." Newton C. Brainard, president of the company in the 1920's, served as mayor of Hartford (as had his predecessor Leverett Brainard); Charles E. Brainard, a company director, is also an officer today of The Smyth Manufacturing Company.

While many folders were custom designed through the 1870's for newspapers, book binders, mildly interested, insisted on machinery that delivered the same folds as their hand folders. (Newspapers used different impositions.) Talbot C. Dexter of Des Moines, Iowa, developed a practical book folder in 1880; a newspaper pressman, Dexter had invented several devices, but not being a "patent rights man," lost credit for them. In 1878 he had begun working on a folder, and with ingenious improvements by his brother Thomas made it almost indispensable to the edition bindery. Dexter's famous "Quadruple Book Folder" (giving either four 16-page signatures or two 32's), fastest and still most efficient for bookwork, appeared in 1896.

A year later Dexter produced a combination folder, gatherer, and wire stitcher, building several for the long-lived Boston magazine, *Youth's Companion* (500,000 circulation): the 25-foot, 10-ton machines—the first of many such—manufactured 4500 magazines per hour. Harper's bindery, formerly true to Chambers, had converted. "Your notes will be easy here," said the periodical superintendent to a reporter in 1909. "Everything is Dexter, Dexter, Dexter!" In 1900, with over 150 patents on record, Dexter moved his factory to Pearl River, New York, to better serve his customers, where today it operates as part of the giant Miehle-Goss-Dexter organization.

Other inventions in folding and paper handling followed rapidly. Richard T. Brown with J. L. Hirt developed a folder in 1883 which became the principal product of the Brown Folding Machine Company, Erie, Pennsylvania. Frederick P. Rosback, another "inventive genius," had developed a knot-tying machine (for machine crop harvesting), the round-hole rotary perforator (for postage stamps), as well as automatic index-tabbing machine, a wire stitcher, and punching machines; he organized his firm in 1881 and moved it to Benton Harbor, Michigan, in 1910, where it subsequently offered a complete line of bindery equipment. The Mentges Folder Company and the Eclipse Folding Machine Company, both at Sidney, Ohio, also were early in the field. By their tireless efforts in undoubtedly the most competitive area of bindery machinery, the many folder manufacturers gave binders their first look at what automatically fed machinery could do.

Bookbinder Edwin Crawley, Sr., Cincinnati, Ohio, also worked indefatigably to automate the recurring rounding and backing job. "After 30 years' incessant labor" he developed an automatic rounder-backer (1891) capable of 450–700 books per hour, settling the problem for a long time thereafter. Having lost control of other inventions, Crawley —his firm dates to 1888—first tried to sell the machine without agents, almost personally. His son Arthur, however, also an inventor, wisely thought it better to stick to manufacturing: E. C. Fuller is generally credited with introducing the successful Crawley rounder-backer to the trade. In 1947 the machine, fully redesigned, was capable of handling books from $3\frac{1}{2}$ x $10\frac{1}{2}$ inches wide, $2\frac{1}{2}$ x $12\frac{3}{4}$ inches long, and $\frac{1}{8}$ to $3\frac{3}{4}$ inches thick. The modern Crawley Book Machinery Company continues to invest heavily in bindery automation—and on a world-wide scale (p 288).

James L. Lee and Paul Shneidewend began as electrotypers and machinery dealers, and in 1893 as the Challenge Machinery Company commenced manufacturing printing presses, paper cutters, drilling machines, and other bindery equipment, locating in Grand Haven, Michigan, in 1903. James' son J. Edgar Lee invented several bindery machines.

The Boston Machine Works Company, Lynn, Massachusetts, founded 1895, makes book-cover turning-in machines and book-corner turning machines.

The E. P. Lawson Company (now a subsidiary of MGD Systems, Inc.), makers of paper cutters, began in 1898.

Bookbinder and machinery designer Edward M. Brackett in 1913 founded a company in his name to manufacture his equipment, the Brackett stripping machine in particular:

"The stripping machine is versatile [says the US GPO]. It will apply strips of paper or cloth to sheets of paper or to the backs of books. It will strip end papers and tip them to the book signatures in one operation. It will make cases for cut-flush bindings and apply back-strips to books from 1/16 to 1 inch thick. It will hinge or guard inserts and fasten the guards to the signatures. . . ."[7]

Guarding is the use of pasted paper strips to insert maps, etc.

John J. Pleger, after advising the Philippine government in setting up its bindery, formed a Chicago company (1926) to make a roller-backer, a back gluer, and a round-corner turning-in machine. In 1953 Gane Brothers & Lane acquired the company.

Paul Gitzendanner and Charles A. Muller for a long time independently manufactured and repaired bookbinding machinery. Together as Gitzendanner-Muller Company their successors now make wire stitchers at Roselle, New Jersey.

Chandler & Price and Brandtjen & Kluge, both manufacturers of clamshell printing presses, have long made heavy duty models for die-stamping work.

The scattered applications of machinery to specific binding problems, as we have seen, tackled the most common, repetitive tasks, but haphazardly. Inventors did not always exploit their ideas wisely—and we do not record here the hundreds who failed altogether. Those who marketed their own invention soon discovered that novelty and intricacy were often mistaken for showmanship and chicanery, as inventors always tend to inflate their claims. Those who were too trusting of sales agents reaped small rewards and debilitating suspicions. Many inventors, reluctant to leave their secluded shops, needed extraordinary understanding if even the most clever work was to see the light of commercial success:

> "Invention results from genius which always hungers for sympathy [said an industrialist to employers at an 1889 trade fair], and is subject to depression. If you have such a workman, take him into your confidence, interest yourself in his family, ascertain his circumstances and encourage his labors. Such treatment will pay you better than any other investment. In some respects inventors are weak. I never knew an inventor who was at the same time a good businessman."[8]

The commercial outcome of any useful invention hinges critically on undisputed ownership (patent), persistent dissemination of information (advertising), and availability of the product (manufacturing and distribution). Strong trade resistance would be a capping hurdle. The complexity of such business problems was more than many of the most inventive minds cared to face; the expanding industrial environment grew too large even for small partnerships as well as individual entrepreneurs. Hence there emerged a few larger organizations composed of gifted mechanics and engineers, but, at the same time, a staff of trained and talented salesmen to market the product sensibly, steadily.

After mid 19th century all technological advances in bookmaking (as in many other industrial areas) were American in origin. With the expanding demand for books throughout the United States there were more bindery tasks than handwork could possibly perform; what is more, the smallest of them grew to sufficient volume to demand mechanical solution. US manufacturers were acquiring the reputation for willingness to design equipment or alter existing models; they had already established themselves, generally, for quality workmanship, interchangeable parts, and "brand-name" association with "lines" of merchandise that persuaded binders with problems that they did not have to slap together "monkey" machinery all the time. As early as the 1876 Philadelphia Centennial American industry was powerfully appreciated abroad: US bindery and boxmaking equipment, viewed by British mechanics before the show opened, appeared so superior to their own machinery they reportedly returned their wares to England unopened.

The giant American companies had strong footholds in their fields. Robert Hoe & Company, New York, was among the first large manufactories to find the bindery a close, profitable, adjunct to the printshop. Robert Hoe (1784–1833) had come from England about 1803 and soon (1823) acquired the small printing press factory at which he worked. The market was increasingly lively and varied. Hoe's purchase of the Isaac Adams enterprise upon the latter's retirement in 1859 thus increased business for both binder's standing (or stationary) and stamping (or embossing) presses as well as printing presses of all description. Adams had endeared himself to binders with a line of stamping and gilding presses; Hoe in 1867 still offered (from the Boston factory) a book-rolling machine, embossing presses in three sizes, a "patent" book and paper cutter capable of trimming three turntable-positioned sides successively, a 21-inch "vibrating" knife (an oscillating guillotine which cut with greater ease), and other smaller accessories, all of which had been Adams' products. But the Hoe company's progress in newspaper work was a far more dramatic—if indirect—contribution to the book binder than the furnishing of a slew of hand- and steam-operated devices of diminishing novelty.

Richard M. Hoe (1812–1886), taking charge of his father's establishment in 1830, exerted immense effort in the development of new equipment. About 1832 he obtained from General Thomas W. (incredibly nicknamed "Toggle-joint") Harvey, father of the inventor of surface-hardened armor, rights to a rotary toggle-joint press, but Harvey, appellation notwithstanding, did not invent the movement, as he claimed: Peter Smith, Robert Hoe's original partner and brother-in-law, had already used the toggle or "knee-action" joint in his 1822 Acorn printing press. The toggle-joint in stamping presses nevertheless provided the stupendous pressure French, British, and American binders needed to fuse a considerable amount of intricate goldwork to millions of fancy book and album covers.

From about 1842 Richard Hoe himself patented printing machinery at a proliferating rate, making the company foremost in commercial and newspaper presses. Richard was father-in-law to J. Henry Harper and uncle to cousins Frank Dodd and Edward Mead, but (excepting a fine book and art collection), he seems to have expressed no particular interest in bookwork. That was to be the unsurpassed domain of his own son (p 150).

Stephen D. Tucker (1818–1902) was apprenticed to Hoe in 1834 and remained 59 years to retire as a senior partner in the firm. Assigned to a new "Experiment Room" in 1842, Tucker, whom *Scientific American* considered "one of the most brilliant mechanics that this country ever produced," took almost 100 patents in perfector and webb-press machinery, plus many others jointly with Richard Hoe. Of especial value was an 1875 rotary newspaper folding attachment, first used at the *Philadelphia Times,* which functioned as fast as the high-speed press itself. To New York's Metropolitan Museum of Art this master craftsman of time and motion left a grand collection of sundials.

Picking up the thread of invention from Hoe and Tucker was yet another press-building "mechanical wizard." Luther C. Crowell had designed an airplane at the age of 22, and five years later (1867) patented a more down-to-earth machine for making square-bottom paper bags. His improvements to sheet delivery and folding equipment led in 1875 to the installation, on a new press for the *Boston Herald,* of another unique rotary folding machine. From 1879 on he designed for Hoe a number of intricate multiple-cylinder and perfecting presses, and pamphlet-printing and wire-stapling presses, obtaining over 280 patents for printing machinery alone. A wrapping and mailing machine, and one for labeling bottles, were also his. For 24 years (until his death in 1903) Crowell, characterized by *Scientific American* as "an ingenious Yankee skipper who could not even read a drawing and had to work from patterns or models," boldly and authoritatively worked out the final details of newspaper and periodical mechanization. The Hoe organization almost single-handedly made the "mammoth" weeklies, the high-speed dailies, and the giant weekly supplements possible. By its competition and its mechanical precedents the newspaper profoundly influenced all bindery work.

Bernard Sheridan—after working as a pattern-maker for Robert Hoe

—in 1835 began to manufacture printer's rollers and bindery equipment. Within three years he placed his first small hand-operated embossing press on the American market, and by 1845 it was a steam-operated giant—18 years before Engel's in France. In 1861 the Sheridan firm took over the competing business (founded 1827) of Frederick J. Austin, maker of a variety of binding machines, who himself announced to the trade:

> ". . . after a severe and protracted illness, from which he is still suffering, having concluded to relinquish the Machine business which he has so long conducted in this city, has sold the same out to his friends Messrs E.R. & T.W. SHERIDAN: comprehending the good will entire, all of his patents, the right to manufacture all of the machines heretofore made by him . . . , all of the patterns necessary for that purpose, and all of his tools and the fixtures of his shop complete."[8]

The new owners moved into Austin's New York factory and there assimilated—and offered for sale for fully 40 years—their predecessor's paper cutters (14 models), embossers (7 models), standing presses (10 models), shears and board cutters (4 models), and a book sawing machine. Austin had, like Adams of Boston, with a vast collection of carefully cast and machined equipment, quietly, unobtrusively, performed the first step in bindery modernization by providing quantities of reliable, efficient tools.

With the entry of two sons into the firm upon Bernard's death just before the Austin purchase, the company remained "E.R. & T.W." until 1882, when, having taken in Charles B., a third son, it settled down as "T.W. & C.B." Theodore W., heading the company for 60 years, was, like his father, highly inventive, "responsible for more improvements and advanced methods in the manufacture and use of bookbinding machinery than any other man," carrying the firm through its most critical period of industrial expansion.

Despite the professed mechanical ingenuity of father and son, however, the Sheridans were in fact salesmen, not inventors. Through the 19th century they supported little engineering experimentation the way Hoe did, preferring instead to continue assimilating working designs which their New York and Chicago salesrooms would display. In 1856 they had bought James E. Mallory's "Vibrator" guillotine, and with some minor modernization reintroduced it as the "Sheridan Improved Vibrator." (Austin, perhaps exasperated by both Hoe and Sheridan, reminded the trade in 1861 that he had in 1839 *originated* the "Sliding or End-vibratory motion.") Similarly, Hervey Law's patent 1864 cutter was purchased and renamed the "Sheridan." Both machines were popular in the 1880's and '90's.

In 1893 Sheridan brought out as its own development—"Not a theory, not an experiment, but a practical working machine"—a case-maker which automatically took pre-cut cloth and boards (at first), glued boards and lining to the fabric, turned in the edges, and shot the finished case through a bank of rollers. Actually invented by Alfred Bredenberg under unusual circumstances (p 215), this machine was a substantial step beyond Sanborn's simple case-smoother. Sheridan promised 1000–1200 cases per hour, making them without warping or blisters, "better and neater than the most skillful man." Early machines went to Donnelley's Lakeside Press, Frank A. Munsey (p 210), and the US Government Printing Office (p 196); it was among the first major machines to find wide acceptance in America and around the world. The Sheridan case-maker was improved in 1905 to enable it (with 3 attendants) to cut cloth from a roll, making 1300 cases hourly.

1893 was also the year of the World's Columbian Exposition, Chicago, at which Sheridan, bidding for leadership in the bindery machine market, boasted the largest exhibit ever assembled in the United States. More significant, perhaps sensitive about their distinction as a manufacturer, every piece of machinery on display was made by Sheridan, and manufactured routinely, not as novelties for the show. In addition to Sheridan's reputation for sturdiness, the company usually could supply parts for their machines up to 50 years, long beyond the requirements of any reasonable trade customs. At the Columbian exhibit were their "Auto" paper cutter (a genuine 1879 Sheridan design), three other guillotine cutters, embossers, inking machines, a roller-backer, and a board cutter, for which display they received 8 awards and 5 medals.

In 1909 Sheridan proclaimed itself agents for the Parkside Casing In machine, a product of British design (p 275). Modifications by 1914 resulted in two Parkside models, the "No. 2" (at 1000 per hour) capable of handling 7 x 4½ to 16 x 9¾ inches, and the "No. 3" (750 per hour) extending the maximum to 22 x 14 inches. These too apparently became Sheridan's own by assimilation.

BERNARD SHERIDAN

Upon Theodore's death in 1914 LeGrand L. Clark, his son-in-law, became president of the company, followed by the latter's own son, Theodore Sheridan Clark; they guided the firm beyond modern manufacturing into an age of creative advertising. In 1927 with a long line of bindery machinery including a gatherer, "the machine that thinks," the T.W. & C.B. Sheridan Company's starry-eyed copywriter waxed eloquently:

"The use of Sheridan improved book binding machinery today means a remarkable advancement in the manufacture of books. The day of the ideal bindery has arrived. The enormous outputs now obtained with Sheridan machinery reduce the cost of production to figures a few years ago deemed impossible. Best of all these enormous outputs, and the tremendous reduction in help, have been accomplished not only with no sacrifice in quality, but the Sheridan machine made book is usually far more uniform and stronger than the old fashioned hand-made book."[10]

Long before, however, Sheridan, Sanborn, Smyth, and other bindery suppliers had provided the bookmaker with an almost fully mechanized workshop. *The Paper Box Maker and American Bookbinder* in 1899 furnished an explicit example of what machine efficiency had done for the binder. To manufacture an edition of 1000 books, twelvmo, cloth-bound, 20 signatures each printed in 16's, cover stamped in two colors of ink plus gold, using a shop containing folders, Smyth sewer, Crawley rounder-backer, and usual smashers and stampers:

| *Materials* | | *Labor* | |
|---|---|---|---|
| Thread | $ .40 | Cutting sheets | $1.00 |
| Glue | 1.50 | Machine folding | 5.00 |
| Crash, headbands | .50 | Gathering, sewing | 5.00 |
| Waste paper | 1.50 | Folding, smashing | 1.00 |
| Board | 2.50 | Inserting waste leaves | .80 |
| Cloth | 17.50 | Rounding, backing | 1.25 |
| Dies | 8.00 | Trimming | 1.50 |
| Gold leaf | 2.50 | Crash, headbanding | 3.50 |
| Ink | 2.00 | Case-making | 3.50 |
| | ———— | Cutting cloth | .70 |
| | $36.40 | Casing in | 3.50 |
| | | Jacketing | .50 |
| Office expenses | 13.42 | Examining books | 1.00 |
| Profit (20%) | 16.10 | Packing, delivery | 1.75 |
| | ———— | | ———— |
| | $29.52 | | $30.00 |

Total: $95.92 or less than 10¢ per book, for the complete binding. Along with this cost analysis, the journal itself editorialized upon the state of American progress in the art of manufacture:

"The growth of the machine industry . . . in the United States has of late years been rapid and extraordinary. The inventive spirit of the people has been the prompting impulse of this movement. . . . It is not a question of bulk or tonnage, but of efficiency. There may be economics in cost and construction, simplicity in detail, and an absence of the ponderous and cumbersome, but it is not over stretching the matter to say that in point of ingenuity and constant improvement, newness of design, and in the elegancies of finish, the American-made machine, from a typewriter to a Baldwin locomotive, is a favorite under all circumstances. . . ."[11]

A bibliophile, noticing no significant French or British bookmaking machinery, heartily agreed: "Yankee wits," he said, "have surpassed all their rivals." This last decade of the 19th century had brought the bindery well into the machine age—and binders were almost tumbling to their destruction. Since the beginning years when binderies nestled close to their erudite patrons, the publishers had not been insensitive to the promises of speed, versatility, and cheapness: a few of them, in fact, had been pushing all the way.[12]

With pride and satisfaction in their work, therefore, the commercial printers and binders, aided by cheap machine-made paper and fast new cylinder presses, realized they could offer publishers mass-produced "cheap books for large numbers of people." Between 1830–1840 schools and leisure reading grew; by the 1850's the biggest publishing boom Americans had ever seen was under way. The "penny" press and other periodicals commenced; annuals and "furniture" books (those with "flashy" woodcuts designed to be seen on coffee tables) strongly inspired by Ackermann's of London, began to sell for less than $1. In spirit with the elaborate wood and steel engravings in vogue, binders soon entertained the "revolutionary" notion that commercially made bindings could also possess an "esthetic excellence" of their own. Their plain and goffered cloths were soon blind-stamped (embossed without pigmentation, tonal effects achieved only from the glazed surface) through 1845–60, although elaborate gilt-stamping designs were also common. (Gold and colors in combination did not start until 1865–1870.) A financial crash in the late 1850's and the interruption of the Civil War, however, were heavy blows to proper book production—leaving the field unattended and exposed to the cheapest stuff of all.

Brothers Erastus F. and Irwin P. Beadle, leaving their Buffalo stereotype shop, in New York issued a "Dime Song Book" so successful they launched, in 1860, a dime novel series of which Archibald Constable would have been proud: "Books for the Million—a dollar book for a dime!!" ran their advertisement (first offering: Stephens, *Malaeska: The Indian Wife of the White Hunter*). The series became long famous in its salmon paper covers, although the best stories were acknowledged to have come out during the first few years. Thousands of dime paperbacks, nevertheless, marched off to war in pockets and knapsacks, with no complaints as to literary or physical quality.

With the book business in the doldrums during and after the Civil War, American publishers slept as a British invasion stole through the states. The cheap English editions, scarcely able to contain themselves in Great Britain, suddenly became available everywhere in the United States. An English-made book selling for 25¢ was adjudged "so excellent that if it had been made in this country," said a critic, "it could not be sold for less than seventy-five cents." American publishers were galvanized to action.

Initial reaction to the cheap British inundation had appeared almost without recognition in the form of subscription and supplement publications. The first subject material—war literature—was well calculated to arouse lethargic readers. Civil War veterans, with a stock of chatty, personal combat anecdotes, traveled the countryside selling book "subscriptions" (books now deliberately segmented to be sold by installment) from door to door. Horace Greeley's *American Conflict* (2 volumes, O.D. Case & Co., 1864–1866) ultimately reached 225,000 copies, mostly sold by subscription. *Picturesque America* (Appleton, 1872), edited by William Cullen Bryant, was sold in 20 parts so successfully it prompted Taylor, *Picturesque Europe* and Wilson, *Picturesque Palestine*. As complete works, each in 2 volumes, *Picturesque America*, in brown crushed levant, and *Picturesque Palestine*, pale green morocco, were judged "very neat and tasteful" at the 1889 Paris Exposition, although the British commentator suspected—half correctly—both English materials and English emigrant labor had made them. General Grant's *Memoirs* (2 volumes, Webster & Co., 1885–1886) sold 650,000 by subscription, but Appleton, ironically, was deprived of colossal sales with General Sherman's reminiscences because the general would not permit harassment of old soldier friends by subscription salesmen.

Even more ambitious was the publishing record of François P. G. Guizot, *Popular History of France* (Estes & Lauriat, 187?), a gigantic work of the historian and statesman, but unappreciated in bookstores; reissued by subscription in 55 parts at 50 cents each, it was a best seller.

With steel engravings and good paper, and "beautiful letterpress," it also sold well, subsequently, as a $39 deluxe edition. A decade later it was issued again (8 volumes, $6.00, John B. Alden) so well printed on good paper and so well bound, said a reviewer, its value "almost staggers the powers of a fervid imagination."

Peter F. Collier similarly carried installment sales to a fine specialty at this time. He began as a young man hawking bibles to poor families with little success. "No, me boy, I have not that much money," said a scrubwoman. "I will give ye a dollar now and fifty cents iviry week till it is paid." With his employer's approval Collier sold 50 bibles in this manner the following day, and found the system successful for Shakespeare, Dickens, and *Collier's Encyclopedia* as well. About 1879 he organized his own manufacturing plant in New York, an enterprise which grew to 700 workers supported by 32 sales offices around the country and 96 sub-offices. From 1880 to 1909, when he died, Collier had produced 52 million books of fair quality—"usefully bound in cloth" said he—sold from door to door, and founded a publishing empire now operating (after discarding several nationwide magazines, *Collier's* and *Women's Home Companion* among them) as the Crowell-Collier and Macmillan Company. Remarkably, for the inspirational scrubwoman Collier built a home and raised her son when she died.

Newspapers too combatted the British imports with "extras" and weekly supplements. In an age of one mechanical and scientific revelation after another, readers awaited voraciously these popularized technical articles selling from 5 to 15 cents. The *New York Tribune* issued its extras in pamphlet on good stock, although J.R.G. Hassard, *The Fast Printing Machine* [The Hoe Web Perfector with folding attachment] (1878, 32pp, 10¢), trimmed to about 5 x 7 inches with 8-point text set to a 2½ x 4½ inch type page, if typical, related them more to Pickering's "Diamond Classics" than to readable literature. (4½-point editions had actually been issued in the 1860's by US publishers imitating Pickering.) More sensational, however, the *Tribune* issued weekly fiction as well as fact—and the entire publishing world gaped to see how it sold. The reading mania via such series was to eclipse its appreciable English forerunner.

With the *Tribune* subscription novels as precedent, publishers rushed to get out periodical series of their own. Oddly enough, the movement began in Chicago: Donnelley, Gassette & Lloyd (whose Lakeside Press, begun in 1864, was named by Reuben R. Donnelley out of admiration for Houghton's Riverside Press) began with their "Lakeside Library." George Munro's "Seaside Library" and "Fireside Companion," his brother Norman L. Munro's "Riverside Library,"

Frank Leslie's "Home Library," and Beadle & Adams' "Fireside Library" quickly followed. All issued standard fiction and new novels in paper covers, at 10 to 20 cents, in quantities of 5000 to 60,000. By 1877 the Lakeside Library contained 100 titles, but dozens of new competitors in cloth or paper were also luring readers, among them T. B. Peterson, Richard Worthington, Thomas D. Hurst & Company, John W. Lovell, Belford, Clarke & Company, John B. Alden, J. S. Ogilvie, Rand, McNally. Some, like Street & Smith, carried on with an impetus that took them well into the 1920's, their so-called "pulp fiction" curtailed at last only by the motion pictures.

Sold on newsstands along with the newspaper supplements, the cheap series were at first only a curiosity to the book trade watching them multiply almost microbiotically:

> "Our list already includes fourteen 'libraries' or series of these broadsheets [said *Publishers' Weekly* in 1877], of which one out-reaches a hundred numbers, while another is increasing just now at a regular rate of eight per week. . . . Their current sale is large, rather through the newsdealers and smaller booksellers, however, than through the important regular trade, as the profit of three cents a copy is not sufficient to induce most booksellers to offer them. . . ."[13]

By 1885 there would be 5000 paperback titles in print.

Gradually, of course, the paperbacks found their way into all the bookstores, although seldom to the bookmen's delight. "As soon as a cloth novel is shown to a customer," said August Brentano, Jr., (nephew of the bookstore's founder) in 1876, "and if he takes ever so great or little fancy to it, in two cases out of three the first question is 'Have you not got this in paper?' " But immediate discomfort would yield to such an innovation: within 10 years a few cheap publishing firms with their own shops (nicknamed "sawmills") would be capable—with typesetting, presswork, and binding almost entirely done by machine—of producing finished paperbacks in 10 hours, if necessary. The sawmills paved the way to complete mechanization of all books.

A model sawmill operation were the publishing offices and plant of George and Norman Munro. George, with 9 brothers and sisters in Nova Scotia, and eclectic training as printer, teacher, and theologian, came to New York in 1856 at the age of 31, with the urge to publish. He worked six years for D. Appleton, probably assigned to the ambitious *New American Cyclopedia* (p 163). From there he gravitated in 1864 to a mundane job at Beadles', writing almost "unmitigated trash" for $16 a week—and characterized by Beadle as happy to remain so occupied. But Munro quit soon after, apparently quite ready and well suited to operate somewhere between Appleton and Beadle in level of reading material.

At the same time Irwin Beadle also left his brother, and with Munro (Irwin P. Beadle & Company) began to publish the "Old Sleuth Library," issuing crime and detection stories. Trained as a bookbinder, Irwin, ironically, of necessity issued all his cheap titles unbound or in paper covers; he died about a year later, and Munro carried on. In 1867 Munro bought the Fireside Companion and in 1877 acquired the ailing Lakeside Library to launch it "Seaside." Both series were very successful, the latter (all British, no royalties) with almost 200 titles. When in 1881 a new translation of the bible appeared, Munro, from proofs smuggled to him by a participating Greek scholar-neighbor, published his own annotated edition exactly one day later. With his gigantic ventures, however, Munro was almost single-handedly flooding the cheap market.

Even before the mid 1880's, however, the stands had appeared so saturated it was necessary to dispose of paperbacks en masse as merchandising premiums: "Book Soap" was so-named just so a free volume could be packaged with it. One wholesaler returned to George Munro over a million unsalable Seaside titles: with amazing audacity the publisher accepted them (disposing some to soap companies) and countered by issuing a new series even more ambitious. Readers, he proclaimed, were not saturated—they were merely tired of the paper-covered quarto. The much smaller—but cloth-covered—duodecimo size was now newly appealing, and Munro exploited it. He reissued 449 titles in one year, while his brother Norman (with obvious fraternal collusion) similarly reissued 266 titles as "Munro's Library" (1884). From about 1882 on, the "cheap twelvmos" or duodecimos captured the public fancy, and all publishers had to change to smaller sizes.

Brother Norman was no less busy. In 1885 he was publishing "The New York Family Story Paper," Munro's Library, and "Munro's Pocket Magazine," claiming to spend more on advertising than any other publisher—$350,000 yearly—on bill posters, newspaper ads, promotional offprints of articles, and premiums. That year he also gave away—every week to the 300,000 subscribers of his story paper—a 16-page novel (pamphlet octavo), the unsalable returns dumped on his brother, to be sure—but what style! The manufacturing plant for schemes of this magnitude would have to be colossal. And it was.

The Munros shared a 9-story Manhattan building, finished in 1882 with "The New York Family Story Paper" emblazoned across its roof in great gilt letters. Departments were distributed by floor much like Harper's, but with significant new machines in the bindery. On the sixth floor the bindery, "with its small army of ever-busy female book-folders," had a Sanborn cutter, five machine folders, and a smasher capable of compressing 80 books a minute. "Another machine then saws holes through the backs of the sheets for the needle to pass through," said the Munros. "This being done, the sheets are sewed together by the Smythe [sic] sewing-machines, five of which, with a combined capacity of sewing 125,000 sheets or an average of 12,500 complete books a day, are operated by girls in the bindery." (Five "No. 1" Smyth machines in a sawmill, while almost a damning testimonial, illustrated that machine sewing from its inception was both cheaper and better than handwork; for their part the Munros must have appreciated that only good sewing could hold a fragile book together long enough to reach the marketplace.)

Covers were then glued on by hand, five girls handling 2500 books an hour. A trimming machine making 50 cuts a minute trimmed the edges. All bindery machinery and 22 presses were powered by a 150-horsepower steam engine in the basement. Norman Munro's family settled in Brooklyn with a number of fine trotting horses and a steam yacht named "Norma." George, called by Exman "the most exasperating of pirates," munificently endowed a Canadian University somewhat embarrassed that a theologian could write dime novels; he died in 1896, age 71.

John W. Lovell also came to New York from Canada, after several ventures under the aegis of his father, John Lovell, a prominent Montreal publisher—a firm still in existence. Boldly establishing a book manufactory at Rouses Point, New York, an absolute wilderness in 1874, the elder Lovell hoped to furnish employment for some of his six sons, all coming of age. The US Book Trade Association, meeting in Philadelphia and unsure of Rouses Point, suspected Lovell of intending by some borderline ruse "to defraud the revenue of both countries and to undersell all the traders who pay their honest dues," and mobilized to "stop his fun." Their fears on geographical grounds were unfounded, however, the location being distinctly 1½ miles below the Canadian border. Lovell meant this to be an American enterprise (yet close to his Montreal headquarters), and would spend $160,000 to house and equip it: the newly christened "Lake Shore Press" (later called "Lake Champlain Press")—like Kingsport Press only 50 years later—capitalized on cheap rural labor and unprecedented volume.

Brothers Joseph, Robert, John W., and Charles W. Lovell were promptly dispatched to the new plant, the last two almost in concert finding suitable Rouses Point girls and marrying in August, 1876. Lesser employees, however, found slim pickings in that northern spot. One of the 80 compositors there—more than Houghton had at Riverside Press—reported:

"Our great printing and publishing concern here is a phenomenon of its kind. New York, Boston, London, in fact cosmopolitan comps., bookbinders, and pressmen find their position outside the office somewhat anomalous. Rouse's Point is a straggling village of some 1,500 inhabitants. . . ."[14]

Food, clothing, and other comforts were scarce or expensive; to pass the desolate winters social activities were furious—clubs, musical band, turkey shoots, ice skating. John Lovell, although managing director of the plant, was not one to long endure this bucolic isolation.

In bustling, temperate New York Lovell quickly found his milieu. As Lovell, Adam & Company he began (age 26) to pirate British literature, rationalizing his cheap twelvmos and other series as "home [Rouses Point] manufacture." Said Lovell, "I believe with the late Charles Knight," whose *Popular History of England* (8 volumes, 1878, $10) was his first plunder, "that the mass of the people should be our first consideration . . .," although Knight had never condoned skipping out on royalties. (Estes & Lauriat's 1873 "authorized" edition of Knight cost $25; the two firms had long subsequent battles.) After failure in 1881 he reorganized as John W. Lovell Company with "Lovell's Library" of cheap (10¢, 20¢, 30¢) paperbacks, for which he managed to obtain a second-class (newspaper) mailing permit.

In 1888 Lovell bought the plates of the Munro Library and other series (including Estes & Lauriat's), and issued books through a number of subsidiaries. His "better" books came from Lovell, Coryell & Company, but nobody was fooled: one title, Raife, *The Sheik's White Slave* (1895, $1.25, cloth), despite its fine design in green and "electric blue," was simply considered one of a "class of poorly executed commercial bindings" for its cheap paper and faulty forwarding and overhang. ("Overhang" is the extension of the boards beyond the trimmed pages, usually 1/8 inch; the projecting boards—which should be equal and parallel all around—are also called the "squares.") So prolific was Lovell's output, nevertheless, he was nicknamed "Book-a-Day" Lovell, and soon sought to enlarge an already staggering production schedule (p 213). Gradually, however, he specialized in publishing socialism, occultism, suffragettism, and also dabbled in real estate on a Mexican Utopian community.

To produce the books of such sawmill publishers, the entire graphic arts industry seemed in suicidal conspiracy. Editorially, "established" publishers were infuriated by the indifferent attitude of the younger pirates who, like Lovell, declined to "Go in heartily for the 'courtesy of the trade' and—starve. . . ." Thus the collapse of that venerable institution brought anarchy where there had been peaceful gentlemen's agreement. Physically, little proofreading was done, the cheapest

wood-pulp paper was used, and many titles were printed from borrowed type or plates, however battered or worn. The result was an
understandable clutter of books and brochures of all sizes, shapes,
colors, prices, to bombard a defenseless public. The paradox was
obvious:

> "These are the golden days of the paper cover, the limp leather, the
> flexible cloth, the 'pocketbook' form and the tuck attachment [fancy
> cover flap buckled to keep a book closed]. The 'Dime,' the 'Half-
> Dime,' the 'Pocket,' the 'Half Asleep,' the 'Handy,' and the 'Unhandy,'
> Series, etc., are now in brisk demand. They are called the 'Libraries,'
> because they are not intended to be stored in libraries. . . ."[15]

The more "respectable" publishers could not watch idly. Usually
maintaining their own manufacturing facilities and reaping already low
unit costs for fair workmanship, they could not stoop lower without
jeopardizing their reputation, author obligations, and plant investment.
Some fought the cheap invasion, some joined it—but carefully. Henry
Holt issued the "Leisure Hour Series" (1883), and Harper & Brothers
brought out the "Franklin Square Library," which almost uninten-
tionally lent the whole cheap movement considerable respectability
(despite some titles at 10¢, Harper still paid royalties on English
works). Houghton Mifflin in 1885 introduced its quality "Riverside
Paper Series," although Houghton said, a few years later, "I have
never been troubled with the multitude of cheap books. People who
buy a cheap book will throw it away soon, and come and buy the
better book we publish, and they will keep it. . . ."

D. Appleton & Company with other dignified publishers had nevertheless tried nobly to fight the trend. With its own printing plant
and bindery—and exclusive book-stitching and book-sewing machinery—Appleton already had an excellent manufacturing posture. The
firm had early sought to stop the cheapness by campaigning, along
with George H. Putnam, for an international copyright law so that
indifferent American (and British) publishers could be regulated. Yet
the American market, from the point of view of manufacturing, was
too lucrative to permit even the honorable exchange of literary property to take place in the form of imported finished books. In an 1871
letter to the London *Times* William H. Appleton explained:

> "The United States now contain nearly forty million inhabitants,
> and they are eminently a book-buying people. The American market
> for English books is already great, and is destined to become immense.
> . . . But [Americans] hold themselves perfectly competent to manu-
> facture the books that shall embody your authors' thoughts in ac-
> cordance with their own needs, habits, and tastes, and in this they
> will not be interfered with."[16]

Appleton could not admit that, aside from the profits of piracy, American authors (except the giants—Cooper, Irving, Bryant, Paulding) had so little appeal in the United States they were often disguised as foreigners; had American publishers not manufactured large-selling British literature they would have become nothing more than importer-wholesalers. The American bookmaking industry might never have developed beyond the handbound needs of rich collectors—and even they were not buying "American."

The Appleton organization nevertheless plunged into the hectic market. Although from 1854 on they offered some items for 6¼ cents apiece, their "quality" series, the "Popular Library of Best Authors," retailed at 50 cents per volume. Other better sets were an 18-volume Dickens ($10, post-paid), and 25 works of Scott in 43 volumes. Unlike the more crass publishers, Appleton was genuinely embarrassed when it once inadvertently issued in its library a title already appearing elsewhere. Yet the library "mania" grew: in 1888 Appleton issued the "Town and Country Library" which, at 50 cents for paper and $1.00 for cloth, ran to 312 titles. With Harper's, Holt, Funk & Wagnalls, and Dodd, Mead, Appleton maintained its reputation as a fine publisher—despite continuing odds.

All the series had been issued regularly, usually one or two volumes per month, to qualify as periodicals in order to get low postage (1874 rates: 3¢ a pound for quarterlies and monthlies, 2¢ for weeklies; new 1885 rate: 1¢ for all second-class mail). By 1890, however, the United States postal authorities were catching up with some publishers who had failed to issue titles periodically, and others who possessed no demonstrable subscription lists. The International Copyright Law of 1891 soon put an end to royalty-free publishing schemes altogether, although even into the early 1900's new, cheap mail-order paperback publishers somehow still managed to offer—unabridged—*Dr. Jekyll and Mr. Hyde* for 1¢, *A Study in Scarlet* and *Treasure Island* for 3¢ each, *Vanity Fair* for 5¢, and 12 volumes of Dickens for 48¢.

The 1893 depression took its toll of pirate publishers, to no one's dismay. The cheap publishing boom had collapsed, but a vast sea of ill feeling and confusion remained for publisher, manufacturer, bookseller, and public alike. The 1884 lament of a *Publishers' Weekly* correspondent would persist for decades:

"The commerce of literature is no longer what it was; the courtesies of the trade are now not known; the trade sales have fallen into disuse; and our gatherings of publishers and retailers, and the common interests that bound them, have all disappeared. . . . In the rage for cheapness we have sacrificed everything for slop, and a dainty bit of bookmaking is like a jewel in the swine's snout. . . ."[17]

With the depression, too, some of the quality publishing houses collapsed as well: both Harper's and Appleton failed, to the intense astonishment of the book world, and were painstakingly refinanced. Disgusted with cheap publishing, Appleton after these difficulties reportedly destroyed 300,000 old books rather than remainder them.

Under such impecunious circumstances Harper's and Appleton (and three other houses—Barnes, Ivison, Blakeman, and Van Antwerp, Bragg) had already yielded up their expensive textbook departments, the quintet in 1890 becoming The American Book Company, New York and Cincinnati, handling schoolbooks exclusively. But an even more drastic separation loomed ahead for publishers with their own manufacturing plants.

In 1876 the Philadelphia Centennial exhibition rules had required house manufacture of books for display, arousing the ire of dozens of publishers without such facilities. At a last moment the rules were changed, and *Publishers' Weekly* explained why:

> "Publishing is a business by itself, the most important of various factors in the production of a book, except the work of the author himself. It consists not so much . . . in manufacturing as in providing for manufacturing; and the responsibility, and therefore the credit, of the various details of printing, binding, etc., are the publisher's rather than his agent's."[18]

Thus publishing proudly recognized itself as a separate industry. Most large publishers thereafter increasingly devoted their energies to the acquisition of manuscripts and the sale of books, finding these activities as sufficiently taxing as had the hundreds of individual entrepreneural publishers. The reasons, however, were not solely prestigious.

As long as the captive bindery had been an inexpensive department in which hand labor presented small capital investment, it thrived. But as greater quantities of expensive machinery became necessary for efficient bookmaking, publishers gradually severed their ties to manufacturing. Willy nilly, impending industrialization had added emphasis to the distinction between the two businesses.

There were exceptions. Ginn retained its plant until 1951, Scribner's until 1955, Little, Brown, until 1960, Houghton Mifflin until 1970— as newer economic pressures forced their hands. Doubleday (p 284) still manufactures its books, as do other giants like Western Printing and Lithographing Company and Rand McNally (p 279), whose publishing operations are almost incidental to manufacturing. An anomaly was G. P. Putnam's Sons, founding the Knickerbocker Press in 1874, and in 1891 against the trend moving it to New Rochelle,

New York, where it was enlarged to handle the work of other firms as well (p 318). By and large, however, the unencumbered publishers were not sorry: country-wide printers' and binders' strikes (in 1906–1907 they sought an 8-hour work day for their $15–21 weekly wage) told of dissatisfaction down to the bottom of the industry.[19]

Events had suddenly moved fast for the binderies of America, not sure whether they had caused vast publishing problems or simply been their chief victim. As a remote department in the publishing of books, and the last station in their production, the sequestered bindery had not been ready for overwhelming industrial revolution, however beneficial. And now that the largely independent industry was no longer dominated by captive conditions—publishers were customers now, not bosses—bindery managements had to think and plan for themselves.

Sister industries provided little help to the binder; on the contrary, they were racing toward mechanization with a zest that inevitably would swamp traditional bookmaking. Although the setting of type had not been successfully mechanized until 1886 (so many inventors throughout the century were at work on the problem it always seemed shortly within their grasp), steam-operated presses and production stereotyping equipment had speeded up presswork even before the Civil War. Although business had been spurred after 1865 by increasing nation-wide communications through the telegraph and the railroad—rapidly followed by telephone, typewriter, and shorthand systems—commercial binders had expected to maintain their relative output more through manual exploitation (hiring more and more hands, as necessary) than through any multiplication of mechanical aids. Indeed, machine work was not always cheaper, or better, than manual labor. Bookbinding—the "art of arranging the pages of a book in proper order, and confining them there by means of thread, glue, paste, pasteboard and leather"—had for centuries been synonymous with hand work.

James B. Nicholson described the operations preparatory to sewing at a period (1856) no longer given to romanticizing about the superior —but mystical, laborious—methods of the "ancients." Sawing the spine to receive the cords was a new, acceptable practice (detestable, as we have seen, only to the French), pragmatically obviating the expense of hand fashioning raised bands on the back. A rotary "tenant-saw" with several prepositioned blades made notches for each cord and slight cuts for lodging the kettle stitches. (To Lippincott it had been a "mimic" saw; to the Munros it was worthy of note but nameless: the several local names suggest that binders more likely built their own versions than bought Austin's "book-sawing" machine.)

Likewise pragmatic was the hand sewing of commercial work. For more or less occasional requirements many fussy methods were reduced to three: (1) overcasting or whip stitching—for rebinding single sheets; (2) sewing on raised bands—slow and expensive, only for books with small gutter margins; (3) sewing linen on guards and then whipping—only for big plate books. The principal sewing method for routine work was called "one sheet on" (adding 1 sheet of 4 pages onto the cords at a time), its description in an 1894 dictionary almost deliberately obfuscatory:

> "The strings [cords] are fastened to the crossbar [of the sewing press] and are stretched vertically downwards to the end of the press, where they are firmly secured. The number of the strings depends principally on the size of the book, and varies from two to ten. The sewer sits in front of the press, lays a folded sheet down on it with the back edge in contact with the strings, opens the sheet in the middle and sews it to the strings, passing a needle and thread to and fro. The needle passes through the back edge of the sheet twice as many times as there are strings, the object being to twist the thread around every string and thus connect them and the sheet together. The first sheet having thus been treated, a second is laid on with the first and sewed in a similar manner; and so on with a third, a fourth, and as many as there are to form the volume, all the threads being fastened to the strings and indirectly to each other; for the thread passes from one sheet to another by a peculiar kind of stitch called a kettle-stitch. . . ."[20]

Hand sewing at the sewing "press" (it performs no pressing motion). Before cords were cut, long loops were pulled between books so that each volume had its own slips for glueing to the boards. [New York Public Library]

WILLIAM O. HICKOK

The kettle stitch took its name from a corruption of "catch-up."

The difficulties of performing this kind of operation mechanically would unquestionably remain paramount. One simplification was the sewing of 2 sheets on (an 8-page section), frowned upon as poor practice. The development of the cloth sewing machine, however, set many inventors to devising a great variety of stitches, one of which might indeed eventually be suitable for bookwork. Meanwhile, for bindery problems of a more routine nature there were a few simpler operations for the joining of sheets in pamphlets and small booklets.

The first mechanical development for the joining of loose sheets was immediately applied to pamphlet work. This was the hand-operated stabbing machine, invented by an Englishman, Philip Watts, in the 1820's, for which he received an £5 prize from the Society of Arts. Before that, bindery girls had used hand awls and mallets to drive holes into thick pamphlets for tying.

William O. Hickok, also born an Englishman, was brought by his parents in 1834 to Harrisburg, Pennsylvania, where he became a foreman in his father's publishing firm. Mechanically gifted, Hickok organized a small bindery machinery factory in 1846; in addition to many ruling machines and devices he offered a full line of commercial bindery accessories and supplies. Hickok invented a stabbing machine in 1860, a waist-high machine with movable head, to which needles were attached in changeable positions. The operator, using a foot treadle, brought the head down upon the sections to be bound, and thus performed neat, uniform holes. Frederick Ullmer in London, 1874, is also credited with a foot-operated stabber. The needles of later fully mechanized models, like Sanborn's, were threaded and automatically tied the sheets with a knot.

The culmination of ingenious machinery along these lines was that of Sterling Elliott, an American whose pamphlet-binding machine was judged "almost human." The Elliott, manufactured in Georgetown, Massachusetts, punched its own holes, sewed about 35 double stitches per minute, finished each pamphlet with a square knot, and cut off the thread, holding one end ready for the next pamphlet. It was the only known bindery machine capable of tying a knot, "but how it is done," said a baffled British binder, "we dare not attempt to describe. . . . It is almost needless to add that the 'Elliott' is an American invention, although now manufactured in England." The stabbing process made all but the thinnest pamphlets cumbersome to handle and read, and was not at all suitable for bookwork. But another marvelous machine was ready to try.

The wire-stitching machine was also the invention of an American. Henry Renno Heyl (pronounced "Hyle") was born in Columbus, September 14, 1842, the second son in a prominent Ohio family. Between the ages of 12 and 18 his fondness for mechanical construction produced a number of sophisticated "toys." To facilitate his woodworking operations he first built an adjustable mitre box, and then a wood-turning lathe, the balance wheel of which he fabricated from part of an old stove. He invented (and built in miniature) a truck-mounted fire ladder, capable of elevation to upper stories by a cranking mechanism at its base. For a local physician he constructed a heliostat, an instrument that concentrated sunlight from a series of mirrors—adjusting themselves to the sun's apparent movement by clockwork—to illuminate the stage of a microscope.

In a moment of sartorial impatience, at the age of 16, Heyl made himself several months' supply of muslin-lined paper collars, very carefully finished with imitation stitching impressed along the edges. Thinking that no one but he would dare to wear paper collars, he abandoned interest in them only to find, a few years later during the Civil War period, that the manufacture of such paper collars would become a considerable business surviving well into the 20th century.

Educated at private institutions and then at Capital University, Columbus, Heyl in 1860 went to Cincinnati to learn the trade of cabinet making. While employed in a furniture shop there, however, he received an injury which obliged him to quit work and which also disqualified him from military service. Upon recovering sufficiently to perform light work, nevertheless, Heyl functioned as a clerk in the office of a Columbus attorney until 1863, when his family moved to Philadelphia. In that thriving metropolis Heyl's wizardry came alive.

One of the earliest and most unusual of Heyl's successful inventions was the first apparatus—anywhere—for projecting moving pictures upon a screen. In 1870 he began posing and photographing live models (himself included) in successive dance and acrobatic positions. Tiny

HENRY R. HEYL

[Courtesy Wolcott M. Heyl]

glass negatives were arranged on a wheel before a stereopticon projector. In February of that year Heyl's "Phasmatrope" was demonstrated to an enthusiastic Philadelphia public of 1600 persons. Considering this device a "recreation" rather than a lucrative invention, Heyl claimed no patent on it or to the stupendous motion-picture industry that followed. The auspicious premier nevertheless won him the hand of Mary Clarena Knauff of Philadelphia, who gave him three sons.

From his short career as law clerk Heyl found his first toe-hold as serious inventor. In 1866 he approached the Franklin Institute, that august body of tinkering Philadelphians—Mathew Carey and Matthias W. Baldwin (who briefly made binder's tools before turning to locomotives) were officers—founded 1824 for "the promotion and encouragement of manufactures, and the mechanical and useful arts." Heyl described a process for temporarily filing or binding papers and manuscripts: "two or three holes are cut with a small circular punch in the 'fold' of each signature. At each of these a 'binding-tag' (or half circle of paper with a loop of cord incorporated so as to leave only an eye projecting from the middle of its straight side) is attached by gum already applied, so that the eye projects through the punched hole." Any number of signatures could thus be strung together on laces which in turn were secured to covers. Heyl here had almost managed to create, loop by loop, what the later book sewer would do mechanically. For home rebinding purposes it nevertheless filled a need.

Heyl quickly established H. R. Heyl & Company to place his "Patent Adhesive binding tags" on the market. He advertised them as ". . . a most simple and perfect contrivance to enable every one to bind their [sic] own Music, Newspapers, Journals, Magazines, &c, one by one, as they are received, without waiting for the completion of the volume. . . ." Within a few years this tiny item would find its way to European as well as American music dealers and stationers. But for its inventor the binding tag was, like the Phasmatrope, purely divertissement from a more baffling and consuming assignment.

In 1865, at the age of 23, Heyl had met C. S. Patterson, a wealthy Philadelphian apparently impressed immediately with the young man's ability. Patterson commissioned Heyl to develop an automatic paper-box making machine; if successful, profits to be shared equally. In modest quarters Heyl labored and tinkered for six long years on "447," the partners' shop designation for the prototype. Their faith and perseverance were extraordinary, as Heyl himself (concealing some justified pride by using the third person) recollected: "During all of this time this one machine was the daily and sole occupation of H. R. Heyl and also the sole business venture of Mr. Patterson, and it is as remarkable as gratifying that although it took six full years and an expenditure of about $30,000 to complete the undertaking, neither of the parties to the agreement was tired of the bargain, nor was ever a word or look of impatience or dissatisfaction exchanged. . . ."

The paper-box maker was patented (No. 120,436) October 1871, and immediately assigned to the American Paper-Box Machine Company—as were a half dozen patents to follow—triumphantly embarking Heyl on a career of paper-manipulation inventions so sweeping in importance their results are today still fundamental to the American marketing economy.

Henry Heyl's early clerical employment inspired another binding device for which he quickly saw applications. "While in this position," he recalled in 1918, "I put into practice the use of wire staples in fastening together legal papers as a substitute for the then common practice of using metal eyelets and red tape. The efficiency and simplicity of this new method appealed to me and I thought out extended uses for these little staples which laid the foundation for the binding of books with staples as now universally used." Heyl built stapling machines for pamphlets, small books, and for fastening the seams of paper boxes. For these machines he assigned patents to the American Paper-Box Machine Company and the Novelty Paper Box Company, both of Philadelphia; they apparently continued to manufacture such equipment until 1894, when the rights expired. Heyl was himself vice president of a third Philadelphia firm, the Standard Box Company. Heyl's machine shop, ironically, was on the imposing site later occupied by the Curtis Publishing Company.

The tiny paper box industry—in Philadelphia as elsewhere—after the Civil War had bravely challenged the widespread commercial practice of wrapping all merchandise (except, perhaps, matches, pills, and tacks, for which small hand-made boxes were available) in plain paper, tied with string. Some of Heyl's early machinery was for making folding paper boxes which could be shipped flat all over the country (at lowest freight rates), and locked into shape at their destination. The staple —in place of glue—was instrumental in the success of this operation. Heyl also developed machinery to turn out lidded boxes, automatically covering boxboard with fancy paper and a label, if desired. He followed with one for the classic one-piece "oyster pail" with string or wire handle, and an automatic matchbox maker.

The matchbox making machine was a particular breakthrough, according to Hector Orr, who reminded a Franklin Institute assembly in September 1873 that his friend Henry Heyl had resolved, more than 7 years before, to make rectangular boxes—theretofore hand-pasted together by boys and girls from pasteboard and paper slips—by automatic machinery. Orr, on a "freezing and thawing" February day of that same year, received word that success was at hand:

> "But what is two miles of snow slush as an impediment, when there is an ingenious machine to be seen at the end of the journey? . . . Within the next hour [I] was on my way to the factory, at whose threshold I met Mr. Heyl, who declared the burden of the day completed by my arrival. I there saw a machine making such boxes as *this* [showing one], at the rate of 3,000 per hour. It is a match box; and I saw the slips of wrapper lifted singly and shaped; then fastened by delicate staples of iron wire, which were made and riveted by the machine; and then said enclosures were touched with glue and sprinkled with sand, and fell down before me ready to be filled with matches!"

Newspaperman Orr's description of Heyl's staple is of particular interest:

> "These minute staples are composed of fine soft wire hardly more rigid than a thread of waxed sewing silk. This wire is wound on a spool, from which the proper length is drawn for each box, and the staples are formed and brought each to its place at right angles with the box material, and at the right moment are made to puncture the wrapper or board, and are immediately clinched on the opposite surface. I think the most adroit set of fingers among us would fail to force or coax the point of this wire through even a thick wrapper, in less than several minutes, while this machine, besides all its other work, does this sixty times per minute. It furnishes one more instance of an act which,
>
> 

'*When* it is done,

'Twere well it were done quickly.'

>
> Indeed, unless it be done quickly, it cannot be done at all. . . ."[21]

The matchbox-making machine, "an emphatic triumph of patience and skill," did the work of 75 persons, and won for Heyl the Institute's John Scott Legacy medal in 1875. Like the early envelope makers it demonstrated, as we have seen, that truly complex tasks could be performed by machine, and furnished incentive to inventors everywhere.

Later with machines to his credit for fabricating paper tubes, cylinders, and cones of all description for packaging (including a three-ply paper cup ready for hotels and restaurants the moment national legislation forbade the use of common drinking utensils in public places), Heyl sought even more enthusiastically to eliminate unsanitary milk bottles. His American Paper Bottle Company was also ready to furnish, by contract, another absurdly simple—but today indispensable—product:

"What this company has to offer is a perfectly clean and sterile [paper] bottle, answering every requirement, weighing but two and a half ounces per quart size, occupying but two-thirds of the space taken by the glass bottle, and cheap enough to be used once and then discarded. . . ."22

During the latter years of his life (he died in 1919, aged 77), Heyl almost obsessively championed his unfortunately premature "single-service" paper milk container, a scheme which did not materialize until decades after his death.

Heyl was for 30 years a director of the Franklin Institute, and in that capacity supervised several of that organization's industrial expositions. During his long and fruitful life he received a number of gold, silver, and bronze medals, and dozens of machinery patents in many non-bindery areas as well. "Mr. Heyl's inventions," he wrote, proudly enough, "have all been pioneer work, not improvements of existing machines, and he is recognized as the Father of the wire book stitching and the self-locking folding paper box industries." (All too often the pioneer inventor was eclipsed by the improver, the hawker, the sharper —Heyl's fate exactly!) His three sons each shared some of their father's genius: Dr. Paul Renno Heyl as a US Bureau of Standards physicist (co-inventor of the earth induction compass), Professor Charles Christian Heyl as principal of a Philadelphia highschool, and Earle Godfrey Heyl, as a Baltimore businessman.

Because of a surprisingly successful American hold on his box-making patents, Heyl created an exclusive market for his boxes. The "knock-down" self-locking box, for example, became a Philadelphia monopoly for 20 years: one New York customer alone took 125,000 boxes (5 tons) daily for 15 years. The paper-box industry outside that city was ironically unaware of both the wire stitcher and the knock-down box—until the late 1880's. The book-stitching apparatuses, for which Heyl took no patent until 1876, might also have been potentially a lucrative secret, but the idea as applied to bookwork—far more captivating than box-making—was not so easily controlled.

Ellicott D. Averell, of Brooklyn, also developed a wire stitcher, about 1874, and was first to get it patented that year (No. 158,013). He quickly assigned it to William Matthews for the exclusive use of D. Appleton & Company (p 163). Although his patent specifies its purpose was for stitching pamphlets "in the fold of the back" (now called saddle-stitching), the inventor should nevertheless have foreseen —as Heyl had—far greater versatility in a mechanism that could join anything capable of penetration by wire. Although Averell in 1876 also developed a machine gatherer, he apparently preferred the steadier business of marketing bindery equipment to inventing. His stitcher

**E. D. AVERELL.**

**Machines for Stitching Books with Metallic Staples**

No. 158,013.                    Patented Dec. 22, 1874.

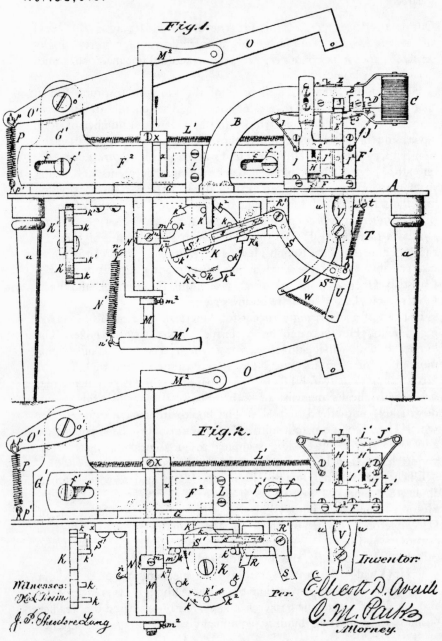

*Fig. 1.*

*Fig. 2.*

Witnesses:                    Inventor:

Per.    Elliott D. Averell
        C. M. Parks
        Attorney.

J. P. Theodore Lang

or its patent nevertheless attracted another genius who perceived at a glance that it could be improved—and used in many ways.

Louis Goddu (1837–1919) as a boy of 16 practiced shoe-making and sewing machine work in Massachusetts, returning to his native Canada to supervise a large shoe factory. In 1866, again in Massachusetts, he began to demonstrate a talent for invention which would run to 300 patents, mostly in sewing, shoe-making, nailing, and tacking machinery. (One of his last was an electrical device for transmitting *mental* energy in the form of "notes and syllables.") Goddu almost inevitably met Gordon McKay, a New England entrepreneur and industrialist who recognized the young man's genius and employed him in 1865 for six years, literally utilizing everything he invented during that time.

About 1874 Goddu improved the wire stitcher, which had come to his attention, although both his and Averell's machines still required the punching of holes by an awl before the wire staples would penetrate a thickness of paper. Henry G. Thompson, of Milford, Connecticut, himself a prolific inventor, purchased the Goddu wire-stitcher patent and with it established a flourishing business under his own name. The device could produce 2000 pamphlets—a day's work by hand—in an hour. Harper's, Barnes, Appleton, and other publishers turning out huge editions of magazines, brochures, school, and copybooks, endorsed it with great satisfaction.

As the 1876 Philadelphia Centennial Exposition approached, compilers of its official catalog faced a dilemma of growing seriousness. At least a million copies of the publication would be needed, yet binding had to be delayed to the last possible moment to accommodate late entries, withdrawals, and other changes. Hand sewing and stabbing would not be fast enough; the conventional sewing machine (p 162) could never handle more than ⅛ inch of paper. Although divided into four separate volumes, the 1200-page illustrated catalog would still be too thick for all known methods of binding. Something extraordinary was necessary.

Henry Heyl promptly attacked the unusual problem. About the beginning of 1875 he reportedly converted a "standard" sewing machine to use fine-gauge wire "thread" such as he had employed on his box-makers, making short, individual "stitches." This description from a 1935 *Bookbinding* (which identified the inventor as "Edwin Heile")

Earliest American patent specifically for wire-stitching books (pamphlets). Foot treadle (M) depresses lever (o) to make two pinholes in the spine fold of a book positioned on table (A) under apparatus (F); a second treadle stroke sends a staple, cut and bent during first operation, down a chute and through holes. [US Patent] was probably an apocryphal re-creation based on hearsay. More likely, Heyl struck upon the idea of saddle-stitching successive sections onto the conventional cords or tapes of multi-section books, for which mode of construction he received a patent in April 1876 (No. 176,632), and a patent for the machinery itself in August of that year (No. 180,765).

Heyl's stitcher, capable of making ¼-inch staples at the rate of 50 per minute, solved the catalog dilemma admirably; with two custom-made companion machines it was shipped to H. O. Houghton's Riverside Press, Cambridge, where the Centennial catalogs were to be manufactured. George W. Prentiss & Company, in nearby Holyoke, furnished the wire—first of its kind to any book bindery. With less than four weeks to go, the catalogs were reported "well along," and copies appeared for the May 10 opening without further event.

Heyl quickly put his multiple-section wire-stitching principle to commercial use. He demonstrated it at the Philadelphia Centennial by exhibiting a cut-away book showing the spine so stitched; "with this book," an admirer wrote to the inventor in 1882, "[you] collected from your friends and acquaintances the means to enable you to prosecute the more important work and perfect the machines. . . ." A Heyl pamphlet briefly summarized the machine's rapid success:

> "Five years of thorough test has won for this system of book sewing the widest popularity, and the unqualified favor of publishers and readers everywhere. Every book is 'sewed flexible' upon tapes or wide bands (sawing the signatures being entirely dispensed with), and the work is equally well done upon all classes of books.
>
> "Every signature is sewed 'all along' by independent tinned-wire staples, uniting them firmly to the tapes or webbing, thus securing the utmost strength and durability in addition to the valuable feature of thorough flexibility.
>
> "This system is equally adapted to all grades of edition and school book binding, from the cheapest to the most costly full bound books. Also for all classes of blank books, music books and pamphlets of one or more signatures. . . ."[23]

Similarly observing that "great simplicity and economy" were attainable, *Publishers' Weekly* described it in adulatory terms it would later regret:

> "Each section is sewed with wire upon tapes, giving more flexibility and durability because the wire is impervious to rust and doubly strong as thread. The machines are adapted to all kinds of work from 32mo up and all thicknesses of paper, and faster, and with less material than when done in the 'ordinary' way."[24]

The "No. 2" Heyl wire book-sewing machine, about 1880, capable of stitching books in sections up to 4½ inches thick at 1600 signatures per hour. "A supply of all materials," said Heyl, ". . . such as Wire, Tape, Webbing, &c., can always be obtained of the Sole Agent." [Heyl catalog]

With all staples attached to the tapes one above the other, however, there would be an awkward swell at those points on thick books, even more troublesome than the swell due to thread. For pamphlet work and other ephemera the stapler was nevertheless an instantaneous success, and earned Heyl another Franklin Institute medal in 1879. The US Government Printing Office promptly acquired 13 Heyl stitchers, which the bindery superintendent found "one of the greatest improvements of the age." Waterlow & Sons, London, acclaimed it "the greatest advance in bookbinding of the century," commending its flexibility, durability, and economy. A. Straker (now Leighton-Straker), London, took 11 machines. By 1881 over 300 Heyl stitchers had been sold.

The No. 2 "Wire Book Sewing Machine" was the popular size (said Heyl), capable of books up to 20 inches in spine length and up to 4½ inches in thickness; its rate was 1600 signatures per hour; a woman could operate it and would be taught to do so by the inventor, who would also attend "personally" to setting up and starting the machine, "free of expense to purchasers." Heyl's one serious mistake, perhaps, was entrusting subsequent sales and service of his equipment to "H. Grant Thompson," New Haven, Connecticut, who had little interest in perpetuating Heyl's belief that he would become known as the "father" of the wire-stitcher industry.

Thompson, as we have seen, had already begun to exploit Goddu's stapler; he was also (p 169) collecting stapling and stitching and sewing patents from many other "yankee" geniuses as well. Heyl's identity (like Goddu's) disappeared in the 1880's, replaced by a far more ubiquitous "Thompson." With 12 different models of staplers handling bulks up to 1½ inches, Thompson machines dominated the field in paper, leather, and light manufacturing applications. Similarly successful were the "Universal" (E. C. Fuller), "New Jersey" (J. L. Shoemaker & Company), "Monitor" (Latham Machinery Company), "Perfection" (J. L. Morrison), the "Acme," the "Monitor," and machines made by E. P. Donnell Company, Leonard Machinery Company, and several foreign versions. But eclipsing all of these was still another, international in design and sales, and remarkable for the machinations of its manufacturers—the Brehmer brothers.

Associated with Heyl in the development of box-making equipment in Philadelphia were two German brothers whose potential was no less than his. August and Hugo Brehmer had immigrated to the United States in 1871 and were engaged by Heyl, assisting in his mechanical projects and sharing jointly in the ownership of some of his patents. Heyl probably spoke German and (judging from witnesses' names on his patents) employed immigrants from the "old" country whom he knew to be good mechanics. The Brehmer brothers worked closely with Heyl on the book stitcher and its success appealed to them (at first) more than the box-making machines. They instinctively knew it would also appeal tremendously to European (especially German) bookbinders who would welcome its obvious, positive, simple operation. Sharing the rights with Heyl, the brothers quickly severed their employment and in 1876 founded their own company, possibly nothing more than a Philadelphia sales office from which they solicited orders. It is feasible that a single factory produced stitchers for the Heyl-Thompson American market and also (at first) for Brehmer's European trade—and whatever customers the brothers could reach before their competitors.

Leaving Hugo to continue his experimentation in Philadelphia, August returned to Germany in 1879 where he promptly organized a factory, Gebrüder Brehmer Maschinenfabrik, Leipzig-Plagwitz. Hugo —suddenly confronted by Smyth's thread-sewing machine—succeeded in developing similar equipment (p 194), the last modification of

Brehmer wire book-sewing machine, about 1894. Similarities to the Heyl were not limited to superficial design, although from about 1882 on Heyl's Philadelphia factory did not make it. [Brockhaus' *Konversations-Lexikon*, 14th Ed.]

which, in 1896, was patented from Lübeck by the executor of his estate.

American-built Brehmer wire stitchers found their way to France and England between 1876–78. The British distributor, John Heywood, heralded the "American Wire-Book-Sewing Machine," adding considerable advertising to the trade journals; the Waterlow and Straker machines, therefore, probably had Brehmer nameplates. As soon as the Leipzig factory was in production (about 1880) the Brehmer organization canvassed all Europe with never another look to Heyl—except, perhaps, at his patents. An unusual letter to Heyl revealed the tense climate at Leipzig over such lucrative stitcher and box-making inventions:

"Leipzig, April 9, 1882

To Mr. H. R. Heyl in Philadelphia

I address you in regard to a matter pertaining to your patents for stitching machines, which, trusting to reciprocal confidence on your part, I hope may not be without practical benefit also to you. . . .

"I was for a considerable number of years foreman in large tool machine manufactories, among others for nine years in the most important German tool machine manufactory of John Zimmermann in

Chemnitz [Karl-Marx-Stadt] where I became acquainted with August Brehmer as a colleague. In 1876 I visited America as a member of the German delegation to the Exhibition in Philadelphia, visiting, at the same time, the principal American manufactories in my line and becoming acquainted with Hugo Brehmer in Philadelphia.

"When the Brothers Brehmer established themselves in Leipzig-Plagwitz, the position of foreman was offered to me, which I finally accepted, in order to make myself familiar with the work-methods of good American precedent. To my experience and to my acquaintance with the conditions of workmen here, the Brothers Brehmer are largely indebted for the rapid success which they obtained in the manufacture of the wire-stitching machines and of the machines for making paper boxes. . . .

"The arrogance and insufferable dogmatism of Hugo Brehmer, however, made the position unpleasant to me. . . . I have learned that the Brothers Brehmer are not the inventors of wire stitching for books, as they have boasted throughout Europe, but that this novelty, which had made the Brehmers rich and famous as inventors in Europe, is your invention. . . .

"The Brothers Brehmer, who manufactured and sold [your paper fastener] in a somewhat changed form, . . . have pretty well glutted the market with it. Of this little apparatus, these gentlemen acted as inventors and had it patented. . . . You will see from this the ambitious efforts of the Brothers Brehmer to adorn themselves even with borrowed plumes which are, at least in part, the intellectual property of others and from which the Brehmers are enriched. . . ."[25]

It is not known whether Heyl formed an alliance or partnership with this hopeful manufacturer, nor whether his patent assignments to the three Philadelphia box firms left him an opportunity to do so.

Heyl, as we have seen, had unfortunately lost his identity in both box and book industries. He reconciled himself with new schemes, for example, stapling and folding the printed product of a web press, although he recognized that "a stoppage [for driving the staple] of one of the several sections of the web would interfere with the continuous movement of the next succeeding section of the web, or else the two sections would for a moment overlap each other, and thus the folding operation [on the press] would be interfered with. . . ." (Performing such work in motion was later a routine matter.) At any rate, Heyl should not have fretted over the book-stitcher, for it was an inferior solution almost immediately supplanted (in America) by the thread sewer.

For the Brehmer Brothers, however, the bookbinding market in Germany could not have been more favorable, and they plunged into it with their stitchers. Within a few years (1888) the No. 4A Brehmer, "the most perfect yet," could handle bulks up to ¾ inches. Using galvanized iron wire, pamphlets were saddle-stitched by a hand-operated machine while books were done on a motorized version. In the book stitcher the staples were driven from the inside of the section through the fold and through the tapes or open fabric (crash or mull) which was stretched and firmly held by clasps directly opposite each stapling head. The projecting legs of the staples were clinched over, thus producing (theoretically) a firm connection between the section and the tapes or fabric. As an improvement over Thompson (Heyl) machines, in order to reduce the swell at the spine, the Brehmer was so constructed that each stapling head made two or three shifts so that the staples were staggered in adjoining sections. Thus there appeared on the spine two or three times as many rows or staples as there were staples in each section.

In Europe too all sorts of commercial work was done on the wire stitcher, including guard books (reinforced scrapbooks), pattern books, and postcard albums. The famous Baedeker guidebooks—and the hardly ephemeral 17-volume reference work, Brockhaus' *Konver-sations-Lexikon*—were wire stitched, at speeds up to 2000 sections per hour. By 1910 a Brehmer advertisement had plenty to boast: "Paris Exhibition 1900, Grand Prix and gold medal"—but more pointedly, over 18,000 wire stitchers sold in the United Kingdom, and 55,000 throughout the world. But by 1910 the worst had already been done.

*Publishers' Weekly*, for one hundred years the voice and repository of exchange among librarians and booksellers as well as publishers and authors, printed the following letter in 1875 from a "western" librarian:

> "The new books that we put into the library frequently come to pieces by the time they have been out of the library three or four times. The sewing is poorly done, sections are often barely caught by the thread, consequently they drop out in reading the book through once or twice, and the thread is often poor, breaking very easily. We have to keep a binder at work all the time. . . . Are we going backward in the art of stitching and sewing books?"[26]

The editors agreed that sewing was one of the worst faults in modern bookwork, but within a few years they reproduced the first of a new

Spine of a book sewed by Brehmer wire stitcher. Staples are in pairs, arranged in three shifts to reduce swelling. Backing material—crash or mull—is omitted for clarity. [Stephen, *Commercial Bookbinding*]

line of complaints, reprinting a letter from a librarian to the British *Bookseller:*

"As far as my experience goes, 'wire-sewn books' are utterly unfit for circulation in libraries. . . . Having received a new copy [of Symond, *Life of Shelley*] from a bookseller, I carefully opened it, and found section D quite loose; both the wires had given way, and I was compelled to send it to the binder's to be sewn; but before doing so I took it to pieces (being well acquainted with every branch of bookbinding) and I was surprised to find that each wire was separate, and that there was nothing whatever to hold the sections together except the lining at the back, through which the wires appeared to be threaded. Surely any one who is acquainted with books knows well enough that this is not sufficient to stand the wear to which a book is subject. . . ."[27]

To this the *Bookseller* editor replied that wire-sewn books ought to be sewn on tapes, and not too closely at that. But this problem may have mystified American readers, since the wire stitcher was just gaining momentum; anyway, hand-sewn books were still under attack. In 1880 *Publishers' Weekly* voiced the criticism of the Boston Public Library bindery foreman:

"Of the thousands of volumes that yearly come under my hands for rebinding, less than 10 per cent are sewed the full length of each signature. I find generally 2 folds—often 3, and sometimes 4—sewed on with one crossing of the thread [that is, sewing 2, 3, or 4 sheets on, or as 8, 12, or 16-page signatures], while the percentage of volumes with folds so thin as to require sewing only 2 folds on, is very small. Volumes that have been sewed 'all along' with good thread, though the leather be entirely gone, can very often be rebacked, lined, and covered, and made as good as new, without taking apart."[28]

(Sewing 8 folds on, that is, in 32-page signatures, is machine practice today.) In the same issue *Publishers' Weekly* finally got off an editorial on the growing "Infirmities of Cloth Binding," saying, in part:

"The chief complaints against cloth bindings which have repeatedly been made by our correspondents, may be summed up as follows:— sewing defective (the sheets not fairly and *bona fide* stitched in the back); the bands cut off too close to the back; books stuck into their cases without care, and only retained by their endpapers; large forms printed on heavy paper (instead of thin sections on flexible paper) preventing a free opening of the book or causing the breaking of the back and loosening of leaves. . . ."[29]

But by 1883 inferior hand sewing was ignored as wire stitcher complaints began with a vehemence never used before: ". . . detestable habit lately introduced of using wire instead of thread . . ."; ". . . and now comes the wire-stitching machine to load our shelves with un-yielding and inelastic bindings . . ."; and from exotic India in 1886: "In Bombay the result is that after the first monsoon there is a stain of iron mould, after the second or third one is fortunate if the leaves of a well-used book do not come out altogether. . . ."

"Glue and wire," said *Studio's* 1899 bookbinding survey, trying to be cheerful, "inadmissible in the ideal [binding] method, may be quite legitimate in the lesser, . . . [resulting] in the higher development of the next thing beneath it in order of worth. . . ." meaning that for ephemera and trash wire was perfectly appropriate. But nobody was prepared to agree, since practitioners were not confining the wire stitchers to the lowest classes of work. So many wire-stitched books were finding their way into the libraries, wire injury to fingers (when tearing bindings apart for rebinding) was a common hazard. Librarians everywhere decried loose and lost pages "anchored" by only 2 poorly clinched staples, the inevitable rusting of the wire, rotting and staining of the paper and backing, and ultimate ruin that even rebinding could not rectify. Yet one further development was possible.

The firm of A. S. Barnes & Company, long operating as text and general publishers, took an ultimate step with "Barnes's Iron Books." Alfred S. Barnes had begun publishing in 1838 at Hartford, Connecti-cut, moved to Philadelphia, then coming (in 1845) to New York. Edwin M. Barnes, his third son, in charge of manufacturing through the 1880's, kept 20 power presses in Brooklyn running continuously on schoolbooks alone, and the company's captive bindery finished them with dispatch. A New Yorker, Howard M. Hoyt, had in 1878 devel-oped a process of "indestructible bookbinding," the chief novelty of which was "a sheath of tin metal slipped over the back of the sheets after they are wired." To pierce the tin, a heavier staple, "practically a metal pin," was required. Hoyt advertised that the scheme was "The only Invention of Practical Utility ever Applied to the Bookbinding Art."

Hoyt was a compelling salesman, apparently. "The point of advan-tage in this binding," he said, "is simply that, in the opening and closing of the book, there is no friction, which is the destructive element in all ordinary binding. . . ." He persuaded the New York Board of Edu-cation—to whom heavy wear and damage must have been a staggering problem—to permit him to rebind worn schoolbooks, and Barnes also utilized the invention by contract, proposing to issue its standard line in indestructible form "at a slight advance on the price of the old."

Yet Barnes's iron books were not the answer, for the wire staple itself was fundamentally unacceptable. (Barnes gave up its manufac-tory in 1893 to become Braunworth & Company.) With knowing anticipation, Douglas Leighton wrote of this distressing state of affairs, "but thread was bound to win, and by the end of the eighties binders were scrapping their wire machines." There were many, furthermore, who, like Morris and Cobden-Sanderson, would not wait for mechanization—albeit with thread—to solve the binding problem.

Reaction to the ugliness of machinery and its products had its proud —and surprisingly durable—American period as well as European. American commercial binders had not "kept pace" with the arts to the satisfaction of a great number of newly affluent and devoted bibliophiles—paradoxically created by the age of industrialization. Too, American hand binders had not even attempted to compete with machine binders: generally they soon accumulated the same labor-saving tools and techniques. To combat these tendencies, the Grolier Club was formed in 1884 in New York by nine lovers of books—Robert Hoe II (bibliophile heir of the press manufacturers, whose precious 14,000 item library would bring $1,932,000 at auction), Theodore Low DeVinne (master typographer and printer); William Loring Andrews (bibliophile and author who commissioned his own 26 books to be executed exquisitely); Arthur B. Turnure (founder of the chic *Vogue* magazine and printer of esthetic books); Alexander W. Drake (art director of *Century* and *St. Nicholas* magazines); Albert Gallup (lawyer and bibliophile), Brayton Ives (banker and bibliophile), Samuel W. Marvin (head of Scribner's manufacturing department); and Edward S. Mead (of Dodd, Mead & Company). Members soon included Walter Gilliss (printer of monumental works and art magazines); William W. Appleton, Louis C. Tiffany, J. Henry Harper, Cornelius Vanderbilt, and Louis Prang.

Organized "for the promotion of the arts pertaining to the production of books," the Grolier Club quickly became "the most distinguished among American book clubs" in tradition as impeccable as its 16th century namesake. Its members were not content merely to collect. "The Grolier Club is interested in books not as literature but as works of art," said member Brander Matthews, and added that, toward this end, it also conducts lectures (William Matthews, for example, on "Modern Bookbinding Practically Considered," later issued by the club in 1889), publishes books, and maintains exhibits. Some members wanted even more.

In 1895 a few individuals proposed that the Grolier Club form a hand bindery to produce the choicest specimens of binding, so rare in the United States. Amateurs and serious owners were still sending sheets to French and English binders for "substantial and tasteful binding," and the plan seemed to fill a need. Dismissing British binders for "carelessness amounting to apathy" for their indifferent preservation of incunabula, the Grolier sponsors beamed at the prospects of French craftsmanship available locally. Club member Edwin B. Holden (bibliophile coal dealer) organized "The Club Bindery" with the assistance of member William Matthews (p 165), who planned the shop's layout and recommended European workmen of his acquaintance, like Frank Mansell, son of William Mansell, one of the best finishers of his day. Member Hoe brought from France Henri Hardy, late of E. Mercier, as foreman, and Léon Maillard, Paris' best finisher; with them came 5000 finishing tools of the finest quality, and boards, paper, gold leaf, and even thread, "the best procurable" in France.

Through the turn of the century the Club Bindery proudly executed superior work, "undoubtedly the finest ever done in this country," wrote collector A. Edward Newton. In 1900 an exhibit of books done for club members was judged unsurpassed even in Europe; T. J. Cobden-Sanderson would visit the shop (1908) much impressed. Gradually, however, the bindery began to work more and more for Robert Hoe, who by 1902 was commissioning lavish designs with tools made in France for his exclusive use. The French artists, delirious with so munificent a patron, made little effort to expand their clientele or, for that matter, conduct their small shop with even moderate financial prudence. (Too, European bindings continued to undersell the Club Bindery's work: under the tariff in effect, a book more than 20 years old or in a foreign language came into the United States duty free, although it might have been bound more recently—at 70 percent less for wages in England; years later hand bindings were taxed separately, up to 30 percent of their value.) The Club Bindery's costs rose prohibitively; it was finally dissolved officially in 1908 and it closed a year later.

This was the end of extravagantly fine binding in America on anything resembling supra-commercial methods. In Boston Frederick J. Quinby's Harcourt Bindery—still operating—charged $500 per volume; his 1903 "bibliomaniac" edition of Paul de Kock (100 volumes, $50,000 per set, only 10 copies printed), taking jobbers two years to accumulate enough French levant morocco, sold out immediately. But stable conditions for the "extra" bindery were rare. Some of the Club Bindery workers moved to Cleveland, home of the Rowfant Club, a group of bibliophiles formed in 1892. After World War I, however, Frank N. Doubleday brought the binders to his new Country Life Press (p 284), Garden City, where they continued to work for a while.

About this time (1923) R. R. Donnelley & Sons, Chicago, also formed an extra (hand) bindery with Alfred de Sauty, a Londoner, in charge: unlike the Club Bindery workers, who not only disdained from giving binding instruction, but actually preferred to work behind closed doors, Donnelley's Lakeside Press soon established a binding school, and continues today under Harold W. Tribolet to turn out extra binding of fine and lasting quality—in addition to over 30 million volumes annually in its two edition binderies at Crawfordsville, Indiana, and Willard, Ohio. There is today plenty of work for extra and edition binders alike, not the least portion of which finds its way, once again, into the libraries.

The growth of public reading rooms, circulating libraries, and book clubs could scarcely keep pace with the growth of mass reading and appreciation for books which developed to staggering proportions at the end of the 19th century. Thanks to wealthy benefactors and spirited civic organizations, libraries bloomed everywhere, although threatened successively by the popularity of the bicycle, the automobile, motion pictures, and other minor crazes.

The bicycle mania was—or should have been—a genuine worry to bookmakers. As peddling grew in popularity no one stayed home to read—even binderies had their cycling clubs. The Hickok people in Harrisburg, boasting a new plant in 1891 "with Electricity as Motive Power and Light," almost abandoned bindery equipment to manufacture bicycles (offering printers and binders a special discount), using as their trade mark a bicycle with square wheels. These were not rational times. The sanity of printed education and entertainment was bound to win, however, and book people, weathering the manias, worried less and less about them.

While the big central city collections and college libraries were accessible to few, the smaller workman's "association" libraries thrived everywhere. In Hartford—home of the book sewer—the municipal Library Association, for patrons thirsty for news, subscribed in 1888 to 12 daily newspapers, 25 weeklies, 2 fortnightlies, 29 monthlies, and 3 quarterlies, and in an average month circulated 2400 books. (Five years later as a free public library it circulated 13,000 books per month.) Seymour Eaton in Philadelphia formed a chain of "subscription" libraries called at first "The Booklovers Library," then "The Tabard Inn Library." Membership was effected by donating a $1.50 book to gain access—for a small rental fee—to all the others so donated. (If you lost your borrowed book, you simply bought another.) Eaton told his stockholders in 1903 that 3015 members were borrowing 10 million books per year; the new Tabard Inn, less than a year old, was already earning $5000 a week. The plan was very popular until the advent of 1939 paperbacks. Whether private or public, readers heartily supported reading programs beyond expectation.

Through the ending years of the 19th century the success of free libraries (a worry only to those booksellers who thought borrowers would never be buyers) was heralded by such capsule notices as this British item in 1890:

"AMERICAN NEWS

The Castleton (N.Y.) Free Public Library is left $500 by Mrs. E. M. McDonald. The Chicago Medical Service loans its books to the Newberry Library. The Hartford (Conn.) Free Library has obtained $368,275 towards its fund. Rev. W. B. Palmore gives the Kansas City (Kan.) Y.M.C.A. 2,000 volumes towards a library. Kansas City is to receive a building for a public library and art gallery from T. H. Swope. Yale College Library receives $10,000 by the will of J. E. English. John Jacob Astor leaves the Astor Library $450,000. The Trenton (Mo.) school receives $50,000 from J. Norris for the formation of a library, and Andrew Carnegie has offered $1,000,000 towards a library for Pittsburg."[30]

Even the smallest towns had a reading room, lyceum, or athenaeum, where newspapers, magazines, and books were available. Before the turn of the century the United States reportedly had about 4000 public libraries housing 1000 books or more, an appreciable minimum of 4 million books in more or less lively circulation. "All reading matter is perfectly free, no ticket of admission being required," announced philanthropist Collis P. Huntington's new 1891 library in the Bronx. Thus disarmed everywhere, the public proceeded to read voraciously.

But library growth could prove even more sensational than library circulation. The New York Public Library, a consolidation in 1895 of private libraries belonging to John Jacob Astor (260,000 books), James Lenox (smaller, but extraordinarily rare), and Samuel J. Tilden (15,-000 books and a $2 million bequest for more), began with 1,200,000 volumes and pamphlets when the colossal Fifth Avenue building opened in 1911; the collection grew to 4,500,000 a half century later. Similarly, Andrew Carnegie's architectural munificence, begun in 1881, had by 1904 provided for the construction of 300 library buildings; by 1923 the number was 1677, and by 1935, 6235 buildings. And such growth has not waned: in 1967 it was calculated that in the United States a new library was being formed every day.

The libraries of New York, Cleveland, Chicago, Los Angeles, Philadelphia, Cincinnati, and Detroit, total over 20 million volumes. Today, too, throughout the world, 320,000 separate titles—not counting newspapers—are produced annually by every practical means short of clay tablet and papyrus scroll. As caretakers of the world's archives librarians have often attempted to insure minimum construction standards —sometimes quite detailed—despite incessant technological changes.

They hope at least to avoid total disintegration; while some 15th-century papers are today still "like new," many books manufactured on cheap wood-pulp paper as late as 1910 today possess only 2 percent of their original strength. More pragmatically librarians ask nowadays for the best cover materials (a dark buckram, "an honest, almost noble cloth"), the best sewing (possibly nylon thread side-stitched), the best binding (end signatures reinforced, chestnut board), the best paper (acid free, rated to last 300 years), wide margins (to permit rebinding), and sometimes, naively, they want more standardization in sizes to fit their inflexible stacks. They refuse nothing, however, that can possibly be shelved, and generally rely hopefully on the publisher's original binding, whatever it may be. And for a reading population always in a hurry, librarians and publishers alike expect their binders to manufacture the world's literature promptly—as if there were a machine "where you can shove a book in at one end and bring it out all finished at the other." A humorist in 1896 nevertheless thought that possibility was near at hand; it almost was.[31]

FRANKLIN INSTITUTE AWARD FOR HEYL'S STITCHER

THE SCOTT PREMIUM
FOR
WIRE
◦ BOOK SEWING ◦
MACHINE,
1879.
ON THE MOST DESERVING

# 5  *Bindery Mechanization*

## *and the Book Sewer*

DAVID MCCONNELL SMYTH WAS BORN JULY 3, 1833, AT NEWTOWN Ards, near Belfast, County Down, Ireland. His parents, John and Jane (née Crawford), came from Scotch-Presbyterian stock which had settled in the north of Ireland centuries before. One of John Smyth's paternal relations had founded a hosiery works at Balbriggan, but the family was not rich or landed.

When two years old David was brought to America by his parents, apparently preceding the mass exodus of Irish, compelled by starvation and ruin, whose emigration began a decade later. The family settled at first in the wilderness of Harford, Pennsylvania (Susquehanna County), where David was apprenticed to his father's new blacksmith and wheelwright shop. Here he quickly discovered his inventive ability and lifelong enthusiasm for mechanical improvement. Here too his appetite for experimentation was providently slaked by the furious restlessness and expansion of the early eighteen-hundreds in America, a manifestation, for some, not entirely geographical in nature. It was the age of mechanical invention.

*Scientific American,* that weekly newspaper begun in 1845 to record the technological progress of the time, reflected the frenzy of discovery and modification in the vigorous "science" of mechanical engineering. Pages after pages were devoted to inventions and improvements in farm machinery, steam engines, wagons and riggings, lamps, scales, clocks, animal traps, grinding and refining machinery, printing presses, looms, nail-stamping, brick-making, barrel-hooping apparatus, iron casting, and a thousand other devices and processes upon which the industrial revolution was founded. So phenomenal was the inventive movement that by 1848 *Scientific American* had received numerous complaints from inventors and had itself protested that the US Patent Office was six months behind in patent examinations. It advocated the allocation of additional funds to hire more examiners, and the expulsion of several other Federal agencies which were crowding the Patent Office out of its own building.

In this climate of mechanical activity David Smyth, 14 years old in 1847, proudly boasted his first invention, the gimlet-pointed screw, "now so familiar."* Benjamin Butterworth, Commissioner of Patents at the end of the 19th century, described it:

> "One of the chief improvements [of the century] is the gimlet-pointed screw, which has almost superseded the old form of the screw ending in a blunt point. It is singular that so simple an improvement as this, which is simply combining the screw point of the gimlet with the screw itself, should have been so recently made."[1]

Butterworth was not crediting its invention to Smyth, but undaunted, Smyth steadfastly considered this his greatest labor-saving device. The boy's first effort—a gem of obvious usefulness—was actually to become a Pandora's box for an unwary tinkerer.

With intentions of patenting his gimlet-screw invention, David exhibited the admirable resourcefulness of typically determined—but poor—boys. He purchased a supply of colored lithographs, peddled them to farm and town neighbors through the storms and snows of the 1847 winter, and succeeded in doubling his original investment. There is no evidence that he did in fact secure the patent (and with reason), but his persistence obviously convinced his father he would get little smithy work from so earnest a thinker. Smyth was given the remainder of his service to his father, and he wasted no time in exploiting his ideas.

After a year's schooling at a "Franklyn Academy"* (possibly a high-school in one of several towns near Harford named "Franklin"),

---

*Smyth's *National Cyclopedia of American Biography* sketch was in 1897 unquestionably published with his approbation. Quotations from it in this chapter, considered autobiographical, are indicated by an asterisk (*).

Smyth set out for New York City in the Autumn of 1848, hoping for an opportunity to develop the gimlet-screw. Walking the whole distance, he paid his way by various money-making ventures, and was employed for over a year at a blacksmith shop in Fishkill Landing (now Beacon), New York. With finances apparently too meagre to complete the journey—and settle—in New York, Smyth then started another peddling tour through New England and eastern New York. He next included, through 1849–1850, a term of school at Erie, Pennsylvania—a long way from the center of commerce he hoped would be fruitful for him. During this time, nevertheless, he invented a platform scale which he was later to manufacture commercially.

Smyth at last made his way to New York, the town he so long appreciated for business enterprise. Fortune was with him: arriving penniless, he found a silver dollar on a ferry dock, and with this omen happily searched for work. Ready employment awaited him in the smithy of John Stephenson, builder of carriages and street cars, and Smyth was soon transferred to the forge room, where he "from his aptness in the work, was given a forge of his own with wages but little less than the foreman of the shop."* Smyth was now twenty-one years old.

About this time (1854) the young inventor and smith was sought by Thomas J. Sloan, owner of an already established screw-making company, who paid him $1000 for the gimlet-screw invention. Sloan himself had been developing such a device long before the two men met, and had, in fact, patented it August 20, 1846 (No. 4704), the year before Smyth claimed its invention. Sloan also built machinery on which pointed screws could be made, as *Scientific American* reported:

> "To Thomas J. Sloan, of New York city, for improvement in machinery for cutting the threads of pointed screws. Patented November 24, 1846 [No. 4864]. Re-issued March 7, 1848."[2]

(The newspaper's own annals credit General Harvey as the inventor of the gimlet-pointed screw and the cam motion, as well as the toggle joint; among other pioneers of screw technology Smyth is not mentioned.) The Sloan-Smyth transaction, nevertheless, brought prestige to Smyth, and gained him the friendship of Samuel F. B. Morse, Elias Howe, and other noteworthy inventors.

Sloan apparently had bought Smyth's interest in the gimlet-screw primarily to consolidate all claims in his own name, although the money he paid Smyth seems, for those times, substantial. Sloan had dozens of patents on screw devices and allied machinery to further establish his position. Yet Sloan—and all other hopeful inventors— had only to read the newspapers to assure himself of the advisability of absolute ownership, for these were also the days of wild claims, infringement, and theft on another promising mechanical gadget—the sewing machine.

The development of the cloth sewing machine, one of the most controversial in American industrial history because of its immediate mechanical and financial success, attracted insatiable interest on the part of inventors for almost half a century. The number of inventors and claimants who found inspiration and training in sewing machine technology is surprising; its intricacies whetted the sharpest minds, and the variety of its uses seemed limitless. No other machine struck the public so forcefully as prima facie evidence that any complicated task could be performed by machine. David Smyth himself could not resist the call of its nervous clatter.

It is generally acknowledged that Elias Howe (1819–1867) patented in 1846 the sewing machine he had developed in the 1830's. A year later Howe's brother in London sold the machine and its British rights to William Thomas, whose Cheapside factory employed 5000, making corsets, valises, umbrellas, shoes, and carpet bags. As its champion in America, Howe had to reckon, in addition to the inventor's usual pecuniary difficulties, with the skepticism and ire of sewing tradespeople who feared their jobs would be abolished by the expensive ($300) machine. And there was stiff manufacturing competition: 27 individuals or companies were involved with the sewing machine before 1856 (and 900 "improvements" were patented by 1868). Thus, although as early as 1850 Howe in New York superintended the construction of 14 machines, to be used for promotional purposes, he did not mass-manufacture sewing machines until 1857.

Isaac M. Singer patented his first machine in 1851. Before him Allen B. Wilson had also invented one and had formed a company with Nathaniel Wheeler, producing the famous "four-motion feed" model in 1854. Infringement among Singer, Wheeler & Wilson, and Howe was inevitable, and litigation followed, almost as complex as the machinery itself.

David Smyth, not one to enjoy working for another no matter how munificent the salary, evidently left the Stevenson shop after two years. It was his last steady job for a long time. He had patented his platform scale (1855) and, selling one-half interest in it to a manufacturer, W. W. Messer, for $2500, the two partners began to market the scale "with fair success."* But with a touch of prosperity Smyth endorsed notes beyond his ability to pay, and "constantly sought to recoup his fortunes by fresh inventions."* A real measure of stability, nevertheless, was the opportunity to marry Miss Orianna Brundidge Slote, of New York city, on December 31, 1855.

DAVID McCONNELL SMYTH

[Courtesy Smyth Manufacturing Company]

1855 was also the year the Howe-Singer-Wheeler & Wilson infringement suits had been instigated—suddenly conciliated the following year by the last two agreeing to pay Howe a royalty, and all three vowing honorable competition. Smyth is said to have actually assisted Howe in his work, although his genius with sewing mechanisms did not materialize until long after Howe's death. In turn Smyth introduced another young genius to the lure of mechanical sewing: together (about 1870) he and Thomas Edison developed an electric-powered sewing machine which failed only because its wet-cell batteries were too cumbersome to be practical. Smyth nevertheless considered himself a close friend of Edison from then on.

About 1873 Smyth tried to adopt the sewing machine to an industrial use, inventing a machine for sewing on the soles of shoes. This effort failed "because he did not think of the seam channel, from which Gordon McKay realized millions."* (Smyth never failed to notice how others made money on devices he himself could—or did—develop.) The first machines patented in the United States for sewing leather had been Wickersham's in 1853 and Butterfield's in 1854. No successful attempt at sewing the sole to the upper seems to have been made before 1858, however, when Lyman R. Blake, a Massachusetts journeyman shoemaker, obtained a patent for such equipment:

> "This machine did not sew around the toe. It [like Smyth's] had no guiding seam channel, and shoes had to be heated on a steam chest to allow the wax threads to pass through easily. Nevertheless it was hailed by the manufacturers as a great step of advancement in the making of shoes, and [said *Scientific American* grandiloquently] it was so."[3]

In 1859 Blake had the good fortune to sell out to McKay, who subsequently improved the machine and indeed made a fortune. Smyth's machine may have been no more perfect than Blake's, but it was, if anything, woefully tardy: Smyth had patented nothing between 1855 and 1864, by which time McKay had already machine-sewed over 450,000 pairs—8 times longer lasting than hand-sewed shoes—for the Union Army. As with the gimlet-screw, Smyth was always sufficiently proud of his mechanical offspring to bemoan their lack of recognition —despite their illegitimacy. In his middle twenties at this time, however, Smyth, still full of ideas, kept trying.

During the experimentation on shoe-making machinery Smyth must have discovered a mechanical motion useful in several ways. This was the rotary looper, a major contribution to the sewing machine itself. But glumly he was again out of the picture: "From his rotary looper for making the twisted stitch manufactured under the name of Willcox & Gibbs automatic sewing machine, Mr. Smyth also received no profit."*

The Willcox & Gibbs machine was first patented June 1857 by James E. A. Gibbs, a farmer from Millpoint, Virginia. In developing the machine "he conceived the idea of placing at the end of the driving shaft, beneath the cloth, a revolving hook which would take hold of the thread after the needle had passed through the cloth and fashion it into a chain stitch. . . . The revolving hook . . . was an entirely novel feature and it became the distinguishing characteristic of sewing machines." Thus Gibbs' own historian leaves little room for Smyth. Later, James Willcox of Philadelphia added some refinements to make the machine as well established as the earlier "big three." It is a fact, however, that the rotary looper was an integral part of Smyth's successful book-sewing machine; he may have considered himself fortunate if only because he was not prohibited from using the disputed motion.

Following the shoe-sewing machine and the rotary looper was another mechanical success for which Smyth's reward was financial disappointment. His machine for setting spangles in hoop skirts was unquestionably sound—he sold it to Jedidiah Wilcox for a small sum, and Wilcox "netted a clear $300,000 a year"* with it. Smyth was understandably very discouraged.

The outbreak of Civil War found Smyth engaged in mundane contract work making tent poles for the Army. (He was, to be sure, to develop a few inventive ideas in the woodworking field later on.) Then, with admirable patriotism—(or intense dissatisfaction)—for a man of 29, married, and with one child, Eugene Leslie (born December 19, 1857), Smyth volunteered to serve his country. He enlisted in the Eighth Regiment of New York State Militia, Volunteers, Colonel Joshua M. Varian commanding. Even at that time it was one of the oldest and most respected units; it was no place to skulk—if Smyth harbored that thought.

Apparently indifferent to his name being spelled "Smythe" (as on the unit's muster roll, and years later in many promotional releases), Smyth was among the half dozen oldest privates in Company E. Off he went, nevertheless, on May 29, 1862, for a three-month enlistment, taking him to occupation duty at Yorktown, Virginia. The following year he enlisted again for a similar term, and participated in the July battle of Gettysburg. These short campaigns gave him time, if only intermittently, to continue some of his private business ventures. In the same period he gained two new sons: Joseph Elmer (July 23, 1862) and David Grant (June 30, 1864). A fourth son, George B[rundidge?] completed his male offspring.

Smyth had developed a machine for making paper collars and in

1862 started a factory in New York city which was subsequently sold to the Metropolitan Collar Company. By this time he might have added to his list of inventions an improved method for shaving veneer woods, a device for cutting wooden toothpicks, and "the adjustable mitre-box, now in universal use."* Curiously Heyl had already preceded him both in paper collars and mitre box. Smyth was again late to the patent office; none were issued to him in these areas.

From his paper collar experience, nevertheless, Smyth had developed several improvements in paper fabrication, among them the use of chilled iron rollers to calendar paper, and an ingenious machine for making imitation lace from paper. His device for decorative stitching on shoes—"whereby an almost unlimited number of intricate fancy stitches could be made with an ordinary sewing machine"—netted large royalties from the shoe manufacturers at last; this led to a shoe-pegging machine and a nail-driving tool, forerunner of present-day machinery in these fields. (Since inventors crave with justification some small recognition in their fields, Smyth had growing cause to complain: in shoe-sewing annals and mitre-box history alike, as with the gimlet-screw, Smyth is unknown.) It may be said that nothing in Smyth's entire repertoire had yet proved an unmitigated pleasure to him, but we may believe the inventor that growing financial difficulties during the development of these inventions forced the decisive turning point in his thinking.

The constant and mounting incidental expenses of inventing were almost too pressing to recollect euphemistically, but Smyth managed: after the shoe-stitching work "his obliging habit of endorsing promissory notes again embarrassed him seriously."* He was possibly on the verge of ruin but he somehow mustered new strength. *Inland Printer* in its extensive obituary noted of Smyth: "An intensely close observer of what came before him and his wonderful ability to see how things might be done mechanically, led him in many different directions." His genius would not fail.

It is not inconceivable than any clever bindery foreman would see in the sewing machine the possibility of stitching pamphlets with virtually no adjustment from cloth to paper. Indeed, up through the 1870's Singer and other hand-operated, single-thread machines were so used. In his illustrated *Harper's* article R. R. Bowker had described this practice succinctly: "For thin pamphlets, a line of stitching is sometimes run across the back by an ordinary sewing machine, built very stout and strong." Pictured in a bindery scene was the conventional "long-necked" cloth sewing machine still popular today. But would an inventor—taking only the concept of machine sewing—

ignore the machine's limitations and turn it, perhaps, into a totally different device capable of sewing books? A bindery foreman could certainly describe the problems to such an inventor.

Modern concepts of fast bookbinding by machine probably appealed to Daniel S. Appleton when he took charge of the manufacturing department of his grandfather's publishing house. With a lawyer's attention to business detail, and a "quickness and acuteness in making estimates and deciding difficult questions," young Appleton was a rare asset to the firm. Appleton had inaugurated several colossal publishing ventures which would heavily tax its factory: Noah Webster's "blueback" speller came out in 1855, the company selling over 35 million copies by 1890; the 16-volume *New American Cyclopedia* began in 1857 under editors Charles A. Dana (editor of the New York *Sun*) and George Ripley (founder of *Harper's Monthly*); the *American Annual Cyclopedia* started in 1861 with a sale of 24,000 copies despite —or because of—the Civil War. Badeau, *Military History of General Grant* (3 volumes, 1868) was important. Appleton's major magazines and series were also impressive: *Appleton's Journal of Popular Literature, Science, and Art* (begun 1869), "Library of Wonders" (1870), *Popular Science Monthly* (1872), "International Scientific Series" (1873), all would have long lives and large editions.

For this appreciable workload Appleton had just established its own bindery (1854) and printing plant (1855), with composition and electrotyping facilities soon thereafter, consolidating its shops in 1867 at Williamsburg, Brooklyn, where over 600 workers occupied a plant almost a block square. In what was called "one of the largest and most completely appointed printing and binding establishments in the world," the company maintained a restaurant ("meals at bare cost"), two sick benefit organizations, a circulating library, and a mission offering free religious services.

The Appleton bindery alone was 250 feet long and five stories high, employing 425 hands by 1884. Absent (and similarly not a depressing problem in most other bookmaking plants, too) were the excess labor practices which characterized the uncontrolled growth of industrialization elsewhere. A reporter from *American Publishers' Circular & Literary Gazette* in 1868 visited the plant:

"Soft throbs of machinery greet [the visitor's] ear, and, on inquiry, he learns that a score of steam 'folders' are performing their work with a speed and accuracy unattainable by human hands. This great [first floor] room, too, is as light as day, and its atmosphere as pure as a garden's; and the 175 girls who feed the folders, or stitch the sheets when folded, or render other services on this floor exhibit the bloom of health and the smile of contentment. . . ."[4]

WILLIAM MATTHEWS

[Courtesy Rotha G. Matthews]

To this aurally sensitive fellow "a monotonous rattle" on the second floor was the steam-operated board-chopping machine, cutting 3000 boards per hour. Finishing was done (quietly) on the third floor, and packing (including—every day—15,000 Webster spellers) on the fifth. With this impressive organization and with exemplary leadership, D. Appleton & Company would be a giant among publishing innovators.

Chiefly responsible for much of the Appleton reputation for outstanding bookwork was William Matthews, the firm's head binder for 36 years. Born in Scotland in 1822, Matthews was apprenticed at Remnant & Edmonds, Paternoster Row, largest and most versatile bookbinders of that time. Their "specialties" ranged from traditional embossed leather to thermally carved wood bindings. Although he excelled at finishing and blocking, Matthews found working conditions poor and unpromising. In 1843 he shipped to New York, where he quickly established himself as a capable worker. Three years later he started in business for himself, and despite slender working capital, became so "surprised and nettled" that America had sent no exhibit to the London Exposition, he organized a substantial display for the 1853 New York Crystal Palace.

Among several of Matthew's perfect hand-bound books at the great fair was Jones, *Alhambra,* a large folio bound in yellow russia with red and blue inlaid morocco designs—wholly composed of straight and curved lines, dots, and circles, yet done (taking six months to finish) without the aid of any especially engraved tools. For this masterpiece William Matthews received a silver medal, the highest award at the Exhibition—and thereby came to Appleton's attention.

In 1854 the Appleton firm engaged Matthews to manage and control all school, cyclopedia, and fine art books, including much miscellaneous work in cloth and levant. His earlier Remnant & Edmonds days had prepared him well for all the techniques he would need, and in fact he never forgot his old British associations. Matthews hired many immigrant English workers, gave sound advice to beginners, and won many friends and admirers. Gentle and respected, he insisted on neatness and thoroughness:

"... in his walks through the long shops very few blemishes escaped his practised observation [noted *Bookbinder*]. He had a peculiar gift of divining where something might be wrong, and after casually looking at a pile of books he would constantly pull out some unfortunate specimen which had been carefully placed about sixth or seventh below the top of the pile. . . ."[5]

A spirited Brooklyn resident, Matthews was at one time president of the Flatbush Water Works Company.

Matthews had hand-bound Appleton's *Picturesque America* for display at the 1876 Philadelphia Centennial: the two volumes, leather mosaic with inlaid lettering, were judged the "finest books exhibited." At the 1889 Paris Exposition the copies of *Picturesque America* and *Picturesque Palestine*, so admired by the suspicious British critic, were his also. Although Matthews' fine bindings, according to William Loring Andrews, were only artistic relaxation and indulgence to friends, they were much sought by collectors everywhere. He long objected to the French reputation for excellence, finding many faults in gallic forwarding; that France had the best binders he considered "all bosh."

William Matthews' long association with D. Appleton & Company terminated in 1890 when he retired (at which time his son Alfred took the coveted post—another son, William, headed the American Book Company bindery). Ironically Matthews, 74, died in 1896 of shock and injuries when he was run down by a bicyclist. An incalculable asset to one publishing firm, William Matthews would teach all America to make better books.

With a bindery superintendent of such capabilities, it is perhaps curious that Appleton entertained, at the same time, any interest in producing books by means of a novelty sewing machine. Like a surprising number of larger binderies, nevertheless, Appleton was ever alert to new machinery for competitive advantage. Such large shops felt all the more onerous the dragging pace of manually executed work—having to perform constantly some tasks smaller binders encountered only occasionally. But for the sewing of books prospects were dim: between 1848 and 1867 few patents for sewers had appeared, each scarcely more than the hand passing of a shuttle behind the folds of machine-held book sections, similar to loom weaving. Nothing was yet available with promise for mass production.

David Smyth and his family were living in Orange, New Jersey, at the end of the 1860's in pleasantly rural but austere conditions. Father no doubt tinkered at home with lathe and drill, making infrequent trips to New York for tools, parts, and materials, or for patent applications. A fifth and last child, Orianna Slote (March 15, 1868), was of uncertain health, but there were four robust sons for whom to provide. Smyth's many inventions had not yet brought big money: from some there were neither profit nor recognition. Smyth, now about 35, was no longer precocious; yet—like Heyl—he had declared inventing his profession and he meant, solemnly perhaps, to stick to it.

If he noticed the phenomenal circulation rise in newspapers, magazines, and books (1000 titles published annually in 1830, 3000 in the 1860's, and approaching 5000 in the 1880's), Smyth perceived that heavy reliance on hand labor in the binderies would constitute a serious bottleneck. In 1860 a million and a half dollars were invested in about 500 binderies employing 5000 men and women in the United States; toward 1880 this capital would triple, employees would double —and still all sewing would be done by hand. Smyth's impoverished education had perhaps given him profound respect for literature; he nevertheless took a look at the manufacture of books and accepted the challenge to improve methods.

Smyth in 1865 (unfortunately transposed as "1856" in the *Inland Printer* obituary and long perpetuated incorrectly as the date of his first sewer) began thinking about a fully mechanical book-sewing machine. At the end of 1867 he completed a workable apparatus and on February 25, 1868, received a patent for it. His patent for the resulting stitchwork, filed at the same time, was strangely not issued until October 1871: its superficial similarity to conventional "all-along" hand sewing may have made it seem at first unpatentable to the examiner. In his machine Smyth had reversed one essential aspect: what other devices did by hand (shuttling the thread) he did mechanically; what they did by machine (holding the work) he did by hand. It was promising.

The first Smyth book-sewing machine incorporated a number of vertical straight needles—long and fragile, one more than the number of cords desired; the notched (sawn) signatures, open and flat, were fed by hand above the needles, positioned so the needles protruded through the saw holes. A spring-loaded, hand-operated rod passed thread to the hooked needles and retracted. The attendant had then to refold the signature, closing it over the stitch, before feeding another. The machine, however, cannot be considered the ingenious product of a man familiar with intricate cloth sewing machines: far from sophisticated, it was actually Smyth's first sewing invention of any description. Remarkably, however, it was a step forward that apparently needed little salesmanship; a customer was already waiting.

The Smyth book sewer came immediately to the attention of publishers D. Appleton & Company, who may have believed it practical as much for its gigantic magazine output as for cheaper books—both places in which its odd stitching pattern (a cord was "missing" at the bottom notch where only a thread ran from one signature to the next) might go unnoticed. "The aim in our day is cheapness;" William Matthews admitted two decades later, perhaps recalling this Smyth sewer, "hence strength in sewing is avoided. The sewing is so effectually covered up in the binding that the public cannot examine its quality, and are therefore easily hoodwinked." Appleton quickly

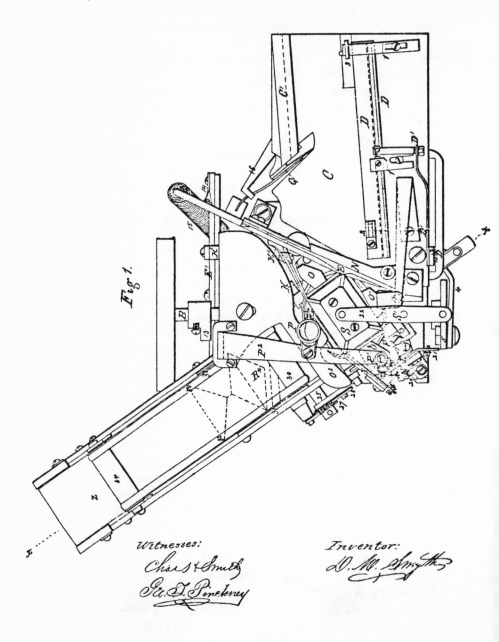

Fig. 1.

Witnesses:

Chas S. Smith

Geo. T. Pinckney

Inventor:

D. M. Smyth

bought the patent rights, gaining exclusive use of the design. Smyth manufactured 15 machines for the publisher—still working, said *American Bookmaker* in 1888—and thus relinquished possession of a marketable product. If he felt this machine to have great commercial promise he was nevertheless not disappointed by his arrangement with Appleton: a year later he repeated it, similarly assigning another important invention, his automatic envelope-making machine, to the publisher. Appleton, apparently delighted with a unique book-sewing machine later recognized somewhat charitably as "one of the most remarkable inventions of the age," was nevertheless discrete: when *Publishers' Weekly* visited the plant in 1873 only hand sewing was shown to the reporter. But the Appleton monopoly was short lived.[6]

David Smyth had begun to recognize paydirt in the sewing-machine motion, as had so many inventors before (and after) him. By June 1869 he improved his basically sound book sewer, performing essentially the same work as the Appleton machine, but transferring two operations, that of the spring-loaded rod, and the raising of sewed sections preparatory to folding them over the stitch, to foot pedals. This version he sold to Henry G. Thompson, who, as we have seen, was increasingly engaged with stitching and sewing devices of all description. A long professional association thus began: many subsequent Smyth patents, including of necessity the 1871 stitchwork scheme, went to Thompson, who was apparently anxious to bring the Smyth machine onto the market.

Five years later, however, the 1869 sewer was still faulty, Thompson himself troubleshooting and explaining one problem:

> "In book-sewing machines the thread is frequently broken by a knot catching in the hook, and by the sudden rapid movement the thread is snapped. If the attendant had any warning, the machine could be stopped or moved slowly, so as to allow the knot to pass the hook, or for another knot to be tied, thus saving considerable time. . . ."[7]

Thompson (with Edward G. Parkhurst, of Hartford) solved this in 1874 with a slotted thread guide waiting to be tripped by pesky knots. Commissioner Butterworth officially acknowledges Thompson with inventing the first true book-sewing machine, although he myster-

Top view of Smyth envelope-making machine, 1869. Strips of blank paper follow feed bar (D) and emerge—see dashed outline—on belt (Z) three sides folded and pasted, the fourth flap (R$^4$) gummed by hand. [US Patent]

iously sets the date at 1872. The commercial success of Thompson's model is not recorded, but he was understandably rushed—perhaps overcome—by new entries in the field.

Not far from Thompson headquarters the Wheeler & Wilson Manufacturing Company, Bridgeport, also well entrenched in sewing equipment, had similarly become interested in bookwork. Several patents issued between 1878 and 1881 to Edward S. Boynton, also of Bridgeport, were developments toward a machine assigned to Wheeler & Wilson (absorbed in 1905 by Singer). These and other sewing developments called David Smyth magnetically to the New England area.

The Smyth family left Orange around 1873, and situated for the next few years in Lynn, Massachusetts, the shoe center of the United States. There is no question Smyth sought to remain identified primarily with the shoe (sewing) industry which at this time had dramatically shifted to New England. A considerable boot and shoe trade had quickly established itself around yankee inventors like McKay, Thompson, and Goddu. It is probable that James Crawford Smyth, already located in Lynn, was an older brother. James also developed sewing and stitching machinery, assigning some patents to Smyth's daughter Orianna, apparently as potential income to combat a chronic illness. (Orianna died shortly thereafter.)

The busy sewing-machine clatter everywhere in Lynn's "shoe town" was siren song to an unsatisfied inventor. For Smyth many cloth and leather sewing inventions followed in rapid succession, most of them sold immediately to manufacturers for commercial exploitation. The fashion world adored fancy stitchwork, multiple ruffles and pleats, and elaborate embroidery. Stickler, Eliott & Wilson, New York, and The Singer Manufacturing Company, Boston, took Smyth's machine-feed mechanisms and pattern embroidery stitchwork; Henry G. Thompson took his boot- and shoe-tacking equipment. From these attachments and improvements Smyth's knowledge of intricate sewing machinery—scarcely evident in his 1868 and 1869 sewers—increased immensely.

David Smyth's activities were further complicated, since he was working, at the same time, with James Smyth on a series of wire stitchers.

"In 1878, it is stated [*Bookbinder* reported], Mr. David M. Smyth . . . constructed a wire-stitcher which differed materially from its predecessors, in the fact that the staples were first made and then placed in a hopper, from whence they passed down an inclined shute to the point where they were driven into the book."[8]

Smyth had in 1864 developed a machine for wire-stapling wood slats to make window blinds; James now borrowed this mechanism for a book stitcher, enabling it to drive staples with sufficient power so as to dispense with awl holes. The staple channel (also used by Averell and Goddu), however, was still obviously poor, here more so because it was hand-fed. David witnessed James' patent (No. 187,189) but his interest in it was minimal.

The Smyth wire-stitcher work nevertheless progressed simultaneously with Heyl's in Philadelphia; both must have followed each other's progress through patent announcements. The earlier staplers of Averell and Goddu, of course, might have been physically present in Thompson's shop, providing a more concrete incentive for the mechanically minded than ponderous patent descriptions. Both Smyths, however, were late in the wire-stitcher race: D. Appleton & Company, David's best client for bookwork applications, had already bought Averell's stitcher in 1874.

James Smyth's last stapling machine (1880), electro-magnetically operated, went immediately to the Book Sewing Machine Company, Boston; the application of electricity (perhaps learned from Edison) may also have been David's contribution, but there is no further indication it was successful.

The Smyth Manufacturing Company believes Smyth's first important book-sewing work to have begun in 1871, since it appears he then began thinking about an "off and on" multiple-stitch book sewer. It is indeed possible to dismiss the two earlier machines which operated, as we have seen, in simple "all along" fashion—probably requiring more stitches, thread, and time than was actually necessary to hold a book together for ordinary use. Unless very fine thread were used, "all-along" sewing also swelled the spine considerably (a book of 256 pages, normally sewed as 64 4-page sections, had 64 lengths of thread running through as many folds). Both early machines stitched to cords in imitation of hand sewing, perpetuating the sunken cord problem along with the nuisance of frequent breakage of the long straight needles. Smyth apparently abandoned the straight needle about 1873, seeking an "off and on" (thread running down only a portion of one signature and then skipping to another) interlocking stitch without the need for cords. He developed the curved-needle machine capable of these objectives by the end of 1878.

The curved needle was another source of irritation for Smyth. The machines of Howe, Singer, and others had used a straight needle with eye at its very tip. Smyth in the 1868 Appleton machine claimed invention of a straight needle with hook at one end and eye at the other (through which the cords were anchored): no great innovation.

Smyth discarded this needle along with the shuttling sewing operation of the early machines. A curved needle—integral to the success of Smyth's new concept—had almost gone unnoticed: it was patented in 1862 by Auguste Destouy, who attempted to apply it to the sewing of shoe soles. Destouy's idea succeeded only when Charles Goodyear, Jr., son of the rubber inventor, modified it: "The great feature of [the improved] machine," *Scientific American* explained, "consists in the employment of a needle, working within a circle of *less than two inches in diameter*, thus overcoming the great difficulty which has always existed in adapting sewing machines to this [shoe] work." An even earlier cloth sewer had used a curved needle, but Singer improved the machine by substituting a straight one. Smyth quietly took back the curved needle and built a book-sewer around it.

Finishing his work about the end of 1878, Smyth drafted and signed his application for patent on January 27, 1879, filing it a week later. Two potentially influential parties had already examined the device about this time: lawyer Charles H. Smith, who witnessed the application, and George Wells Root, to whom the patent was assigned. Root, heir of a prominent and wealthy New England family long successful in commercial enterprises, while professing to no mechanical ability, perceived the machine's success more by his faith and confidence in its inventor. Smith, and another lawyer, Charles E. Gross, had both examined and witnessed many such patents originating in the Hartford, Connecticut, area: their enthusiasm was grounded on more substantial comparisons. For fund-raising purposes Smyth constructed a small model of the curved-needle book-sewing machine which Root often fondly remarked "he could put in his hat." None of Smyth's patents had been launched more affectionately.

Toward the fall of 1879 official notices, like this one from *Scientific American*, began to herald the yearly event which inventors and spectators awaited with nervous apprehension:

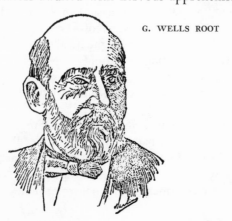

G. WELLS ROOT

"The 48th exhibition of the American Institute will open September 17 in New York. Parties having novelties which they intend to bring to public notice should at once address the General Superintendent for blanks and information. The medals, it is said, have been increased, and special awards will be made upon a number of articles."[9]

The American Institute of the City of New York had been incorporated in 1828, like Philadelphia's Franklin Institute, to encourage and promote domestic industry in the United States in agriculture, commerce, manufactures, and the arts. Immensely popular, the Institute's annual "inventors' fairs" had already introduced Morse's telegraph, Mc-Cormick's reaper, Singer's sewing machine, Remington's typewriter, and Bell's telephone to a gadget hungry public. Although Smyth had reportedly displayed his 1868 sewer at the 1869 fair (where Thompson might first have spotted it), there is no evidence. The great exposition in any case was an ideal medium in which to display his new model and attract backers. The inventor had perhaps learned something more of promotion and publicity in ten years, driven at the same time by the most pressing personal financial situation. He was, at any rate, more mercenary in 1879, later recalling his triumph as desperate utilization of genius available only under duress: "feeling the necessity of inventing something with some promise of pecuniary return, he set to work on a book-sewing machine, which, being patented, was pronounced a success, and in 1879 won the 'great gold medal of honor' of the American Institute of New York."* Duly listed in Group 4 of Department III ("Dresses and Handicraft") was No. 1117, Book Sewing Machine, David M. Smyth, Hartford, Connecticut. So Smyth found himself before the public, oblivious to the fact that few passers by appreciated good book sewing; fewer still had need of a machine for it.

*Scientific American*, usually sensitive to mechanical marvels, had unfortunately exhausted itself covering the 20-year battle of the sewing machines. A bored reporter noted that

"Agricultural machinery is not so abundantly represented as it has been, and there are fewer pumps, looms, printing presses, washing machines, and, not to speak disrespectfully of the foregoing, fewer catch-penny shows. . . . As usual, there is an interminable display of sewing machines and attachments, and other contrivances for saving (or increasing) domestic labor."[10]

The American Institute judges, however, were more alert. Viewing the Smyth sewer at work, they recognized a device capable (in the words of the award) ". . . by long continued operation and practical adaptation, to be so important in its use or application as virtually to supplant every article or process previously used. . . ." The machine met every criterion.

The Smyth Manufacturing Company would indeed advertise for years with the proud boast, "American Institute Gold Medal, 1879," and thousands of hours' operation in all sorts of binderies, under all conditions, would eventually prove the judges correct. More important, perhaps, was the opinion of publishing and binding people at the exposition who pronounced the sewer "the very thing they have been looking for for years." Such hearty trade endorsement, recognizing the Smyth as "one of the greatest inventions of the century," promised its inventor welcome fame at last, and more directly led to the formation of a company for its production.

The American Institute exhibit performed its most critical mission— not so much attracting backers (who were largely friends of Root and who put up little money anyway), namely, performing the publicity and promotion by which the bookmaking world discovered, almost as a body, the existence of a labor-saving machine for sewing books at extraordinary speed. With the promise of enthusiastic trade interest, the incorporation of a company to manufacture the machine was almost anticlimactic.

As one of the largest industrial sites in the east, Hartford, Connecticut, with good communication and transportation networks, reservoir of technically trained workers and new immigrant laborers, was a provident location. It was fertile terrain: the Patent Office would later observe that "While Mississippi takes one patent for every 20,469 of her population, Connecticut takes one for every 1,018 of hers, . . . and New York, 1,635." Smyth, pursuing the urgency of his need for money, welcomed Root's business associates and beamed at the panorama of the thriving Connecticut community. But before long he learned that his Hartford backers had far more enthusiasm than substance.

George Wells Root, frank, out-going, public-spirited spokesman for the group, had in 1843 entered a Hartford dry goods shop at 17. He soon became a member of the firm, and grew with it in jobbing and commission work which quickly required large New York city offices and salesrooms. A director of several Hartford commercial, banking, and municipal organizations, Root radiated inspiration: he was, said an admirer, generous in helping others all his life. "He had gone into

Side view of 1879 Smyth book-sewing machine. Dashed lines show feed arms bringing a section (heavy dashes) under needles; above upper (solid) arms two curved needles are retracted, two are stitching. [US Patent]

# D. McC. SMYTH.
## Book-Sewing Machine.

No. 220,312. Patented Oct. 7, 1879.

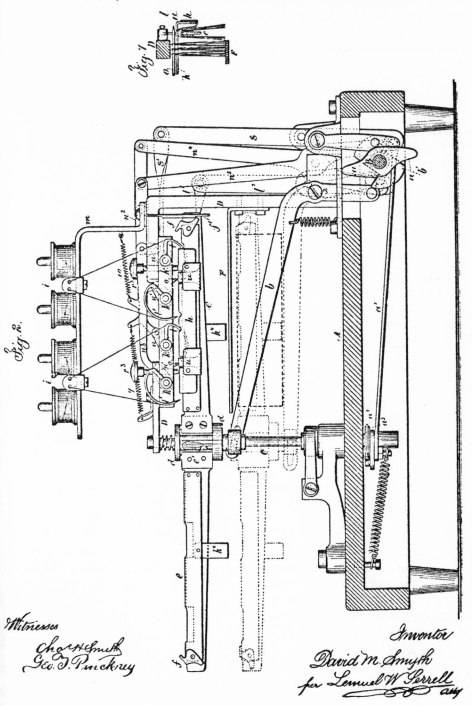

Witnesses
Chas H Smith
Geo. T. Pinckney

Inventor
David M. Smyth
per Lemuel W. Serrell
atty

many enterprises more to give a lift to those engaged in them than because he really expected any large returns for his money. . . ." Obvious infatuation with the throbbing book sewer in his hat—and Smyth's unimpeachable sincerity—had prompted Root to acquaint his friends with the fascinating device.

With Root, as we have seen, were lawyers Charles H. Smith, and Charles E. Gross; George S. Gilman was also a lawyer. Ebenezer Roberts and H. W. Conklin came along. Carlos C. Kimball, J. S. Tryon, and James S. Bryant became first president, secretary, and treasurer, respectively. All gathered, apparently, as diversions from their regular business occupations in town. On December 3, 1879, they issued 3000 shares of common stock valued at $100 each; three days later they voted to buy Smyth's patent (No. 220,312), paying all their capital—$300,000—for it. Ironically, however, Root and Orianna Smyth between them furnished the money: Root subscribed for 1460 shares of stock, Orianna (apparently entrusted with the Smyth bank account) 1458. Smyth himself took 2, and the eight remaining participants, 10 each. While not an officer of the company, Smyth was appointed General Superintendent with an annual salary of $2500—the only paid member of the unusual group. He had at last emerged from the realm of the speculative to the land of promise; he had, strangely, full-time employment again and plenty of work ahead.

David Smyth found himself, willy nilly, General Superintendent of a phantom machine works—for the company had no resources left to erect a plant of any description. The Smyth Manufacturing Company's office was only a small rented room behind a Hartford bank. The Sigourney Tool Company, another of Root's Hartford enterprises, was engaged to perform all manufacturing operations for the book sewer. With its one "employee," nevertheless, the new company, not actually incorporated under the laws of Connecticut until January 1883, almost immediately began to attract some unexpected notoriety.

In December 1879 the American Institute exhibition sewer was shipped to Hartford to be set up at Case, Lockwood & Brainard for continued demonstrations. It was probably the only working machine in existence, and would enjoy a steady audience. Suddenly, however, H. O. Houghton, whose wire-stitched centennial catalogs three years before had been a prestigious coup, appeared on the scene—almost within days of the company's creation—with another idea. He proposed that the Smyth machine be used to sew a 50,000 edition of the quarterly *U.S. Official Postal Guide*, a publication Riverside handled from 1874 to 1886. The Press would pay only shipping charges for the machine, but the publicity for Smyth would be well worth the trip. The demonstration machine was promptly diverted to Cambridge where it performed the first commercial work of its kind in the world. (By 1886 Riverside Press would possess 7 Smyth sewers, all paid for.)

The first Smyth book sewing machines appeared in the Spring of 1880. Considering the time necessary for procurement of materials, machinery, and manpower, and for tooling, seasoning of castings, assembly, painting, finishing, and adjustment, these first machines, not serial-numbered, must instead have been largely hand made and fitted. Designated the "No. 1," the sewer could handle octavo signatures up to 7½ x 10 inches; the "No. 2" was identical, but could accommodate larger sections. Both machines possessed four brass radial feeding arms, and, of course, the famous curved needles which have become the trademark of the company. They sewed "off and on," alternating 3 stitches on one signature and 3 on the next, to minimize spine swelling. The length of the stitches is governed by the curvature of the needles, and is therefore invariable. These first machines were not to be quietly buried under tons of work in diverse binderies—they would be most important promotion models.

Smyth was 46 years old when The Smyth Manufacturing Company was formed, and he appears to have enthusiastically diverted his attention—for a while—from inventing to publicizing and marketing its machines. In April 1880 a meeting of the board of directors—none of whom knew anything about binderies or book sewing—resolved that "Mr. Smyth be hereby authorized to take one of the machines now made and owned by the Company to any and all foreign countries for the purpose of exhibiting the same or procuring further letters patent [in England, France, Germany, Austria, Italy, Belgium, Canada] therefor. . . ." (Apparently the domestic market had already been sufficiently primed to await the delivery of machines.) Providently Smyth resisted the immediate temptation of further tinkering—although the machine was far from perfect—and promptly took it to Europe, where he dutifully acted as directed. He was not only the sole manager who could superintend its manufacture, he was also the sole salesman who could explain and demonstrate the machine's capabilities. In September the directors welcomed him back:

> "The meeting was called upon Mr. D. M. Smyth's return from Europe to hear his report of his trip. Mr. Smyth's recital of his experiences in Great Britain and Continental Europe were listened to with great interest. . . ."[11]

Smyth's experiences, alas, were not recorded, but they unquestionably indicated sufficient sewer interest in Europe to require, as the first production machines came off the assembly line in October, 1882, that five be sent to Frederic R. Daldy, London, and in November, five to

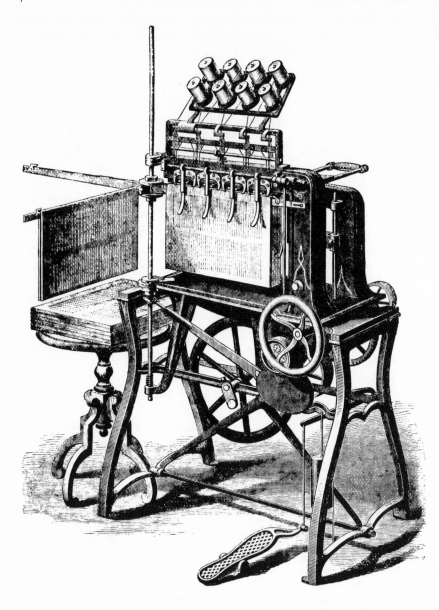

The "No. 1" Smyth book-sewing machine. Thread holes had to be pre-sawn before sections could be fed to radial arms. The sewer was immediately judged "remarkable not only for the great ingenuity of its construction, but for the rapidity with which it operates and the strength of its finished work." [New York Public Library]

Richard Horstmann, Berlin. With the establishment of these two agents the foreign market was actually accommodated before the domestic. Smyth had also traveled around the United States where he was similarly well received, considering the geographical distribution of initial orders that followed:[12]

| *Serial No.* | *Purchaser* |
|---|---|
| 1–5 . . . | Trow Directory, Printing & Binding Company, New York |
| 7–9, 15–16 | (overseas shipment; purchaser not recorded) |
| 10–13 | A. S. Barnes, New York |
| 14 | Gibson, Miller & Richardson, Omaha, Nebraska |
| 17, 39–40 | E. E. Tomlinson, New York |
| 18 . . . | H. W. Rokker, Springfield, Illinois |
| 21 . . . | George W. Crane, Topeka, Kansas |
| 25 . . . | John & Somerville, New York |
| 27 | J. L. Regan & Company, Chicago, Illinois |
| 28, 30–33 | The Public Printer (US GPO), Washington, DC |
| 29 | William B. Burford Printing Company, Indianapolis, Indiana |
| 34 | John F. Busch & Son, Philadelphia, Pennsylvania |

Others soon went to E. Fleming & Company, Boston (later Colonial Press); P. F. Collier, New York; American Bible Society, New York; George McKibbin, New York; William Rutter, Philadelphia; Harper & Brothers, New York; Norman L. Munro, New York; Riverside Press, Cambridge; T. Y. Crowell, Boston; Methodist Book Concern, New York; J. B. Lippincott, Philadelphia; W. B. Conkey, Chicago; Becktold Company, St. Louis; Rand, McNally & Company, Indiana; Hunter, Rose, Toronto; J. J. Little & Ives, New York; Thomas Russell, New York; and so forth. The list was a veritable Smith's *Blue Book of Printing Trades* for the 1880's, and a remarkable phenomenon: in an age of testimonials, with no prior experience possible, the purchase of a machine—3 to 5 of them, in some cases—was an act of pure faith out of desperate need by both quality houses and sawmills alike.

Little notice appeared in the American trade literature, perhaps too reserved to share the young company's hopes that any claims could have a sober foundation. *The* [Hartford] *Evening Post*, however, hailing a native industry, had innocently put the firm's bold intentions immediately (December 1879) into print:

"A HARTFORD INVENTION

. . . This machine will revolutionize the book-making business. There have been other machines introduced which sew with wire, but they do not meet the requirements of the Trade. Mr. Smyth has invented the only machine ever made for sewing books with linen thread, and the one just brought out is so perfect and will add so vastly to the working capacity of any establishment in which it may be used that no concern of any magnitude can afford to be without it. . . ."[13]

Surprisingly enough, all of this was true, but only slowly, after actual working conditions proved the claims, would such praise come from outside the company. *Scientific American* in 1883 praised the sewing machine for handling leather to lace, carpets to brooms, and (only vaguely) pamphlets to books. *Publishers' Weekly*, however, never did notice the Smyth editorially, or thought it too unimportant to mention: the machinations of cheap publishers was consuming all its attention.

In commemorative publications few of the original plucky purchasers felt the reception of Smyth machines significant enough to mention by name. Many, like the American Bible Society, only hinted: "During this period [1871–1891] . . . newly perfected printing presses and machines for the bindery were brought and substituted for the older styles." Yet the advantage of machine sewing was incalculable: Caleb T. Rowe, for 44 years General Agent of the Society, supervised during that time the production of 42 million bibles—many in foreign languages—on which the sewing of over 3000 books per week represented considerable labor.

The original plan of The Smyth Manufacturing Company in 1879 was not to sell the book sewer, but to lease it to bindery customers. A small initial charge would cover maintenance and damage, and a royalty based on usage would repay the company's great initial investment. Smyth was ready with a counting device, "a very ingenious automatic register," to record numbers of signatures sewn, but the plan did not materialize.

Although about 350 machines were sold between 1882–1887, the company was disappointed, to some extent, in the Smyth's initial reception. Kimball was disturbed in his own travels to American and European binderies, to find that the sewer's operation seemed so fantastic to workers they doubted they could keep it running. Too, some improvement was immediately called for: according to Ian D. Mackenzie, an E. C. Fuller officer, Smyth had overlooked "the human element."

Since the original machines had no apparatus for stabbing holes to facilitate passage of the needles, hand-made saw cuts on the spine of signatures (as with commercial hand sewing) were necessary, performed by pre-positioned blades on a circular saw. The Montague-Fuller catalog offered this accessory: "To secure accurate saw cuts for this machine, Smyth makes a saw machine, complete, $160." (If

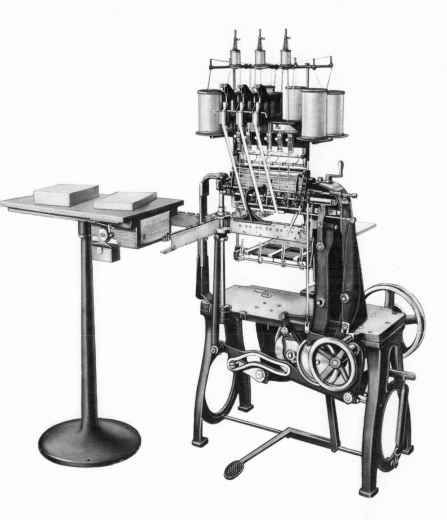

The "Improved No. 3" Smyth sewer shown loaded with three tapes. "Although every part of the Improved No. 3 has been changed from the original," says the company, "yet the principles of design and construction which made the original No. 3 a success from the start, have proved themselves through years of use a perfect mechanism for their purpose." [Smyth Manufacturing Company]

ordered with a sewer, it cost only $125.) Through indifferently sharpened blades and careless feeding, however, saw operators were making irregular or deep cuts which often mutilated the spine of a book. There was no choice but to mechanize this crucial preliminary operation if the Smyth were to be truly successful.

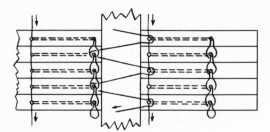

Machine sewing by "No. 3" Smyth sewer, one-half of spine shown. Stitches are made independently of each other, with double threads. Braiding stitch, sewn zig-zag over tape (*center*), was optional. [Stephen, *Commercial Bookbinding*]

Kimball brought this problem (also recognized by Smyth) to John J. Reynolds, chief engineer at the growing Smyth enterprise. Nicknamed "frog's hair Johnny" for the precision of his specifications, Reynolds developed the punch system, now incorporated into the radial arms, which eliminates the hand sawing. It was immediately installed in 1886 and distinguished as a new model, "No. 3," which was to be distributed throughout the world in large numbers. According to Mackenzie, the No. 3 specifically "can honestly be said to have revolutionized bookbinding." To Joseph Rogers it was the machine that launched the great period of American supremacy in bookbinding technology. Its operation was fully and simply described everywhere in the trade literature.

The operator places consecutive sections over each of the four horizontal feed arms which project from a vertical shaft, thus providing continuous feeding of books, section by section. In a one-quarter revolution the arm brings the section under a series of curved needles, and pushes it upward to insure that the sewing will begin exactly at the center of the fold. To facilitate the needles, a series of holes is punched along the fold during the upward movement, by punches in the feed arm. These stabbed holes give the added advantage of pushing the burs outside the fold, reducing the thickness of the spine.

The needles then travel in an arced movement along the fold, passing into some of the holes, and emerging at others. A series of loopers holds open the loops from the previous signature's stitches, in order to

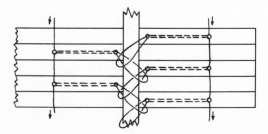

Machine sewing by "No. 7" Smyth sewer, one-half of spine shown. This is plain sewing over cord (*at center*). Tapes and cords are no longer used in machine sewing. [Stephen, *Commercial Bookbinding*]

allow the needles to pass through the loops. The loopers then withdraw, leaving their looped threads around the needles, and coming forward again to take new loops from the needles. The needles then recede, leaving their loops around the loopers, and occupy their original position in readiness for the next signature. It is the looping action which joins one signature to its neighbor.

Spine sewn on tapes, by hand (*below*). Note that one continuous thread is used; signatures are held together only by kettle stitches at head and tail. [Stephen, *Commercial Bookbinding*]

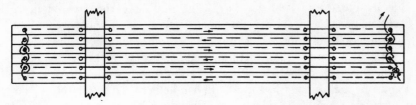

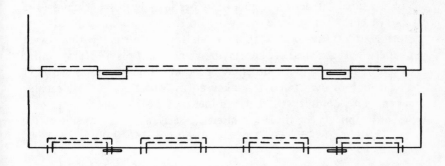

Hand and machine sewing compared. A hand-sewn thread (*above*) will unravel completely if broken; independent machine stitches (*below*) with double threads have tighter, more even tension, and remainder are not affected if one breaks. [Stephen, *Commercial Bookbinding*]

The first and last signatures of a book are tipped with paste by the operator before placing them on the feed arm, in order to prevent unraveling of the end stitches, although successive books are sewn without having the thread cut between them. The sewed sections are pushed back along a horizontal table, and if the sewing were done on tapes, extra tape lengths had to be pulled by hand between books for later pasting to the book's boards.

The tapes soon became a nuisance. Originally the binding of books hand-sewed on cords or tapes was stronger because these "bands" were securely laced, that is, run through a hole in the board and splayed on the other side, or buried in the split spine edge of the boards. The cased-in book, however, whether made by hand or machine, simply had the tapes pasted to the surface of the boards, covering them (only poorly) with endpapers; because of the tape's thickness, a wide "French" joint was necessary, usually a space ⅛-inch between board and back of book. By the 1930's both British and American binders considered the sewing on tapes of dubious—weakening—value, judged against the work of the triple lining machine (p 283) which lays 2 mulls and 1 brown crepe paper over the sewn spine, each layer individually glued and rubbed down. The mulls are then pasted neatly between board and endpaper to make a very serviceable joint. Sewing on cords disappeared about 1882, and sewing on tapes is no longer considered a good method even for heavy books.

The No. 3 machine featured six needles which would make stitches about one inch in length, and would handle between 55 and 60 sections a minute. It could be adjusted to accommodate sections as small as 2 inches long with one stitch; 7½ inches long with four stitches (plus 3 tapes or cords, if desired); and 12 inches long with six stitches (and 5 tapes or cords). The style of sewing on the No. 3 was changed from the original "off and on" pattern to "all along" (although there were gaps between stitches). The sewing may be "plain" (also called "French"), meaning without tapes or other material, or, as we have seen, through or over tapes or sunken cords. The machine was capable of even more complex stitches: braided sewing which zig-zags over tapes and connects the thread of alternate sections on either side of the tapes. The No. 3 sold for $1200, no increase in price over the original Nos. 1 and 2.

According to company history, more No. 3 Smyth book-sewing machines have been sold than any other in the world. The first No. 3 (beginning with serial number 500) was sent for exhibition at Edinburgh, Scotland, in 1886, where considerable British bookwork existed (p 201). Meanwhile, however, many suggestions from the trade must have bombarded the firm along with Smyth's own revisions: "The Smyth Company kept on improving and redesigning. It was a young company, but it availed itself of the best mechanical talent to be found in a locality famous for practical ingenuity and fine workmanship. Before long, five models of book sewers were being built. . . ."

The "No. 4," "No. 5," and "No. 6" machines differed slightly from their predecessors. They are single feed-arm machines, built sturdier and slower operating for heavier work like ledgers, account books, and other special applications, although they will perform all of the sewing done by the previously described machines. They also sew "all along," each stitch being slightly less than 1½ inches long. The needles are adjustable in relation to each other, and one or more can be used at a time. The estimated speed of the original No. 4 was 30–45 sections per minute, and it sold for $1600 in 1892. Introduced in 1891, the first No. 4 machines went to Plimpton and Riverside Presses.

These heavier machines were improved (as was the No. 3) in the 1930's with light-weight duralumin (an aluminum alloy) feeding arms, adding 10–15 signatures per minute to their output. The three models will do plain sewing, sewing over tapes or webbing (single or double), or over raised or sunken cords. They have the following capacities:

| No. 4 | six needles | handling books | 2 to 14 inches in length |
|-------|-------------|----------------|--------------------------|
| No. 5 | six needles |                | 2 to 16                  |
| No. 6 | ten needles |                | 2 to 18                  |

The "No. 7" has four feed arms like the first three machines, but they are shorter in length to enable it to run at higher speeds—up to 70–80 sections per minute (a speed no operator could long maintain). It will handle section lengths from 5½ to 10½ inches in a style called "two sheets on," that is, each pair of threads being interlooped, one thread of each pair going into every other section, and the other thread into alternate sections. The machine is constructed for plain sewing, sewing through mull or crash, or over raised or sunken cords, or through tapes.

While the Smyth Manufacturing Company still offers the Nos. 3 and 4 machines, much progress has been made in recent years. The most up-to-date basic machines offered to the trade are the "No. 12" and the "No. 18," both available as semi-automatic and fully automatic when they first appeared. The No. 12, introduced in 1928, will accommodate sections from 3 x 3½ inches to 10½ x 14 inches, and one version, the "12C," has adjustable needle blocks for extremely accurate positioning of stitches. The fully automatic No. 12 handles the same minimum section size, but the maximum is 10½ x 13½ inches. It achieves a speed of up to 95 sections per minute, 10 more than the semi-automatic. The fully automatic operations are the feeding, pasting of end signatures, and cutting apart of books, although the feeding may be done by hand if necessary. An electrical safety system is employed to stop the machine in the event of a jammed or missed signature. These machines were developed by Carl Schramm, who joined Smyth in 1922 and replaced Reynolds shortly thereafter as chief engineer, holding the position until 1958.

The No. 18 machines have been developed to sew "two up," that is, two separate—but not yet cut apart—books (necessarily imposed for printing "two up") at the same time, and to accommodate a larger

range of sizes. They handle sections from 3 to 10½ inches in width to
7½ to 19 inches in length at a speed of up to 85 signatures a minute.
Needle blocks are adjustable on all No. 18's. The fully automatic
model sews "two up" with the same automatic functions as the automatic No. 12. Both the "12" and the "18" employ straight needles, a
radical departure after 48 years of curved needle sewing.

Introduced in the 1940's, the No. 18 was just about as modern as a
machine could be. "Don't let booksewing bottleneck your profits," said
the company in 1941 to binders who found the old No. 3 machine
slow. Ironically there was still room for improvement, fittingly recognized by David Smyth himself, and later pursued independently of the

The "No. 12" Smyth book-sewing machine with semi-automatic feed;
pasting and thread cut-off are actuated by treadles. Developed in 1928,
this and the "No. 18" (similar, but capable of "two-up" sewing) use
straight needles instead of the classic curved ones. [Smyth Manufacturing Company]

Hartford company (p 290). The inventor, nevertheless, would first enjoy the fruits of his spectacular success.

With the splendid prospects of financial security at last, Smyth, perhaps in need of a prolonged vacation, retreated to East Northwood, New Hampshire (another "shoe town"), after the flurried activity of company organization, production, and sales trips. He had established a summer residence there about 1877. From New Hampshire Smyth frequently issued patent improvements on his book sewer until about 1892. He apparently earned such prestige and influence he became a member of the New Hampshire legislature in 1889.

In 1891 David Smyth removed to Pasadena, California, where for his declining years he built a beautiful home in the shadows of the San Gabriel mountains. Why he chose this area is speculative: Nathaniel C. Carter had gone to California in 1871 (upon doctor's advice), so impressed by the climate and improvement of his own health he began "bombarding" eastern newspapers with letters, and in 1874 ran excursions from Massachusetts to California. Carter, on Pasadena's official "Reception Committee," had been a sewing-machine agent in Lowell, Massachusetts, and may have snared Smyth in his popular lure. Too, Eugene Leslie Smyth toured the West—he wrote and illustrated *The Missions of California* (A. Belford & Co., Chicago, 1899)—and may also have coaxed his father there. Nevertheless, after the death of his wife in 1897, Smyth divided his time between summers at his East Northwood home and his winters in California or the South.

Smyth's accomplishments were many and varied; his automatic clutch was probably the first developed for instantly stopping machinery; along with the sewing and stapling machines, his gas petcock, water pump, and ore-crushing apparatus were all uniquely motivated electro-magnetically. More remarkably, he was also poet and artist, publishing in 1897 a touching memorial to his wife, and in 1901 a book of poems entitled "The Hermit of the Saco," reportedly containing "many lines of unusual merit." Many of his paintings were highly praised.

David Smyth (identified rather comically by the trade journal *Paper and Press* in 1891 as a "manufacturer of sewing machines") had been a director of the American Association of Inventors and Manufacturers, an organization emerging from the 1891 Patent Centennial in Washington, DC. It held its first meeting January 19, 1892 with Dr. Richard Gatling (machine guns) as first president; Commissioner Butterworth was also an officer. Smyth was also first president of the Pasadena Fruit Exchange, which changed its name in 1909 to Pasadena Orange Growers Association, proprietors of the famous trade name "Sunkist."

Smyth's sons led equally commendable lives, each ironically incorporating some facet of his father's genius: Eugene Leslie as author and artist of marines and landscapes; Joseph Elmer as inventor of bookbinding machines and founder of a company for their production (p 195); Professor David Grant as Superintendent of Schools in Hartford and inventor of telegraph equipment and other devices (p 290); however, of George B., also living in Hartford, little is known.

David McConnell Smyth died October 11, 1907, of an apoplectic stroke, at the home of his son David. He was 74 years old. Interred with his wife and daughter at Pasadena, his name is far from forgotten. Charles E. Brainard, retiring in 1970 as Chairman of the Board of Smyth after 32 years of service, has observed: "It is significant, however, that the major contribution which he made to the art of production bookbinding is still referred to as 'Smyth-sewn' as part of the language of the trade."[14]


The Smyth Manufacturing Company went on to develop many other bookbinding machines, many of them almost as important as the sewer itself. Once the Smyth sewer illustrated the fact that bindery problems, no matter how intricate, could be solved mechanically, additional equipment could be called into being almost upon order. But some mechanical wizardry would still help. Among "Yankee geniuses" capable of creating new revolutionary equipment was Arthur I. Jacobs, an inevitable addition to the Smyth firm.

Born in Connecticut in 1858, Jacobs worked for a local loom works where he made many mechanical improvements. At the same time he invented a book-sewing machine which he patented (1887), manufactured, and sold throughout Massachusetts. These activities could not escape Smyth's attention: "So impressed [wrote Jacobs, confidently] with the value of this invention," the company bought the patent rights and engaged Jacobs to assist in perfecting its own models. He remained at Smyth until 1901, during which time he invented a number of machines, a book coverer, a book sewer, a cloth cutter, and a casing-in machine among them. He also developed the machinery for manufacturing the curved needles. In 1901 he produced the famous Jacobs "Improved Drill Chuck," and left the Smyth organization in order to form a company for manufacturing and marketing it. The Jacobs chuck is universally used today.

The Smyth Manufacturing Company brought out its "No. 1" and "No. 2" case-making machines making 12–15 cases per minute, in 1896 and 1899, respectively. The American Book Company bought the first No. 1—which followed Sheridan's case-maker by almost two years

—and three years later, the first No. 2. In 1901 the "No. 1" cloth cutter appeared (the "No. 3" is the current model).

In 1903 the Smyth glueing and pasting machine, and the "No. 1" casing-in machine were produced. A single operator feeding uncased books could collect 4000 finished tomes by day's end; two men pasting and pressing by hand were lucky to do half that. This first casing-in machine—anywhere—had been bought by Ginn & Company, but was returned to the factory for adjustments; by 1905 it was again on the market, successfully. The "No. 3" appeared in 1940; the newest machine is the "M–68," handling books up to 13¾ x 10¾ x 4 inches.

The first book trimming machine was shipped in 1909, and in 1916 the first case back-forming machine. The company also makes a rounder and backer, a book jacketing machine, and the triple lining and headbanding machine.

Of its manufacturing policy, the Smyth people say, "A tremendous amount of thought, work, time, and expense goes into the development of every Smyth machine before it is made available to the industry. Exhaustive tests in both the factory and the field are completed before the design is frozen and the production tools are built. Five years is considered to be a short time between the conception and the production of a Smyth machine." Much of the prototypal testing has taken place at The Plimpton Press, an unusually enterprising book manufacturer nearby.

The Plimpton family had been a vital New England graphic arts force. George A. Plimpton (1856–1936) began as a textbook salesman for Ginn & Company in 1876 and was admitted to the firm five years later; his keen interest in schoolbooks manifested itself in a precious collection of horn books and primers which he later gave to Columbia University. In 1886 Ginn encouraged Plimpton to organize a book manufactory: he turned naturally to his brother Herbert M. Plimpton (1859–1948) who had already established H. M. Plimpton & Company (later Plimpton Press), Norwood, Massachusetts, the year Smyth sewers first emerged. Herbert had believed heavily in the magic of the machine (and in diversification—he owned Holliston Mills), installing early Nos. 3 and 4 book-sewers, and the first Crawley rounding and backing machine.

In 1891 Ginn bought Plimpton's bindery, acquiring in the transaction a third brother, Howard E. Plimpton (1862–1899), as its plant superintendent. Despite the new Smyth and Crawley machinery Ginn believed the shop to be crying for modernization:

"At this time machines for folding flat sheets and for sewing books were recent and had not come into general use, so that a considerable part of the folding and sewing was still done by hand. Books were rounded by hand, and the backing machine was worked by hand. The cutting of paper and of the edges of books and the stamping of covers were about the only other operations done by machines. . . ."[15]

This attitude seems designed to justify new investment, and a site at Cambridge, Massachusetts, was selected in 1896 for a modern plant. Ginn's new Athenaeum Press soon began turning out 40,000 books a day. (In 1951 Athenaeum became Cuneo Press of New England.)

Herbert Plimpton quickly replaced his bindery, enabling book designer and author William Dana Orcutt, a Plimpton employee, to introduce to the publishing trade the concept of "complete manufacture," in which all work could be handled at one plant. (Today's book

The Smyth "No. 1" case-making machine, hand fed, about 1896. Cloth must be pre-cut. Along with an automatic-feed model, it has undergone little modification in over fifty years. The "No. 2" case-maker accommodated larger cases. [Smyth Manufacturing Company]

manufactories must also offer offset lithography in addition to letter-press—as well as "hard" and "soft" bindery lines—to qualify as "complete.") The two Plimpton brothers themselves invented an early gathering machine used in their shop and later manufactured commercially. Plimpton Press also cooperated with Smyth in developing its first casing-in machine, and a prototype new-style casing-in machine operated there in the 1920's. More recently Smyth's endpaper printing and folding machine and jacketing machine were tested there. In 1942 Plimpton installed a pioneer package bundler developed by the Package Machinery Corporation, Springfield, Massachusetts, equipment Plimpton had been trying to fabricate for years. In 1960 Plimpton acquired the bindery of Little, Brown, and after brief ownership by the McCall Corporation (1964–1970) functions today as an independent firm.

The Smyth Manufacturing Company in 1956 moved to new quarters in Bloomfield, Connecticut, a few miles north of Hartford, where today it continues to produce precision bindery equipment—machines on which (since 1955) enlarged "Smyth" nameplates boldly broadcast Smyth quality around the world.

The Smyth company, as we have seen, had quickly established European connections by which foreign markets might be exploited—cognizant perhaps that for so special a machine nothing less than world-wide sales would provide sufficient volume. With other bookbinding machinery manufacturers encroaching with similar or alternative equipment, Smyth providently engaged one of the most successful agents in the graphic arts area to manage its sales.

Montague & Fuller, New York city, suppliers of printing and binding equipment since 1886, were chosen as general agents for the United States and Canada. Capitalizing on what they called, with some justification, "the six Perfect Machines" (Smyth sewer, Thompson wire-stitcher, Elliott thread stitcher, Chambers folder, Acme paper cutter, Giant signature press), the partners set up so grand a display at the 1893 World's Columbian Exposition they won 9 medals and 11 diplomas. Egbert Cuthbert Fuller, a Thompson stitcher representative from Hopedale, Massachusetts, was himself inventor of an automatic paper feed mechanism for printing presses. With a name like his, it was said, Fuller *had* to be a "tough egg," but he was all salesman: dressed in top hat, cutaway, and florid scarf, he would mount a sewer in a hired carriage and drive from shop to shop demonstrating—and selling —it. In 1894 he bought out his aging partner to become the E. C. Fuller Company, with offices in New York and Chicago.

Fuller sales and service had long been an extraordinary combination of competence and consistency, offering customers technical help no less qualified than the original plant engineers. Carl G. Dunderberg had come from Sweden and stayed 40 years with Fuller; throughout the United States and Canada he erected bookbinding machinery and retired a vice president of the company. With some interlocking of officer positions with The Smyth Manufacturing Company, Fuller continues to be the sole agent in North and South America. After World War II, however, it also handled the sales of an appreciative aggregation of important bindery names: Joseph E. Smyth Company (p 195), The Rosback Company, W. O. Hickok, John J. Pleger Company, Sieb Manufacturing Company, Crawley Book Machinery Company, Gitzendanner Corporation, Standard Machine Company, and others. (Many of these have since established their own sales agencies.) By the 1930's the E. C. Fuller agency claimed there were 2500 No. 3 sewers in operation, suggesting sales averaging about 50 per year.

In London F. R. Daldy after a few years began to share his 1884 appointment with W. C. Horne, Cannon Street; in an 1887 *Bookbinder* he advertised: "The Smyth Thread Sewing Machine (by Steam); Gold Medal American Institute. W. C. Horne, Agent." A year later Horne's stand at the Manchester Book Exhibition was probably the first wide presentation of the sewer in Europe. John Heywood, official printer and bookbinder to the show, was invited to supervise the operation of what *Bookbinder* called the "Smythe Patent Book-Sewing Machine as used by Messrs. Virtue and Son, and other celebrated printing firms." Horne also had a Martini folding machine and Harper New Patent Wire-Stitching Machines, all operating at once. "The work is turned off from the respective machines in such a way by the operator (Miss Bowker)," said *Bookbinder,* with some praise for female dexterity, "in baskets for dispatch to the 'Excelsior' Printing Works, as to cause much admiration." But many in England needed a little more; they were receptive, but not quite sold.

Many highly reputed bookbinders and binding firms found opportunity or excuse to profess strict adherence to hand methods—the bibliophiles were, after all, constantly shopping about for exquisite work. In the face of growing claims from competing and conflicting manufacturers—and the impending invasion of American machinery heralded by the Smyth book sewer, the British indeed remained dignified throughout, standing especially on the dictum that the highest quality work had to be hand sewn. After five years of Smyth sales operations in England *Bookbinder* remained reserved, although it knew all the Smyth arguments: "The inventor claims that the machine is capable of doing at least six times as much work as an expert hand-sewer performs;" it noted in 1889, possibly having met Smyth, "that the stitch is stronger and more regular than in hand sewing; that the machine sews easily at the rate of 45 signatures a minute, and that the automatic tension controls the thread perfectly."

Undaunted, for the Paris Exposition in 1889 Horne bundled a No. 2 sewer which he exhibited as "a new and original machine for sewing together the sheets or signatures of a book." But France was barren territory; the French might have been far more impressed had they been able to see Miss Bowker's performance along with that of the sewer.

Roderick W. Horne, a son, had been sent to America to learn Smyth methods at first hand; he worked for a time in the Hartford factory. In 1905, with George Kimball, Carlos' son, he incorporated the manufacturer's name with his own, and a Smyth-Horne Ltd. advertisement soon boasted: "Nearly 3,000 Smyth sewers in use, a number of repeat orders having been obtained." This figure suggests European (or world?) sales of about 120 machines per year during the first quarter century of the company's existence; in the 1920's Smyth-Horne's count was over 4000—approximately a hundred a year.

Smyth-Horne Ltd. continues to represent the Smyth Manufacturing Company with two London offices and a branch in Paris. A. M. Satterthwaite & Company, Christ Church, handles New Zealand; B. J. Ball Ltd., at Sidney, handles Australia. Ault & Wiborg Company, New York, serves the Far East from Manila and Tokyo. For a time, Africa was also serviced.

As early as 1892, therefore, Montague & Fuller proclaimed that, from the viewpoint of service and quality the Smyth sewer—originally produced and demonstrated by the inventor almost unassisted—was now the product of an organization second to none. "These machines," said the catalog, "are now in use in every country throughout the civilized world where books are made. Many operators sew over 20,000 signatures per day. . . ." As far as quality was concerned, "All of the Smyth Sewing Machines are made in the most perfect manner [Montague & Fuller continued], every part being made interchangeable, and are pronounced by expert engineers to be the most perfectly made machines in the country." (Proof of this was necessarily decades away, but it came in: a No. 3 sewer at Case, Lockwood & Brainard—installed in the 1880's—and a No. 4 at Plimpton—installed 1891—were still going strong in 1926. Another No. 4, manufactured 1895, underwent overhaul 30 years later by the E. C. Fuller Company: every improvement ever made to No. 4's could be added to it.) Neither Montague & Fuller nor the Smyth Manufacturing Company could afford to rest on laurels despite the magnitude of substantiated claims. Many other sewing developments had made the sewing of books a very competitive field.

Although the Brehmer wire book-stitching machine was a mechanical success, as we have seen, it had, in the United States especially, been condemned for even most commercial bookwork by people in all phases of the trade. As a result August Brehmer in Leipzig promptly developed his brother Hugo's thread-sewing machine, putting it on the market in 1884, two years after the Smyth. At the Manchester Exhibition the fickle Mr. Heywood himself abandoned the Smyth to work the Brehmer sewer, turning out memorandum books at "a high speed." The machine's performance was as versatile as the Smyth, and did not require saw cuts, but it sewed "all along" with a single thread (instead of separate double threads for each stitch). This manner of sewing was suitable for ephemera, according to Stephen, for, while it kept spine swell to a minimum and accommodated thin papers better, the single thread was not as strong as Smyth's double thread, and its continuous stitching would not keep a book intact (as would the Smyth) if a thread broke.

The Brehmer operation had another disadvantage when used for edition work. The machine had to make slits in the head and tail of each section in order to allow the continuous thread to pass from one section to another without being cut by the guillotine in trimming the book. According to Stephen the slits did not need to be more than a quarter of an inch, but operators were frequently making them much longer. The long slits prohibited kettle stitches close to the ends of the folds where they ought to be for proper library rebinding.

At the turn of the century Brehmer had three newer models which sewed with double thread, and which made no head and tail slits, thus overcoming the major objections to the first version. A Brehmer advertisement claimed "Speed up to 2400 stitches per hour . . . and not liable to breakdowns or expensive repairs," possibly a slam at Smyth meaningful only to foreign binders who may have had to wait for parts from Hartford. Brehmer book-sewing machines—capable of 100 signatures per minute—continue to be manufactured in Leipzig by VEB Leipziger Buchbindereimaschinenwerke, and are widely sold throughout Europe despite Communist control of the large firm.

The modern Brehmer, since 1948, is also manufactured in England (slogan: "You can't beat a British Brehmer"), fully redesigned and improved. The "No. 38–¾–H–50" features speeds of 50, 65, 75, and 90 signatures per minute, comparable to the Smyth No. 12, a thread-breakage warning light, and automatic pasting apparatus. In 1959, in association with Rudolf Hepp Gmbh, West Berlin, the German Brehmer company introduced completely new thread book-sewing machines: the model "39" with 7 heads and automatic cutoff between books; the "39¼" with one additional stitch for sewing on tape, and the "39¾" with an additional alternating stitch. All include the thread-breakage warning device, but more important, these machines are automatically fed. For its long history of service to edition book binders, the Brehmer continues to hold a strong place in bookbinding machinery.

From quite another quarter of Europe another important sewing machine reached the American market at the turn of the century. Joseph E. Smyth, David's son, strangely chose to follow his father's precarious calling; his soundly launched gathering machine, however, had failed to match the book sewer's success (p 207). Joseph, 38 in 1900, nevertheless remained in the difficult bookbinding market. He organized the Joseph E. Smyth Company in Chicago to manufacture

The Martini National book-sewing machine about 1903, depicting its charming operators with confidence and serenity—just before massive strikes disrupted the binding industry. [New York Public Library]

the "National" book-sewing machine originally developed by mechanical engineer Frederic de Martini. Famous for his invention of a breech-loading rifle long (1871–1889) in British service, Martini (originally from Trieste) had a decade before begun in the bindery machinery business with an accomplished senior partner.

In 1862 Martini and Johann H. Tanner—inventor of folding machines—in Frauenfeld, Switzerland, founded a company to make Tanner's combination folding and stitching machine. Vibrating needles carried thread across each section before the final fold was made (the machine was patented in the United States but not exploited here). In Switzerland folders and embroidery sewers were quickly overshadowed by the company's success in firearms until 1890, when an improved book-sewer was announced. Within the following years both British and American agents were anxious to handle the National.

In 1904 the National "No. 1" book sewer was introduced to the British market, its performance similar to other straight-needle machines. As Martini's American agent, Joseph Smyth had contracted not merely to sell the machine in America, but to manufacture it as well. While tooling up in 1903, he theatrically placed 12 machines in the US Government Printing Office bindery. The growing public printing office could use them.

The Government Printing Office, Washington, DC, proposed by Congress in 1818 but not actually begun until 1861, like commercial shops throughout the United States, frequently reconstructed its facilities around successive periods of trade mechanization. Often machinery was donated for experimentation or prestige value. So voluminous was its work, nevertheless, there was value in every piece of equipment however acquired. The bindery occupied the entire third floor of the large old plant built in 1861, and there were also bookbinding branches at the Library of Congress and the Senate Library.

In 1878 the GPO bindery's 500 women sewers were organized into "companies" of 40 girls with a captain in charge; in fire drills (much enjoyed by crowds watching the girls in long petticoats negotiate the outside fire escapes) they could all evacuate the building in 1 minute. That same year the bindery bought 9 wire stitchers for pamphlet work, and within three years the number of girls was reduced to 240. As additional sewing machinery entered the shop the girls became understandably piqued. To improve their "discipline" in 1883 (now over 13 wire stitchers and 2 thread sewers on hand), 130 girls were put on piece work instead of the usual $11 weekly salary. "Careful sewers," said an official, "can earn as much [as $11], . . . while those who were not returning a quid pro quo with the needle very naturally fell back to their places in the rear." Although the GPO was first to institute an

8-hour work day (1868), some technological unemployment in the bindery, especially among women, was almost inevitable.

In the 1920's, the GPO bindery—located in new 1905 quarters—had 47 Smyth sewing machines (as well as 4 case-makers, 3 casing-in machines, 3 cloth-cutting machines, 2 glueing machines, and 1 case back-forming machine—all Smyths), and today it acknowledges without commercialism that it has 24 machines of one model alone (probably Smyth No. 12's), turning out 10,000 to 18,000 signatures a day. Joseph Smyth's National sewers had done their part of the GPO's work too, and testimonials to that effect did theirs.

The Martini National book-sewing machine proved to be considerably well received. With vertical, straight needles, "the machine for good work" succeeded in keeping spine swelling to a minimum, because its hole punches (like those of Reynold's on the Smyth sewer) threw burs outside the fold, and its "off and on" sewing distributed the stitches over the spine. It was a "handsome, well-built machine, quiet and easy in operation, with practically no jar or racking, and . . . all its wearing and operating parts [were] in full sight," said *Inland Printer* in 1903, of the European prototype. Soon testimonials trickled in: "Our customers are delighted with our books," said the Lutheran Publishing House, Decorah, Iowa, "since we started sewing them on the Martini, because they are stronger and entirely flat opening." Gradually more impressive binderies also praised it: Braunworth & Company, Edwin Ives & Son, The Roycrofters. Success was rapid—ironically attested by an infringement suit brought (and won) in 1906 by The Smyth Manufacturing Company against T.W. & C.B. Sheridan (Joseph Smyth's agents), who were enjoined from selling it with the specific punching features developed, as we have seen, by Smyth engineers Reynolds and Jacobs.

By 1925 the Chicago company, which now also handled a line of bindery equipment, moved to new quarters, making it the "largest factory in the country used exclusively for the manufacture of book sewing machines." Joseph Smyth, having "found his greatest pleasure in his home, and there devoted the greatest portion of his spare time," died in 1916. Under the general managership of John E. Smyth (Joseph's son), the plant continued to manufacture the National, originally available in three sizes, and later increased to four: 16, 18, 20, and 28-inch capacity. Sewing with or without tapes at 50–60 revolutions per minute, it handled edition work, catalogs, schoolbooks, and annuals with ease.

About 1920 Martini's chief designer, Kugler, had invented a spiral hook needle which simplified the mechanism and contributed greatly to the company's machinery. For the following 30 years—until 1950—

Martini made book sewers exclusively, more than 8500 of which were delivered all over the world. The National in Chicago, however, from 1937 on—alongside David Smyth's sewer—was handled by the E. C. Fuller Company, but with diminishing sales. In 1961 the declining Joseph E. Smyth Company was merged with Fuller, the latter continuing to manufacture and sell American-made Martini sewing machines until the mid 1960's.

The current European model, "HA–35," is manufactured by the Martini Bookbinding Machinery Company, Frauenfeld, and distributed in the United States by The Sheridan Company. It features semi-automatic feed, one-shot lubrication, thread-breakage light, and "straight spiral needles," doing 110 signatures per minute, with even, tight sewing, left or right-hand delivery. The T.W. & C.B. Sheridan Company in 1911 apparently discarded the distributorship of the National (which Dexter then assumed), offering instead the "Sheridan International Sewing Machine" in three styles and four sizes. It claimed "Better and tighter sewing . . . capacity greater than any other machine on the market today." In 1960 Sheridan resumed its handling of the Swiss Martini, "product of seventy five years of experience and installation throughout the world," Sheridan and Martini having exchanged stock and become closely associated with each other (p 255).

For edition bookwork, the Smyth, Brehmer, and National/Martini sewers seemed capable of satisfying the requirements of any bindery, American or foreign. For more specialized types of book sewing it was inevitable that, since the machine had indeed distinguished itself in so complex a task, more specialized book-sewing machines would be developed. The H. L. Roberts Company, Mount Vernon, New York, in 1908 perfected a silk-stitching machine designed for double stitching of pamphlets. Using silk floss, mercerized cotton, or commercial thread, and putting a knot in the center of each spine, it could stitch a day's hand work in an hour, doing dance programs, keepsakes, and other fancy applications. Horace L. Roberts was no stranger to the trade: through the 1880's and '90's a machinist, erector, and instructor for Chambers, Montague & Fuller, and Dexter, successively, Roberts had observed the need for such a sewer, and in 1941 also developed a side-stitching machine using cord or thread on spines up to 1⅛ inches, a sewer very useful for rebinding.

In 1914 the Samson-Back Book-Sewing Machine, created by James H. Renninger, was announced to the market by The Dexter Folding Machine Company. Handling bulks up to 2 inches, it sewed 6 books a minute with light or heavy cord or with wire, although it had no needle; it was "so apparently superior to human hands that it almost seems uncanny," said *Inland Printer*, although the magazine had seen

many mechanical marvels in its earlier days, some all the more extraordinary as pioneers. Nevertheless, two strong men could not pull
a book apart. A year later the machine was redesignated a book binding machine ("and a wonderful binding!") although its product still
looked like saddle sewing.

The Oversewing Machine Company (with factory until 1958 in
Los Angeles), about 1919 began manufacturing a book-sewing machine whose specialty required a formal definition:

> "Oversewing—A new method of machine sewing . . . instead of sew-
> ing through the back fold of the sections the needles pass obliquely
> through the section itself forming a lock stitch with each separate
> section and independent lock stitches 'all along' the back; *a superior
> method to the ordinary type of sewing, and very advantageous for
> single leaves and sections of varying sizes and thicknesses.*"[15]

The company also produced a book-sanding machine, and with a new
1926 patent it offered the "Nu-Way" Book Sewer capable of 3000
books per day, hand fed—"a genuine novelty." Frank M. Barnard,
president of Chivers (p 200), Frank J. Barnard & Company, and vice
president of Oversewing, was inventor of several machines, among
them an adjustable rounder-backer. Today the Oversewing Machine
Company of America, Medford, Massachusetts, offers a hydraulic
building-in press, a book paster (for casing-in), in addition to its oversewing (also called overcasting) machine, which accommodates any
thickness up to 4½ inches. It is especially recommended for library
work: "Oversew now . . . or sew over later," the company warns.

In 1926 Wes W. McCain, from a family long engaged as bindery
machinery agents, founded the Chicago Machinery Laboratory to produce a side-sewing machine, capable of stitching through both thin
and thick books—up to 2 inches—at high speed. It uses a single thread,
without bobbin. "For Strength and Economy in Book Manufacturing
Side-Sew on the McCain," said its advertisements. R. R. Donnelley &
Sons committed themselves to it in 1934 for manufacturing the *Encyclopedia Britannica*, and within a month the *Encyclopedia Americana*
also converted to it. The latest model will sew ¼ to 2¼ inches in bulk,
making 1- or 1¼-inch stitches; another model sews 1200 books per
hour, making ¾ inch stitches at the rate of 250 per minute. In 1969
the company changed its name to McCain Manufacturing Corporation; much of its marketing is done by Dexter.

Other book-sewing machines have been manufactured under the
names Edler, Elliott, and Friedheim (now London agents for Martini
and other firms). Still useful is the Singer: for heavy books—up to 1½
inches thick—Singer in 1931 introduced its "6–18" lockstitch machine

with drill for boring needle holes; it made 75–80 1-inch stitches per minute. Other Singer machines, properly, are still simply conventional sewing machines useful for bookwork. Moffett Precision Products, Inc., Batavia, Illinois, now makes a high-speed side sewer using a Singer "7–33" mechanism, operating on books up to 1¼-inch thick, and in 1971 announced a new machine that sews *flat* sections which are then folded into book pages.

The appearance of a dozen intricate machines whose only capability is sewing books indicates the size and stability of a marketed product approaching its centennial anniversary. Acceptance, as with any novelty, was not so fast or convincing. There were powerful forces to be persuaded, forces constituting the respected traditions long entrenched in both edition and library bookwork. The British market was most prestigious—and formidable.

Joseph W. Zaehnsdorf, Jr., a confirmed hand binder, in his binding manual acknowledged "Smythe" as the latest word in sewing, but his careless spelling betrayed strong feelings. Zaehnsdorf's father, born in Austria-Hungary, had founded a bindery in London (1844), winning a succession of awards for excellence. The son continued the shop with almost complete disregard for modern invention. "We use no machinery," he said, simply, when moving to larger quarters in 1890. "Ours is all hand work." At a discussion of machine sewers in 1908 Zaehnsdorf still admitted he had none in his house and knew nothing about them, but, compensating in strictness for lack of modernity, went on: if any of his girls, he warned, "put in their stitches so unevenly that they were a quarter of an inch out one way and an eighth of an inch out the other way," they would not remain very long in his employ.

Cedric Chivers, of Portway, Bath (six times the town's mayor), son of a binder, was the first English employer to adopt the 8-hour work day. He pioneered in binding materials deterioration research, invented many bindery devices, and introduced a "vellucent" binding process (transparent vellum over colorful designs). Chivers opened a branch bindery in New York (1905) which he relinquished in 1924, although his name was retained. He championed his own "Duro-Flexile" sewing—a kind of overcasting—which, in lacing each signature to the kettle stitch, to the tapes or cords, and also to its neighboring signatures, solved the problem of handling "spongy" paper "once and for all." "No leaf of a book should carry more than itself," he maintained. The American *Library Journal* commended it. Both Zaehnsdorf and Chivers (like Riviére and de Coverly), through the great library explosion, served librarians and bibliophiles well and fared comfortably, although their superior hand sewing became "definitive" for very few of the world's books.

British edition binders, whether they talked about it or not, were buying book-sewers with diminishing fear. Messrs. Blackie & Son, Glasgow, had Smyths and Brehmers, but still did much hand sewing; W. & R. Chambers, Ltd., in 1890 had a Brehmer, 2 Smyths for tape work and a larger Smyth as well, "but the better work is folded and sewn by hand." Another binder had no reservations: "We have four of Smyth's sewing machines going, and they do very good work, especially in the matter of speed." William Collins Sons & Company accumulated (by 1953) more Smyth sewers (Nos. 3, 4, 8, 12, 18) than any other binder—90 of them—with a happy motto, "A stitch by Smyth saves time." Some of the original No. 3 Smyth sewing machines sold to British and Scottish shops in the 1880's were still running after World War II. Thus resistance to the machine by the end of the 19th century had almost completely disappeared.

The commercial firm, in fact, that clung exclusively to hand sewing beyond the 1880's was rare indeed. The Chief Inspector of Factories and Workshops in England had reported on "female labour" in 1888:

> "This industry [bookbinding] employed an army of workers now greatly reduced by the introduction of motive power to stitching machines; the value of hand-sewing has fallen in consequence, producing a redundancy of labour and causing much misery during slack times. . . .

> "The commercial book-sewer finds regular employment, and can earn 15 s. a week at machine work; the publishers' sewers are subject to the uncertainties of trade. Generally, girls work in threes, two of them at machines, one to prepare work, changing places by rotation; they earn 12 s. to 15 s. each, but hand-sewing has fallen to 8 s. to 10 s. . . . I believe that publishers' binding work is now amongst the poorest paid of city industries."[17]

In the United States the story was similar. A recent immigrant complained of wire stitching: "We did only the best of work [in Dublin]. . . . We women did the folding and the sewing and a little pasting. But now, the machines have changed it all. If ye'll look at a pamphlet, ye'll see that where we girls used to stitch with a sharp needle and a linen thread there's naught but a piece of wire." And when there were only odd jobs left for the unskilled, they became, like the women at the GPO, understandably recalcitrant. One foreman was extraordinarily empathetic for his time:

> "Our girls earn on an average $6 a week. Some of them earn $22; the beginners earn $3; all of them work by piece. They can do any

sort of work, and the finest books we have are sewed by them. They cover the pamphlets, but the bound books are done entirely by men. The stamping and such work is done by machinery. Our girls work 10 hours a day, and sit down during the whole of that time, or at least the greater part of it. The girls who work on the 'dry press' are obliged to stand. The dry press is a machine for pressing the matter overnight after it has been folded."

"What sort of girls are they? [asked the reporter]"

"Good, quiet-going girls, for the most part. The majority of them live at home. They are as neatly dressed as any girls you see from the shops."

"Do you employ them steadily?"

"—Well, some of them we do. Of course, when it is dull we let our girls go; but when we have a big job we advertise, and get a lot for the time being, or if we know of some good hands we send for them. . . .

"Some of the girls are very dull, and have to be shown over and over how to do the simplest thing. They learn to do just one little thing, and seem to have no ambition to extend their knowledge. Fifteen years ago a bindery girl used to learn to sew, stitch, fold, and paste. Now she does only one of these several things, and is helpless when any of the other duties are required of her. It is partly stupidity, partly indifference, and partly shiftlessness. Of course you will not understand me to mean that that refers to any of our old experienced hands that we keep continually with us, but to those girls who cling to the skirts of the trade, as it were, and pick up jobs here and there.

"Perhaps you imagine they jump at a job. Not a bit of it, I assure you. They read your advertisement in the paper, come around and critically examine the sort of work you have in hand, and if they don't like it they tell you so in graphic language. Their manners are very self-possessed, to put it mildly, and I think a candid person might even go so far as to call them cheeky. But then, too, there are some very sweet girls who go about taking the chance jobs, and who are very glad to take anything they can get and work hard at."[18]

The "very sweet girls" who were willing to operate the Smyth book-sewing machine crossed a very real threshold when they entered the machine world. They were disarmed, perhaps, by Montague & Fuller, who felt, in 1892, that "The machines are easily understood and operated by any fairly intelligent girl, who is taught how to run them without charge." A sociologist two decades later found a certain amount of trauma in the bindery:

"To touch the back of a section with paste and then to place it over the revolving arm of the machine, while picking up the next section, watching the threads, and throwing aside badly folded or mutilated sheets, requires the sort of cooperation of head and hand which cannot be acquired without long practice."[19]

George Stephen, a British librarian, was the first to take a long, critical look at the processes of machine sewing. His first treatise, "Machine Book-Sewing," a paper read in 1908 when he was 28, described the difficulties of securing data from manufacturers; two years later his book, *Commercial Bookbinding*, contained a practical evaluation of machine sewing:

> "The principle of machine sewing is good, because the thread is always held under even tension, which may be varied to suit, and no section will come out until every stitch in the section is broken, whereas sewing by hand requires training before even tension is achieved. If the thread in a hand sewn book is broken, not only will the section come out, but the whole sewing will loosen. The chain stitch (which the machine makers erroneously call a kettle stitch) at the head and tail is not as strong as the hand kettle stitch, but this is not too objectionable."[20]

Many others praised machine sewing with fewer technical grounds.

At a paper read before the Bookseller's League in New York, binder Robert Rutter, speaking of unwieldy spines, said, "Happily those days are passed, and ignorance is (if it ever was) no longer bliss. To the American Book Company, more than to any other house, this reform is due [with text bookwork the most demanding of "quality control"]; but in a complete measure the modern book-sewing machine accomplished the easy-opening back combined with great durability." G. P. Putnam's Sons in 1904 was telling authors they would get speedy sewing "accomplished by the aid of a most ingeniously constructed sewing-machine," giving them books that would open easily—an "advantage" authors usually take for granted.

Henry Blackwell, an American binder ranking behind Matthews and Zahn, in 1900 boldly praised the entire area in which so many others had little good to say:

> "Machinery has produced better books, better bound, and artistic in the highest degree. It can safely be said that the cloth bindings of today have reached the highest pinnacle as regards art, and the workmanship in every detail perfect, and the work of today in New York excels that of any other country, in point of binding and decoration. . . ."[21]

Critics could agree, however, that the Smyth machines "have created a revolution in the world of binding books," substantiating the proud claim of the Smyth Manufacturing Company, "Standard of the World in Bookbinding Machinery." But in the 20th century revolution was all too frequent. Just as David McConnell Smyth, his work done, retired—"a devoted lover of nature and never so happy as when he could roam through the woods, fishing, or in search of rare wild flowers"—a spectre invaded his bindery domain. It was exactly the antithesis of his life's work: it was a stitchless, threadless binding machine.[22]

# 6 *Periodical Production*

# *and Adhesive Binding*

FROM THE TIME OF THE FIRST ROLLING AND ROUNDING MACHINES, THE first standing and stamping presses, and the first stitching and sewing machines, their proud inventors, owners, and medal-bestowing progress committees were too delighted with the whir and clatter to notice the lost time inherent in such reciprocating devices. An operator fed his machine manually, the work was admirably performed, and the tender got his product returned to him. But "return" time was often as long as entry time, and the operator was waiting there—quite unprofitably —all the while. An 1858 "yankee" wit's proposal for continuous, "straight-through" production was woefully premature: "Drive a sheep in at one end, and he shall immediately come out at the other, four quarters of lamb, a felt hat, a leather apron, and a quarto bible." The concept was not as ludicrous as its byproducts made it seem.

The number of operations in the binding of a book, even by machine, was too high to expect that one piece of equipment might ever do them all. The folding machine, the sewing machine, the roller-backer, and the stamping press, had solved only the most technical or laborious problems. Hidden between these principal operations, however, were many mechanical steps still handled by troops of bindery females who had managed to hang on: in 1900 there were over 15,000 girls engaged in US bindery work, 26 percent of them in New York city. Folding, almost fully mechanized by the end of the century, left the women only "knocking up" —jogging and stacking sections as they came from the folder—(the girls were called "knockers"). But gathering and collating still remained a hand chore of considerable proportions.

Technically, gathering was the act of collecting in correct sequence the component sections of a book. Properly, a set of 4, 8, 12, 16, or 32 printed pages, when folded, constituted a "section," while a "signature" was only the sequential identification mark printed on the top page of a section; today, however, little distinction is made between the two words. Many thousands of women employed in gathering, walking up and down long tables on which successive sections were piled— "like convicts taking exercise," someone said—seemed money lost to the harried binder.

Collating was the formal checking of the gathered sections against a model, prior to sewing: collected signatures were bent at the corner, and as pages sprang back, the eye had time to glance at the letters "B," "C," "D," and so forth (the unlabeled "A" section was always better identified by its halftitle). As long as human hands did the gathering, human eyes did the collating—a wise, if expensive step. But if the gathering could be mechanized—a foolproof routine incapable of error—both jobs could be eliminated. Some thought it could be done.

Gathering machines, like folders, were sufficient challenge to the inventive mind from a mechanical point of view; that they would replace another segment of manual work was at first hardly a consideration. Ellicott D. Averell, developer of the wire stitcher, produced the first gatherer in 1875 which, although hampered by a faulty feed system (sections were loaded in boxes standing on their edges), showed the workability of the device. Another inventor, F. Wood, solved Averell's problem in 1886 by feeding signatures flat from the bottom of the box, the method used on most of today's machines. The Acme Gathering Machine (manufactured by the Brown Folding Machine Company) in the 1890's had 60 boxes and a speed of 100 sections per minute—apparently capable of collecting as large a publication as has ever been put together. The Seybold Machine Company, Dayton, Ohio, manufacturers of bindery equipment, offered a halfway measure in its 1893 gatherer, a vertical "ferris" wheel of 20 revolving shelves, from which quick-fingered girls had to pluck signatures manually to assemble a book. Gathering machines were feasible, said *Inland Printer* as late as 1900, but opined—rashly, as events proved—that "The cost of gathering, however, is so slight that it will never pay to construct expensive and complicated machines to do the work." None of these machines, apparently conceived for the job and magazine bindery, possessed anywhere near the efficiency needed if deadlines were to be met.

In 1896 Joseph E. Smyth developed another gathering machine, one which seemed to present no particular breakthrough for the bindery. Working at his father's home in Pasadena, Joseph elicited much sage advice and counsel in the machine's construction. David Smyth, in fact, occasionally boasted he had contributed the essential designwork. Joseph, for his part nevertheless, capitalized handsomely on the Smyth reputation. To manufacture the gatherer, "which promises to equal in value the book-sewing machine," said announcements, Smyth formed a company with himself as secretary, his father as vice president, and Horace J. Evans as president and treasurer. Joseph was ready in 1896 to incorporate the Smyth Automatic Machinery Company, with capital amounting to $300,000 (exactly what the Smyth sewer had required just 17 years before). The machine, "said to be the only one of its kind in existence," was heralded that year as gathering correctly 100,000 signatures in 10 hours, doing the work of 12 or more girls. Many orders had already been received.

By 1900 the Smyth Automatic Machinery Company now located in Chicago, was ready to sell manufactured units. In extensive *Inland Printer* and *American Printer* advertisements it claimed:

"A great achievement in bookbinding. The Smyth Automatic Signature Gathering Machine. Its three cardinal points:—speed—accuracy—compactness. Bookbinders the country over will be interested in our property. One year ago this month the 'Smyth' was perfected and put into continuous daily use. It is the first and only AUTOMATIC signature GATHERING machine ever made that bookbinders have found thoroughly practical, though nearly fifty years have been spent by different inventors in endeavoring to build a perfect working one.

"Briefly stated, this machine occupies 4 × 14 feet of floor space; is run by 1½ H.P.; can be operated by two persons [a girl to feed, a boy to control], and will gather 17,000 complete books of 24 signatures each per day. It works equally well on the heaviest and the thinnest of book papers, and will gather in all sizes from 4½ × 7 to 7½ × 11 inches."[1]

Endorsements were included from Rand, McNally & Company and R. R. Donnelley & Sons, in whose binderies the machine was tested. ". . . it does the work in a most perfect manner," said Rand, McNally. "It never makes a slip, nor a hitch, nor a stop, except when there is an imperfectly folded signature running through, when the machine will automatically stop instantly and at the same time indicate on a dial, plainly in view, the location of the trouble. . . ." The *Inland Printer* reporter, touring the Rand, McNally installation with Joseph Smyth, found it "simply marvelous"—and magnanimously retracted the magazine's earlier impolitic remark.

Through 1901–1902 Joseph continued to work on the gatherer, one patent alone (No. 679,039) covering 29 modifications. But, although the company was "being taxed to the full limit," sales were not so rapid as hoped; the gatherer was apparently still a premature invention to conservative binders. In the 1893 depression climate many publishers, as we have seen, had dragged their binders into financial difficulty with them. Few daring souls (there were some) felt that large purchases of better equipment were a way out of trouble. In the light of what others were doing for newspapers, and what Bredenberg and Juengst were about to do for magazines, the gatherer did not perform a sufficient portion of the binding operation. But for job binders with heavy gathering work, it had its place.

Subsequent advertising affirmed the Smyth machine's large sales on both sides of the Atlantic for books, magazine, catalog, and pamphlet work. The London agent cabled, "Tests were severe but satisfactory. Machine accepted. . . ." In 1907 the Juengst Gatherer, Collator and Stitcher (p 219) and the gatherer of Alexander Gullberg and Charles L. Smith (patents 811,509 and 875,384) were also introduced to the trade, and the 6000 rpm Cheshire Book-Gathering Machine followed in 1915; this competition was serious.

Advertised as "the only machine that can successfully handle any sheet or signature," the Gullberg and Smith required one operator, a girl to feed every five boxes, and another to remove finished work, all of whom the company would train upon purchase of a machine. Frank A. Munsey took 4 of them, Butterick, 2, and several other New York and Philadelphia binderies, 1 each.

Butterick was no stranger to bindery mechanization. Ebenezer Butterick, a Massachusetts tailor, in 1859 had begun selling paper patterns for shirts and children's and ladies' garments, soon to be cut and sewed by millions of housewives. In 1867 salesman Jones W. Wilder and Abner W. Pollard, a Butterick nephew, joined to form a company, adding a Brooklyn factory and a fashion magazine which became the *Delineator* (1906 circulation reaching 1.5 million) with British, French, and Spanish editions as well. George W. Wilder, Jones' son, bought (from Erman J. Ridgway) *Adventure, Romance,* and *Everybody's Magazine* (founded 1896, circulation 1 million), the latter a popular monthly whose issues sometimes reached 352 pages. Because of tight schedules and increasing workload, the company believed in using the best machinery available—almost nothing in the plant was more than

ALFRED BREDENBERG

[Courtesy John T. Zurlo]

CHARLES A. JUENGST

[Kingman]

five years old. With a new (1904) Manhattan headquarters Butterick's 2500 employees and 91 presses in 1910 made the firm second only to the US Government Printing Office in size, producing 50 million tissue patterns and 22 periodicals annually. The Gullberg and Smith went right to work.

The gathering machine went to work in small shops too. One bought a gatherer in 1904 which saved him $30 per day in girls' wages (and that meant dismissing up to 30 women making about $5 each per week). "The machines have cut our force in half," said another. "Seven or eight years ago we employed 60 or 70 girls. Now we have 30 with just as large an output." As the roller-backer had displaced men some 60 years before, so had mechanization caught up with women in the bindery. For all but the dismissed worker it was a two-sided problem that union leaders and manufacturers would long dispute. On behalf of the terminated employee one sociologist brought the inventor into the fray:

> "To save labor often means to dismiss a laborer [wrote Van Kleeck in a classic 1913 sociological study], and behind the stories of the triumphs of the inventors one may expect to find the equally human, if less cheering, stories of the displaced workers. . . ."[2]

On top of this struggle was the additional economic factor of the depression.

The depression of the 1890's was hard on magazines as on books, but in the graphic arts arsenal there were some new weapons: paper and printing costs were lower than ever; the invention of the halftone screen brought lavish, realistic photographic coverage at a fraction of wood-engraving prices. Best of all, with new waves of immigration and new scientific advances, the public clamor for both light and serious periodical reading remained undiminished. Publishers, unfortunately, had thoughtlessly raised their subscription rates with every financial squeeze, and could not seem to repair their declining circulations. One maverick publisher showed them how.

At 28 a crack telegraph operator, Frank A. Munsey had, like others before him, come down from Maine in 1882 with an urge to publish, but no experience. With a borrowed $260 he started the *Golden Argosy*, a children's magazine which brought him no profit for almost 10 years. Between 1894 and 1907, however, it yielded almost $9 million, with which Munsey methodically began to trade magazines and metropolitan newspapers with uncanny skill. In the midst of depression he boldly lowered the newsstand price of *Munsey's Magazine* from 25¢ to 10¢ (making competitors do likewise)—and raised its circulation to 700,000; the magazine often contained well over 256 pages per issue. Other Munsey properties also grew to great manufacturing proportions.

As tyrannical, egocentric head of a gigantic publishing domain of cheap periodicals and newspapers, Munsey—called "The Chief" by affectionate subordinates—had keen appreciation for the latest technological advances. "His plants were always equipped with the newest machinery," said his friend, printer Erman J. Ridgway, "if the newest was the best and the fastest." For his immense New York pressroom he ruthlessly threw out old machinery in 1908 and bought from Robert Hoe & Company eight large 96-page presses and one 384-page multicolor perfector (really four presses in one) which delivered 156,000 16-page signatures per hour, folded, cut, and counted in bundles. Munsey's success was in divining what the public wanted (i.e., popular, lurid material profusely illustrated; he introduced the "artistic" nude), but his manufacturing acumen was no small asset. His fortune—$40 million—he quixotically willed to New York's Metropolitan Museum of Art; about the finer arts he knew precious little.

The periodical industry at the turn of the century had been content at first to fold, gather, wire-stitch, and hand-cover magazines on up to 4 or 5 separate machines, in tandem. Each set of grippers released its precise hold on the unfinished work, only to require positioning and set-up on the next machine in line. The inefficiency was obvious. Many of the larger bindery equipment houses soon offered custom-made or standard machinery for combinations of functions, reducing re-set-up time considerably. For the Curtis Publishing Company's *Ladies' Home Journal*, for example, with circulation close to .75 million, Chambers Brothers in 1906 spent a year developing a giant "combination" (folding and stitching) machine. With eight automatic feeders (5 to feed 16-page sheets, 1 each for 8-page and 4-page sheets, and 1 for covers) it could deliver any combination of signatures to make a complete issue of up to 96 pages. With 5 adjustable wire-stitching heads the machine folded, collated, covered, stapled, and bunched the magazines, ready for trimming.

Later combination machines, no longer novelties but proven in high-speed production, were available generally: the Kast Insetting, Gathering, and Stitching Machine (available from Dexter in 1915) folded covers, inserted any number of folded signatures, headed up (jogged to the head) all sections, wire-stitched with staples staggered to avoid bulging, and deflected imperfect copies. In 1924 Curtis' 16 such Kast machines each performed at a rate of 50 magazines per minute; today they do more than twice that. Edward R. Kast (1879–1944) had been chief engineer of the Dexter Folder Company. But for the many periodicals over 96 pages, the wire-stitched product was not an unmitigated joy.

Gradually many magazines and catalogs grew too thick for wire staples, and although even hand-operated stitchers could penetrate up to 2½ inches of paper, there was no sales appeal in thick, unwieldy magazines. *Harper's*, *Scribner's*, and *Century Magazine*, the three most popular monthlies of the early 1900's, could not—for lack of time—be thread-sewed, yet were bulging with advertisements and almost novel-length fiction. Saddle stitching could not handle multiple signatures; side-wire stitching of any bulk often snapped shut in readers' hands. "Let us hold to the more courageous and hopeful belief," said *Inland Printer* in 1902, "that American ingenuity and humanitarianism will soon invent a machine that will sew even the cheap magazines in a civilized way. . . ." The need was desperate, but help was close.

Lovell-Bredenberg automatic periodical covering machine (patented 1890 as a "book-binding machine"), capable of applying covers to 1500 magazines per hour, sewn or wire-stitched. [Courtesy T. Blair Hawkes]

Alfred Bredenberg came from a Swedish family involved for generations in iron foundry work. Born in 1855, he was at 12 straightening and cleaning iron bars at a Swedish rolling mill; he ran a steam hammer and a 40-foot tugboat by the time he was 16. Assigned next to a rail spike-making machine newly imported from England, Bredenberg for several weeks could not produce a single spike—becoming a laughing-stock of the village. The disgrace jogged him doubly—he not only got the machine to work with prodigious output, but became painfully aware that his love for mechanics was frustrated by a skimpy education and small-town conditions which would lead him nowhere.

Bredenberg found promising new work in machine shops, during which time he married—only to face sudden economic depression and poverty. His first child died in infancy. At this point—finding the future in Sweden holding no hope—Bredenberg about 1879 thought of America.

In 1880 Bredenberg brought his proud but unsure family—wife and infant—to the United States, accompanied by a small coterie of similarly minded relatives and friends. Profound personal religious faith had sustained him through meagre years, and would fortify him against adversity in the future: he spoke no English and had only $4 in his pocket when his band disembarked at New York. His experiences and expectations—not unlike Smyth's—were strange, agonizing background for a potential inventor.

Providently, Bredenberg was working within a week, and able to settle comfortably in a small Brooklyn apartment. He was shortly enrolled in English and drafting at Cooper Union and eventually able to buy a home in Brooklyn. Holding a machinery design job for ten years, Bredenberg gained the technical skills he would need to develop his own inventions—bookbinding equipment "bringing education, pleasure and comfort to countless millions," he proudly boasted. He knew education would be his new country's foremost need, as it had been his own.

Bredenberg warmed to his inventive potential with two utilitarian items: a paper-bag machine (1890) and a shoe-counter former (1891), both of which he patented. About 1889 his draftsmanship apparently came to the attention of Charles W. Lovell, who, like his brother John, had evidently also escaped the Rouses Point book manufactory to settle in New York. A bookbinder and tinkerer, by 1893 he formed the Lovell Manufacturing Company as a bindery, and engaged Bredenberg to help develop ideas for book-making machinery.

The Lovells in fact had need of an inventive genius who could on demand produce the most ingenious machinery yet conceived. John W. Lovell had just formed the United States Book Company (1890),

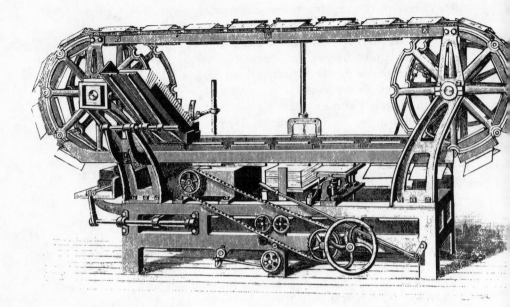

Lovell-Bredenberg automatic periodical covering machine (patented 1893 as a "book covering machine"), capable of applying covers to 2400 magazines per hour, sewn or wire-stitched. [Sheridan catalog]

a $3,250,000 trust in which other "cheap" publishers were invited to pool their printing plates in order to control discounts and prices. Methodically Lovell began buying out publishers who would not cooperate. He corralled 16 by March 1890, including some original cheap publishers, Worthington, Hurst, Belford, Clarke, Alden, the Munros, as well as Estes & Lauriat and Lippincott—both probably glad to be rid of thorny enterprises. In hopeful *Publishers' Weekly* advertisements Lovell promised fine book paper and good binding, planning "as creditable specimens of book-making as can be obtained." Never so acutely would "Book-a-Day" Lovell need truly modern, mass-produced book-manufacturing equipment. Charles Lovell's bindery could be expected to handle a substantial part of this work.

For Charles Lovell Bredenberg designed what he himself considered "revolutionary" machines during a 3½-year collaboration. Some patents specified Lovell as co-inventor, and all of them assigned a portion to John Lovell:

428,741   Book-binding Machine (1890)
466,719   Sheet-gathering Machine (1892)
476,208   Book Binding and Covering Machine (1892)
490,877   Book-trimming Machine (1893)

490,895   Book Covering [case-making] Machine (1893)
493,553   Book Covering Machine (1893)

Through these years of Bredenberg's earliest work David McConnell
Smyth had just begun to enjoy the success for which he had labored
so long. If successful, Bredenberg's machines would replace Smyth's
sewer, technically, performing on an even newer and cheaper principle
(although not intended for books). His binding and covering machine,
specifically, was indeed revolutionary—it was a threadless binder. Its
scheme of operation, furthermore, was "straight-through," inline
performance; a traveling clamp carries each book from station to
station where wire-stitching, covering, trimming, and other operations
were performed. ". . . there is no back motion or movement of the
machine," said the inventor in his patent, "it moving always forwardly
and accomplishing work at each step, so that there is no loss in time.
. . ." Patent specifications attest to its complexity, consisting of 14
pages of text and 11 pages of diagrams. Bredenberg had finished a
staggering—and costly—assignment.

Never before had private individuals not in the business of making
bookbinding equipment invested so heavily in machinery research and
development. Neither the Appleton investment in a book sewer, nor
the Riverside Press purchase of a book stitcher had been so speculative. Yet, although magazine production across the United States was
at record quantities, the "Lovell pamphlet covering machine" appeared only fleetingly in the trade press—the depression destroying
any chance of success.

Without manufacturing facilities of his own (the Rouses Point
plant apparently failed after just a few years), publisher John Lovell
—perhaps expecting his brother momentarily to signal readiness to
fabricate books with unprecedented automation—was unfortunately
indebted by October 1892 to The Trow Directory, Printing and
Binding Company (p 219) for $200,000 in work executed—at which
point the publisher failed. Too lavish, too acquisitive, Lovell had been
badly hurt by the new copyright law and mortally struck by the
1893 panic. Ironically, Trow, to whom other shaky publishers had
forfeited the plates of hundreds of cheap books, probably engineered
the entire US Book Company scheme. The collapse of the publishing
venture had the inevitable effect on his brother as well.

Charles Lovell was also financially destitute. A $10,000 promissory
note he had given Bredenberg as payment for services rendered was
not likely to be met. Bredenberg began to worry over his uncertain
future as he had not long before, in Sweden; he now had five children,
and an expecting wife. Shortly after giving birth, his wife Anna died of

pneumonia. Bredenberg was spiritually crushed; after placing his children with friends, he took a three-month leave of absence from Lovell to visit his family in Sweden. During the trip he met a young woman named Hilda to whom he described his unhappy situation, and she agreed to marry him when they returned to the United States. Bredenberg's grief was mitigated by the relief that his children would be properly cared for. Health and spirits revived.

When the inventor returned to America, however, Lovell could only surrender one patent, the case-maker, for the worthless note, having already contracted with T.W. & C.B. Sheridan to manufacture and sell the other machines on a royalty basis. Lovell himself then returned to more dependable printing and bindery business, which he continued for many years. Bredenberg, however, was not forgotten. Sheridan quickly recognized the value of taking the inventor along with his machinery, and quietly surrounded him with mountains of work (p 230). As for the trade, at first, only someone examining the patents themselves would really have known the potential value of the Bredenberg equipment. For Charles Juengst they were required reading.[3]

Charles A. Juengst (pronounced "Yengst") was born January 2, 1859, in New York city, where he spent his early boyhood. His father, George Juengst, a German, had patented—of all things—a sewing machine which he began to manufacture in the 1860's. The "Empire" sewer became so successful, apparently, Juengst could no longer produce it in cramped New York quarters. About 1864 he bought property at Croton Falls, New York, where he remodeled some old mill buildings and blocked the Muscoot River to obtain the best water-power in the county. His masonry dam, bolted and cemented, had stones weighing up to 4 tons; water racing through its narrow gorge soon wore "fantastic shapes" in the solid rock bed. This sound and colorful factory complex he named "Empireville."

In 1866 Juengst formed the Empire Sewing Machine Company, and with 70 to 100 workers began production at once. Raw materials came in from Katonah, a stop on the Harlem Railroad, and 80–100 finished machines per week were shipped from there to New York. We have already seen what a thriving business was the sewing machine industry.

About 1870, however, the city of New York bought considerable real estate nearby for reservoir development; Juengst's precious water-power suddenly disappeared. "The gigantic wheel," said an old account, "which, with its systems of cogs and belts, gave the hum of busy trade to the numerous lathes and spindles in the great factory, ceased its revolutions." (Why Juengst could not profitably convert his prosperous plant to steam power is curious.) He sold his sewing machine rights, along with the property, to the Remington family of Ilion, New York (where typewriters would soon be manufactured); a "merged" Remington-Empire sewing machine was produced for many years thereafter. Juengst, nevertheless, was out of the sewing machine race.

Juengst relocated nearby, on the Croton River, again with good waterpower. Here he commenced making machine tools and steel planers for the growing machining trade. In 1884 he shifted his shops to another site a half mile upstream, retained until 1927. For this factory Juengst—having waited out the age of steampower—in 1894 installed electric generators powerful enough to fill his needs and still supply the neighboring community with electricity. With about 20 employees Juengst did a modest machine-shop business as his sons George Jr. grew to become an expert machinist and businessman, and Charles began to develop his special genius for mechanical invention. The Juengst family lived until 1893—when reservoir needs again took the property—in an old homestead of Enoch Crosby, the Revolutionary War spy portrayed in Fenimore Cooper's *The Spy*. George Juengst died in 1905, but his sons carried on the firm with its original name, George Juengst & Sons.

Charles Juengst's first patent, and dozens of others through the

Sheridan case-making machine about 1915, designed by Bredenberg. Note roll of cloth feeding from left, and stacks of pre-cut binder's board. Earlier version required pre-cut cloth. [Sheridan catalog]

following thirty years, were improvements to machine shop equipment: Variable Reciprocating Planer-Motion (1884), Shaping and Slotting Machine (1890), Self-Adjusting Feed Mechanism (1894), Metal Planer (1899), Cold-Metal-Sawing Machine (1905), and so on. His Cold-Metal-Saw Blade (1904) was exactly the blade used today in portable electric circular saws. Most of these patents, assigned to the Higley Machine Company of Croton Falls, a tool manufacturer, were fully and immediately useful.

Around 1886 Juengst began to tinker with a mechanical adding machine, working out its major elements in about 8 months. In 1893 he patented a Cash Register and Indicator which engineer John E. Kingman magnanimously considered "basic" to all cash registers, although the National Cash Register Company, Dayton, Ohio, had by the 1890's already been making machines for almost 10 years—successfully fending off over 80 competitors without Juengst's help. Notwithstanding, Juengst's interests, like those of most prolific inventors of his time, recognized no territorial bounds: he also developed several improvements to the internal combustion engine (1917) although he felt automobiles still too chimerical for serious attention.

"One thousand feet up the river" from his father's shops was another building where young Juengst carried on his major bindery experimentation. This work Kingman (noting that *The Patent Office Gazette* was gathered, stitched, and covered on a Juengst machine) characterized as establishing Juengst not merely a dreamer, but "an inventor of the useful class." Here he did not dabble or tinker; here the inventor—after frequent hours on his father's little bridge over the Croton River, watching the waters cascade and thinking out his plans step by step—applied himself determinedly almost throughout his life in a steady program of bindery machinery development.

Juengst first fabricated a gathering machine which he apparently built exclusively for—and to the specifications of—Frank Munsey in 1901. Similar machines, weighing 8 tons, were soon made for Sears, Roebuck & Company, and the New York Telephone Company. With these custom installations Juengst, like David Smyth, may have realized there was profit in a new bindery revolution he himself might engineer. Patent after patent, undoubtedly engendered by the Munsey work, followed with dogged regularity:

768,461   Signature-Gathering Machine (1904)*
761,496   Signature-Gatherer (1904)
763,673   Stop Mechanism [to deflect imperfect signatures] (1904)
768,462   Pneumatic Sheet-Separator (1904)
768,463   Curved Plate for [delivery of] Signatures or Sheets (1904)

*Patent date; patents are listed in order of filing.

779,784  Paper-Feeding Mechanism (1905)
789,095  Signature or Paper-Sheet Separating Apparatus (1905)
783,206  Sucker Device for Signature or Sheet-Gathering Machines (1905)
813,215  Stapling-Machine (1906)
828,665  Signature-Gathering Machine (1906)
846,923  Signature-Conveying and Wire-Stitching Machine (1907)
893,510  Signature-Gathering Machine (1908)

Utilizing virtually all of his first 12 binding-machine patents, Juengst's Gatherer-Collator was heralded in 1907 as "astonishing and revolutionary." Featured were "Four operations [gathering, collating, jogging, stitching] at one and the same time, consequently a great saving of time and labor." Replacing 15–20 girls, it needed only one feeder for every 6 boxes, and one porter to carry off finished books. Because of its unique ability to detect faulty signatures, it turned out "perfect books only." In a time of heavy reliance on testimonial advertising, Juengst boasted three machines at the US Government Printing Office (doing the *Congressional Record* as well as the *Gazette*), and pairs of them at several New York binderies.

At the Hill Publishing Company (publishers of several industrial and technical magazines before merging book operations in 1909 with the similar McGraw Publishing Company), the Juengst, like all other equipment entering this scientifically coordinated plant, had to be painted white as an aid to safety and efficiency. But at the Trow plant visiting reporters were transported into absolute wonderment watching the whirring of the Juengst and Sheridan innovations.

John F. Trow (1809–1886) began his first print shop in 1834. Issuing a sumptuous 1856 specimen book (title page in 5 colors, frontispiece in 7), he boasted machine-set composition and Adams improved power presses—the first in New York on both counts—the latter already printing for D. Appleton & Company (particularly *New American Cyclopedia*, the largest original work in the United States to that time), as well as for Scribner's, Harper's, Putnam's, and other New York and Boston publishers. With bookbinder Jonathan Leavitt, Daniel

JOHN F. TROW

Appleton's brother-in-law, he began publishing a commercial New York city directory (1847) which grew to four separate tomes annually—a substantial bindery operation.

In 1870 Trow was somehow forced to surrender ownership for a short while to a Tammany-controlled management which renamed it the New York Printing Company. (When *Harper's* magazine attacked the political party the New York Board of Education was ordered to reject all Harper bids and to destroy $50,000 worth of Harper textbooks on hand; New York Printing got the coveted business.) In 1901, having bought the Brooklyn plant jettisoned by Appleton—and with it a contract to manufacture all Appleton work—the Trow Directory, Printing and Binding Company found the Appleton bindery still ideal (had not Matthews designed it?) for long-run bookwork. Trow's own gigantic Manhattan shop was also a model of efficiency: the bindery, with 9 Smyth sewers ("without which no modern bindery can expect to compete successfully") and numerous folders, culminated with 2 Juengst gathering machines and 2 Sheridan coverers.

To a *Printing Trade News* reporter the Trow plant manager said of the Juengst: "It never fails to grasp the sheets, and should a signature be defective in any way the machine will stop automatically and an indicator show which signature is the offending one." Similarly, another visitor reached philosophical heights over the tandem performance of this equipment:

> "As the writer stood with the foreman of the bindery and watched the working of these two remarkable machines and listened to the glowing eulogy bestowed on both for their simplicity of construction, intelligence of operation and economy of production, he could not help marveling at the great change that has taken place in the printing business through the advent of the various labor-saving—dollar saving! —machines, and wondering where it was all going to stop, his perplexity being heightened by the operation of this wonderful Juengst gatherer that goes around and, with almost human intelligence, gathers up the sheets of a magazine, carries them along mechanically and at the end of their journey stitches them with wire and turns them out at the rate of seventy-five a minute. The Juengst machine having done all this, the stitched magazines are automatically fed into Sheridan's covering machine, which, with equal intelligence, simplicity, speed and economy, glues, covers and completes the binding operation."[4]

Juengst, now 48, had too much work to enjoy reportorial reflections and speculations. His patents now included "conventional" wire-stitching and machine-sewing techniques—the Juengst family experience with sewing machines giving him added perspective. His solutions for wire-stitching multiple-signature books (complicated with staggered rows of single staples perpendicular or diagonal to the spine, each straddling two sections) and for thread sewing (far more complex than Smyth's) were, however, never exploited:

893,511   Stapled Signature for Books (1908)
893,512   Method of Sewing Signatures to Form Books (1908)
893,513   Method of Sewing Signatures to Form Books (1908)

Suddenly the Juengst company found occasion to institute infringement proceedings against Gullberg and Smith over the use of Juengst's "Detector or Caliper." The court in 1909 examined Juengst's patents and a small display model, the latter "to my mind [said the judge], . . . of little practical benefit." He considered neither party pioneer of the caliper device, and Juengst lost his case. Gullberg and Smith users— Munsey, Butterick, Tapley, Donnelley, US GPO, and others—were somewhat relieved, since Juengst had sought to hold accountable both sellers and operators of infringing equipment. A year later, however, Juengst returned with a reversed decision by a higher court, obliging Gullberg and Smith to provide past and future customers with a stop mechanism they "believed" simpler and more reliable. "We Win!" said a single Juengst advertisement, gleefully, in 1910—without a trace of the German accent with which Juengst would have uttered those words. The brothers again resumed their serious work.

Like Bredenberg, Charles Juengst was not satisfied to create a single device which, once completed, would perform a single function. He was instead attempting to perfect an entire system of operations formerly handled separately in the bindery: stitching, glueing, covering, trimming—all to be executed automatically, continuously, and perfectly. He had admittedly borrowed the straight-through concept from Bredenberg, but he had made it his own obsession too.

In 1910 Juengst topped his 1907 announcements by offering a combination machine with "Five operations [gathering, collating, jogging, stitching, covering] at one and the same time. Production on Magazines, Pamphlets, Catalogs, etc., 3,000 to 3,500 books per hour." In three sizes, 7 x 10, 9 x 12, and 10 x 14 inches, the 15,850-pound machine, making 60–90 revolutions per minute, manufactured magazines, by the firm's own calculations, at a rate of 20 for about 1 cent. "No inventor has yet put on the market a machine into one end of which the materials may be dumped and from the other end a finished book taken," said *Inland Printer* that year, with a nervous glance at Croton Falls. "Still, the advances made in automatic machinery during the past few years have been tremendous. . . ."

As if to apply greater persuasion to prospective customers by deed rather than promotion (a tactical error, perhaps; George Juengst &

C. A. JUENGST.
SIGNATURE GATHERER.
APPLICATION FILED MAY 15, 1901

NO MODEL.

2 SHEETS—SHEET 1.

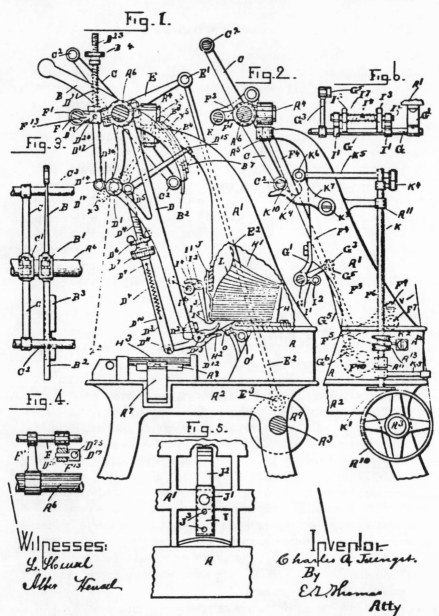

Fig. 1.

Fig. 2.

Fig. 6.

Fig. 3.

Fig. 4.

Fig. 5.

Witnesses:

Inventor
Charles A. Juengst.
By
E. L. Thomas
Atty

Sons—without the original "Empireville" flair—used no agents and advertised only modestly), Juengst again returned to his laboratory.

| | |
|---|---|
| 1,029,130 | Gripper (developed 1907, patented 1912) |
| 1,126,026 | Delivery Mechanism for Signature-Gathering or Other Machine (1908; 1915) |
| 1,040,689 | Signature-Gathering Machine (1908; 1912) |
| 1,109,127 | Signature-Gathering Machine (1908; 1914) |
| 1,071,555 | Signature-Gathering Machine (1909; 1913) |
| 1,049,492 | Signature-Gathering Machine (1909; 1913) |
| 1,193,395 | Book or Pamphlet Covering Machine (1910; 1916) |
| 1,023,568 | Signature-Gathering Machine (1911; 1912) |
| 1,023,569 | Device for Applying Adhesive Material to the Backs of Books in Covering Machines (1911; 1912) |
| 1,055,639 | Machine for Feeding Sheets to Folders, Presses, Etc. (1911; 1913) |
| 1,068,778 | Signature-Gathering or Other Machine (1911; 1913) |

In December 1912 Juengst revealed a Gatherer-Stitcher-Coverer capable of 3000 hourly, and a Gatherer-Binder doing 2500 (later 3000, with five operators). With surprising audacity in January he altered his half-page *Inland Printer* advertisement to rename the second of these machines the "Gatherer-Perfect Binder" ("on which a flat open book is produced. . . ."). But unsure perhaps whether Sheridan—barely six months ahead of him (p 232)—had proprietory rights to the term "perfect binding," Juengst in February rechristened it again, "Wireless Binder," a name he maintained thereafter, although he frequently had to explain that it did "Perfect Binding, so called."

Significant was Juengst's aim that all three of his latest machines (gatherer-collator, jogger-stitcher, wireless-binder) could be used separately or connected in tandem to perform the complete manufacture of a magazine or pamphlet; there was an option, of course, in obtaining a stitched or stitchless product with the complete equipment. (Ironically, "pamphlet" derives from the French *par filet*, "[sewed] with thread"; similarly "brochure" is from the French *brocher*, "to stitch.") In a 1913 testimonial the Charles Francis Press, New York, one of 9 early purchasers of the triple combination, said:

> "In the matter of your combined gatherer, wire stitcher and covering machine, which you placed in our establishment somewhere about four years since, we can say that for a machine that accomplishes so

Juengst's gatherer patent containing his important "Detector or Caliper." In Figure 1, plates $B^3$ and $B^4$ jam if suction cup o (beneath signatures) takes an incorrect thickness from the bottom of a stack of signatures ($H^1$). [US Patent] much, our product has been entirely satisfactory and fully up to your statements. Trouble has been a minimum.

"We should be pleased to say a good word for the machine any time or to show it running in our establishment.

"Our second machine has been in about two years."[5]

While the Sheridan company did indeed claim ownership of the term "perfect binding," the process of binding books without thread or wire was far from novel to binders, and often far from perfect in its execution.

As early as 1836 William Hancock, one of five English brothers all of whom pioneered in the uses of "India rubber," described caoutchouc or rubber applied to the trimmed edge of a book after the fold was cut away. The individual sheets were rounded with a concave forming tool, rasped to give roughness to the spine edge, and moistened with a thin latex (uncured rubber) solution. When dry, a slightly stronger rubber solution was painted on, sometimes up to four applications. With the last coating a cloth strip was cemented to the spine which, when dry, would have boards glued to it, whereby ". . . books so bound," said Hancock in his patent, "are made to open perfectly flat, or more nearly so than books bound by any other method heretofore in use. (Perfect flatness seems to have engendered the later, unnecessarily controversial name, "perfect" binding; adding to the confusion was the papermaker's label "perfect paper" for a ream of 516 sheets, and the printer's use of "perfect" to describe a sheet printed on both sides.

Although we should today be delighted to find a caoutchouc binding in any condition, Hancock's first effort, Richie, *Versailles: Picturesque and Romantic* (1839), was discovered by Middleton in 1963 to be "falling apart." Nevertheless, the technique was popular: George Dodd, visiting Westley & Clark in 1843, found their "caoutchouc-shop" enjoying a steady demand for india-rubber bindings. One of the first monumental works to attract wide attention to threadless binding, auspiciously, was Wyatt, *The Industrial Arts of the Nineteenth Century* (2 volumes, Day & Son, 1853), commemorating both the 1851 Exposition and the industrial revolution itself. An impressive 19 x 13-inch collection of chromolithographic plates, McLean found it "too big and heavy ever to be easily looked at." Like ornate binding, however, sheer grossness too has often protected a book from hasty, impulsive destruction.

In the United States William Matthews' award-winning *Alhambra*, shown as we have seen, at the Crystal Palace, was 23½ x 16½ inches, and nearly 3 inches thick. Bound with rubber, it was, according to Matthews in 1885, despite its weight and size, easy to open, lying perfectly flat, and durable: "Contrary to the usual result of rubber binding," said Matthews, "though this heavy volume has been used for thirty-four years, every leaf is as firmly bound as when exhibited in 1853." Similarly, Charles Goodyear extolled the virtues of rubber for books, in 1855 issuing one made entirely—pages and covers—out of rubber, although sewn conventionally. In 1945 it was almost irretrievably stuck together.

The London house of Matthew Bell was licensed to perform the patented caoutchouc work. This shop, begun in 1843 by an apprentice to Leighton named Eeles, was among the first to install (not without sharp labor problems) machines for backing and trimming; it bound the 1851 Exposition catalog—the first copies so tardy the black and blue cover ink, not yet dry, came off on people's gloves, cheeks, and noses. In 1867 Matthew Bell (brother of publisher George Bell) joined as partner, and assumed complete control by 1870. Bell highly recommended the India-rubber process for large atlases and plate books, permitting a *Bookbinder* reporter in 1890 to test some samples "with a result that satisfied us that the ordinary overcasting could not compare with this system. . . ." Others were also impressed enough to seek similar adhesive compounds to circumvent the Hancock patent (p 235).

Caoutchouc was much appreciated both in England and the United States for its flexibility and durability, characteristics which depend greatly on the purity of the rubber. It was a fairly expensive process. As long as the cement remained flexible, the integrity of the book was safe. Although many formulas, including gutta percha (like rubber, the gum of a tropical tree) were tried, they were not suitable. When the adhesive dried, the book disintegrated. "Many a handsome Victorian volume is now a dismembered wreck," McLean wrote, and in John Carter's words, the whole concept was "hideously unsatisfactory." Its loss of public acceptance for good books occurred simultaneously with that of the wire stitcher. Also at work destroying the reputation for adhesive binding was the hand binder's admitted expedient, called "fiddling," similarly securing the leaves of a book by animal glue only.

It is possible that a chemist would see in these developments the likely approach of improving rubber solutions or finding better substitutes. Charles Juengst, however, was not a chemist; when he met resistance he returned to his engineering shops and turned out more mechanical devices:

| | | |
|---|---|---|
| 1,200,200 | Paper-Cutting Machine (developed 1913; patented 1916) |
| 1,244,861 | Pamphlet-Coverer (1913; 1917) |
| 1,215,547 | Conveyer (1914; 1917) |
| 1,195,926 | Web Feeding and Cutting Device (1914; 1916) |
| 1,232,560 | Sheet-Feeding Machine (1914; 1917) |

1,277,939   Adhesive-Applying Device (1914; 1918)
1,313,487   Delivery Mechanism (1914; 1919)
1,275,988   Delivery Mechanism (1916; 1918)
1,277,217   Delivery Mechanism (1916; 1918)
1,280,753   Grooving [backs of books] Device (1916; 1918)
1,389,762   Book Covering and Binding Machine (1919; 1921)
1,394,309   Cutting Mechanism [for books] (1919; 1921)

Juengst had tackled little problems one by one. In one patent (No.
1,277,939) he found it "advantageous to heat the book before the glue
is applied"; in another (No. 1,023,569), with an auxiliary roller, he
made an end of "hot glue [forming] long globules or lines,—called
'whiskers' in the trade,—which drop and smear up other parts of the
machine." These enabled him to present grand solutions for bigger
problems. No. 1,244,861 consisted of 10 pages of text and 15 pages of
accompanying plates:

"The present invention . . . has for its main object the provision of means whereby the book to be covered may have the back cut off and roughened, an adhesive applied to the back, a reinforcing strip attached to the back, and a cover applied, all while the book is traveling continuously."[6]

(No. 1,193,395 had done the same continuously, but for a stitched book and hence without cutting and roughening the back.) But the complications of multiple, continuous, coordinated motion was undoubtedly consuming; the Juengst brothers had already spent too much time in the shop.

In 1916 the American Assembling Machine Company, formed by a group of Memphis, Tennessee, businessmen headed by J.H.T. Martin, took over George Juengst & Sons. According to inventor and engineer Paul E. Kleineberg, who had serviced—and improved—Juengst's Patent Office installation (and with American Assembling went along to

Sheridan-Juengst gathering machine (*rear*) and Sheridan automatic side-wire stitcher. A third machine, a coverer (*not shown*) can be added to the line—for a total length of over 52 feet—for complete periodical manufacture. [The Sheridan Company]

Sheridan), the Memphis company, unsure of developments outside the newspaper industry, had independently named the process of gathering (and itself) "assembling." Nevertheless, Juengst's gathering machines, collators, stitchers, pamphlet-covering machines, and binders (in addition to American Assembling's own gatherers, stitchers, coverers, and newspaper stuffing machines—the last used to insert separately printed sections so as to assemble a complete newspaper) continued to be manufactured at the Croton Falls plant until 1927, when a new factory was built at Easton, Pennsylvania. Juengst's continuous side-stitcher was with new vigor claimed to be the only one capable of driving 1, 2, 3, or 4 staples without stopping the book's movement through the machine. American Assembling also made the Cahen rounding and casing-in machine (p 313).

In this merger Charles A. Juengst, now 57, remained as consulting engineer, but continued to live at Croton Falls until about 1931, when he died. Ironically, Juengst and Bredenberg had strong professional admiration for each other, but the former's death precluded, by just a few years, the possibility of their working together for the same company. George Juengst, Jr., who also served as member and president of the North Salem, New York, Board of Education for over half a century, died in 1939.

The number of major machines manufactured at Croton Falls and Easton cannot easily determined, although in the three decades involved they probably did not exceed 25 per year. Five 20-pocket gatherers turned up in France in 1926 (distributed by Smyth-Horne) where their automatic assembling of 70 books per minute was a spectacular anachronism in the French bindery. Elsewhere these machines, labeled "epoch-making" by veteran binders, were truly the workhorses their creators claimed, many of them still in use throughout the United States today.

The American Assembling Machine Company soon removed its headquarters to Memphis, but was quickly in trouble when the depression struck. Sheridan in 1933 acquired all rights to Juengst machines and other American Assembling properties, including the Easton factory. Larry Martin, a son, with some remaining adhesive-binding and newspaper machinery assets in Chicago joined the Dexter Company (known for a few years as Dexter-Martin). Sheridan nevertheless now dominated the perfect-binding market—such as it was.

The T.W. & C.B. Sheridan Company had not ignored the growing periodical industry by any means. As agents it had carried, simultaneously, the Gullberg and Smith, and the British Mercer gathering machines, although long litigation with Juengst over the caliper device had been a costly drain—a trap for any sales agent who could not control the legal rights and claims to machinery as designs evolved. Sheridan also offered the "Lovel-Bredenberg [sic] Automatic Book Covering Machine—the only pamphlet covering machine on the market," by its misspelling obviously unhappy paying royalties to the originators from its $3500 pricetag, despite impressive production records at *Munsey's, Cosmopolitan,* and *Godey's.* Sheridan had not long before seen the value of developing and manufacturing its own products. Reliance on independent inventors would always be expensive and unpredictable; as trade requirements grew more complex, individuals, however gifted, would not likely possess the experience or capital to succeed with any idea.

In 1887, having outgrown its New York shop, Sheridan bought half interest in a foundry at Champlain, New York, coincidentally only five miles from Lovell's Rouses Point enterprise. One of the last of many neighborhood founders making farm tools and other small items, James Averill, Jr., owner and manager, was desperate for more substantial work. Sheridan, apparently looking for such a shop, was quick to respond, disregarding what must have been very questionable logistics: with poor local ore, iron pigs were shipped in via Buffalo; coal was transported upstate on Lake Champlain; only sand was available nearby. A long railroad haul brought finished machinery to New York or Boston (Sheridan's reputed heaviness in castings for the sake of strength and stability would spell even higher shipping tolls). The Sheridan Iron Works was nevertheless a reality.

A half interest in the plant, however, was only a half step forward. As with Sanborn-Standard, the relationship between Sheridan and Averill was one of only partial commitment: patent rights were scrupulously divided between them—until the 1920's, when Sheridan finally acquired complete ownership. Both Sheridan and Sanborn would have agreed that manufacturing bookbinding equipment exclusively through the 19th century was risky specialization. Like bookbinding work itself, the unique machinery was largely useless for any other trade or purpose. As characterized by its 1927 advertisement, as we have seen, Sheridan only at that late date had fully committed itself to the manufacturing and sales of bookbinding machinery—and had the boldness to state to the trade that unusual decision. By that time, of course, the company had much in its favor.

Principal items manufactured by Sheridan in the early 1890's, as we have seen, were paper cutters: Alexander Malm, a New York inventor, had assigned his five consecutive patents 1890–1892, and Charles L. Smith assigned one in 1894. These were apparently instrumental in permitting Sheridan to exhibit so magnificently at the 1893 Columbian Exposition. Such cutters, however, were approaching a state of sophis-

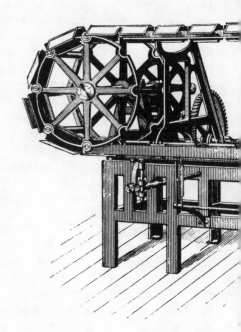

The Sheridan Perfect-Binder, about 1915. "Very similar in construction to the Covering Machine," the company explained, *"will bind and put covers on Pamphlets without thread or wire,* and make a flat opening and serviceable book." [Sheridan catalog]

tication possibly beyond Averill's inclinations (the company gradually abandoned guillotine cutters about 1930); he and his simply equipped shop were reaching their limit. Alfred Bredenberg's new patents for combination stitching, glueing, covering, trimming, binding equipment —a nightmare of interrelated machine cycles, speeds, strokes, strains, and tolerances—would be unfathomable to all but the inventor himself. Although he at first furnished instructions from Brooklyn (his home was near T.W.'s; C.B. lived in Orange, New Jersey—was it he who introduced neighbor Smyth to bookbinding problems?) when he entered Sheridan's employ in 1894, Bredenberg was soon asked to move to Champlain. A year later, 40 years old, Bredenberg became chief engineer of the Sheridan Iron Works, a post he held for about 35 years. Averill was so glad to have him he secured a house in town and saw to it that the inventor and his large family had every comfort.

Bredenberg's first problem in the Champlain shop was the poor state of tools and equipment. Like Juengst, he first constructed many special machine tools. He had to design an elliptical gear-cutting machine (essential for the paper cutters), since no commercial machinery maker

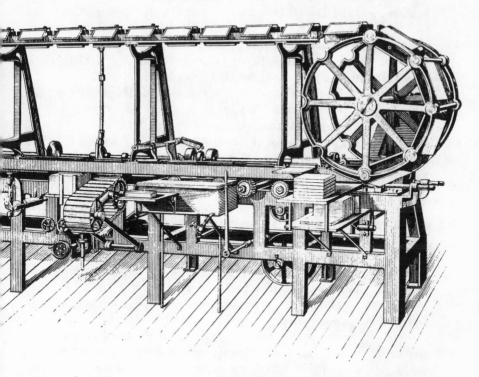

cared for the job. As his own bookbinding equipment came off the assembly line Bredenberg, like Smyth, would be obliged to follow it around the country, traveling for months on end to show new customers how to use it. Frequently he was recalled during years of labor disputes when workers sabotaged the machinery—often by no more than tossing a cup of oil into the glue pot. His fanatical love for solving mechanical problems—happy to work almost without remuneration—was a consuming inventor's weakness. Nevertheless, Bredenberg's royalties from the case-maker helped pay for the little house, and between business and family he enjoyed some measure of happiness at last. He even found time for fresh inventions:

816,708   Paper-Cutting Machine (1906)
821,079   Embossing Press (1906)
821,080   Book Trimmer (1906)

Many such bookbinding inventions continued until 1918. The Sheridan sales force, meanwhile, had been at work marketing Bredenberg's early machinery with fair success. The Lovell-inspired equipment began to appear in 1895, the date to which the company traces its perfect-binding experience. *World Almanac*, Montgomery, Ward, Donnelley, Munsey, and the US GPO were, not surprisingly, first customers for the $6500 pamphlet-covering machine. The 1908 Book and Covering machine ("No brushes. No glue pots. Great saving in glue. . . .") could handle 22,000 pieces daily; Butterick took 7, Munsey 4, Harper's 2, Street & Smith 4, Trow 2, and the US GPO had one as well.

In 1911 Sheridan proclaimed the culmination of design for the periodical publisher—Bredenberg's masterpiece. For magazines the company announced its "Perfect" binder, capable of between 1400 and 2000 books per hour, under the control of one man with three girls. Eighteen feet long and elliptical in shape, the machine had 30 pairs of vertical clamps or jaws traveling continuously; as each pair approached one of the girls it opened to receive, fed by hand, one complete issue (without cover); the work was then carried to a horizontal knife which cut off the folds; then roughened by a small circular saw to receive adhesive. A piece of mull (crash), and the cover, were picked up and slapped onto the wet spine. The Sheridan "automatically binds and covers in one operation," said an advertisement, "dispensing with wire or thread, and at the same time turns out a flat opening book." It was— or could be—"The Perfect way to bind a magazine," but, as with India-rubber, the adhesive was the key factor.

Glue—the gelatinous substance obtained from boiled animal skins, sinews, bones, or hoofs—was known and used for centuries. Applied hot, it penetrates paper, cloth, leather, and wood fibres and dries positively, firmly. For binders it came granulated (soak in water before heating; but if soaked too long, bacterial action decomposes it); it was available bleached (the acid treatment also reduced its strength), or opaque (adulterated with colors). It might get frozen (discard; frozen glue never regains its strength); it might get frothy (erroneously considered "live" when it bubbles, froth actually indicates fat and acid impurities); it might get overheated (above 140–150°F it deteriorates). Plain brown untampered glue was best; when pure it was called "hard" and with additives like glycerine it could be made "flexible." For bookwork needs, binderies usually kept two or three glue pots heated constantly, and with only minor unpleasantries: "The perfume(?) shed by a glue kettle burning dry was something one *never* forgets," said an old-timer.

In 1923 a committee of the National Association of Glue Manufacturers began to study and classify glues then on the market. Based on viscosity and gel strength (1 percent or more gelatin in a glue will form a firm gel), they found that hide made better glue than bone, and adopted a range of 21 grades with "21" best at a gel strength of over 600 grams. Such industry self-regulation removed much of the secrecy and mystery remaining from centuries of obscure trade customs. But glue was not so easily tamed; tricks of the trade were still sufficiently elusive to the uninitiated to require slavish attention:

"SOME GLUE DONT'S

Don't heat flexible glue over 145 degrees—important.

Don't have glue department or bindery under 70 degrees—prevents chilling.

Don't use soap or oil on cutting machine knives, especially for tabbing —prevents sticking.

Don't throw pieces of glue into glue machine tanks unless properly dissolved—makes bubbles and foam.

Don't put ground glue in with dissolved flexible glue unless it is properly dissolved first, then add—this prevents stringiness.

Don't use glue *too heavy*, especially on tabbing glue. Two thin coats give better results.

Don't use *scalding hot* water in mixing glue or thinning it—lukewarm.

Don't fail to read directions on flexible glue packages."[7]

"Animal glue is best for you," rhymed the glue association perhaps with forced jollity in 1931, but so it seemed for many years. Sheridan, unlike Juengst, had with a forceful sales organization interested many of the biggest publishing houses—not in machines, simply—but systems of complete bindery operations. For Sheridan too, the chemistry of adhesives would be all the more crucial. But there were few chemists anywhere in this engineer-oriented world of mechanical ingenuity.

The Curtis Publishing Company, Philadelphia, was obviously a prime customer for the perfect binder. Cyrus H. K. Curtis with a weekly, *People's Ledger* (begun 1872)—noteworthy in that each issue contained a complete novel—had perceived well the potential of mass magazines. His *Ladies' Home Journal* with 25,000 subscriptions in 1883 swelled to 200,000 in a few years, then (after doubling its format) to 1 million in 1893. *The Saturday Evening Post*, acquired 1897, was also a growing enterprise: for it in 1909 Curtis ordered four 56-page Hoe rotary web perfectors equipped with folders, wire stitchers, and—a breakthrough for automation—a special feed mechanism to introduce the magazine's customary "high-grade covers" (card stock preprinted in 2–4 colors) and advertising inserts, so that the complete issue could be entirely manufactured on the press. (This venerable publication expired 1969, largely a victim of television.)

The *Ladies' Home Journal*, however, only two years after the installation of the Chambers combination machine, as we have seen, was again in trouble. New four-color sheet-fed presses, two-color rotaries, and one-color presses with folding attachments were again delivering too fast for the bindery. Curtis appealed to Sheridan for a solution. With Bredenberg already at work on the concept of a straight-through, combination "threadless" binder, the company was well disposed to respond, although the completion of such a machine would still take two years more. For Curtis Sheridan about 1911 built one of the first perfect-binders: with a crew of 10 to handle, in addition, a special prepositioned gatherer, and 20 collection boxes, it could bind up to 12,000 magazines in a 9½-hour day. (The special gatherer may have been the child of Paul Gitzendanner, Jr., engineer for the Butterick bindery, chief novelty of which was a method of rejecting a defective book without stopping.)

At about the same time Sheridan furnished perfect binders to Butterick (for *Everybody's Magazine*) and Country Life Press (*World's Work Magazine*), the latter, turning out copies prior to March 1911, possibly the very first in operation. These were the undisputed marvels of the bindery world—behemoths to match the mammoth presses of 50 years before. With them Sheridan daringly had committed itself to machinery for exploiting long runs of ephemeral work—at a time when short high-quality runs were much more common.

The Sheridan "mechanical contrivance" for threadless binding quickly found its way to England in the hands of C. B. Sheridan, who personally directed the European market. He sold a gatherer to George Newnes, and then the controversial coverer-binder itself, first used there (also 1911) on *The Strand Magazine*, an illustrated 6-penny monthly begun in 1891 by Newnes in imitation of *Harper's*. At the turn of the century *The Strand* had become so popular it was said that every other person on a British train was likely to be reading it. In its twenty-first "majority" anniversary in 1911 the magazine complimented itself for having introduced Sherlock Holmes to the world and apologized for its heavy advertising (a "necessary evil" to its editors), but like literary people everywhere, found its own manufacture—in its own plant—too mundane (or too complex?) to describe. The perspicacious London *Times*, however, in its classic 1912 "Printing Number," had not missed the importance of the new *Strand* production equipment:

"An ingenious machine, known as the Sheridan 'Perfect Binder,' is used for binding the *Strand Magazine*, and, when seen by the writer at Messrs. Newnes' premises, was working at a rate averaging about 1,400 copies per hour. This machine, which has revolutionized the methods of binding magazines, secures the leaves by processes similar to those of the indiarubber binding, patented many years ago by Mr. Hancock. . . ."[8]

(*The Strand,* also a victim of modern communications, ceased publication 1950.)[9]

But the new adhesive binding process still had a serious flaw—the glue. When applied to the backs of perfect-bound books animal glue failed dismally, all the more exasperating because the trouble was often undetected until the product was in the buyer's hands. Juengst's "whiskers" were nothing so insidious as adhesive that would not hold. The problem was in the fibers of the paper and the flexibility of the glue.

Merchandise catalogs and telephone directories, manufactured on the perfect binder, had actually been eminently successful. Needed in tremendous quantities, these books were given away free and were seldom expected to last more than a year. The selection of cheap, coarse text papers—not much better than newsprint—provided the perfect-binding process with stocks most receptive to the glue. Loose fibers further roughened by the machine's cutters ensured sufficient penetration of glue to hold under almost all conditions.

Magazine publishers, however, could not use the cheap papers. They needed smooth, slick, calendered stock for whiteness, fine halftone and color printing, and appeal to the eye and hand. These papers, unfortunately, demonstrated no similar attraction for glue. Because of this, an unprecedented degree of care in the handling of perfect-binding glue would be essential if it were to work for the periodicals. Marian Lawson, then Managing Director of Sheridan's British affiliate, reminisced:

"The Newnes machine in its experimental stages was still under the care of Sheridan, and we had a lot of difficulty in persuading the operators and those responsible to give the requisite attention to the glue. We had to persuade them that it was not enough to throw slabs of hard glue into the tanks, and then add hot water to melt it. The glues for the Sheridan 'Perfect Binder' at Newnes [ultimately] were especially prepared with various ingredients, including rubber, and were mixed to special formulae. . . ."[10]

The search for better adhesives than simple animal glue was of critical importance. But research in this area had been painfully limited.

Original "hard" animal glue had to be "softened" usually with glycerine, to make it flexible. Other compounds—rubber, gutta percha, isinglass, resin, shellac, linseed oil, varnish—had also been tried in various attempts to avoid licensing fees attached to Hancock's patent; Archibald Leighton himself is reported to have used treacle for this purpose. A Londoner, E. W. Edwardson, toward the end of the 19th century, while working for Roderick Horne, developed a flexible glue for use on the lining machine; he thereupon formed his own company (still in business) to exploit it. Such additives, being hygroscopic, simply hold moisture—especially during periods of low humidity—preventing the glue from ever really drying. Flexible animal glue has long been used successfully in "glueing-off" the spine of hard-bound books; it is applied immediately after sewing (to help keep the stitches in place) and is flexible enough to endure the rounding and backing operations which follow.

Because of the nation-wide distribution of the American mass magazine, however, minimal flexibility was not sufficient, and special formula compounds were prohibitively expensive. In cold climates the glue became stiff; the spine cracked and broke into segments upon use. In hot climates the glue never really set at all, and individual pages fell out as if scarcely touched by the adhesive. *Ladies' Home Journal*, in the face of ruthless competition, could not risk the glue pot's infidelity, and returned to side-wire stitching, its tight mechanical grip at least security against fragmentation. India rubber a half century before had done no worse. Yet so tempting was the idea of cheaply manufactured mass-produced magazines by this method, that the wrath of periodical readers (perhaps not so vehement as irate book lovers) was repeatedly courted.

Sheridan continued to advertise as if there were no glue problem at all. The 1913 announcement of its Circular Coverer (40 books per minute; 12-inch model, $3500, 16½-inch, $4500) offered a saving of 50 percent on glue, since "numerous glue pots and brushes are dispensed with." Claims that year were indeed impressive:

"Three Million New York Telephone Books Covered in One Year on Sheridan 16½ in. Circular Covering Machines;

One and Three-Quarter Million 'Ladies' Home Journals' Bound and Gathered [but not actually perfect-bound] Every Month on Sheridan 16½ in. Combination Binders and Gatherers;

Over a Million 'Cosmopolitan Magazines' Covered Every Month on Sheridan 12 in. Horizontal Coverers;

Five Million Sears, Roebuck Mail-Order Catalogs Bound in One Year on Sheridan 14½ in. 'Perfect Binders.' "[11]

With almost no exception, said a Sheridan advertisement, all large magazines, mail-order catalogs, and telephone directories were being bound or covered on Sheridan equipment. Aside from the popular slick magazines, whose managements were understandly unhappy with perfect binding, the remaining catalog and directory work was indeed suitable and sufficiently large in volume to justify Sheridan's marketing campaigns. And no one knew better than they that there was risk in their growing commitment to long-run bindery work. Until the adhesive problem were solved, however, the "quality" periodical publishers would never be interested.

There were some adhesives of merit that did not derive from animal materials. Arabol, invented in Germany about 1891 was the first of a family of flexible vegetable glues. The Arabol Manufacturing Company, New York, introduced it to America in 1897 for padding and other minor uses. It did not mold in hot weather, nor become hard in cold temperatures—it was for its time "unsurpassed for strength and flexibility." But it was not cheap. Not until 1938, however, did Arabol itself announce, after a belated year of research, the perfection of a flexible glue formula designed expressly for Sheridan equipment. The Bakelite Corporation at about the same time also developed flexible non-animal glues.

Sheridan, with most at stake, ironically did not believe ambitious chemical research necessary to solve its unique flexible glue problem. In 1932 the firm hoped (once more) to supply The Curtis Publishing Company a latex adhesive for perfect-binding *Ladies' Home Journal* (again), but the publisher was (once more) unhappy with the results. Since Curtis manufactured its own paper, reusing large quantities of its magazines as scrap, and since latex is not dispersible in water (that is, it will not dissolve and wash away in the papermaking operation), quantities of latex would contaminate newly made paper. Later adhesives (p 249) also had this disadvantage, and Curtis opposed them too.

Sheridan did not seriously investigate adhesive problems until 1942, when it formed an adhesives division—operated by the National Starch Company, a large independent glue manufacturer. But it was too late: with a difficult war economy and scarce materials it would be impossible to develop new materials of any description. Wartime people would read anything they could find, and old machinery (and old techniques) would have to produce it.

Sheridan had announced an improved combination gatherer-binder in 1930 capable of 100–120 books per minute (3000–4500 per hour); this was the most "advanced" perfect binder yet. Alfred Bredenberg, 75 that year, retired from his work only gradually, continuing to patent bookbinding machinery and improvements up to 1935, the year he died. T. Blair Hawkes, whom Bredenberg picked to replace himself as chief engineer at Champlain, after a few miscellaneous bookbinding assignments, soon concentrated his attention on the Sheridan perfect-binder, and over the following years became a world-wide authority on stitchless binding. Hawkes, who remembers Bredenberg affectionately as "Uncle Alfred," himself retired recently.

In 1938, however, on the brink of war for which the company

would manufacture decorticating machines and sheet-metal forming presses, Sheridan had an impressively long, but woefully indiscriminate assortment of equipment in its catalog (much of which would become obsolete as the war progressed).

For magazine work:

Sheridan gathering machine
Sheridan rotary gatherer
Sheridan single and double stitchers
Sheridan continuous coverer
Sheridan small stitcher-coverer
Sheridan continuous binder
Juengst gatherer
Juengst stitcher
Juengst coverer
Juengst binder
American Assembling Machine gatherer
American Assembling Machine stitcher
American Assembling Machine straight line coverer
Sheridan straight line continuous trimmer

For edition bookwork:

Sheridan gatherer
Sheridan wire stitcher
Sheridan continuous belt-feed smasher
Sheridan rounder and backer
Sheridan two-up rounder and backer
Sheridan backliner with headbanding attachment
Sheridan rounder and backer/backliner combination
Sheridan continuous casemaker
Sheridan automatic case-feed stamping press
Sheridan heavy-duty stamping press
Sheridan cutting machines
McCain sewing machine
Murray backliner with headbanding attachment
Bundlers, standing presses, etc.[12]

As inventories and parts supply became hopeless when depression economy turned to national defense, lethargic reading habits surprisingly turned to extraordinary publishing vitality. A new generation of publishers, having weathered—or by their youth escaped—depression, panic, and first world war, now gloomily faced post-war price escalations (p 278) with justifiable trepidation. To some of them the prospect of cheap publishing by eliminating boards and cloth had (again) particular appeal—at least those who had seen paperback operations in France and Germany.

In England Ernest Benn had begun publishing 6-penny books in the 1920's, but failed. Victor Gollancz, then working for Benn, started his own scheme in 1927, shocking his friends and public alike with enormous, ugly—but effective—newspaper advertisements, his black or magenta typematter on standardized yellow jackets ("gems" designed for him by Stanley Morison), and his uniform black cloth bindings. Along with aggressive personal endorsements for his inexpensive books he achieved considerable sales largely through gigantic book clubs. Although a confessed admirer of Tauchnitz' delicately designed series, Gollancz himself relied heavily on substantial volume and sales, marketing factors no mass-manufacturer could afford to overlook.

Allen Lane, nephew of John Lane (to whom he was apprenticed), publisher of the startling *Yellow Book* a generation before, surmised about 1930 that little reading was done by a large segment of the British population for two reasons: (1) book prices were high; (2) bookstores by their dinginess discouraged prospective readers unaccustomed to habitual browsing. He began to explore a more deliberate program to remedy the situation.

Strongly influenced by the Albatross series, Lane early in 1935 proposed a series of 7⅛ x 4⅜-inch 6-penny books. Trade book people agreed it would fail as had Ernest Benn's: other series had never been truly successful, competition with hardbound books (not a problem for Albatross) would exist. But good design (as with Albatross) could help: the "Penguin" (borrowed from a comic strip) would identify a bright, simple, modern, distinctive, and sound series of popular paperbacks. The format was designed by Edward Young to look a lot like the Albatross series.

The first titles for Lane's Penguins were an important decision. They had to be "new," yet "safe." Chosen were books that had been good hard-bound sellers:

André Maurois, *Ariel*
Ernest Hemingway, *A Farewell to Arms*
Susan Ertz, *Madame Claire*
Eric Linklater, *Poet's Pub*
Dorothy Sayers, *The Unpleasantness at the Bellona Club*
Agatha Christie, *The Mysterious Affair at Styles*
Mary Webb, *Gone to Earth*
Beverley Nichols, *Twenty-five*
E. H. Young, *William*
Compton McKenzie, *Carnival*

Booksellers—as predicted—were disinterested in the proposal: they liked the list, to be sure, but were unimpressed by the price and format. Lane took the project to the British F. W. Woolworth Department Store organization, where the format and price were welcomed, but not the titles. At a last minute, however, the gamble was accepted, and distribution of the series was assured. First printings were 20,000 each, with 17,500 calculated to be the "break-even" quantity. The books began to sell. In October 1935 a second group of 10 was published, and with the project hopefully launched, Penguin Books, Limited, was formed on January 1, 1936, by Allen (later Sir Allen) with his brothers Richard and John.

Establishing its headquarters at Harmondsworth, Middlesex, the firm next brought out non-fiction "Pelicans," and "Penguin Specials," featuring political and contemporary topics (1937). "King Penguins," dealing with the arts, was a hard-cover series (1939) in imitation of the popular German Insel books. In 1937 over 100 titles were available, and two years later the several series were brought to the United States.

Ian Ballantine, with a master's thesis in the 1930's on paperback publishing, became Lane's first American branch manager. Although sales of the 25¢ imported books were good, war conditions forced the company to reverse its operations, printing some titles in the United States and exporting them to England. In 1954 Ballantine, with Walter Pitkin, Jr., and Sidney Kramer, left Penguin to form Ballantine Books, Inc. Kurt Enoch, formerly of Albatross, replaced Ballantine.

In 1948 Penguin sold its US operations to New American Library of World Literature (NAL), and two years later again formed its own American company, situated in Baltimore. Under Harry Paroissien (who retired 1970) the Maryland office produced 20 percent of the company's output, printing in 40,000–85,000 quantities. With its stunning success in both England and America, Penguin—having borrowed boldly from Germany—provided all of Europe and the United States with a new and exciting concept in book publishing.

In 1947 as the series faced a post-war reading boom and inevitable increased competition, Lane engaged Jan Tschichold to improve the design and production quality. There were now "Penguin Classics" (1946) and "Penguin Millions"—printings of that size for George Bernard Shaw, H. G. Wells, Agatha Christie, and others. By 1956 the complete Penguin catalog contained almost 2400 titles, of which over 1000 were in print. By that time, too, 65 various Penguin publications had won design awards. Despite competition from other paperbacks—over 30 British publishers alone were issuing them— as well as hard-bound books, the plucky Penguins are still manufactured in 50,000–65,000 printings, still relatively conservatively covered, and still much in demand (p 33|3|) despite a certain snob-bishness: a 1964 Penguin prospectus stated, "They are not a product for the masses. Eleven million Penguins sold in the United Kingdom in one year represent only one Penguin bought by one Englishman out of five. The Penguins are made for a (relatively large) minority, a select minority." American paperback publishers pretended to no such ex-clusivity.

The modern paperback in the United States had several fitful starts. It had appeared in the 1830's and '40's as a cheap temporary binding, but was quickly outsold by the new cased-in book which thereafter relegated the paperback to reprints and ephemera. In the 1860's and '70's, as we have seen, it took advantage of the scarcity of cloth and the exigencies of travel, but low quality and overstock left no room for endurance. Again in the 1880's and '90's the paperback almost flour-ished, but suffered under severe competition and the copyright law. Always a distress to the bookseller, the paperback seemed incapable of becoming anything more than an erratically recurring fad.

Bookstores were strangely a problem for the paperback, too. John Lovell had tried to sell 25¢ paperbacks through them; proteges George Dunlap and Alexander Grosset, after working in Lovell's enterprises, as their own first venture perversely tried rebinding paperbacks as hard-bound books. These succeeded, but the recurring problem was the fact that there were—as recently as the 1920's—only 700 bookstores in the United States, catering to a small, albeit steady, reading public. Indeed, Lehmann-Haupt and Alan Dutscher agreed that this condition had long before produced quite a startling effect:

> "That is [wrote Dutscher], the real significance of the public library development in the United States is to be seen in the fact that America had to subsidize book outlets at a loss, at a time when the population of every other advanced nation in the world could profitably support them."[13]

Robert L. Duffus and the Cheney Report (p 269) both saw that book publishing had still lagged behind newspapers, magazines, motion pic-tures, and radio, because of the "failure of those who distribute books to devise a system for reaching large numbers of people." For mass-produced paperbacks, bookstores were anathema.

E. Haldeman-Julius, in Girard, Kansas, in 1920 started a fantastic series of over 1200 5¢ "Little Blue Books," printed on a special press in quantities up to 30,000. Each book's sales—almost entirely by mail—were carefully analyzed (women, for example, bought only 30 per-cent) and many titles were changed to make them more alluring. Through the depression years, however, along with other paper attractions, the Little Blue Books were not so much cheaper than inexpensive cloth-bound, sewn books, and presented no threat to established publishers. Indeed, Cheney found—seriously—that when the American public paid 25 cents or more it wanted a cloth-bound book, concluding, "What have nickel books and cheap reprints really proved about ordinary publishing?" The Little Blue Books gave no impetus to what was to come.

Simon & Schuster, Farrar & Rinehart, and Doubleday, Doran tried cheap (one-dollar) hard-bound books in the early 1930's, but the idea —like the "Reader's Library" (p 309)—seemed only a "noble experiment." Another 1930 enterprise, Blue Ribbon Books (an amalgam of Harper's, Harcourt, Dodd, Mead, and Little, Brown) also tried to sell $1.00 hard-bound books in drug stores, and in 1937 added "Triangle Books," 39¢ hardbound books. Eugene Reynal, who headed the operation, had bought Blue Ribbon Books in 1933 from the four founders, and sold it in 1939 to Doubleday, moving on to other ventures. Much of the one-dollar operations seemed like passing hot potatoes. "Only the best, most modern bindings and jackets will sell," *Business Week* had said, in December 1930. "The public wants a book cheap but it does not want it to look cheap. . . ." Books "were not a drug store proposition yet," the magazine concluded prophetically.

Albert and Charles Boni in 1929 started publishing inexpensive (50-cent) editions in paper covers. Designed by Rockwell Kent, the "Boni Paper Books" were not produced in large editions, nor were they sold in any but conventional bookstores. The project was soon abandoned; Bennett Cerf bought the list to start Random House, Inc., and "The Modern Library," maintaining 475 active titles as late as the 1960's. Ironically, although the rigidly uniform 4¾ x 7-inch series furnishes a considerable part of the company's income, Cerf claimed himself firmly against standardization: "We pride ourselves, and take special efforts to publish books distinctive and unique in design and typography. . . ." Such statements are common to assure the public (who seldom compare one book to another, physically), that standardization does not necessarily mean mediocrity.

Harold K. Guinzburg, founder of Viking Press (1925), after observing the success of contemporary German book clubs, started Literary Guild a year later, and Junior Literary Guild, finally selling these clubs to Doubleday in the 1930's. (The first modern US book club had been Book-of-the-Month Club, 1921.) During service in the Office of War Information in 1944, Guinzburg "discovered" an important book fact: "there is no substitute for the printed word," and articulated yet another warning important to paperback publishing—the US book business, last to adapt to mass marketing, had never, as in Europe, developed an adequate bookstore system. He suspected that thousands of potential readers were "lost" to the trade, as Allen Lane had surmised in England. (A 1946 survey substantiated that about 70 percent of all US books were read by 21 percent of the population.) Guinzburg himself had, with bookclubs, substituted the post office for the bookshop, and the drugstore would also serve if the "formula" were right.

Robert F. de Graff, a nephew of Frank N. Doubleday, had headed Garden City Publishing Company's "Star Dollar Books," then moved to Blue Ribbon Books. In 1938 he began to analyze the American market more carefully for its paperback potentialities. Format and content, and, especially, marketplace were foremost considerations. He had watched Boni's paperbacks, "The Modern Library," and the cheap European publications, particularly the Penguins, noticing increased sales in every series as the book's price went down. In an April 1939 *Publishers' Weekly* de Graff coyly asked:

"Has anyone ever considered publishing a special cheap edition . . . which people would buy instead of lend, that would not interfere with the sale of regular editions[?] . . . then the author and the publisher through the sale of their cheap edition would get a revenue, however small, from each person who reads the book."[14]

Apparently receiving no answer to his satisfaction, de Graff launched Pocket Books, Inc., within weeks issuing its first 10 titles, like Penguin's, a crucial selection:

James Hilton, *Lost Horizon*
Dorothea Brande, *Wake Up and Live!*
William Shakespeare, *Five Great Tragedies*
Thorn Smith, *Topper*
Agatha Christie, *The Murder of Roger Ackroyd*
Dorothy Parker, *Enough Rope*
Emily Brontë, *Wuthering Heights*
Samuel Butler, *The Way of All Flesh*
Thornton Wilder, *The Bridge of San Luis Rey*
Felix Salten, *Bambi*

Of their format, de Graff explained years later, "My idea was to put out 25-cent books which could fit easily into a pocket or purse and to provide them with attractive picture covers. . . ." Because of their uneconomical manufacture—special presses were later built for them—de Graff accepted a loss on the early titles in order to prove the validity of his market research, but the gamble was sound.

Colonial Press, Clinton, Massachusetts, manufactured the first paperbacks for de Graff, using essentially conventional equipment. Founded

1930 by J. J. Little & Ives (p 308) as a wholly owned subsidiary, The Colonial Press, Inc. was bought the following year by Roy C. Baker and Lewis M. Adams, who resigned as president of Little & Ives to do so. By 1962 the complete book manufactory—with a one-floor bindery occupying 4½ acres—produced 300,000 books daily, with 1200 hands working three shifts. For paperbacks, however, there were new handling problems: the operation had to be completely conveyorized from gathering to finish, including two-up trimming, staining, stacking, and packing. When a breakdown occurred, stockpiles of unfinished books at each station insured that production—hand-fed if necessary—would continue. Colonial today continues to produce a tremendous quantity of adhesive-bound paperbacks in addition to all other kinds of bookwork.

For larger quantities more efficiently produced, two giant printing firms began to handle the new paperbacks almost from the beginning. James W. Clement bought a Buffalo shop in 1879 which, as the new century began, captured many nation-wide commercial accounts, most of which eventually spelled tremendous catalog and periodical work. The firm expanded in 1946 to manufacture 18 million paperbacks annually, but these are still a small part of the company's output. (Owned since 1965 by the Arcata National Corporation, Menlo Park, California, J. W. Clement's name in 1970 was changed to Arcata Graphics Corporation.) Like Clement, W. F. Hall Printing Company, Chicago, dates to 1895 when William F. Hall reorganized an earlier firm. Printing of paperbacks by both companies was from stereotypes, electrotypes, or rubber plates, on high-speed presses, printing 18,000 128-page books per hour, two-up. Standardization of format and "even" printing forms are essential; covers are usually printed 16 at a time, 8 titles up. Both companies use Sheridan adhesive binders doing 12,000 per hour.

Although World War II paper shortages hampered unlimited growth, Pocket Books was a phenomenal success. Designed by Robert Josephy (p 268), the paperbacks sold for 25 cents—a low price justified by the company by low profits and royalties—and elimination of "costly cloth" and seven expensive traditional bindery operations. The 4¼ x 6½-inch books, Smyth sewn at first but later "perfect" bound, edges tinted red all around, and endpapers pasted to glossy laminated covers, suddenly appeared everywhere in variety and drugstores as well as newsstands. An immensely active war-time reading public carried them off almost habitually, as conveniently, at least, as the company's symbolic kangaroo—really a wallaby, said de Graff—"Gertrude," a design finalized by Walt Disney. Indeed, along with handy paperback "Armed Services Editions" of many kinds of literature for troops, the way was paved for mass post-war exploitation by paperbacks. Publishers had told de Graff his plan wouldn't work; that New York was not a realistic trial city—yet R. H. Macy sold 4100 books in six days. In 1940 4.5 million books were bought; in 1949, 45 million. In those first ten years 600 titles appeared, totalling 260 million books—more, according to Pocket Books, than the combined total of all US bestsellers since 1880. Over 50 titles have sold more than a million copies apiece.

Imitators quickly jumped into the exciting movement. A Milwaukee publisher duplicated Penguin's trim size exactly, although the series ("Red Arrow Books") did not survive. Avon Publications, Inc. (1941) was prohibited by injunction in 1942, brought by Pocket Books, from selling paperbacks "with red or similar tinged edges and the word 'Pocket' appearing on the front cover." NAL began in 1948 with Victor Weybright as Editor in Chief and Chairman of the Board, and Kurt Enoch (today a director of the parent Times-Mirror Company) as President. Pocket Books and Bantam Books (1945) both established British branches in 1949—Europeans were now buying more US paperbacks than US hard-bound books. Dell (1943), Graphic, Pyramid, Lion followed, as did Ballantine (starting an unusual simultaneous paper/hardbound publishing operation in 1952) and others—throwing a considerable burden on a retrenching postwar market.

And a curious market it had become. Had paperbacks been distributed to the handful of reputable bookstores, frequented only by a small literate clientele, their life would have been short indeed—more so, because neither bookseller nor "bibliophile" cared for them. But distributed with magazines, the paperbacks would find themselves in an entirely different world. Ever since Paternoster Row's magazine days the periodicals had elicited popular interest and enthusiastic response that books would seldom know. Available—almost the day of publication—at newsstands and shops everywhere, they reach masses who will pay a few cents for a few hours' entertainment.

On the early 25-cent paperbacks the publisher's cost was $10\frac{1}{2}$ to $12\frac{1}{2}$ cents, plus 2 cents for royalty; the wholesaler paid the publisher $15\frac{1}{2}$ cents and got 19 cents from the retailer, who made a 6-cent profit. But with the privilege of placing every title in the series on the market, the publisher had to consider that, because no one in the shop was familiar with the books, they would get no special attention from clerks. Like unsold magazines, they would have to be fully returnable or exchangeable. These handicaps were brilliantly compensated for by format and design: small enough to fit special racks and shelves for maximum exposure; bright covers to call attention; provocative lead paragraphs to sell the curious reader; lamination and stained edges for "elegance" (to hide fingerprints and suggestion of yellow aging). And the casual shopper has unlimited time to browse in familiar, friendly surroundings. Instead of a disadvantage, any retail outlet in fact became a workable market for paperbacks, since no special knowledge or major investment was necessary.

Despite the necessity for large presses and press runs, the new paperback was capable of surprisingly fast production—not unlike the magazines—when the occasion demanded. Pocket Books demonstrated extraordinary speed seldom expected in bookwork: upon the death of President Roosevelt (Friday, April 12, 1945), George and Stefan Salter were called on Saturday to design cover and text, respectively, for a 250-page commemorative volume. Composition and proofreading at Colonial Press began on Sunday; platemaking and presswork ran through the week, with binding and shipping finished on Friday. On the following Monday morning—after 6 production days—60,000 copies were on sale; the total edition of *Franklin Delano Roosevelt— A Memorial* (325,000 copies) was curtailed only by paper shortages.

With these unique approaches and capabilities in distribution and marketing, and with new sales forces supervising title selection, distribution, display, and sales in territories scarcely touched before— rather than by manufacturing economies, however substantial—the paperback book industry really found its strength. "In mass merchandising," claimed Freeman ("Doc") Lewis, vice president of Pocket Books (now retired), restating the thesis Munsey had demonstrated with magazines, "it is wisdom to make a little on a lot; it is suicide to try to make a lot on a little." Yet the beginning success was too easy. During World War II with shortages of other amusements bringing enforced reading, the demand for books could not be met—a favorable situation for any struggling enterprise. After the war, however, the aspect changed drastically.

With the introduction of new entertainments, people were suddenly reading less; drugstores themselves returned to more profitable luxury items again available; competition became keen and reckless. Returns and overstocks forced marginal publishers out of business. Although the end of the 1940's brought some stability, rising costs forced book prices to jump to 35 and 50 cents, and with cheap reprints all but exhausted, publishers were coaxing original authors with attractive royalties difficult to defray even at advanced prices. Also at work was the gradual abandonment of publishers' usual propriety. The 1952 Congressional Gathings Committee, investigating pornography, criticized paperbacks for their "three S's"—sex, sadism, and the smoking revolver. The result was duplication, overproduction, and self-chastisement, and it was ruthless.

By 1953 the paperback market was so glutted 15 million books were returned to publishers—for full credit. Warehouses were full. Ballantine recalled 14 titles, accumulating great piles of books in its offices. Smaller companies declared "publishing holidays" and fired many. New outlets, like supermarkets, were desperately developed. According to Lewis, whose recommendations for industry-wide cooperation went unheeded, tons of Pocket Books were buried in an abandoned canal near Buffalo, and 60 million books of other publishers were also probably destroyed. Said David Dempsey, "It is the fate of the trade publisher in the United States to be chronically ailing without ever becoming critically ill." So it was with paperback publishing. The six dozen or so firms engaged in the paperback industry clamored for economic relief: cheaper paper, smaller type, unprinted endpapers, unlaminated covers. It was like the 1870's and '80's all over again.[15]

As the economic situation gradually righted itself, publishers began anew with more sober plans. Greeting them was good news from the chemists, led by Frederick R. Blaylock: the adhesive problem had been solved. Blaylock, a research associate employed by the Book Manufacturers Institute (formed 1933 to replace the earlier Employing Bookbinders of America, principally to set minimum bindery wages— 37.5¢ per hour for men, 30¢ for women—and ethical business practices under desperate depression conditions), worked at a US GPO laboratory to investigate the warping of covers (p 277), the tarnishing of foils, and other bindery thorns. He was instrumental too in developing the startling new synthetic resin (polyvinyl, acrylic, and epoxy) adhesives. Everyone stopped to look—and try the ultimate test for stitchless books: hold an entire tome by a single leaf. It held.

The polyvinyl family had begun just before World War II to substitute for animal glue as animal materials and glycerine shortages became acute. Another compound, sorbitol, replaced glycerine as flexible agent. In conjunction with BMI, the Government Printing Office developed several resinous adhesives based on a water emulsion of polyvinyl acetate ("PVA"), a heavy milky white substance drying to a hard, brittle film, quite unsuitable for flexibility applications. But the 8 percent addition of a plasticizer—dibutyl phthalate, glycerol triacetate ("triacetin"), or 2-methyl, 2,4-pentanediol ("hexylene glycol")—produced a dry, resinous film that was permanently flexible. Readily diluted in water, easy to apply, and safe from noxious or inflammable components, the plasticized PVA has yet another surprising characteristic: it actually increased 10–15 percent in strength after several weeks, as it continues to "bite" into paper fibers long after the binding is completed. It was a substantial breakthrough for the binding industry.

The synthetic adhesives did have some disadvantages: although unaffected by aging, they are generally slow in setting, requiring either long storage time (several hours), or the installation of costly dielectric (high-frequency) heating equipment to harden them—in seconds. (In a curious return to bookbinding history, the Willcox & Gibbs Sewing Machine Company now offers the trade its "Thermatron Electronic Drier" which sets glues "instantly.") The adhesives, nevertheless, were a new approach to old bindery problems, and even if suitable for only the most specialized jobs, they were welcome.

Better still were the PVA "hot melt" adhesives also developed at the GPO, around 1944. E. I. duPont de Nemours & Company shortly thereafter furnished special formulas to W. F. Hall and Clement which were also hot melts. About the same time (1949) the Battelle Memorial Institute, Columbus, Ohio, developed in conjunction with duPont and Sheridan, a hot melt for Kingsport Press (p 309): hard-bound books were being glued-off at a rate of 80 per minute—a speed breakthrough—with flexible hot-melt adhesive applied at 300°. Similarly at high temperatures (350–400°F) for paperbacks, the hot melts set or cooled rapidly, permitting trimming without intermediate storage. They use a minimum of water (wetness distorts paper and cardboard, resulting in ripples and warping), were tough, mildew-resistant, and best of all, they remain permanently flexible. But like animal glue the early hot melts had some faults: they required priming (application of a preliminary thin coat to promote fiber penetration), and their fumes were malodorous and toxic. It became desirable not to apply it from the melting pot, but to install a pre-melt pot, although overheating and premelting too much made for difficulties too. They also had some intolerable temperature eccentricities: "cold flow" (distortion under strain in hot climates) and "cold crack" (tendency to crack even in moderate climates). Another solution seemed necessary.

Subsequent development came in the form of "one-shot" hot melts, where, essentially, the primer is eliminated. The one-shot hot melts came close to being the ideal adhesive; as solids they contain no water or other solvents which contribute to warping problems. Books can be manufactured at 200 per minute, they trim well, and about 80 percent of the "hard-to-bind" papers take to it. Some formulas have no cold flow whatever, and no cold crack down to 10 or 15°F, although they do have some disadvantages. As with some PVA emulsions and hot melts, the one-shot hot melts, recent research discloses, will deteriorate if books are stored at high temperatures. (High temperatures in general are critically harmful to paper as well as glue: heating paper at 100°C (212°F) for a period of 36 days is estimated by Barrow research people—William J. Barrow Research Laboratories, Richmond, Virginia—to be equivalent to 300 years of natural aging.) More serious, perhaps, the PVA's, like latex, will not dissolve in water.

Because of the non-dispersibility of PVA adhesives in water, waste paper containing PVA cannot be sold as scrap. Such waste, however is valuable, accounting for up to 35 percent of the pulp used annually in papermaking. Two pounds of original PVA could ruin up to 200,000 pounds of newly made paper: it emerges as spots on the paper which are not receptive to ink. (duPont has solved this with an alkali-dispersible variation of PVA called polyvinyl acetate-crotonic acid copolymer.) But the revitalized adhesives industry could not really complain of such faults—there were specialized formulas for every application: Thomas W. Dunn Company made "Dunnflex"; Paisley Products, Inc., had "Paisley Pliable Cement"; Federal Adhesive Corporation's was "Federal Book Flex"; Special Chemical Company had "Flexbond"; Swift & Company made "Morflex"; William C. Hart Company with "Hartflex"; as well as synthetics by United Paste and Glue Company, Arvey Corporation, the Cudahy Packing Company, Bakelite Corporation, and Arabol, whose original vegetable glues may have been the spark that started chemists thinking.

Even with different formulas for a variety of papers, however, there were still many problems to solve. Recent microphotographic research of preliminary spine roughening action shows that just a few broken teeth on the roughener blade will affect adherence. It is no wonder that, in the shop, such unnoticed defects contribute to puzzling adhesive failures, often vaguely diagnosed. As late as 1959 Sheridan recorded an instance where 300,000 books, ready to be shipped, were found to be falling apart upon exposure to cold weather. "The truth is," said one binder, as if to disarm the culprit with candor, "that we have trouble; not on all books but on some. . . ." By the mid 1950's, however, over 250 million paperbacks were selling annually; no longer a small experiment, they were accounting for 20 to 25 percent of the magazine distributor's business, and there were 1200 wholesalers tending to 100,000 retail outlets, all anxious to participate. There was enthusiasm and money enough for full research.

Soon, of course, even animal glue with special softeners would be made flexible enough for certain applications. It dries fast for inline bindery operations. *Adhesives Age* magazine, reporting authoritatively on the new glues, in 1959 disregarded its allegiance to the inorganic chemical world and conservatively switched from side-stitching to animal glue, applied at 140–145°F after a "slotted binding process" (signatures perforated along the gutter—but not trimmed—on the

folder so adhesive could seep into inner pages). Unlike most telephone books and catalogs (95 percent of which use flexible animal
glue), and popular magazines which also prefer animal glue (since
tremendous quantities are likely to end up scrap), a few pacesetters
have converted to PVA, *Fortune* and *Reader's Digest* in particular.

*Fortune* has found "pre-priming" of its slick stock necessary, despite
a cost twice that of side-stitching. *Reader's Digest,* since 1957 perfect-
bound at the Dayton, Ohio, plant of The McCall Corporation, runs
to well over 13,500,000: Peter de Florez (p 285) considered it "the most
advanced bindery production operation in the world." Even so, after
much difficulty with cracking and running adhesives to which some
readers found themselves allergic, *Reader's Digest* in 1967 offered an
improved "crack proof, run proof, sneeze proof magazine." *Popular
Science Monthly,* having changed its format several times since Appleton started it in 1872, is now 8¼ x 11 inches, adhesive bound. *Inland
Printer* (now merged with *American Lithographer*), hardly demonstrating more technological daring than *Adhesives Age,* coyly asked
in October 1968: "Notice anything different about *IP/AL* this
month?" It was perfect bound. The dignified spokesman of the printing industry had at last found the binding it sought three-quarters
of a century ago.

The handling of books, even paperbacks, like magazines, however,
left something to be desired for readers who were faithful to their
bookstores but found the cost of well made books rising beyond their
grasp. Periodical techniques—fast turnover, consignment, free delivery,
low discounts, fixed short-time exposure—were not best for books.
Why not bring paperbacks back to the traditional bookstore where
conditions were ideal for book buying? Someone would try.

In 1953 Doubleday brought out its "Anchor Books," a series of
serious reprints selling from 65¢ to $1.45, done on better paper, with
some graphic taste. These were "quality" paperbacks, a title, according
to Jason Epstein, their creator, referring not to literary quality (many
world classics appear in cheap editions) but to the fact that printings
are modest and street-corner sites are not likely markets. They are,
in effect, paper-covered "trade" books.

By the end of the 1950's the publishing world was still reeling with
wonderment over the "paperback revolution," cheap or qualitative.
Many publishers still had not entered the field: some, especially the
university presses (characterized by Yale University Press' Chester
Kerr as "the most fool-hardy form of publishing: . . . the smallest
editions at the greatest cost, . . . the highest prices . . . [for] the
people who can least afford them") frustrated by readers' shifting to
paperbacks even for scholarly uses, were still wondering if paperbacks

would be "menace or manna" for them. Gradually they all came into the race with one or another series, their commitments indeed decisive. "Paperbound publishing seems destined to sweep American publishing," said Arthur A. Cohen, President of Meridian Books in 1959, "to obliterate cloth trade publishing as we presently know it. . . ." Others agreed that "For some categories of books the days of cloth over board are numbered." Many publishers already issue paper and hard editions of a work, knowing that the trade will prefer the former and the libraries the latter.

The libraries perceived they could benefit immediately with paperbacks. "In thousands of small towns the public library—usually a Carnegie library—was the only source of new or unusual books," wrote Lou La Brant, "and unless the town happened to have an energetic committee and some good angel with money, choices were limited to the tried and true, often to the dull and moralizing [Butman]." Today, however, libraries large and small are introducing inexpensive paperbacks wherever possible. Some titles circulate as few as two times, but others as many as 30, before they disintegrate. While some librarians don't even catalog paperback titles (and don't dun delinquent borrowers for them), others strive to protect them with reinforced wire-stitching and plastic binders. In England paperbacks were so successfully rebound for library use publishers took legal action to object: Penguin now manufactures a special library edition —"threadsewn, not unsewn-bound." "Staples for adhesive binding, hard binding for the paperback—it is all rather paradoxical," said Lee E. Grove, of the Council on Library Resources (p 300). But library patrons, young and old, mysteriously prefer the unassuming paperback to the same book in a durable hardbound edition.

Elementary and highschool teachers, like librarians, have found the inculcating of good reading habits to be almost effortless with paperbacks. Classroom paperback libraries and bookclubs abound. Fiction, nonfiction, languages, history, science—all fit nicely into reading programs, both integral and supplementary. Although the modern paperback could easily be compared realistically with yellowbacks and dime novels, Alexander Butman, an executive of Bantam Books, in 1963 found it unnecessary to refer to the last century's cheap publishing:

"The paperback book has gone through a continuous series of evolutions and 'revolutions' since its introduction in this country in the summer of 1939. The first paperbacks appeared in crude bindings, with colorful jackets [sic] resplendent in peelable cellophane and cover art demonstrating the key situation in an over-glamorized or provocative manner. Today's educational paperback, with its attractive cover illustrating the essential nature of the book; its highly improved 'perfect' binding which will usually last as long as the paper; its new laminated cover impregnated with a varnish that is strong and pliable; and the use of new techniques in high-speed printing, new inks, new vinyl adhesives, new improved papers and new presses in its manufacture, is a far cry from the early editions."[16]

Paperbacks in the schools, he predicted, were not just a new package for an old item, they were a new educational dimension. Teachers, students, and parents were all delighted with them.

The paperback had indeed swept the public's fancy. It came home with the week's groceries and with the businessman's overnight bag. It fit handily into purses and (only when clothing manufacturers increased pocket sizes for it) into trousers and overcoats. It took the subway to work and it enjoyed vacations as well. It nestled compactly on the tiniest shelves ("If you eliminate cardboard covers, you can store approximately five additional books, average type, on a three-foot shelf," said designer Raymond Loewy, whose French childhood taught him—only half correctly—that boards were quite expendable), or it could be discarded without puritanical feelings of guilt. Frank L. Schick, whose laudatory paperback history (not manufactured, alas, in paperback form) is encyclopedic, believed strongly in the future of his ephemeral subject:

"As mass media seem to supplement rather than support each other, the demand for impermanent reading matter seems to grow and may reach the point where most, if not all, fiction will appear in this temporary format. . . . Paperbacks have democratized the approach to learning, self-improvement and entertainment. They fit well into the smaller American homes of today. . . . [They] hardly ever outlast the life of their purchasers, but the ideas they convey often do. If they are worth the reader's attention this alone justifies their existence and expansion."[17]

Britons noted disappointedly that the paperback in the late 1960's in American hands had not only returned to the British Isles to out-perform all the seminal European series, it had also killed "coffee-table" books (large picture nonbooks jointly financed by international publishers) which they had learned to appreciate as the French had cherished their *livres de peintre* 50 years before. Additional developments, furthermore, show that new adhesive bindings may indeed outlast their purchasers, who may soon choose between paper covers or more sturdy cases (p 326). The revolution in paperback publishing was real and permanent—as dramatic as the revolution a century before when cloth replaced leather.

To assure the continued existence and expansion of the paperback, bookbinding machinery manufacturers have rushed to provide equipment for every need. Some binders are committed only to the mass production of general paperback titles, while others cater to medium or short-run paperback jobs, and still others accommodate single-copy requests or runs under 100 for libraries, in-house use, or special presentations. Because of the prodigious output of a single adhesive binder, as we have seen, machinery sales are highly competitive—although limited in number. *Book Production Industry* in 1966 estimated that in the United States there were no more than 1000 perfect binders in operation—the preponderance of them, of course, Sheridans costing $110,000 to $125,000 apiece.

Sheridan-Bredenberg-Juengst equipment over a period of fifty years had long proved a precious asset both to the company and to the binding trade. It has been used variously for gathering everything from blueprints, calendars, and music, to greeting cards and mimeograph work, and it has bound quantities and varieties of printed matter that would boggle the mind. Never more than today, however, has Sheridan shown proper concern for its position and leadership. In 1961 the firm refurbished an 1832 barn near its Easton plant for use as a machine shop and test facility. Oscilloscopes, stroboscopes, and high-speed cameras are the new tools of the engineer and inventor (al-

The Sheridan high-speed perfect-binder will connect to either arm or rotary gathering machine. With Sheridan stretch-cloth applier it will also bind books for later casing-in. It produces 12,000 books per hour. [The Sheridan Company]

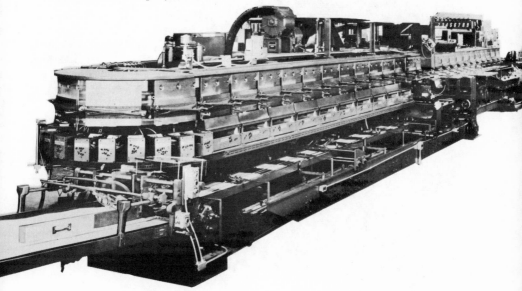

though the barn itself was recently abandoned). In 1964 the Harris-Intertype Corporation bought the 129 year old company and the brothers' initials were dropped.

Principal product of The Sheridan Company today for periodical work is the "High Speed All Steel Rack Driven Perfect Binder," available with 45 or 57 clamps. Old models had required 1 to 2 hours for adjustment, with a special rachet wrench on each of 40–50 clamps, of paper thickness; now clamps automatically adjust themselves as they pass a point on the machine. "This most perfect of the perfect binders," the company quips, handles sizes from 7 x 4½ x ¼ inches to 17½ x 7 x 2¾ inches—at speeds up to 200 per minute—using any of the animal or polyvinyl, primed or one-shot, adhesives, and will also cover side-stitched books or case-bind them with the addition of a stretch-cloth applier.

In gatherers Sheridan offers the Accu-Speed high-speed automatic which, with vacuum instead of mechanical signature feeding, handles up to 7500 sets per hour. This is eclipsed by the Sheridan XG gatherer, introduced in 1968, which uses an "orbital vacuum rotating head" to pick up signatures and set them in motion before they are actually fed

Sheridan standard rotary gatherer pulls signatures from their hoppers and sends them onto the raceway at top speed. [The Sheridan Company]

into the collection raceway. As a result of this new technique gathering speeds approach 12,000 per hour.

The Sheridan Model 5E Mark II combination inserter, stitcher, trimmer handles periodicals at the rate of 10,000 per hour; the "Pacesetter" high-speed combination inserter, saddle-stitcher, trimmer has a speed of 13,000 per hour. For edition paperback work a high-speed inline system is offered to binders as a companion to the company's hardbound production line (p 316). For the handling of books or magazines between manufacturing processes, Sheridan-Loach automatic conveyorizing machinery is available.

In 1950 the 88-year old Martini Bookbinding Machinery Company, Switzerland, designed its first adhesive binder. For medium and long runs this first fully automatic European machine, connected with a gatherer and automatic cover-applying equipment, was ready three years later. High-frequency adhesive-drying apparatus became available for it in 1958. Some models (the "BBA" and "Autobinder") are capable of 9000 books per hour. The Martini has been very well accepted, over 200 machines sold to a worldwide market in the two post-war decades. Many European shops have more than one Martini, while one German binder, Burda Druck, Offenburg/Darmstadt, has no less than six of them.

The Autobinder, introduced in 1959 for medium and small applications, handles telephone directories, magazines, and paperback books from 17 x 10 x 1¾ inches down to 3½ x 3⅛ x 9/16 inches. It is fed by hand. Its high-speed circular knife and fiber-roughening cutters handle all grades of paper, including coated stocks. Unlike Sheridan Perfect Binders, the Martinis deliver finished books standing on their backs, which the manufacturer claims insures good adhesion and obviates any further rubbing down of the spines.

Today Martini continues to diversify its bookbinding equipment. In its newly enlarged Frauenfeld factory it continues to produce its famous book sewer, including a new semi-automatic model; since 1960 it has (by license with Sheridan) manufactured a "Martini-Sheridan" gathering machine; it also produces a jacketing machine and (by license with the Magnacraft Manufacturing Company, Chicago, makers of tipping, mailing, and labeling machines) a counter-stacker. For mass magazines and catalogs Martini offers a new "Comet High Speed Perfect Binding line," capable of 10,000 per hour. For short runs the Martini "Econobinder" performs at the rate of 2400 per hour. For the cheerful and energetic Swiss, the future seems busy enough in the world bookbinding machinery market.

The Dexter Company offers extensive inline gathering, stitching, covering, and adhesive-binding equipment. For a paperback line either

Dexter's single-raceway gatherer or its high-speed dual raceway planetary gathering machine may be used, the latter giving speeds up to 200 books per minute. Components like joggers, calipers, pockets, adhesive systems, dryers, stitchers, are changeable.

The Dexter high-speed adhesive binder, introduced 1964, is available with 21 to 65 clamps, producing up to 200 books per minute. Both long and short runs are possible because of quick adjustments: single handwheels, for example, control pile guides and pockets. The machine also features an open-clamp detector which drops a vacant clamp out of operation, preventing jams and applicators from building up excess glue. Modular construction allows pockets, adhesive systems, dryers, and other attachments to be added or removed as necessary. The heart of the Dexter adhesive binder is a system of backbone preparation originally inspired for a special hard-bound application (p 315).

Gane Brothers & Lane, Inc., Chicago (auspiciously celebrating its 125th year in 1971 and claiming to be the largest graphic arts

suppliers in the business) furnishes to the American trade the British Sulby Bindmaster (Sulby Engineering Development Company, London), capable of 3000 books per hour. Another model does 1500. For smaller runs a new version introduced in 1963, the Sulby Auto-Minabinda, has a fully automatic feed clamp which carries gathered signatures over a milling cutter, over the adhesive, and then to the covering station. It uses a one-shot hot melt for instant drying and immediate trimming, turning out 500 per hour. A still smaller Minabinda, hand-operated, with two girls can do 250 books per hour.

The machine works of August Kolbus, with plants at Rahden, Bassum, and Minden, Germany, and over 70 years' experience, manufactures a wide range of bindery equipment, offered in the United States by Schuler Sales and Service Company, Bergenfield, New

New gatherer-binder control cabinet for latest Sheridan standard adhesive binding line. Fault/jam detection lights (1-8) on console and atop machine indicate defects: faulty incoming book (1); infeed or clamp problem (2, 3); missing cover (4); glueing or cover problem (5, 6, 7); book stuck in clamp (8). The combination operates at 10,000 books per hour. (Gatherer not shown.) [The Sheridan Company]

Jersey. Included are board and cloth cutters, case-makers, embossing presses, nipping, smashing, and glueing machines, rounder-backers, backlining and headbanding machines, casing-in machines, most of which can be assembled into automatic book production lines. In 1969 Schuler introduced a casing-in, building-in, and rounder-backer in-line combination capable of 70 books per minute. The new Kolbus adhesive binder, model RP 2415, does 3000 books per hour, up to $9\frac{7}{8}$ x $15\frac{3}{4}$ x $2\frac{1}{8}$ inches.

Other European adhesive binders continue to appear rapidly—the German trade, starved for sewing machines, especially welcomes threadless binding. After World War II a German engineer, Hans Ehlermann, began to manufacture "Quick Binder" machinery from 1938 patents of an inventor named Lumbeck: at the heart of it is a novel back-and-forth fanning operation over rollers (instead of roughening action) to force glue onto the sides of pages. Ehlermann's "Fanflex" with 23 clamps does 1500–3600 per hour; his "Fanquick" does 700. The German Flexstabil (K. G. Hollmann, Darmstadt) adds a deeper milling unit to the Martini for large, thick books. The German "Masso" makes notches on a rilled guillotine; the German "Plana-Flexibu" is for hand work. Consolidated-Mueller makes a "Jet-Binder" with a ferris-wheel apparatus for cooling hot-melt adhesives at the rate of 8000–10,000 books per hour.

The Swiss Thouvenin Company's Model R-24 replaces its earlier Model 300. The Swiss semi-automatic Bufalo "Sewingless" adhesive binder (W. Gantenbein, Maschinenbau) does 800 per hour. Les Machines Ledeuil, Paris, makes an adhesive binder for small applications like check books. A Japanese firm, Toyomenka, Inc., offers two adhesive binder models, MB-1 claiming 30,000 per hour, and MB-2, 1600–4800 per hour. Many of these will succeed in finding a lasting place in world binderies, others will not.

The adhesive-binding industry today is the fastest growing bindery operation in the United States. Shops divide themselves generally according to size of run. For quantities over 100,000—considered "large" runs—only Sheridan or Martini equipment is likely to be feasible. This is still principally the realm of national magazines, directories, and catalogs. For quantities below 2000, semi-automatic or hand-operated units probably will suffice. Generically, four principal techniques may be distinguished on present-day machinery: (1) trimming the fold and roughening the spine surface (Sheridan); (2) trimming the fold and fanning the pages (some German machines); (3) cutting of notches into conventionally folded signatures (Cahen-Dexter, p 314); (4) Cutting of notches into accordion-folded sheets (Cameron, p 320). Of these, and of the many manufacturers around the world, only Sheridan, by its many years in the trade and the extent of its experience in the adhesive binding area, seems to have the capacity to furnish binders the equipment they want during a span of bookwork that may evolve beyond today's processes.

With the perfection of adhesive binding many of the traditional bookmaking steps are forgotten. New speed breakthroughs were achieved. With 25 people—and an adhesive binder/gatherer, a band saw, a three-knife trimmer, and (optional) facilities for edge-staining—a modern book bindery could manufacture and pack 135,000 books in 7½ hours, about 720 books (384 pages) per man-hour. And such quantities were not merely academic: the process would solve another tremendous World's Fair production dilemma.

Electronic Perfect Binders, Inc., Brooklyn, New York, was the special creation of Henry M. Newman, who founded the firm. Sheridan furnished a perfect binder in 1963 to Newman's unique specifications, calling for fully automated electronic circuits (costing $50,000 beyond the basic binder price) which handle starting and stopping, speed control, adhesives temperature, roughener pattern and speed, and scoring, hinging, tipping, and inserting operations of which the machine was capable. One of Newman's own components was a waste removal system in which shavings and paper dust are blown through overhead ducts to a furnace, while larger scraps are baled. With these features Newman's staff was reduced to 12, and in two shifts Electronic can bind most kinds of work at a rate of 168,000 books per day. "You put in paper," said an employee, "it comes out books."

As in 1876, it was most appropriate that such revolutionary equipment be available for another auspicious World's Fair. The 1964 fair guidebooks, 5 x 8 inches, 312 pages plus cover, were automatically gathered and adhesive-bound continuously at Electronic until 4 million copies were manufactured—one of the longest runs on record. With books manufactured like periodicals, why return to traditional bookwork with its costly, laborious, semi-manual techniques? But the traditional bindery had had its revolution too.[18]

["His gestures are few, but significant. Sometimes he stands with his hands in his breast pockets; once or twice he walked a few steps to and fro. He did not mind the distant noises and the litter and machinery, but doubtless rather enjoyed them. He was perfectly self-possessed. . . ."]

*Part III*

# MODERN BOOKS
# AND PUBLISHING

"*You shall watch how the printer sets type, and learn what a compos-*
*ing stick is;*
*You shall mark, in amazement, the Hoe press whirling its cylinders,*
*shedding the printed leaves steady and fast:*
*The photograph, model, watch, pin, nail, shall be created for you. . . .*
*Mark—mark the spirit of invention everywhere—thy rapid patents,*
*Thy continual workshops, foundries, risen or rising;*
*See, from their chimneys, how the tall flamefires stream! . . .*"

[Walt Whitman]

# 7 America:

## The Automated Line

To PROTECT VALUABLE MANUSCRIPTS AND DECORATED LEATHER bindings, cardboard and leather boxes or slipcases have long been used, some of them as ornate and costly as their contents. One type, the solander (named after a British Museum official who developed it for storing prints), with tight-fitting cover, completely surrounds the book for which it is carefully molded. Under most conditions it is fire resistant, giving it a usefulness far beyond its beauty. Quaritch as a test once threw a $1200 book, encased in one of Zaehnsdorf's solanders, onto a roaring fire and then quenched it explosively with water: to Zaehnsdorf's intense relief the book came out unscathed. Collectors today still value the solander for this kind of emergency. For cheaper mass-produced books, however, far more humble protection was deemed adequate.

The beginning use of cloth, especially watered silk (popular between 1825–1850 for "Ladies' Boudoir Libraries"), probably necessitated some immediate protection against dirt and abrasion. At first glassine, kraft, or plain paper wrappers were put over the covers of books, the last sometimes simply printed with title on front, spine blank, and conventional advertisements for other books on the back. Such is the earliest existing jacket, printed in red on buff stock: Heath's *Keepsake* (Longmans, 1833). Gradually jackets appeared more frequently, printed by the binder from the dies themselves, usually in black ink on colored papers. There seemed little sense spending more on a "dust wrapper" functioning only to protect the binding beneath. Thus within seven years of the introduction of cloth, nevertheless, the British (and American) book as a package was not unlike today's product, physically, and so it remained, modestly, until the end of the century.

The art of the poster through the 1890's—thanks to several color printing processes—soon revolutionized the possibilities of all forms of advertising. In France Jules Chéret, already a poster expert with his own chromolithography shop, had begun illustrating book jackets about 1885 for Jules and Michel Lévy, maverick publishers of cheap books. Considered particularly appropriate for calendar, theater, magazine, and book sales, the poster in England developed uniquely in the hands of book illustrators (who also dominated the magazine world). Beardsley and his followers had dramatically brought bookish skills to everyone's attention; their employment exploded with great flair on the American magazine stands both as poster art and magazine cover as well.

Top-ranking US periodicals had long retained uniform, staid, unchanging covers to maintain their "identity" on the crowded newsstands. *Ladies' Home Journal* in the 1890's began bravely to change its cover every month, inviting considerable apprehension and speculation. "Perhaps," said Brander Matthews, naively, "the paper cover [was meant] to serve also as a pictorial poster to draw the attention of those who pass by the stall on which it is exposed. . . ." He conceded the value of this ploy, but deplored similar tactics in dime and shilling books, whose covers he considered too lurid to be appraised artistically. Bernard Grasset, considered a French "Walter Crane," had executed a special cover for *Harpers* (1889); Toulouse Lautrec did one for the US *Chap Book* (1896), and with such respectable names all barriers disappeared. Soon *Century, Lippincott's, Scribner's,* and other magazines were engaging the best artists for covers and posters—a scheme which survives today, although, as we have seen, the general-interest publication is fast disappearing from the nation's newsstands.

The influence of magazine treatment on books was inevitable, as was the general direction for both to gravitate toward the garish, the overly suggestive—excesses which colored the cheaper books of the 20th century right up to the recent paperback inundations. In 1948 a Jacket Designers Guild, meeting in New York, disclaimed any connection with the "top-heavy ladies draped in undress" school which seemed unwilling to utilize good design features like "integration [with the story]," or "expression [of the theme]," both of which made the jacket a link among author, publisher, bookstore, and reader. Despite a noble philosophy, however, the guild a few years later admitted that no "wrapper" by itself could sell a book, although the public had become so accustomed to the jacket it felt "cheated" when buying a book without one.

Modern book artists, E. R. Weiss and George Salter among them, saw the jacket as a cohesive part of the book—albeit the most blatant part—and attempted to coordinate their design. For popular literature, however, their intentions were frustrated: the abyss between jacket and book had long before been charted with mock humor—but genuine horror.

William A. Dwiggins in 1927 was clearly not sympathetic with the jacket artist:

> "The book jacket . . . began its career as a protective wrapping pure and simple. In its present evolved state it retains something of its purity—if the edition moves with reasonable speed—but it cannot by any means be called simple. . . . A walk down the aisle between the tables of best-sellers gives you something of the kick of a cocktail. . . . The jackets are very jolly things. There is only one count against them: they have taken the joy out of book covers. . . ."

Dwiggins earlier—in 1910—had concluded that "all books of the present day are Badly Made," following with a sequel in 1939 in which he was again obviously pained by the money spent on jackets (instead of bindings), but he himself (in 1927) had explained why this was so:

> "There was a time not many years ago when book covers did a bit of reveling on their own account. . . . There were bright-colored cloths, and colored inks, and colored foils, and gold. And were they not handsome? As a matter of fact, they weren't. The colored inks were sticky and dull; the foils flaked off; the designs were feeble indications of the New Art of the period. . . ."[1]

There was indeed a period of technological difficulty.

Gold and other metallic colors as roll leaf—made from metal powders and sizing sprinkled on glassine paper with a thin beeswax coating —had been invented about 1880 in Germany: Ernest Oeser was the pioneer foil maker, "perfecting" white in 1890 and bronze in 1905. An American product, Peerless Roll Leaf, was not on the market until 1916, and even then deprecated by finer binders and publishers as a poor substitute for gold leaf. Flaking off, and, as with the French metallic ink stampings of earlier decades, loss of lustre and discoloration

were common among all the imitation foils. (Today, on modern embossers, by judicious application of pressure—usually 9–12 tons, temperatures—240–300°F, and contact time or "dwell"—1/10th of a second,
new imitation metal foils can be released from their backing film under
optimum conditions at 2500 impressions per hour, and except under
conditions of hostile chemical ambience, they retain their grip and their
luster admirably.)

In the first half of the 20th century, however, book designers wanted
far more decoration for both stamped covers and printed paper covers.
Beardsley, Crane, A. E. Housman, and "greatest of all," Charles Ricketts (whose limited edition of Oscar Wilde, *Sphinx* is his masterpiece, according to Douglas Leighton) designed stamped covers in
6–8 colors, and when even greater tonal effects were wanted, resorted
to full-color printed designs which had to be applied to cloth bindings
as paper labels. Hundreds of cheap novels in England and the United
States were similarly successful, like Macquoid, *Berris* (US Book Company, 1895) whose printed cover depicted "a young girl walking forward, her wind-blown skirts, flying cape and picture hat contrasting
finely with her quiet, absorbed face, which is bent toward a book she
is intently reading. . . . . ," considered very artistic and not at all too
ambitious. Gradually the multicolor label, however, yielded to the
multicolor jacket as a far simpler manufacturing problem.

With colorful jackets everywhere the costly rendition of heavy
design on book bindings was relieved. The binding, as Dwiggins lamented, never again received prime attention, although during the
1931 depression, when any sales device was welcome, Doubleday,
Doran, with books designed by A. P. Tedesco, urged purchasers to
"take off the wrappers . . . show the exquisite bindings." Occasionally
today blind stamped, pre-printed, or silk-screened designs—when particularly suited to their graphic process—have called appropriate and
harmonious attention to themselves. Artists, however, engaged to create jackets often without regard for the design of the book's interior,
were seldom expected to attempt any "cohesion" whatsoever. More
unfortunate, perhaps, it appeared at first that no one was responsible
for the interior portions either.

Until well beyond the turn of the century publishers were less concerned with typography than with utility. Token respect was paid to
"fidelity and truth," "grace of line," and "imagination" as the peculiar
essentials of "American" design. But once electrotypes or stereotypes
had been cast an edition was expected to remain in print for 30–40
years, a span of time no design could survive. But as costs went up
publishers took more aggressive economic control—if not physically
by in-house production—of their bookwork, and finally faced the

spectre of complete book design. Some of them had no trouble at all.

With Bruce Rogers in their employ from 1895–1914, Houghton Mifflin turned out countless books well wrought, about 60 Riverside Press editions of especial beauty done by him. Stone & Kimball in Chicago (1893–1896) issued small twelvemos in Pickering's style, much recognized and prized by collectors. In Boston Copeland & Day's (1893–1899) books were also among the best. Both these small firms also had precious literary journals fashioned after *Yellow Book*. These and a few other scattered efforts at fine bookwork, however, represented the end of a lavish Victorian era rather than the start of excellence in machine-made products.

After World War I inflation had eaten away much of the industry's capacity for better bookmaking. The J. F. Tapley Company in 1920 explained to publishers (as would Kingsport Press a quarter-century later) that the only solutions were machine production and inexpensive materials: "even now," said the company, trying not to be ominous, "many publishers are using embossed papers instead of cloth and . . . imitation gold and ink. . . ." As the depression followed, the private presses were soon abandoned, and several semi-commercial ones, like Updike's Merrymount in Boston (machinery sold to Norwood Press) and William E. Rudge's Sons (sold to Geffen, Dunn & Company) also faded away like old soldiers, their crusading work largely accomplished. Paradoxically, Lehmann-Haupt pointed out that increased mechanization and industrialization has only increased the importance of design; the experimental presses may have never been needed for that particular lesson. For their mechanically made books, nevertheless, trade publishers began to engage book designers.

In England B. H. Newdigate's exploratory articles, "Book Production Notes," through the 1920's had begun to train publishing people in a craft that had scarcely existed outside the compositor's shop. A little irony salted his lessons: "The Utopian book is not a mere congeries of paper, print and binding. . . . The binding is decorated rather more lavishly than with us and with far better taste. . . ." Dwiggins too made contributions to the subject: the designer, he said, is faced with the conflict of making the book functional (for easy reading) and at the same time conspicuous (for sales). For this kind of enigmatic work Richard Ellis, for over 60 years a designer and producer of exceptional books, maintained that the appropriate name should be "book architecture." Frederic G. Melcher warned in 1927 that another paradox must be scuttled:

"And in spite of what is occasionally averred, a well-designed book does cost more than a poorly designed book, because good design requires the time and intelligence of especially competent persons, and time and intelligence must cost money. . . ."[2]

But lest designers be carried away with praise and attention, Arthur A. Cohen of Meridian Books put book design in sober perspective: "Good design may affect the appeal of a book," he said in 1957, "but good design will not sell a bad book." There was nevertheless no disputing the publisher's need for designers to settle the minutiae of typeface selection, margins, and compatibility of materials.

Robert Josephy, who claims to be the first professional book designer to be retained by a manufacturer (J. J. Little & Ives) for the service of publishers, had for many years found his calling so unfamiliar to publishers he was almost unrecognized even among his clients. Retiring in 1960 from a thoroughly industrialized bindery world, Josephy found himself far more cynical—despite a long and distinguished career—than Cobden-Sanderson: "I don't think there will be any radical changes in book production methods," said Josephy, "as long as everybody is making a lot of money. . . ." The economics of contemporary publishing had been sufficiently traumatic, however, with depression and war before paperback boom, so that many modern publishing people are often understandably unsure about the role—and effect—of designer, salesman, and production manager.

The heart of publishing is deciding what books are to be published (the acquisition area in which publishers most proudly identify themselves), how many are to be manufactured, and how the market is to be reached. Still recovering from the depression of 1893, Putnam's in 1904 told their authors how painful these decisions could be: in their observation half the books published yearly in America failed to return their cost, and half the remainder brought no profit. The entire industry was thus obliged to survive on the remaining quarter. To Swinnerton the averages seemed more kind: "A few good books do not sell"; he said, "many bad books do sell; but since the majority of the books published are neither very good nor very bad, . . . I think there is a kind of rough justice in the fates of most of them."

Of the publisher's remaining decisions, however, the size of the edition or quantity first brings him squarely to face the economic realities of book design and manufacture. "There is nothing so easy or so common," said Charles Knight in 1854, when the prospect of books by the million first began to loom as an obtainable goal, "as to over-rate a demand in the commerce of books." Most publishers have found themselves far too optimistic about the number of times "everyone from eight to eighty" will want to buy a new publication. Excess stocks and warehouse costs have all too frequently tied up capital better used for newer projects. Also involved is the publisher's obligation to pay both authors and suppliers at least partially in advance of sales, and to publicize, promote, and advertise on a pitifully limited budget.

The depression of the 1930's, like the one that ended the 19th century, put every sales tenet to the test. Few publishers had George Macy's opportunity, with Limited Editions Club (founded 1929), to capitalize on unemployed artists and low production costs to produce gems for the collector. The reaction of publishers with broad trade experience had been a bombardment of cheap paperbacks, as we have seen, and cheaper hardbound books.

Coincidental with depression conditions, banker and lawyer Orion H. Cheney had just spent 15 months making an analysis, inaugurated by the National Association of Book Publishers, of pre-depression publishing. His 320-page report, with 17 pages of recommendations for the industry, was full of witticisms at which many couldn't laugh:

> "The idea that a book is good because it is well-bound or cleverly illustrated or in a limited edition is destructive of standards. . . . A primary confusion is that between a good-looking book and a well-made book—even among the technicians."

> "If a book achieves good sales, under present conditions it is anybody's guess as to what caused the magic. . . . Best-sellerism [because it mislabels books not truly selling best, was an] intolerable curse on the industry."

> "The love of books is the industry's strength because it is the most powerful incentive to the expression of the feeling of craftsmanship in publishing [but it was also the industry's great weakness]."

> "Between these two points [the binder's warehouse and the book buyer] is the tragedy of the book industry . . . a tragedy without a villain."

A last specimen of Cheney epigram would alienate (or confound) anyone:

> "There is no consumer industry of any importance in this country which does not show as discouraging a record of blindness, planlessness, waste and inefficiency as that of the book industry."[3]

Cheney surmised that people bought books for (1) self-improvement, (2) curiosity, (3) recreation, (4) escape, (5) identification, (6) vicarious thrills, (7) status—but accused the industry of ignoring these motivations in sales campaigns. (Other surveys over several decades produced similarly disturbing results—and depression was not a factor: the United States had the lowest proportion of book readers of any major democracy—1950; almost 90 percent of all homes designed and built for the medium or "popular" price level in the United States had no built-in bookshelves—1957.) Cheney concluded that distribution was the chief difficulty in all four methods: (1) direct from publisher to customer ("direct sales"); (2) from publisher through wholesale and retail outlets (the "trade," with its customary 40 percent discount); (3) used books in the old and rare book markets and auctions; (4) newsstands—at that time something of an experiment. Cheney criticized lack of coordination, unplanned "list-making" and promotion, and general inefficiency. But many resented his smug analyses and sarcastic tone. The report had almost no immediate effect.

Equally disturbing to publishers were the design and manufacturing comments of critics of a new age. The Bauhaus lesson that mechanically made things could be beautiful had not brought with it any surge of esthetically made books after all. The 1933 *Penrose Annual* instead described national characteristics of bookmaking with damning perspicacity:

(1) Germany (although then "divided and torn by politics"): "The German book is like a man who knows how to dress well and decently, even with limited means, according to his social position, renouncing any falsely distinguished appearance. . . ."

(2) England: "The elegance of the well-dressed man who wears his clothes with the force and freedom of habit. . . ."

(3) America: "The elegance of the man specially dressed up for a party."[4]

Americans had indeed found it hard to be "comfortable" with books. Melcher with Newbery (1921) and Caldecott (1936) medals hoped to draw public attention to excellence without affectation in children's books, as have American Institute of Graphic Arts' "Fifty Books of the Year" exhibitions. Despite the superiority of American bookmaking machinery, despite the Riverside Press' fine example, the United States lacked confidence and taste in making books—right up to World War II. After the war there was ample time and attention to attack the problem.

Too much American design, said Merle Armitage in 1949, spoke with a British accent. His charges against American publishers and bookmakers were perhaps the most vehement of all:

"The book, . . . the principal tool by which man has educated himself, . . . the grand escalator that has brought us all up from darkness and slavery into light and freedom, has, in our time, lost its leadership, and is uncertain of its function and its direction.

"Books of today are not reflecting their time . . . a source of vitality they have always possessed, nor do they possess an honest character.

They are anonymous among their fellows, and are becoming comparatively impotent as a means of communication. All this is transpiring at a moment in history when they are about to meet their severest test.

"This is a situation that must engage every person who believes in books, who loves them as fascinating creations, and who is convinced that an appropriately designed and manufactured book really has no rival among all the known vehicles, or methods, of communication.

"America is possibly the most resourceful and inventive country in the world. Yet in America, the book has received the least attention from men of imagination and power. . . ."

"The book today is, for the most part, a failure. Most designers, printers, publishers and others responsible for the decadence of the book seem singularly unaware of today's problems. . . ."[5]

Armitage placed the blame largely on publishers "who purchase manuscripts they have never read [and] assign them to designers who will never read them."

Similarly perplexing were features of the book which production manager Arthur W. Rushmore found questionable. He believed the wide outside and foot margins we so appreciate today resulted only because noblemen before the age of soap and silverware had perpetually greasy fingers. He also attacked other fundamentals:

"Why do we like books that are upright rectangular in shape? Why not square ones? . . . Why are the tops trimmed and smooth to the touch where you do not touch them, while the front and foot have messy, furry and uneven edges that shed fluff all over your blue serge? . . ."[6]

All were based on sound reasons, no doubt, but now long forgotten; we call them, said Rushmore, matters of "taste."

William Dwiggins also attacked tenets that had seldom been seriously challenged, and found, specifically, that in the United States (as perhaps in Holland) some books were bound all too well:

"Aided by the machine (and limited to one single manner of making by the machine) [trade book covers] and bindings are excellent mechanically. Try to break a book down and you will see. But, if you look at those books as I do—as Ephemera—does it strike you that their covers are *functionally* in line with the purpose to be served? Functionally they are *too* good. They don't need to last so long. Their cost is all out of proportion to the work they do. . . ."[7]

The trade book, meant to be read and cast aside, should be bound more simply, Dwiggins concluded, in keeping with its short life expectancy; the paperback today must answer his description all too well. "Let there be cooperation among those whose work makes the final form of a book:" said Gyorgy Kepes, with intentions, apparently, of ending a sharp criticism on a harmonious note, "the author, the book designer, the printer, the photoengraver." Somehow he had slighted the binder, in whose custody the entire package is placed. Few bookmen, nevertheless, realized that such post-war exploratory questions signalled the end of an era.

At work in the manufacture of cheap editions from the start of the Industrial Revolution was the fact that bookwork, thanks to Gutenberg, was already entirely cloistered in the chapels and guilds of printing and bindery trades—for which esthetics became a minor concern. Beauty as the mechanician saw it was in the sometimes ingenious skill of keeping steam engines from exploding, fan belts from snapping, rounder-backers from pounding spines into pulp, and embossers from driving dies cleanly through cloth and board. (Similarly, we are today so consumed by the electronic performance of computers we don't seem to notice how ugly and unwieldy the printouts are.) At the same time the shifting economics of labor, materials, and elusive publishers' orders made it appear periodically that the entire industry of untested "sawmills" and unsure sales techniques would collapse. With worries such as these it is no wonder that the appearance of books in Europe and America degenerated into the slavish 19th-century repetition that McLean called "no taste at all."

As the technical aspects of bookmaking and the expenses of new machinery increased toward the end of the century there was no inherent inducement to alter the perspectives. William Morris rightly questioned the disregard for care in bookmaking—but his violent, theatrical return to the days of Gutenberg (and before) was no solution. Yet so persuasive was the charm of his arts and crafts movement two world war intervened before the book could be examined without longings for leather and deckle edge. Only the temporal detachment of 75 years (neither geographical or cultural distance nor mechanical superiority were sufficient) and the incidental economic evolutions of modern living would oblige American book people to return to the problem Morris had not solved. It had to be solved again—for America.

In too large a country to expect a single man either with *précieuseté* or *buchkunst* to guide the future of bookmaking, Americans even at mid-20th century would have difficulty recognizing trends or improvements couched in purely esthetic terms. Merle Armitage came closest to tabulating American design inadequacies, but his design solutions were too personal for others to find inspirational. Pragmatically, the searching questions about the look of the book only remind us that the sewed, cased-in product is essentially a British invention dating, as we have seen, to the 1820's. (So it will always be.) The development of book sewer, case-making, and casing-in equipment were ingenious and flattering attempts to perfect that uniquely foreign package; and such attempts continued well after World War II to reduce its cost and speed its production in binderies all around the world (p 279). The truly American book to emerge from these explorations—the start of a new era—was not far off, but, as if to demonstrate that Britons still knew best how to make cased-in books—even with American machinery—another important plant emerged. Cobden-Sanderson's "unexpected" took place in an unexpected locale: Edinburgh.[8]

Thomas Nelson about 1798 opened a second-hand bookshop in the Scottish capital, and soon turned to publishing classics and religious works. His sons William and Thomas joined him between 1835–40 with such enthusiasm (Thomas Jr. is credited with inventing a rotary printing press exhibited at the 1851 London Exposition) they built a manufactory outside of town employing 600 hands. A calamitous fire in 1878, however, destroyed the shop (but not the printing plates of hundreds of titles in several popular series), obliging the Nelsons to rebuild.

The new plant at nearby Parkside was tremendous, even by 20th-century standards. A reporter from *The British Printer* found book-binding alone "on a scale almost unprecedented in our experience." But Thomas Nelson & Sons had not yet shown him an even greater operation—its "New Factory."

For truly cheap books by the million—in dimensions that redeemed Constable's dream and dwarfed even J. M. Dent's enterprise, Nelson in 1907 designed a new self-contained annex to the Parkside plant. There the Scottish firm planned to mass-manufacture 6 and 7 penny cloth-bound "classics" literally without anyone touching them. Within a few years the company was able to proclaim:

> "The New Factory is practically one gigantic bookmaking machine, turning out 30,000 books a day. Labour-saving machinery has abolished all porterage and hard manual labour; the employees simply feed machines. . . ."[9]

Elbert Hubbard's strongest critics would certainly have joined him in censuring both Nelson's bookbinding "philosophy" and its workers who (like those in Chicago) seemed on a colossal scale indifferent to their lack of involvement and craftsmanship. But Nelson—before the Bauhaus, before Francis Meynell—had already come to terms privately with the machine.

The merit of the Nelson plant was scarcely a semblance of "tender loving care," to be sure; its sweeping organization and efficiency appealed not to booklovers, but to mechanical engineers and accountants.

Nelson's automation for books was already an enactment of the concept Bredenberg and Juengst had visualized for magazines. Composition facilities and foundry departments were exemplary. Rotary printing presses (unusual for bookwork) with built-in Dexter folding apparatus provided the fastest possible presswork. For an automated high-speed bindery, however, there was very little equipment commercially available to assure comparable output.

As a start, however, Nelson took 25 Smyth book sewers, 5 Sheridan roll-fed case-makers, a Smyth three-sided trimmer—one of the very first—and new Crawley rounder-backers: all but the sewing machines, or course, introduced to the British market only months before. Similarly, the 1897 gathering machine of John Mercer (at this time chairman of James Burn & Company) was brought in, one of the few non-American machines available. Of these, the Sheridan case-maker drew particular attention, "indeed a *multum in parvo*," said the *British Printer* visitor:

> "It glues the cloth, places the strawboard and back lining in exact position, cuts off the corners, turns over the edges, presses and delivers the case, . . . [at 1200 pieces per hour]."[10]

But all this equipment, individually designed by competitive companies, was hardly compatible for the degree of inline production Nelson contemplated. Something more was necessary.

For the Parkside New Factory much binding equipment had to be custom designed. The Parkside lining (glueing) machine, the Parkside casing-in machine, the Parkside gatherer, and the Parkside endpapering machine shortly materialized, developed by the plant's chief engineer, John Murray—whose work, according to Marian Lawson, was "an original contribution of first rate importance in the development of bookbinding machinery." Equally significant, perhaps, was the Nelson/Murray concept of complete conveyorization from one machine—and one department—to another. With electric tramway for heavy loads, overhead runways, and floor conveyors, there were three lanes of automated materials handling which for many years to come would still be unknown in the best American shops. At Parkside the conveyor system culminated with an ingenious "zig-zag book chute" which flopped books from one side to the other as it carried them between floors to inspectors and stackers.

Thanks mostly to the mechanical processing of materials by belt conveyor equipment, production time dropped considerably. "The new materials enter one end of the room," said the company, "and in twenty minutes finished books can be ready to slide down chutes into stock at the other end." The plant, "Greatest Book Factory in the

World," produced 200,000 books per week with ease, many of them in a 6½ x 4¼-inch format so familiar to readers it was called "Nelson size." (A generation later readers would label these dimensions "Pocket Book size.") Nelson almost surprised itself with its capacity for speed: upon the death of King Edward VII in 1910, 120,000 copies of a biography were on the market within three days.

The production of 10 million volumes a year, no small challenge to world-wide Nelson salesmanship (its New York branch dates to 1854) under the most prosperous conditions, became an obvious dilemma during the war and depression. The plant was eventually forced to curtail operations, and the firm soon abandoned its printing capability altogether.

During the first decades of the 20th century John Murray undertook to manufacture commercially some of the machines he had designed for the Nelson plant. T. W. & C. B. Sheridan, as it had for Mercer's gatherer, handled sales for Murray both in Europe and in the United States. The hand-fed Parkside casing-in machine, almost noiseless, was touted in 1909:

> "A neater book than has hitherto been obtainable by any process is insured by the case-forming device on this machine [said Sheridan]. The same result is obtained that formerly could only be had by passing books after casing thru a rounding and backing machine."[11]

After World War II the Murray casing-in machine, capable of 24 books per minute, was again distributed in America for a while.

Despite his genius, however, Murray lacked the capital and business acumen to become the giant of English bookbinding machinery the British trade might have welcomed. Nelson's automation experiences were quietly forgotten too; they furnished other binders no guide, even in principal, except, perhaps, that speed must necessarily be coupled only with elephantine proportions—and even then there was no guarantee of success.

Although the Parkside facilities had been modernistically organized in sprawling one- and two-story buildings recognizable today wherever industry operates, Nelson officials later believed, nostalgically, perhaps, that a multistoried factory would have expedited materials handling even more efficiently. Elevators and zig-zag chutes were indeed compact and practical, and gravity would always work for nothing. Considering the sleepy development of most binderies, however, the architectural problem was quite academic.

We have already seen how, in the United States, the biggest shops had indeed organized themselves into efficient floor-by-floor departments through which edition bookwork passed. Few proprietors, however, welcomed the prospect of modernizing except at the cost of fire or some other catastrophe to compel efficiency. Smaller shops seldom reaped such rewards in any case. Often the adjuncts of larger press-rooms, their binderies grew fitfully. Second-hand machinery was usually bought, crude tables erected from scrap lumber, gathering "wheels" became homemade novelties, and waste floor space allocated only as necessary. But the vertical production line, however well conceived, fared poorly in principle as improved machinery accomplished more and more work in less and less space. (Expensive multiple-story structures, requiring reinforcement for heavy equipment and extraordinary elevators for materials, would be obviated in most instances by relocating in suburban communities.) For a long time, however, binderies worked furiously—into the 1920's—with little thought of planning for expansion.

The H. Wolff Book Manufacturing Company, New York, suddenly accomplished a modernization program with talent and flair. Founded 1893 by Harris Wolff and Nathan Schrifte to wire-stitch juveniles for The Hurst Publishing Company, it soon developed other clients as well, many of whom, like Alfred A. Knopf, appreciated its good bookwork. For a completely new Manhattan plant Walter Steinmann, a young engineer and inventor, in 1926 organized all the bookmaking machinery into "straight-through" production lines, inspired—not, alas, by Nelson—largely by the success of such assembly line systems in the automobile industry.

> "We have a special plant engineer [said a Wolff executive, grandly] whose entire time is devoted to studying production possibilities and the turning out of work in better and more efficient style. Several of our machines are the only ones of their kind in the country since they were built for our special needs by the manufacturers. . . . We are believers in the latest and most modern bookbinding equipment."[12]

Fundamentally, it was a question of machine delivery facing subsequent machine feed, but it was escalated into geometrical proportions by the company's 14 folders, 2 Sheridan gatherers, 46 Smyth sewers, 5 Singer sewers, and other pieces. Designed were expedient interconnections of conveyor belts, strategically placed stockpiles, wheeled bins, and other materials-handling equipment. For Wolff Steinmann also developed a glueing machine and a case-maker for flexible books. (In 1968 American Book-Stratford Press acquired the H. Wolff Book Manufacturing Company.)

In 1937 Steinmann set up demonstration bindery equipment at the *New York Times* National Book Fair, New York, where, with straight-through features, volumes were manufactured with efficiency and public approbation. Steinmann, like Murray, was almost ahead of his time in modernizing the bindery, despite the fact, as we have seen, that newspaper and periodical shops had considered the inline concept indispensable fully a quarter of a century before. Such modernization involved careful planning, obviously, but—surprisingly—almost no expenditure for major equipment. In any event, the intervention of World War II put an end to such thinking—although at the same time it furnished to a newly awakening industry some tempting opportunity for speculation about great inline binderies of the future.

Similarly overshadowed by the war was research in another area critical to the impending success of the straight-line bindery. Following their codification of glues, as we have seen, bookbinders and glue manufacturers working with US GPO facilities next tackled the vexing problem of "yawning" covers, a warping of cloth-covered boards, after casing-in, that defied explanation for many years. (Its cause was suspected but unproved for decades.) This was a paste problem, and paste, a water mixture made from various starches or grain flours, like glue was very old—and long misunderstood. BMI chemist Blaylock in 1941 at last described the ailment:

"When paste comes in contact with the end sheets of the book, during the casing-in operation, some of the water in the paste is absorbed by the paper and the sheets expand. . . . When the end sheets are pressed against the boards in the book cover, the boards also absorb water from the paste. . . . When moistened on both sides, the loss in strength [of the boards] amounts to 15 or 20 percent. In other words, when moist they become less able to resist bending. While the cover boards are still moist and the end papers are stretched to their maximum degree of expansion, the paste sets and holds the end sheets firmly in place. The end papers then begin to dry out and attempt to contract to their orginal size. This places a pull or stress on the boards at a time when they are least able to resist strain. The result is a warped book cover."[13]

Glucose-glycol, a non-warping paste containing a low (50 percent) water content, was developed, and another mysterious old bindery problem disappeared.

In Europe, however, the nagging problem of warp has never been satisfactorily settled. Confronted with cheaper materials and humid climate, a British binder in 1958 described the dilemma: "We have to choose between Kent chipboard which we can't get and Dutch strawboard which we don't like." Paper and press limitations, too, often result in books bound against the grain—paper direction at a right angle to the book's spine—which adds tensions as components absorb or release moisture in different directions. In any case, books manufactured not to warp in England will invariably do so if brought to more or less humid countries. It has been said of French cased-in books, on the other hand, that they are so extremely rounded (to protect the sewing—hence for long-range preservation) and so tightly backed they are difficult to open and almost impossible to read; they also warp inward so strongly they clutch the book like pincers. The moisture content of materials and adhesives is nevertheless the most persistent problem for binders all around the world.

Appraised of PVA research for the periodical and paperback industry, edition binders were quick to ask what the new compounds could do for hardbound work. The answer was speed; glueing-off adhesives could be made to dry in 5 seconds (instead of a 30-minute wait for animal glue), and such fast lining-up and casing-in adhesives followed in 1947. But high-speed conditions with almost instantaneous inline drying capabilities could be expected to engender strange—incompatible—components: resins, animal glues, hot melts, in a multiplication of formulas would demand care. And faulty glueing-off, either as "breaks" (nonglued gaps between signatures) or "starts" (signatures glued out of jogged alignment), could ruin a binder's reputation. Continuing research at the end of World War II, however, while promising, scarcely reflected the contemporary state of the industry, for which the obligatory phrase, "This is a war-time book," concealed paper allocations, priorities and shortages, and other manufacturing frustrations.

Upon the return to peacetime manufacturing conditions hostilities erupted where a century of harmony had once reigned. Clamoring for low post-war prices, publishers suddenly accused their manufacturers of waste and obsolescence, a broad charge perhaps easily substantiated. Most binders had indeed modernized very little since the turn of the century—when they acquired their plants from the publishers. (Although postwar technological improvements would enable binders almost to double their output, bindery workers would more than double their weekly wages.) Binders retorted that publisher mismanagement was actually at fault—had not Cheney shown distribution to be the worst area? Financiers looked at both parties, and before blessing the rabid mergers that were to follow, frowned on such bickering: "The great problem facing the [publishing] industry is not monopoly," said Bound, "it is failure to cooperate." But at odds in this sudden technological crisis were publishers whose knowledge of bookbinding was limited, and binders not really aware of their customers' new competition problems. Fortunately coolness prevailed.

Colonel E. W. Palmer, president of Kingsport Press, in 1948 spoke grandiloquently for his fellow binders, pointing out that the bindery— much like the composition and printing trades—in the last 50 years had indeed developed little that could promise immediate relief. "Technical advancement," he pointed out slyly, "is most commonly understood by publishers to mean immediate and tangible evidences of new mechanical devices that eliminate labor, speed up production, and are almost immediately reflected in reduced costs of bookmaking. . . ." He could not refrain from recollecting those 50 years:

> "It is probable that very few who read this statement will remember that as late as 1910 much of the machine folding of printed sheets was still accomplished on 'point-feed' folders—hand fed; that thintext and India Bible papers were folded by hand; that an 'extra-binding' department was to be found in every large modern bindery; that a bevy of gray-haired ladies were kept constantly employed at old-fashioned hand-sewing 'benches' sewing books that today are all done by machine; that all lining-up and headbanding was done by hand crews, as was much of the casing-in; that all books were rounded and backed on the hand-fed Crawley backers, or the slower, hand-operated, roller backer; that the best and fastest book trimmer was the old 'duplex' which handled two piles of books at a time, with the holding table turned by hand after each cut; that gold and leaf for stamping book covers was still laid on by hand!"[14]

Colonel Palmer was able, furthermore, to cite a few genuine technical advances on recent Sheridan and Smyth casing-in equipment, but the binding shops themselves, revitalized by wonderful self-generated enthusiasm, began to modernize dramatically—and without waiting for new machinery.

George McKibbin & Son (founded 1890) at the end of World War II converted its Brooklyn shop to straight-through organization, thereby realizing the sensational increase of 25 percent more production from existing equipment. (Between 1951 and 1970 this plant expanded and relocated in Brattleboro, Vermont, as The Book Press, since 1969 a division of General Educational Services Corp.) While new equipment was not yet forthcoming from the manufacturers, McKibbin's replication of H. Wolff's reorganization two decades before was sufficient for many other binders. Dozens of shops followed McKibbin: Doubleday, 1948 (p 285), Donnelley, 1950, American Book Company, 1953 (p 281), Quinn & Boden, 1958, Cuneo, 1958, Becktold, 1960. At Rand McNally the concept, after 10 years, was similarly applied—but with the additional legitimization of organizational "principles."

Printers since 1864, Rand McNally & Company began to publish in 1877, soon contributing an 1886 cheap "Globe Library" which reached 398 titles by 1895. For Andrew McNally and William H. Rand, however, atlases, guides, and texts long became the worthy specialty of the

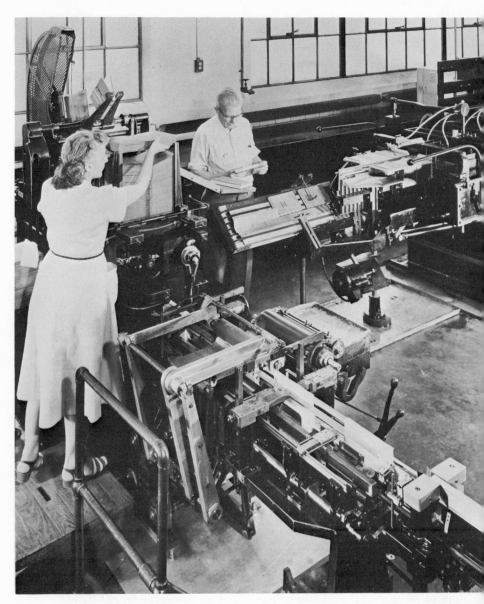

The "Smyth" corner at American Book Company, first fully designed inline operation using ultra-modern equipment. Books are seen at lower right moving from automatic backer (*not shown*) into book back gluer, then to "No. 24" casing-in machine, where girl is stacking cases. Inspector checks the squares as books emerge and head for book presser. [Smyth Manufacturing Company]

firm. In 1949 the W. B. Conkey Company was acquired, giving Rand McNally a plant in Hammond, Indiana, along with its others in Versailles, Kentucky, and Skokie, Illinois. In drastic 1956 modernizing the company pompously established three "principles" of inline, straight-through application: (1) automatic feed added to all equipment; (2) portable conveyors to make any number and variation of machinery connections; and (3) heavy-duty roller conveyors for handling all heavy loads, like paper skids. By this time, of course, all the bindery machinery makers had production lines well under way. They had much to offer.

The Smyth Manufacturing Company in 1944 had revealed the "future" for Smyth customers: (1) a new jacketing machine, (2) a fully automatic No. 12 sewer (p 290), and (3) a No. 40 combination casing-in and pressing machine (also called a building-in machine), which eliminated the building-in press. The last was already being tested at Country Life Press. These were old ideas, however (the casing-in and pressing machine dated to 1938), and the company prudently did not dwell on them. But Smyth before the war had thus recognized the importance of interconnected equipment—that many machines, defying the laws of mathematics, are more valuable together than they are individually.

In 1952 Smyth first applied the principles of automation to book-binding equipment. Involved was the interconnection of five conventional machines—a concept really no more profound than the binders' own reorganizations. But considerable alignment of components, timing of speeds, control features, and quality checks were required to make it fool-proof. From the Smyth No. 38 automatic rounder-backer books are conveyed to the No. 32 triple liner and headbander, the No. 24 casing-in machine, the No. 57 book former and presser, and finally, the No. 46 jacketer. Automatic hopper feeding mechanisms, and conveyor-feeders between machines, eliminate hand feeding at each machine, avoid bottlenecks, and free valuable floor space for storage or stacking.

For the American Book Company, Cincinnati (now a division of Litton Educational Publishing, Inc.), Smyth engineers in 1953 installed the first such automated five-machine inline operation: in 30 linear feet with one right angle, this "Smyth corner" manufactures side-sewn books untouched by hands—so satisfactorily it was duplicated within months at Colonial Press, H. Wolff, and R. R. Donnelley, all of whom agreed that the product, especially with regard to the joints, was superior to work done on individual machines. In Europe both Brodart & Taupin and James Burn & Son, among many others, put in similar lines in 1958. For trade books the line could include automatic jacketing and packing into cartons, if desired.

Despite complex mechanical actions—more than one observer has called the work of the case-maker "almost human"—over 150 Smyth automated lines, with some variations, have been installed around the world, 59 of them in the United States alone. These lines are now able to push a book through rounding and backing, lining-up, casing-in, and building-in, in 1 minute 55 seconds. Fred P. Hofferth, director of manufacturing at American Book Company, was apparently not impressed: "Too much of today's workmanship is bad;" he said in 1965, shortly before he retired, "today's fast machines don't do the job formerly possible on hand-operated equipment. . . ." For the international scope of its activities, nevertheless, The Smyth Manufacturing Company has been awarded the President's "E" flag for "excellence in exporting and for outstanding contributions to the increase of United States trade abroad."

Today Smyth offers, in addition to the Nos. 12 and 18 sewers, Nos.

The Smyth "M-66" casing-in machine performs joint pasting and back glueing at high speed. Another model, "M-68," handles larger books. [Smyth Manufacturing Company]

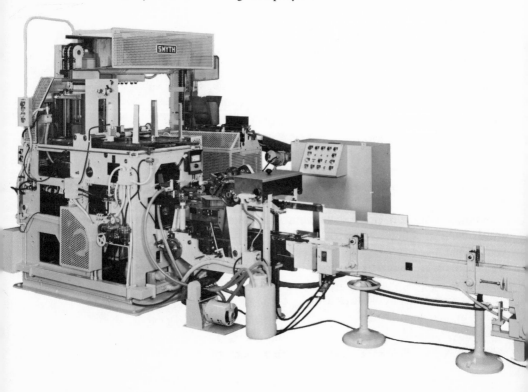

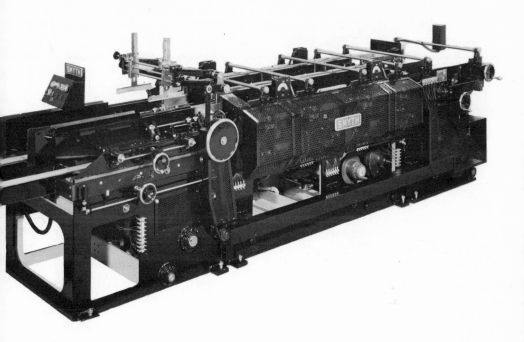

After casing-in, the "M-67" Smyth book forming and pressing machine forms, presses, and heat-sets the joints of two books at a time in two 6-station channels. [Smyth Manufacturing Company]

9 and 28 case-makers, Nos. 38 and 64 rounder-backers, Nos. 32 and 65 triple liner and headbanders, Nos. 24, 41, 66, and 68 casing-in machines, and Nos. 57, 59, 67, and 70 book former and pressers.

Redesignated M-9, the old No. 2 Smyth hand-fed or semi-automatic case-maker makes up to 18 cases per minute, from 7 x 11 to 14 x 22 inches. The automatic No. 28 does 21 per minute, 5½ x 7½ to 9½ x 15½ inches. Both machines have extended capabilities with accessory equipment.

Smyth casing-in equipment is extensive. A fully automatic rounding and backing machine does 36 books per minute, and can be equipped with a conveyor-feeder mechanism uniting it to the Smyth triple liner and headbander, which applies 1 or 2 crash linings and 1 paper, or 1 crash with 1 or 2 paper linings, both with or without headbands. Its speed is up to 40 books a minute. A conveyor leading to a Smyth casing-in machine is available.

The Nos. 3 and 24 casing-in machines are backbones of the edition book bindery. The No. 3 operates up to 25 books per minute, for work between ¼ and 2 inches in thickness, covers 4 x 7 to 14 x 22 inches in size. The No. 24 does 35 per minute, as small as 3¾ x 5½ x 11¼ inches.

In 1965 Smyth introduced a new single-blade casing-in machine, the M-68, capable of 35 books per minute. It handles bulks from ¼ to 3 inches. In the same year the company introduced the M-66 casing-in machine, producing 60 per minute. On both machines the case backs are pre-formed by thermostatically controlled electrically heated formers.

In 1957 Smyth had brought out its M-57 rotary book forming and pressing machine, a 9-pocket unit which applies heat and pressure through thermostatically controlled "creasers" to form the book. This new concept replaced the "venerable" standing presses with their accompanying brass-edged building-in boards. One model also has an index tabbing mechanism for up to 44 books per minute. Two years later the M-59, a 5-pocket inline presser capable of 25 books per minute, was offered. In 1967 a new dual channel presser, the M-67, with 12 stations, was introduced especially to run with the M-66 casing-in machine at 60 books per minute. The M-70 6-station pressing machine doing 36 books an hour was designed to run with the M-68 casing-in machine. Other bindery equipment manufacturers were also pressing toward similar high-speed straight-through goals. Impressive was the work for Doubleday, engineered largely by Peter de Florez and his associates.

Frank Nelson Doubleday, powerful, creative, egocentric, toiled patiently at Scribner's—for 20 years—until 1897, when he formed a publishing company with a succession of partners. John Farrar, an admirer, said of Doubleday: ". . . in a deep and emotional sense Effendi [his initials mean "master" in Turkish] loved publishing. He lived it and breathed it, poring over every intricate process of editing and manufacture. . . ." But more than this was needed: Doubleday himself claimed that in many lesser publishing houses "courage" was the missing element. Contrary to the trend, Doubleday felt he must have his own manufacturing facilities, and designed them—courageously.

Like Dent's operation at Letchworth, Doubleday's Garden City plant, the Country Life Press, erected 1910, was graced by bucolic greenery—and an extraordinary typographic sundial. Here young Alfred A. Knopf worked, after a 1912 London trip in which he began to notice the design of books. In Country Life's production department Knopf began to indulge an interest in bookmaking which has never flagged. (Knopf left Doubleday after 18 months to start his own firm in 1915; he is credited with introducing unfinished—"natural" finish—book cloths, long popular in Europe, to America.)

With hand bindery, as we have seen, as well as complete machine facilities, the Garden City shop was a showplace of modern mass book-work on a grand scale. Cheap books in series tumbled out, many under subsidiary imprints: Star Dollar Books, Sundial Books, DeLuxe, Crime Club, Dollar Mystery Club, and others, kept the shop busy. Many of these projects reached new markets developed by Doubleday's son Nelson, who formed the subsidiary Garden City Publishing Company, and who demonstrated as much genius at book sales as his father.

In 1948 Doubleday began to build new, modern facilities at Berry-ville, Virginia, and Hanover, Pennsylvania, and in 1956 closed its Gar-den City operations. Considering the bleak post-war conditions, as we have seen, of paperback overproduction, rising manufacturing costs, and (elsewhere), publisher-binder mistrust, Doubleday's expansion program, like Putnam's Sons fifty years before, raised a few eyebrows. Dutscher, gloomily describing the poor state of American publishing, elaborated upon Doubleday's added "vertical monopolization" burden:

> "The fact that the firm is in possession of its own manufacturing plant means that it is confronted with yet another enormously expen-sive overhead charge which renders it imperative that the presses be kept running continuously if the business is to remain profitable."[15]

He expected the company's numerous book clubs to be of only limited help in consuming the plant's output, even if they (like the Munros) gave books away as bonuses and dividends. The giant company never-theless tackled its construction program with dispatch.

For the Hanover plant Doubleday engaged Peter de Florez, a con-sultant whose knowledge of bookbinding machinery and methods is considerable. For the mass of inexpensive hard-cover and paperback books Doubleday anticipated, de Florez developed a number of special machines: (1) a conveyorized air-pressure spraying machine for top-staining applications (later available commercially); (2) a jacketing machine capable of 3500 books per hour (in 1945 Country Life had tested the first book jacketer, developed by the Pathe Tool Manufac-turing Company, New York, capable of 1000 per hour); (3) apparatus to convert a case-maker from sheet to roll-feed (for "Permabooks," a cheap hard-cover series in which preprinted paper sides had to be accurately positioned on the boards); (4) combination casing-in and building-in equipment (later duplicated for American Book-Stratford Press, Western Printing and Lithographing Company, and others). It was a long and important assignment.

In 1953 de Florez's consulting firm was merged with The Dexter Folder Company (making it, along with Smyth, Crawley, Lawson, Harris-Seybold, and Sheridan, one of the post-war "big six" of bookbinding equipment). Specializing in research and development, de Florez deplored the fact that the bindery industry was generally too small to support any research at all. Much equipment was still the extemporaneous extension of arms and hands, inelegantly called "monkey machinery" by those professional salesmen who saw paper clips and chewing gum holding such apparatuses together. To encourage more orderly bindery planning, de Florez divided machinery requirements into five categories:

(1) simple, slow tools; mechanical aids for the hand or extra binder.
(2) 1000 per hour range; for short runs or oversize books.
(3) 2000 per hour range; the core of large binderies for decades.
(4) 4000 per hour range; new machinery now on the drawing boards.
(5) 6000 plus; the bindery revolution of the future.[16]

Because of the complexity of many bindery jobs and the unpredictable behavior of paper under various internal and external conditions, de Florez in a moment of despair considered it impractical to automate the bindery beyond the pre-programming of basic settings and sizes. As if to prove himself wrong, however, de Florez himself began to turn out for Dexter many modern and revolutionary machines with considerable versatility.

In 1959 de Florez designed a planetary or "drum-type" gatherer using a rotary motion capable of far greater speed than Juengst's "arm" gathering machine. By 1968 this equipment was processing 200 books per minute—well beyond de Florez's fifth category. In 1965 Dexter revealed an experimental high-speed (category 5) automated line: it handled casing-in, building-in, and jacketing, at 2 books per second. The entire combination was 84 feet long (using a 26-foot building-in section). A year later de Florez announced that such "supersonic" lines would shortly become reality in commercial applications.

For hardbound books Dexter also makes a sheet-fed case-maker in two models (3600 cases per hour), and a casing-in, building-in machine containing integral inline features to eliminate, among other operations, hand squaring (checking the squares before the adhesive dries) on most jobs. The company also handles, in addition to its own folders and arm gatherers, Cleveland folders, Brackett equipment, and the Dexter-Christensen varnisher.

Dexter's most recent developments in inline techniques are not at present applicable to edition binding, but they promise to influence edition bookwork by their general approach to the interrelation of machinery. In particular, a 1969 solution for the coupling of two complex inline machines, developed for catalog manufacturers, maintains a continuous rate of production even though a portion of the system fails. In this "machine integration" system, a "double track" gatherer (a single machine with two separate 32-clamp gathering raceways, one above the other) collects one-half of a book on each track; only half speed is required to turn out 12,000 books per hour. Each half book is given 1 wire staple to keep signatures together and in position. The gatherer is positioned directly before a Dexter adhesive binder, but not coupled mechanically to it.

The gatherer raceways feed two separate hoppers over a conveyor belt leading to the binder. Monitoring the capacity of the hoppers (and two additional manually fed hoppers) is a system of photoelectric cells which control gatherer and binder speeds. When one raceway jams (the usual malfunction), the binder continues, fed from the hoppers. When the hoppers drop below a minimum quantity the binder slows to half speed until the malfunction is repaired (usually a matter of seconds). Although the hourly output of the system continually varies with conditions, there is literally no "down" time. Thus many problems connected with restarting (overheating or drying of adhesive, buildup of adhesive on applicators, poor application of adhesive until maximum speed is reached) do not develop. Such hoppers may also be the solution for feeding any number of machines in tandem, for edition as well as paperback work. (In 1969 Peter de Florez resigned to return to consultory work.)

Similarly, the Harris-Seybold Division of Harris-Intertype Corporation in 1969 developed a system for saddle-stitched pamphlets which contains a radical departure from traditional techniques. Under the Macey label the division produces much collating (a term now used to refer to the gathering of single sheets), stitching, and trimming equipment for the trade binder. The Macey Multibinder is a combination 9, 11, or 13-pocket collator, folder, and saddle-stitcher. It takes press sheets imposed in multiples of four-page signatures which are cut apart on a guillotine; the Multibinder collates them (making a single centerfold for the entire book at once) and stitches them, all at a rate of between 1700–4500 per hour, handling flat sheet signatures from 5 x 8 to 12 x 18 inches. Thus folding as a separate operation (and the machine folder) were eliminated.

"The secret to increased productivity in the smaller bindery [said a Macey official] is not the development of a faster piece of equipment but to get away from the standard folded signature. When you have to process a folded signature you place rigid limitations on the potential output of many production operations."[17]

A similarly dramatic departure was also applied to bookwork in the form of the Cameron book production system.

After World War II the Crawley Book Machinery Company expanded its manufacturing capabilities to keep up with the growing book business. In 1954 it absorbed the [Henry] Sieb Manufacturing Company, Hammond, Indiana, makers of indexing machines, glueing-off machines (actually designed at the W. B. Conkey Company), and Singer saddle sewer attachments. Two years later it introduced a series of building-in machines and added a line of rotary board cutters. The Crawley "12–9–12" high-speed building-in machine (12 nipping and 12 smashing stations, handling books up to 9 x 12 inches) can do over 60 books per minute: with a "true" squaring device, says the company, "It is the first realistic approach duplicating a person's fingers in the usual squaring operation."

Upon celebration of the company's 75th anniversary in 1964, with Arthur III as president, Crawley dramatically enlarged its Newport, Kentucky, plant, and at the same time began to offer an impressive list of bindery-related equipment which it handles as sales agents:

A Sheridan T-shaped "inline" setup for sewn hard-bound forwarding consists of hopper-fed two-up smasher (*left rear*), gluer-dryer (*center*), and trimmer (*at back, alongside smasher*). Optional conveyor at right foreground feeds covers when machine is set for sewn paperbacks. [The Sheridan Company]

Moffett; Hepp; Camco Machinery, Letchworth, England (folders); Norwood & Gildmore (roll-fed endsheet and gilding equipment); Joseph Hunkeler, Switzerland (endsheet pasting and inserting machine), and Atlas-MaK Maschinenbau, Bremer, Germany (three-knife trimmers, automatic rounder and backer, automatic casing-in machine, automatic book liner). One of its newest affiliates has an interesting new binding process.

Leipziger Buchbindereimaschinenwerke, a division of VEB Polygraph, Leipzig, is another Crawley client. Almost a century old and claiming title to the original Brehmer name, this company with its 3000 employees manufactures folders, gatherers, book sewers, wire stitchers, adhesive binders, and a unique binding technique called "fold" or "thread" sealing. Introduced in 1969, the 271-FK automatic fold-sealing machine apparently succeeds at what the 1868 Tanner-Martini folder-sewer attempted. Flat sheets (16-page signatures) are fed automatically and given two right-angle folds; before the third (last) fold a stitching operation takes place. Four staples, made from plastic "thread," are driven through the gutter and their ends, splayed outward, heat-welded to the paper. The signatures are then adhesive-bound by conventional equipment. Another model of fold-sealer, 434-FP, won a gold medal at the 1970 Leipzig fair.

Recent Crawley products include the 1967 "6–11–14" heavy-duty building-in machine, and 1968 casing-in machines. Banking on the future of automation in straight-through bindery equipment, Crawley expects its entire production line to perform at 50–60 books per minute; rounder-backers, nipper-gluer, re-nippers (for final reshaping of the book); casing-in machines, dryers, and counter-stackers. But along with two others of today's "big six" bindery suppliers, Crawley proudly manages to offer a solution for the most baffling of bindery problems: automation of the book sewing machine.[18]

Despite the unquestioned success of the Smyth book sewer, one man —the inventor—perceived in it a nagging shortcoming. Encomiums had been frequent for decades: "one of the most valuable labor-saving machines for the binder ever invented," said J. F. Tapley as late as 1906, perhaps unaware that the machine was still undergoing improvement almost until that date, nearly three decades after its conception. Smyth himself told *American Bookmaker* in 1888 that $500,000 had already been spent on the sewer's development, and he continued to assign to the Hartford company two dozen additional patents pertaining to it up to 1900. On that auspicious date he felt his work for the Smyth Manufacturing Company at last at an end; despite his wide range of interests, ironically, the company that bears his name obtained from him only the book sewer.

But David McConnell Smyth was far from finished with Hartford or book sewing. In 1900 and again in 1903 he obtained patents for automatic feeding apparatus which would have made it unnecessary for an attendant to feed the sewer signature by signature. These patents were assigned to the Smyth Machine Company (an Arizona corporation), an independent enterprise apparently engineered by his son, David G. Smyth, who shared some inventive proclivities with his father, including participation in the automatic feeder. (In 1903 the senior Smyth, alone in California, evidently returned to the east, possibly living at his son's Hartford residence until his death.) The new company and its product, however, did not succeed, and neither Smyth nor any other firm achieved any measure of automation for the book sewer until 1928, when the Nos. 12 and 18 sewers were brought onto the market.

"Don't let booksewing bottleneck your profits," the company had said as late as 1941, in what even then must have sounded repetitive and hollow. But there were still problems in the sewer's persistent resistance to automation as it had long before resisted mechanization. While complete hopper-loaded automatic feeding was claimed for the 12 and 18, the touted breakthrough was not so versatile as hoped. Only certain work—particular text papers, ideally folded—could be automated; excess tail or outside margins, for example (normally trimmed off after sewing), made it difficult for the machine to "find" the center fold. Signatures had to be collated in reverse order to be fed automatically, and if, when fed to the sewer, the job was discovered to be less than perfect, the gathering had to be reversed before it could be hand-fed to another machine. (The reverse gathering requirement was subsequently altered in later models.)

Although in Great Britain the No. 12 operators often read books in their laps to lessen fatigue as they tended the machine—and produced 30–40 percent more than No. 3 operators—their American sisters were not so accomplished. In some shops the No. 12 operators had trouble coping with the three foot pedals which controlled starting-stopping, endpaper pasting, and thread cut-off. To combat this complaint, William B. Hildman, of Chicago, in 1944 patented electrical control equipment which he assigned to Brock & Rankin, large commercial binders of that city. This replaced two pedals with back-of-the-hand controls for pasting and cut-off. But operations were still far from speedy.

Another development of the 1940's was the introduction of nylon thread, strong, elastic, durable: sewn under high tension, it tightens the book even further as it "recovers" its normal tension. But binders were still not happy. Many of them, without the wherewithall to experiment, felt the growing pinch on the sewing line: some had found it necessary to put two sewers side by side to keep up with the production rates of other equipment. "Smyth sewing still remains an isolated operation, requiring hand feeding," said *Book Production Industry* in 1968. Peter de Florez agreed: "Probably the most awkward and inefficient step in the process . . . the bottleneck." Others admitted it was instrumental in sending many paperbacks, ordinarily Smyth sewn, into the adhesive-binding line. But a few experts on the "inside," de Florez among them, knew that help was on the way.

Dexter (now part of MGD [Miehle-Goss-Dexter] Graphic Systems, a division of North American Rockwell Corporation, Chicago) had been at work on automatic feeding and manufacturing operations since the end of World War II. In 1949 Dexter offered McCain automatic inserting equipment for feeding to Christensen gang saddle stitchers; also integrated into the unit was a McCain 3-knife trimmer, furnishing complete automated manufacture for saddle-stitched jobs. Later called "Speedbinder," it could do 9000 books per hour. In 1964 Dexter announced another sophisticated combination: two McCain feeders coupled with a high-speed Singer two-thread chain stitcher, all together capable of feeding signatures, opening them so that up to two inserts (or signatures) could be included, rotating them 180 degrees and sewing through the center fold, cutting the thread and applying adhesive to thread ends, delivering up to 125 finished books per minute. Dexter's 1967 "McCain Unitized" line could manufacture wire-stitched pamphlets similarly at speeds up to 13,500 per hour. This was the kind of expertise that could solve any feeding problem.

In 1968 Dexter followed its fast combination machines with an electronically programmed feeder for the No. 12 Smyth sewer—a unit almost five times the size of the sewer itself. Mechanically similar to the 1964 machinery, the Dexter feeder operation is controlled by a "memory device" consisting of a belt of snap-on plastic links whose nine-hole positions activate suction, deflection, pasting, cut-off, caliper, etc., as required by each set of signatures. Sewing automation had been solved.

Almost simultaneous with Dexter, the German Hepp Company, Berlin, represented in the United States by Crawley, revealed a fully automatic book-sewing machine feeder ready in 1968:

"The completely automatic machine amalgamates an entirely new Thread Book Sewing Machine manufactured by the famous 'Brehmer-Leipzig' factory with the well proven 'Hepp' rotary Section Feeder and an electro-mechanical control system for count of sections per book. . . . The Hepp Rotary Section Feeder is unique in that it provides friction-free extraction of the sheets [signatures] from the pile and has, during one revolution, three sections under control. The first is in the opened position for feeding over the [sewing] saddle, the second is approaching the opening position and the third is being rolled off friction-free, from below the pile."[19]

It worked with Smyth Nos. 12 and 18 machines as well as with Brehmers and Martinis. Smyth, long at work in Europe and America on the same nagging problem, was galvanized to action by the Dexter and Hepp disclosures.

In 1967 the Bloomfield company had also revealed development of its fully automatic book sewer in a machine—the No. 18 using vacuum suckers and/or mechanical grippers—now electronically programmed against bad signatures. It was the product of international engineering and cooperation, perhaps the first such bindery product to enjoy multilingual development. In 1958 Smyth, with Smyth-Horne (England) and Casa Editrice Marietti and Oswaldo Tealdi (both of Italy), had joined to form Smyth Europea, a company based in Casale Monferrato, Italy, to manufacture and market the Freccia book sewer.

The No. 20 Freccia (20-inch maximum spine length—for sewing two-up) had much the same features as the No. 18 Smyth, but, said E. C. Fuller, "cuts your sewing costs by 50%." In 1969 Smyth Europea demonstrated prototype No. 14 and No. 20 Freccia automatic book-sewing machines to an enthusiastic trade at a Milan fair (Freccia also showed a sheet-fed case-maker, introduced 1967, capable of 1900 cases per hour). The Freccia automatic feeder is also available for the Smyth No. 18 (which takes a spine up to 19¼ inches only). In 1970 Smyth announced its No. 7700 paste and cut-off programmer that eliminates

Completely automated "No. 20" Freccia book-sewing machine (*left*). Feeding mechanism and control console are at right. Not present in this installation is an additional "reforming station" between feeder and sewer, necessary in most American shops where compactly folded signatures need to be opened slightly for efficient feeding to the sewer. [Smyth Manufacturing Company]

the sewing-machine foot treadle (except for start-stop), thus reducing operator fatigue and eliminating errors.

With a surprising new sewing process Smyth in 1971 addressed its skills in book sewing to the library binding market. Pioneered by the American Library Association's technological committee and developed by Smyth, the "Smyth Cleat Method" of sewing (or resewing) library books is much like notched adhesive binding, its novelty in wrapping thread around the notches. Smyth president Worthington M. Adams described it:

> "At the first station, cleats ⅛-inch deep are cut in the spine of the book by carbide-tipped circular saws. The unique sewing head laces the thread, which has been immersed in adhesive, around the cleats and through the separate pages, to produce a book which meets the essential requirements of strength, minimal margin use, and improved openability."[20]

Hertzberg-New Method Inc., large library binders, will explore its commercial use.

To handle international sales more directly, Smyth in 1971 merged with its subsidiary, E. C. Fuller, to face increasingly difficult world bindery equipment conditions. Nevertheless, with the sudden burst of automated energy on the part of the three major book-sewing machine suppliers, the solution to automatic machine sewing has finally arrived.

Future sewing machines may be used far more versatilely. They may be coupled to folders, joining the sheets of only a single signature; after gathering, the signatures themselves would be joined in a glueing-off process or by another method. Such a combination machine has been developed. Too, gathering and sewing might be integrated into a single operation: one expensive solution (long ago attempted by Juengst) would be to put two sewing heads at each gathering pocket, sewing each signature as it is picked up. But book-sewing mechanisms seem incapable of simplification. An observation on cloth-sewing machines describes the book-sewing situation as well: "If the machines are simple," said the British journal *Engineer* in 1915, "the needles are of fantastic construction, or if the needles are comparatively straight and simple, the machines themselves bristle with complicated mechanisms." The concensus, however, is that the adhesive-binding processes will take over so much work formerly done by sewing it will never pay to automate the book-sewing operation beyond what is available today.

The success of automatic sewing, nevertheless, restores to the conventionally constructed book a new extension on life, as new equipment can now manufacture case-bound books at a rate of 120 per minute (7200 per hour). "The case-bound book," noted *Book Production Industry* in 1966, "the glamor job that has failed to lie down and die, despite dire predictions, is produced with a great deal more automation and straight line equipment than heretofore." According to Curtis G. Benjamin, former president of The McGraw-Hill Book Company, although the public thinks the hard-cover book is disappearing, in recent years it has furnished 90 percent of the book industry's sales and 95 percent of its profits. With the last "bottleneck" removed, the hard-cover book is ready for almost fully automated manufacture.

The glamour word "automation" had at last penetrated into an industry traditionally considered a handicraft not so long before, and the bindery world finds itself in a state of unprecedented excitement. The old "stop and go" reciprocating machinery, delivering "work and store" batch production, had survived for a century. Automation in practice, however, has proved—so far—to be essentially nothing more than the connecting of existing machines by a series of linking conveyor belts, the whole network more or less flexible by the application of power—and controls—either to the entire complex or to individual components. In the late 1960's individual machines were restyled "modular units" lending themselves to block-like building of elements to obtain a specific product. Operations could be overlapped: machines could be stocked or fed while running continuously (avoiding "down" time), and pre-programming by means of magnetic tapes and plastic links customized the machine to the job. The future is yet lively for the conventional edition bindery producing books for the millions.

But coming along fast were new developments which took the ephemeral india-rubber binding and—with new adhesives—turned the old throwaway paperback into something more lasting. (One giant publisher-binder—J. J. Little & Ives—knew how to perform this unusual feat even before paperbacks had their own 20th-century revolution.) But there was growing indication that the communications-hungry world would not wait.

Any expectation of celebrations over the preeminent position of American publishing and bookmaking at the end of the 1960's had little cause to materialize, however. Other media forces at work—arriving almost simultaneously with the success of the American book designer (freeing himself at last from old world traditions) and the application of automation to the manufacture of books—themselves fully American in origin and excitingly new in concept, had already begun to attack the revered position of the book as a learning and recreational tool. The bicycle, the radio, the motion picture—even television—had not troubled bookmen the way more subtle influences into the academic environment were gaining strength. Many in 1969 lamented that the book was losing its "*primacy*" as a communication medium as photo-duplication, electronic teaching machines, and computerized data retrieval arrived. The school teacher and the librarian, formerly good friends of the book publisher, were beginning to look elsewhere for their materials.[21]

# 8 *Books for the*

# *Millions*

When publishers profess to deprecate "nonbooks," which began to flourish after World War II for much the same trade as coffee-table albums a century before, they refer to scissors and paste collections of ephemera, cartoon and picture anthologies, and other productions requiring little or no author skill. According to Curtis G. Benjamin, however, such nonbooks through the 1960's increased 380 percent, enabling their "reprehensible" creators to "laugh all the way to the bank over this disdainful characterization." Carping at the subject matter of competitors' books, of course, is harmless and understandable, for publishers alone and together (so many international nonbooks have been generated by publishers meeting at the Frankfurt Book Fair, said a British publisher, they might be called "Frankfurters") often value the literary and nonliterary alike, at different times, or even at the same time, for different markets. But there was another form of nonbook.

The competition of other entertainment and instructional media—after the introduction of radio—had, like the earlier threatening fads, been more a spectre than reality. "Now that the book business has

survived price cutting, book clubs, quarter books, and high manufacturing costs," wrote Bernard Berelson in 1951, "the new menace is
television." Frederick B. Adams, Jr., director of the Morgan Library,
New York, agreed, in 1968 expressing the bookman's uncompromising
suspicion of nonbook surrealism:

> "The book faces more insidious rivals than the computer and its ac-
> complices in the reproductive processes. There are the new electric
> media, which have the potential not only to convey messages but to
> be messages. . . ."[1]

Although Marshall McLuhan acknowledges the book as "the first
teaching machine and also the first mass-produced commodity," and
foresees that automation will in the future free men to pursue unprecedented liberal education, he too fears for the book's permanence
—except as paperback (p 334). McLuhan's enigma of media as messages nevertheless worries educated persons who indeed wonder
whether television-trained children today will care for books tomorrow.

Although there are no conclusive reports, it appears that the many
communications media actually stimulate and reinforce one another;
paperback sales often soar after the motion picture enjoys its own
success. Where more serious books were involved Berelson found that
"college-educated, better-off, middle-aged people living in the city"
were the principal American book readers, a composition not likely
to be influenced for a long time by movies or television, or whatever
their successors might be.

But of more serious import for publishers on whatever side of
literary-nonliterary creations, there were growing signs that nonbooks
of quite another description would make serious incursions on bookwork altogether. These nonbooks were exactly that: training or entertainment vehicles other than the printed book: records, audio-visual
aids, films, blocks and flash cards—some in very ingenious combinations. In the world of education, where the printed word had enjoyed
supremacy for centuries, the book was increasingly conspicuous by
its absence in projections of future educational techniques.

Predictions for the future school year include compulsory summer
sessions, day and night classes, team teaching, ungraded lessons, post-
graduate acceptance examinations, and job-placement courses complete
with appropriate subsequent employment. All are calculated to accommodate an unprecedented volume and flexibility in school enrollments.
In the school-house a variety of nonbook teaching aids (some already
at work) will fascinate the student. The simplest educational "skills
package" is a box of cards, templates, pads of diagnostic tests, a stu-

dent record book (and a saddle-stitched teacher's manual), all of which together enable the average pupil to work largely by himself, at his own rate, charting his progress as he goes. Other "three-dimensional" kits for science (specimens), mathematics (puzzles), spelling (games), and pupil guidance, will offer sight, sound, touch, and constructional uses far beyond the capabilities of a 20th-century schoolbook.

Other learning situations utilize transparent films in a number of ways. Multicolor printing on acetate can make a transparent album of exploded or sequential views, or it can furnish slides for enlarged projections. The "paralax panoramagram," a three-dimensional effect achieved by a plastic coating (obviating special glasses) may also find important teaching uses. Cartridges of prepared materials "played" through conventional television receivers will be common, as will motion-picture projection from cartridges which need no threading or rewinding. The historian C. P. Snow in 1965 predicted:

"I believe we are about to see an application of narrow-gage film to education and industry which will be as revolutionary as the paperback has become in publishing, and which will come far more speedily."[2]

In the light of other developments, however, even the trouble-free motion picture, despite sound, color, and possible three-dimensional effects, already demonstrates a lack of technological glamor to educators who have been won over to electronics and computer.

Television and facsimile transmission will bring into the classroom colorful records of past or current happenings around the world—or on the moon and elsewhere. "Computer assisted instruction" involves a perplexing array of hardware—teletypewriters, computers, cathode-ray displays—to provide the student with integrated drill and practice work, sophisticated laboratory experiments, and self-correcting games and simulation programs. These devices culminate in a fully integrated teaching environment:

"The school of the future [Seligman wrote, obviously distressed] would offer televised lessons emanating from four or five master studios, with color if necessary. The teacher, if there was one, could use the resources of an automatic library by consulting a television directory and dialing a number. A microfilm of the requested book would then appear on a screen, page by page. . . ."

The extraordinary versatility and capacity to handle any number of individually programmed channels makes it almost unnecessary for students to congregate; Seligman further portrayed the inevitable goal of this kind of instruction:

"The child will be enclosed in an egg-shaped 'studysphere,' with a complete retrieval system for information from any part of the world.

Temperature controls will provide a purer atmosphere to facilitate learning. The 'studysphere' will contain antenna, television and film screen, microphone, tape recorder, and speakers, as well as adjustable seat. Great teachers will be able to lecture to students plugged in anywhere, without leaving their homes. . . ."[3]

If small future domiciles cannot contain much more than a studysphere and its racks of "required" programming, perhaps the brighter student will find his way to the neighborhood library.

Like the classroom, the library of the future is rapidly changing its methods of operation in order to accommodate changing concepts as to how best to perform its public role. Only the library's purpose remains the same: by definition of the Council on Library Resources (an organization established in 1956 in Washington, DC, to guide library planning), a library "consists of messages sent at some time during the past, and intended for receipt continually into the future." Noticeably missing is any requirement that such messages be in book form, no less bound in a particularly durable package. ("Package," the publisher's own synonym for a smartly conceived book, may indeed have reinforced the thinking of other communications people—and the public—that the physical configuration of assembled data need not be a "book" at all.)

The library situation, however, is genuinely desperate. The world production of books in the late 1960's was estimated at 320,000 titles annually—almost 1000 per day. Newspapers (33,000) and periodicals (70,000), plus maps, music, research reports, and filmstrips, are additional. In the United States alone 30,000 books, 20,000 periodicals, and 80,000 technical papers are issued yearly. All such materials make storage a frantic problem, especially since libraries of the future, recollecting 19th-century bindery mistakes, bottlenecks, and breakthroughs, are likely still to be at the mercy of publishers—and now, nonbook manufacturers—who govern the physical form of the product.

For most large libraries new acquisitions stretch lineally two miles every year. The once charming New York Public Library has already become the largest in the world, with over 7,230,000 volumes by 1963. It has been calculated that building costs, overhead, salaries, and cataloging procedures add twice the original price of a book to its cost when it is placed on the library shelf. Because of these burdening conditions, photography and computerization have been enlisted to help, but they function in a way that will make the future library almost unrecognizable.

For the expeditious handling of the world's literature as well as ephemera (much of which, today, the library does not collect; statistical data like market research, business accounts, hospital records, government memoranda, etc., are forever lost to future historians), books and unpublished materials must either be microfilmed or produced directly into machine-readable forms. Both of these paths, which dictate format for all publications worthy of preservation, involve a non-esthetic book design treatment which scarcely need consider appeal to the human hand or eye.

The production of literature in some form of roll for machine threading has suggested that a great cycle has been completed: information would again be on rolls as it had once been on papyrus volumes (from the Latin *volvere,* to roll) stored in cylinders in the earliest libraries of the world. But there is little room for romantic satisfaction. Microfilm and microfiche store hundreds of pages cheaply on small spools and individual cards; most systems furthermore retrieve these materials automatically, expose them to a copying machine, and return them to storage—without risk of theft, smudges, dog ears, coffee stains, and other human abuses. Libraries will actually give away the duplicated copies to their readers, since the administration of checking out and returning, as with paperbacks in libraries today, would be an unnecessary expense. (Today's microfilm, unfortunately, is almost as perishable as paper, and new, lasting photographic materials must be developed if this scheme is to work for centuries to come.)

For educational purposes the world of the computer has barely been explored, although by the mid-1960's well over 100 commercial companies were producing electronic and mechanical teaching machines— a multimillion dollar enterprise for the dozen largest firms. Electronic reading machines distinguish among typewriter characters at the rate of 200 letters per second, and will eventually perform almost instantaneous language translation work, even when cyrillic or oriental alphabets are involved. One type of optical page reader available today is programmed to recognize 200 different typefaces, although, alas, it may in the future find few of them in use. While the computer, ironically, has been touted as assisting the book designer by offering systems in which basic book formats—designed by people— will simply be programmed for computerized typesetting equipment (and promising more, not less typographic variety), other computer applications assure us that more and more non-human reading or searching will make typographic variety unnecessary if not confusing.

Special libraries housing vast quantities of technical information are particularly hopeful about electronic reading machines, employing them in several spectacular schemes to cope with the information explosion. The Avco Corporation, Cincinnati, has developed an electronic system consisting of a camera to photograph (at 1 exposure per second) each page fed into it, reducing it to 1/40th size on sheets of film 10 inches square—each with the capacity to hold 10,000 such pages. One cubed stack of such film holds a million pages. The National Library of Health, Bethesda, Maryland, acquires medical works, feeds key phrases into a computer (now storing 150,000 citations per year) which then automatically indexes them and prints its gigantic rumination as a book, the *Index Medicus*. Similarly, the National Library of Medicine uses computers to sort, arrange, and retrieve medical data in a system called MEDLARS (Medical Literature Analysis and Retrieval System); it will soon have to assimilate 6000 medical journals publishing 2 million pages annually. Libraries in other scientific areas also contemplate similar programs.

By such electronic automated systems the special libraries will manage to provide instantaneous and exhaustive access to any and all data wanted, no matter how old or new, no matter what original form. Their efficiency, book romance and esthetics aside, is a proper complement to the nature of scientific work and a necessary terminal requirement if scientific data is to be immediately and economically available. By extension, however, their efficiency is also becoming a model for the entire publishing industry. Many people even in the most traditional circles expect that the publisher must now also concern himself with magnetic and paper tapes, memory cores, sound and picture projections, and kinescope recordings, to be examined in countless study booths or printed out (at 6000 words per minute) if a durable copy is wanted. Such thinkers, however, have put aside the convention (established decades ago by international copyrightists like Cornelius Mathews) that publishers are purveyors of thought, not "hardware."

The acquisition of publishing houses by electronics firms revealed the issue of publishers' roles once more. "We are not interested in the book business," a General Electric executive admitted in 1966, ominously. "We are interested mainly in the information business. I predict that you people [publishers] will be chiefly information publishers in the future. . . ." He acknowledged that publishers can best collect and present learning materials, but with computerization the "electronikers" would do better at "transmitting" (did he mean distributing?) them. "We may well be your printers in the future," he concluded.

If the electronics firms aspire to print—and there is much evidence to that effect—but not bind their products, it is possible traditional book binderies, constituting the publisher's closest manufacturing ally, will be expected to engage in nonbook production. They can do so, of course, but at considerable cost. We have already seen how binderies— like machinery manufacturers—only at the last possible moment committed themselves irretrievably to bookwork; they must make the same decision again to enter the nonbook world. If such nonbook work is scattered among many publishers, initial orders will necessarily be comparatively small, reminiscent of modest edition bookwork carried on side by side with classic hand forwarding and finishing. Any phenominal success in nonbook areas will prompt manufacturers to abandon their less profitable bookwork—if they had bothered to be book producers in the first place.

The rapidity of developments predicted for the future will make it almost impossible for any service organization to be assured of long continuity of any type of product. Large electronic firms, like Xerox, have also entered the publishing world with considerable impetus. The tremendous Xerox Corporation admirably demonstrates the speed of technological development in graphic arts and electronic communications—and illustrates with what rapidity an aware management keeps itself in a superior position to engineer such changes. Far beyond the stage of simple xerographic reproduction which it introduced after World War II, Xerox now offers multiple-purpose copying equipment which can take 60 fan-folded computer print-out pages (11 x 15 inches) and in 30 minutes automatically turn out 20 collated sets of 60 pages each, reduced to 8½ x 11 inches for easier reading and storage.

In a 1967 statement Xerox (still without commenting that it had—with automatic collating attachments—entered the bindery field as well) broadly realigned its scope:

> "We, therefore, define our basic business as *graphic communications:* the all-inclusive recording and handling of visual information from point of origin to point of conclusive action. Our purposes extend to creating, copying, duplicating, printing, transmitting, displaying and retaining knowledge and information in graphic form. . . ."[4]

The versatility of the office copying machine, of whatever sophistication, nevertheless challenges the conventional publisher with a new brand of piracy, more insidious than that of the 19th century, since the modern act is usually done for "internal" corporate or private use and never comes to the attention of the copyright holder. While copyright discussions and amendments have followed regularly since 1891 and promise an eventual solution for office copying and other threats to literary property, other publishers, like old Charpentier, have taken more positive steps to counter piracy.

To approach the threats of computer and photocopying, some publishers have (by merger with computer firms) perforce advocated the information "explosion." Unlike the book binder contemplating entry

into nonbook areas—simply fabricating a product to the client's specifications, the publisher entering the computerized teaching world will
(to paraphrase Blackwell) carry author, supplier, manufacturer, and
sales staffs hanging on his media-message judgment. These publishers
feel—perhaps rightly—that the book, with its antiquated copyright
protection, is not really the principal stock in trade. *Data* is the main
product, probably best preserved for commercial use not in standing
plates or lithographic flats, but (thanks to library experience) on
magnetic tape or microfilm. With an itch to maintain his own composition facilities—or at least the keyboarding portion—the publisher
(like his manufacturing ancestor of a few generations before) can
inexpensively record in a system tailored to his needs, and remain in
possession, physically and legally, of his master tapes. For a single
customer of a slowly moving title or for a mass edition the publisher
can play out wanted data in the final form of any conventional media
—book, pamphlet, magazine, newspaper, or audio-visual, radio, or
television transmission.

Lest this versatility seem dehumanizingly automatic among designers
and manufacturers who produce such materials (as it surely must seem
dehumanizingly automatic to the student facing his studysphere),
*Book Production Industry* warns its readers that people must make it
work:

> "Publishers must be able to shift their product lines, information banks,
> and sales and distribution organizations to match new market align-
> ments as they develop. This will call for a free-form pattern of or-
> ganization in publishing, and a very flexible type of manager to control
> it. Publishing in the future will no longer offer the comfortable pigeon-
> hole careers that made life dependable and predictable for many of
> the people in it. Personnel development will be by far the toughest
> of all problems in publishing. . . ."[5]

Since the American publisher has never enjoyed a steady stream of
trained, qualified young people into any of his three major departments (editorial, manufacturing, marketing), personnel development
has always been a special problem. Perhaps the future will find college or post-graduate programs in publishing much more prevalent
than they are now. With a capability to reproduce one copy or books
for the millions, nevertheless, the publisher will indeed enjoy new
ventures never before commercially possible.

For the small specialized university session publishers will offer
"papertexts," short selections chosen by the instructor from a wide
variety of important readings in the subject area; the pamphlets are
conveniently retained by the student in a loose-leaf binder. Also available for larger audiences will be "selected academic readings," similar

instructor-tailored reading material, adhesive-bound in quantities small enough to accommodate only a single class, if necessary. These special editions can be designed for production by small sequentially paged presses (p 319), executed "on order" so as to eliminate warehousing.

For the medium-run semi-technical book, nonfiction with some popular appeal, for example, simultaneous paperback and hard-cover editions will be cheaply and quickly produced, using bindery-line standardization techniques already successful. For the general trade —with millions of readers now at liberty to enjoy unprecedented leisure time—the publisher can proudly continue to furnish fiction and popular divertissements in paperback form, literally by the millions. Bantam Books in 1969 issued the record-breaking first printing of 3 million copies (Arthur Haily, *Airport*)—and with other firms promises regularly to exceed this figure for such mass-appeal items. Marcus H. Jaffe, a Bantam vice president, has said, furthermore, that "There is not one mass market but many," suggesting that more than "sex, sadism, and the smoking revolver" will also enjoy colossal printings in the future. (Paperbacks alone in the last 25 years have expanded from 8000 to 80,000 titles in print.) With a growing reading population increasingly accessible in remote hamlets as well as urban centers (book stores—only about 1500 good ones, irregularly distributed in the 25 largest US metropolitan areas—today account for 75 percent of all hardbound sales without touching the hinterlands), other paperback publishers too may be expected to seek out all or part of the many mass markets.

Even the most enthusiastic modernists have rallied 'round the book. It still had advantages, apparently: "passive, permanent, and portable," said one; "unquestionably the most important medium of communication," said another, a banker. It was still the primary reliance for scholars, said a research agency. "The best storage medium today," said an educator, pointing out it can be searched for "back information" and "corrected" with marginal notes far more easily than magnetic or paper tapes. Designer Hermann Zapf has consoled graphic arts people:

"The answer . . . will be new methods for storing knowledge, both in the form of books, and in new-style information storage centers which one day will be available to everybody. But also in the future, the book will remain superior to all information stored in a computer, because the book can present instructive details for comparison and especially illustrations in color in a clearly arranged and always visible form. . . ."[6]

For the academic world too the book emerges as a tool far from obsolete. Seligman's final remarks about electronic teaching devices are critical:

"Teaching machines, however, merely store and regurgitate facts: They do not teach; they can only test one's ability to memorize. They teach about as well as a book might, yet no one who has ever been involved with the classroom will assert that learning can be imparted solely through a book. Mechanical teaching can be so rigid as to create a vast distaste for the acquisition of knowledge."[7]

Darrel E. Peterson, president of Scott, Foresman & Company, opined: "The textbook is still the central core—it is convenient to use and still the cheapest way to provide material for students. It will probably remain the core for the foreseeable future. . . ."

The foregoing survey of futuristic learning and information techniques, as with all utopian dreams, contains more optimism and oversimplification than realistic planners have dared to contemplate. Aside from occasional parenthetical remarks, it seems purely objectionist for book people to carp at electronic learning processes which, as they materialize, will have to stand the test of public acceptance (and student sufferance) or fail if they cannot be remedied. It seems likely that conversion from Gutenberg's world of the book to McLuhan's world of simulcast may be the most difficult aspect and may take generations to accomplish. All of this, of course, is futuristic and speculative. By "future," for example, library planners generally mean not before the year 2000; electronics people—even the most enthusiastic—cannot even hazard a date for passing information "from brain to brain through a device with a storage of electrical impulses"—although they are already working on it and "selling" the idea to the public. Present-day aspects of our approach to computerized, automated learning and information retrieval show that we are far from happy realization of technology's benefits.

Problems at the United States Government Printing Office, today the nation's largest publisher-printer, illustrate many technological snags that impede any immediate conversion to computerized, electronic production. Computer print-outs often contain newly generated data requiring wide and prompt dissemination, but, the GPO discovered, they are usually wasteful of space and monotonous to read. With this problem at hand, the GPO in 1966 formulated an Electronic Composing System program in which analysis showed that print-outs reproduced without modification required 40 percent more pages—hence more paper, platemaking, presswork, binding materials, and labor—than conventional typography. "The age of automation is upon us," said James L. Harrison, Public Printer in 1962, but there was little evidence of it in the GPO bindery.

Harrison described conditions in its antiquated Washington shop:

"Our bindery, like the rest of our facilities, is jammed and not set up efficiently for flow-line production. That is understandable since our bindery is scattered over four different floors, and we have some 20,000 jobs in the bindery at any given time. However, the bindery is doing a magnificent job in controlling production inventory or it would be a bedlam. . . ."[8]

Although it had sampled adhesive binding in the first quarter of the century (finding the product understandably unsuitable for government work), it had, nevertheless, sponsored PVA research which ultimately contributed to the success of the process. In the 1960's the GPO again considered threadless binding for ephemeral work. Toward the end of the decade, with 7800 employees, the GPO was weighing modernization of its old plant versus the building of a completely new suburban complex. In 1970 Adolph N. Spence II, new Public Printer, announced the old shop would be refurbished.

The whole bindery world similarly viewed the future cautiously. In the face of computer typography, nonbook teaching methods, and microform storage systems, the bindery machinery industry seemed unaware that the life of the book was in jeopardy. The chidings of publishers after World War II had, as far as alarmists were concerned, failed to impress equipment manufacturers; they were still selling "castings," said consultant Eugene F. Sitterley in 1970, albeit slightly bigger and faster than earlier models:

"Except for a few mechanical improvements and some slight increases in speeds, I see no brilliant research or development or advanced thinking coming from our bindery machinery manufacturers."[9]

Yet, Sitterley added, binderies had growing problems with their high-speed machines that only standardization and computerization (of equipment controls) could tame. (No one thought to call "foul play" at comparing actual bindery progress to *projected* nonbook technology aims.) The recently completed inline production programs of the "big six" of bindery manufacturers was apparently not enough for those who wanted greater assurances that there would be book manufactories even in the McLuhanesk world. New concepts—the more radical the better—were what's wanted; and one radical concept (introduced from "outside" the industry, said Sitterley) was obligingly revealed in 1969 to provide bookmen with evidence that the industry was indeed coping. Portions of the extraordinary concept actually dated to 1923—and perhaps had even earlier origins.[10]

J. J. Little & Ives was a 1908 merger of J. J. Little & Company, publishers since 1878, and Edwin S. Ives & Sons Book Bindery, whose founder, ordained a lay preacher, had started in 1868. Ives died 1907.

Joseph J. Little had come to New York city in 1855 from Otsego, New York, worked in a printing shop, and after the Civil War established his own book printing firm with a succession of partners. Civic minded, Little was president of the New York City Board of Education and a congressman; he died in 1913. Often encouraging his publisher friends to give up their manufacturing plants, Little gave his own publishing-manufacturing company a taste for corporate megalomania which no other firm in publishing or bookmaking could imitate until well after World War II.

Long successful without spectacular inventions and mechanical shortcuts, J. J. Little & Ives was an efficient manufactory: in 1917 it set, printed, and bound T. R. Roosevelt, *The Foes of Our Own Household* (Doran, 348 pp) in five days. In 1930 it absorbed C. T. Baker & Sons (formerly the E. Fleming bindery) and, adding facilities to it, created The Colonial Press, Clinton, which, as we have seen, it promptly sold a year later to Lewis M. Adams. In 1933 it acquired the Daniel S. Brassil Bindery (founded 1895) and three years later startled both publishers and manufacturers with plans to concentrate its considerable forces in the field of books as commercial premiums. It was not exactly publishing, said *Publishers' Weekly*, trying to be helpful, "They are really going to be a sort of clearing house for non-expired copyright plates. . . ." The company would create, edit, and manufacture books (and series, such as encyclopedias) to be given away or sold by retailing firms in connection with other merchandise. By the 1960's, selling through 17,000 supermarkets and direct-mail programs, J. J. Little & Ives continues to enjoy this neglected specialty.

Having often demonstrated its corporate capabilities, the impressive company was long accustomed, like Little himself, to give advice on fairly grandiose projects. One such scheme materialized in 1922 at the hands of an old professional publisher, and J. J. Little & Ives listened attentively.

Joseph H. Sears had started work at *Youth's Companion;* he spent 10 years at Harper's and was president of Appleton's when that firm reorganized in 1900. Hearing after World War I that a large factory at Kingsport, Tennessee, was vacant, he developed a plan for its use. Kingsport had originated at the turn of the century as a community more utopian than Dent's Letchworth or Doubleday's Garden City: beside careful zoning to restrict factories and utilitarian areas, inhabitants received blanketing insurance and medical coverage. So remote was this manufacturing center, however, the only raw materials in the vicinity were water, wood, cotton, and coal. Remarkably, these were exactly the ingredients for making books.

Sears believed the American reading public could sustain yet one more series of inexpensive books; generations had passed since the cheap publishers of the 19th century faded away. Royalty-free classics, printed on locally made paper and bound in locally made cloth, might possibly sell in great quantities, not in bookstores (still not present in great numbers) but through variety stores, mail-order houses, and other national merchandising chains.

With financial backing and J. J. Little & Ives to set up and run the plant, Sears began to organize a New York sales force (J. H. Sears & Company) to exploit the output of the Tennessee plant. Its location, 600 miles from the traditional publishing center of the United States, nevertheless assured relatively inexpensive labor; railroad carloads would speed bulk deliveries anywhere across the country. (Were Lovell's Rouses Point experiences a guide?) By 1923 Kingsport Press was fully equipped at a cost of $3 million to manufacture—including fabrics and stamping foils—100,000 books a day.

Sears' program, "Reader's Library," would be marketed largely through Woolworth's Department Stores and Sears, Roebuck & Company. The first title selected for the gigantic publishing operation was Stevenson, *Treasure Island.* "By using special machinery," said Lewis M. Adams, president of Kingsport (and also of J. J. Little & Ives), "we can produce this book to sell to the public at ten cents, but only if we print in millions." Adams' "special machinery" may have sounded mysterious or miraculous to the public; to old-time binders it was perhaps at most not-so-old machinery put to new use. The new series, measuring approximately 4 x 6½ inches, was to be perfect-bound and then cased-in into inexpensive cloth covers. Manufactured at a cost of 5½ cents (for 256 pages)—de Graff's first paperbacks only 16 years later cost 10½ cents—it was hard to see how a cheaper product could be made and still be called a hardbound book.

Although the adhesive-binding process required no sewing, Kingsport officials recognized the desirability of training a large number of sewing-machine operators indispensable to any potentially versatile bindery. To accomplish this, thousands of early volumes destined to be perfect-bound were nevertheless first Smyth sewn for training only; the spine with its sewing was trimmed off and discarded during the conventional adhesive binding which followed. To be sure, the books, made with animal glues, would prove no more durable than periodicals similarly bound. With cloth cases, however, stamped, rounded, and backed like sewn volumes, they promised to be a more attractive, salable package. And packaging had time and time again rewarded publishers of cheap books with mass response.

By the Spring of 1925 165 titles had been manufactured, of which 40 alone sold almost 10 million books. A new series launched that year,

"American Home Classics: The Popular American Library of Worth-while Books," bound in red, green, maroon, and blue "fine quality linen" at 35 cents each, was expected to do as well. At the same time, however, there were signs that the plan could not continue; in the affluent 1920's "the bottom fell out" of the cheap book market and the ambitious series faced collapse. Sears seemed no more successful than Lovell in relying on weighty mass alone to propel an invincible marketing machine.

Despite the apparent impetus of the program—in 1925 still heralded as a publishing wonder to trade bookstores (now newly invited to participate)—there was trouble ahead. Drastic plans were drawn up to rechannel the company out of mass publishing-production into more stable, balanced operations. Upon the retirement of Adams (due to temporarily poor health) in 1925, Elbridge W. Palmer (1887–1953), after many years as president of J. F. Tapley, was installed as Kingsport president, a post he then held for 28 years. Palmer's heavy bindery and technical background was an invaluable foundation; his knowledge of labor and government relations, his appreciation for research and development, and his sound administrative abilities made him a leader in the bookbinding world, just as his new firm was its leader in size. Author of a bookbinding text for many years the standard shop training manual, Palmer was later commissioned a colonel in World War II for his Army work.

Complete reorganization followed. The cloth factory (Clinchfield Mills) was sold to Holliston Mills, and the original cheap series discontinued. The New York sales company was merged with the plant, all to become Kingsport Press, Inc. Sales attention turned to the securing of varied—but more profitable—business from large and small publishers, in long and short editions, cloth and paperback work, and commercial and miscellaneous jobs as well. Good management and willing workers were a sign of hope. Employees in 1926 put on a benefit play, "The Paste Princess, a Musical Comedy in Glue and Paste with More or Less Ink" dedicated to Palmer, in which a New Yorker coming to work at the Press falls in love with an East Tennessee girl— almost a reenactment of Lovell-Rouses Point marriages—with many company and town notables humorously portrayed. (Such harmony was shattered in 1963 when over 1600 workers in five unions struck— for more than two years—for better hours and wages.) The delicate transition from publishing-manufacturing octopus to hard-working book manufacturer had nevertheless been accomplished.

The new Kingsport image soon became one of considerable size but lasting quality. The original perfect-bound cased-in book, however, fragile and cheap, was lost to memory as quickly as its paper yellowed and its spine disintegrated. Although admirably simplified for automatic production, it could not compete with depression-age Smyth-sewn books selling for only pennies more. But the concept inevitably returned when conditions favored it.

After World War II hard-struck binders reexamined the conventional construction of books. In 1945 the Book Machinery Company, London, announced the development of the Flexiback Book Lining Machine, conceived in the 1930's by A. J. Kitcat, whose family bindery now encompassed more than a century's experience. Eliminating hand glueing-off, the machine applied to the backs of sewed, smashed books a quick-setting flexible animal glue, followed automatically by a pleated calico or crimped paper strip capable of expanding laterally when the book was rounded. Lewis Kitcat, at work a decade later in the same area, had to remind many who had forgotten (or never knew) the importance of good rounding and backing: pages firmly rounded into the spine do not sag and wear on the shelf, and a book well backed (folded edge of outer signatures turned outward after rounding) receives a firm ridge which maintains the strength of the rounded spine and protects the cover joints. Rounding and backing thus preserve the upright rigidity of the book and relieve strain on the spine sewing or adhesive. Kitcat strove to retain these features.

Kitcat combined a trimmed spine and the book lining idea with an improved process for rounding; called "Steamset," it used live steam to keep the adhesive flexible during the rounding process. The result, according to the inventor, was "a backed book of exceptional appearance and durability." In the United States this "unsewn binder" with ordinary hot glue was not popular, but in 1952 the Book Machinery Company, with Sheridan as sales agents, introduced an improved Flexiback Thermoplastic Binder to America; using cold PVA adhesives (which do not yield to steam) it nevertheless contained some of the earlier Kitcat features which had merit.

With over 60 machines going successfully in Europe, the Flexiback Thermoplastic binder had much to commend it. The Riverside Press, with penchant for being first in crucially important areas, set up a Flexiback in 1955 and began to run with a journeyman and two girls. At 1200 books per hour (minimum 5 x 3 x $\frac{3}{16}$ inches, maximum 15 x 15 x 2 inches) it was most satisfactory for small cased-in editions. But adhesive binding, however auspicious, was not the harbinger of good times that wire stitching and book sewing had been for Riverside. After some financial difficulties it acceded to purchase by Rand McNally in 1970 for development as a major east-coast book manufactory (coinciding with Rand McNally's association with George L.

Levison, the same year, to create a west-coast bindery in Reno, Nevada).

The Flexiback takes gathered signatures between two parallel horizontal conveyor belts, carrying them past a milling head (8 radial tooth-like cutters) which removes about $\frac{1}{8}$ inch from the back. The book then passes a glueing station where a cold emulsion adhesive is applied; two laminating plates then spread the leaves to force glue into the sawtooth edges of the pages. The sharp points of the laminating plates also open the leaves sufficiently to allow a minute quantity of the adhesive to flow onto the sides of the sheets, thus "tipping" them together. A strip of back lining material, drawn from a roll, passes a glueing station and then around a roller which places it against the back of the book. Turn-in rollers form the lining onto the back, overlapping the outer sides of the book linings by about $\frac{1}{2}$ inch. The book then passes a heated former to accelerate drying. The semi-automatic feeder spaces the books about 1 inch apart so that, just before delivery, a rotary knife cuts the back lining apart. The $\frac{1}{2}$-inch tails of lining are removed during later trimming. Since the book does not have to be lined (also obviated: sewing, nipping, smashing, glueing), it can be processed further on a combination backer (for slight rounding) and casing-in machine. Despite Riverside's enthusiasm, the remainder of the American bindery industry was quite undecided as to whether publisher clients or the general public would care for such a product. There were always complications.

Although many machinery manufacturers after World War II were steadily engaged in research and testing, their work was comparatively slow. Never sure themselves what their bindery customers wanted, they continually oblige themselves to offer extraordinary speed while at the same time promising strict adherence to the traditional principles of fine bookwork which often prohibited innovations and shortcuts. Few binders, when consulted, ever suggest machinery with radical capabilities; fewer still had visions of what the future would require. What the largest binderies clamor for, or develop themselves, nevertheless would find its way to the market. (Tapley, for example, in 1921 persuaded Sheridan to bring over Murray's straight-line backlining machine, after Wessmann had seen it in England.) The Kingsport cased-in perfect binding and the Kitcat Flexiback had both been bindery-developed inventions, and should have indicated to other binders and machinery suppliers alike that a threadless hard-cover book might indeed be a way through manufacturing bottlenecks. But without publisher consultation, bookmaking people in the late 1960's still found only continuing confusion and indecision.

Dexter Robinson, president of The World Publishing Company,

Cleveland, enumerated the restraints which continued to prevent the bindery industry from progressing:

(1) Book manufacturing is not really a cohesive industry; it encompasses many skills, trades, unions, and supply agencies.
(2) Begun as small family businesses, most binderies tend to concentrate power and decision-making in one top man.
(3) Feather-bedding is present because of the cyclical nature of bookmaking; union demands, furthermore, often conflict.
(4) Bookwork is mechanically oriented; its lack of glamor discourages skilled innovators.
(5) Lack of standardization among publishers makes almost every operation unique for a given book.
(6) The nature of edition binding of hundreds of small runs does not lend itself to automation.
(7) Many organizations grew without planning; they are still unsure of commitment to exclusive edition bookwork.
(8) Relative to American industry, the bindery is not a big area for research money.[11]

Yet World had for decades contributed heavily to bindery mechanization and progress, in many ways contradicting Robinson's own theses.

Alfred H. Cahen had come to the United States from Poland in 1902, having worked for a while, in the course of his travels, for Zaehnsdorf. In Cleveland he founded the Commercial Book Bindery in 1905, at the age of 25. Within 5 years he had invented a tipping machine which pasted a single or folded sheet inside or outside of a section, and other pesky pasting jobs (Joseph E. Smyth Company, sales agents). Other devices followed. "We have . . . a great many improvements of our own that we have developed in recent years in the way of labor saving devices, machinery, and attachments on other machines. . . ." said Cahen modestly. Long active in bindery research and management, Cahen in 1940 renamed his enterprise The World Publishing Company (he had bought World Syndicate Publishing Company in 1920), but continued also to bind and invent with special deliberation.

About 1920 Cahen developed a rounding and a casing-in machine (American Assembling Machine Company, sales agents), in 1961, with his son Herman, he produced a gold edge-laying machine, the first time this ticklish work had been mechanized in any way. Cahen's gilding machine applies genuine gold leaf (on a Mylar roll) in an in-line set-up (another gilding machine introduced the same year, the British Gildmore Press, was not nearly as functional as Cahen's). The gilding apparatus, however, had been more a challenge to tame the last of the traditional hand operations (although World is the nation's largest manufacturer of bibles). Another direction of Cahen's inventiveness had some time before demonstrated greater promise.

Upon the announcement of Cahen's most ambitious development, Ben Zevin, World's president and Cahen's son-in-law, in 1948 made some prefatory remarks. He acknowledged what Colonel Palmer had taken pains to conceal: "The big bottleneck in the mass production of books," said Zevin, "is in the bindery, where methods differ only in degree from the binding methods of an outmoded day. . . ." World Publishing was now proud to announce it had perfected the adhesive-bound hardback book, a project Cahen had been working on for years.

Designed and patented by Alfred H. Cahen, then 68 and chairman of the board of World Publishing, the company's new binding process was not unfamiliar to those who had watched related developments. Conventionally printed and folded signatures were first put through a stamping machine which—at 100 signatures a minute—notched the spine fold $\frac{1}{16}$ inch deep, $\frac{1}{2}$ to $\frac{5}{8}$ inches long, about every half inch along the spine (except at the ends). These notches, staggered on adjacent signatures, permit the entry of adhesive onto inner pages without the necessity of trimming off the entire spine fold. Notched, collated books were then sent through a Sheridan perfect binder (by-passing its own trimmer and roughener), where hot-melt adhesive was applied, the spine was rounded and backed, a strip of gauze applied, and then cased-in into conventional cloth-covered cases.

As with claims for paperbacks, a finished book so bound could be held suspended by a single page; it would, furthermore, look and feel like a sewed book, with the flexing characteristics of a sewed book. And there was great economy, of course. World Publishing announced at the same time that two new editions, *Webster's Approved Dictionary* and *Webster's Illustrated Tower Dictionary*, would be first to get the new binding treatment. (In 1971 The Bookwalter Company, an affiliate of Printing Corporation of America, bought World's Cleveland manufactory; World is now a subsidiary of The Times-Mirror Company, Los Angeles.)

The Dexter Folder Company were at first agents for commercial application of the Cahen binding process (the inventor retired in 1962 and died a year later). As world-wide interest grew in the adhesive binding area, Dexter realized that with its own gathering and covering equipment—some of it from pre-war Martin patents—it lacked only a spine preparation system of its own to produce the complete system for mass manufacture of threadless books. The Cahen notching scheme gave Dexter a technique it could call its own, although T. Blair Hawkes has noted that the notched "approach" had recurred periodically for almost a century (Sheridan holding an 1877 patent for it) albeit unsuccessful until the advent of PVA's. By 1964 nevertheless Dexter had improved its adhesive binder as a one-shot hot-melt machine for both long and short runs, from 5 x 7 to 12 x 17½ inches, ⅛ to 2 inches in bulk. It can do 200 books per minute.

The Dexter adhesive binder uses the backbone preparation system perfected by Comstock & Westcott, Inc., Cambridge, Massachusetts. The ideal arrangement employs three C&W cutters in tandem: the first uses a conventional circular saw to remove the fold and gross stock on the spine; the second uses a special cutter head to trim the book to exact page width, and the third mills the notched pattern which Cahen had previously obtained on a separate stamping machine.

The C&W system of "punch and die shearing" used on the two last cutters utilizes a fixed backup plate and a carbide-toothed cutting head (a circular saw with teeth mounted peripherally on one side instead of on the circumference) to trim the spine and mill the notched pattern. The company says:

> "The [backup plate] simultaneously supports the book, preventing it from bending, and forms the die against which the cutters impinge with zero clearance. The cutter teeth then act like multiple punches performing a transverse shearing operation against the backup plate which provides the reaction force."[12]

The alternate high and low cutting teeth in the third unit give a notched edge to the trimmed spine, "lengthening" and making the glue "line" three-dimensional. "The [paper] tabs generated by pattern roughening," says Comstock & Westcott, "extend into the adhesive and are trapped on three sides. They add stiffness to the backbone and transfer some of the bending stresses from the adhesive to the paper." The result is an excellent adhesive-bound book—and competition for the original perfect binder.

Enjoying its hard-won success with machinery for the periodical industry, Sheridan had moved slowly to improve its line for hard-bound books. Its own gatherer (perhaps a hybrid Gullberg and Smith) had appeared in 1927; a new rounder and backer, handling 35–40 books per minute (up to 2 inches thick) was heralded in 1932 as "the machine you have been waiting for." A straight-through continuous trimmer (capacity up to 12 x 16 inches) delivering 30–35 stacks per minute in piles 5–6 inches high, appeared the next year for *periodicals*—with obvious features the book industry would have to await for 20 years. For bookwork there was no commensurate thinking.

After World War II the dozens of individual bindery machines which Sheridan had acquired through mergers and its own engineering were carefully pruned, consolidated, and smartened with electric controls and streamlined cabinetry. Extraordinary versatility, short "down" time, and simple adjustments had also to be incorporated into the post-war family. These objectives have largely been met.

The Sheridan Company today offers sophisticated equipment by which hardbound books (Smyth or McCain sewn or adhesive-bound) can be expeditiously manufactured in high-speed production lines. These are (1) a combination rounder-backer-liner; (2) a combination smasher-gluer-trimmer; and (3) the Accu-Shear trimmer.

In 1964 the company simply extended its inline treatment to cover both sewed and unsewn paperback applications. The Sheridan "free cycle" automation for sewn paperbacks begins with a combination smasher, glueing off-coverer-trimmer and counter-stacker. Folding, gathering, and sewing, as with the "Smyth corner," are done conventionally, as they do not lend themselves to comparable automation. (If the same paperbacks were to be perfect bound, the cycle could begin earlier, at the gathering stage.) Working with an overall speed of 6000 books per hour, this new Sheridan equipment for automated adhesive binding includes a dielectric, infrared, gas, or heated-air dryer-cooler apparatus following 2 to 3 coats of PVA; it concludes with a shear-action knife for splitting jobs imposed two-up, and a continuous backer-liner, and an endsheet applicator for stretch paper (rounder-backer) operations.

Forwarding for any of the three hardbound styles is accomplished on the rounder-backer-liner, a single machine 50 feet long with steel frame, 57-clamps—similar to the Sheridan perfect binder. After "pre-rounding" (spine shaped by convex/concave irons) each book is held continuously by its clamps as it undergoes all subsequent operations. Rounding and backing proceed while the book is in forward motion, achieved by a novel, patented series of 12 spinning "backing disks," working like so many fingers both rubbing roundness into the spine and turning the end signatures back for the hinge.

Next, at lining and glueing stations, crash, paper, and/or headbands are applied. Animal glues or hot melts may be used, as appropriate. The latter, although excellent in adhesion, ironically present a problem to rounding: the molecular structure of the adhesive has a "memory" as to how it set. After mechanical rounding the spine tends to return to the prerounded (flat) configuration in which the adhesive was applied. This stress tends to force the pages out of the case. (Memory is an advantage, of course, when a book is abused: it will return to its proper shape.)

As the book for casing-in continues through rounder-backer-liner, a knife bar automatically cuts liners and headbands from rolls, neatly synchronized to the constant movement of the book. "When the knifebar cranks are at top dead center, the knife bar has a velocity equal to that of the clamps," says the catalog, "so that when the material is applied to the book it is traveling at the same speed as the book." Should an empty clamp appear, material, glue, and knife bar units do not function. These applications, finally, are cemented firmly by the pressing action of a sponge-rubber sealing belt, after which the books—100 per minute—are released, ready for casing-in or covering.

For the rounder-backer-liner a variety of infeed hoppers, conveyors, and transfer units is available for feeding, "gating" (changing book entry speed into subsequent units not synchronized with the rounder-backer-liner) turning, or delivering the product.

Forwarding for any of the three soft binding styles is accomplished on another combination of machines, collectively designated the Sheridan smasher-gluer-trimmer. It consists of a hopper-fed, high speed two-up smasher connected to a gluer-dryer, and in turn to a trimmer. The smasher or book press is a cam-operated toggle-linkage press (capable of 150 tons pressure) applied in a gradual squeeze to insure permanent compactness.

The gluer applies a film of cold glue which is promptly dried by a bank of infrared lamps. For separating two-up jobs the "GT Splitter" operates at up to 150 cuts per minute and can do 200 if modified. It "processes books continuously through the unit without stopping the book or changing its velocity. . . . There is a point in the forward stroke of the knife system when the housing matches the book's velocity. At this point the knife is pulled cutting the book." Thus the performance of static work on moving books (which so plagued Heyl and Juengst) has long been settled. The cut is clean and dust-free—no material (as in sawing) is lost on either side.

For final trimming the "CT trimmer" is the Sheridan Accu-Shear, a standard three-knife trimmer operating between 80 and 100 cycles per minute.

To finish the hardbound manufacture of books Sheridan offers casemakers in two models. One, 15 x 24 inches maximum, with pre-cut boards fed from the short cloth end, runs 25–45 cycles per minute. It takes cloth and/or paper from up to three webs (for 3-piece cases). It is extremely versatile and productive. The de Florez electronic register control, for positioning pre-printed cloth on the boards in close register, can be incorporated into it. The second model, a conventional bookbinder's case-maker, feeds boards at a right angle at the 25-inch cloth side. Among their many other products, straight-line five-knife continuous trimmers (for paperbacks), newspaper stuffers and counter-stackers, high-speed single book trimmers (for periodicals), and a wide range of embossing presses are the principal pieces. Sheridan does not make casing-in or building-in machinery.

Illustrating the successful combination of Sheridan equipment in two particular straight-through inline systems are the facilities at American Book-Stratford Press, a large organization long acquainted with bindery evolution and manufacturing problems.

Louis Satenstein came to the United States from Russia when he was 14, in 1889. Ten years later he purchased a small shop which he named American Book Bindery and shortly added the Stratford Press to his organization. With work and time the plant expanded, and three sons, Sidney, Edward S., and Frank could step into executive positions. Louis died in 1947, age 72.

The second generation moved boldly. In 1950 the Cornwall Press and Bindery were added and—considered the largest transaction in US bookmaking history up to that time—The Knickerbocker Printing Corporation was acquired the same year. Long the pride of the Putnam family, the press had moved to New Rochelle in 1891. George P. Putnam II reminisced in 1942:

> "As a boy I loved K.P. [as the family called it]. The smells were good. There were the odors of ink in the pressroom; glue and paper in the bindery; and the special fragrance of leather in the corner by the west windows looking out over the New York, New Haven and Hartford where the McLeans, father and son [hand binders], worked at a bench with rolls of levant, calf-skin and buckram, and sheets of cunningly 'marbled' paper and binder's cloth on racks above them, and the steel tools, as fine as dentists' instruments, at hand with mallets and presses and thread for handstitching, all components of their craftsmanship. . . ."[13]

The plant had been started and directed by George's father, Bishop Putnam. "His own taste in the making of books was excellent," George wrote of his father, "and he has been credited with doing not a little towards the development of a higher standard of bookmaking for the United States." But George acknowledged both manufacturing wastes and "unwise optimism" in edition quantities which might have been avoided. Putnam's surrendered its interest in the independently operating plant in 1930.

The giant enterprise became American Book-Knickerbocker Press, Inc., with Sidney as president and Edward as vice president and treasurer. With all facilities assimilated by 1959, the versatile organization was turning out 100,000 books a day. Particularly noteworthy in the 1950's was Pocket Books' charming "$1 'Collector's Edition,'" hardcover versions of selected paperback classics cased into imitation-leather bindings: although Smyth-sewn, this tidy package (so traditional in design even neo-Morrises could approve) helped establish public acceptance of a "paperback" product. By 1963 American Book-Stratford Press (reverting to its earlier name) with over 1600 employees in seven plants was manufacturing 130,000–150,000 hardbound books daily. But still more growth was to come.

At Saddle Brook, New Jersey, the company built completely new facilities, finishing with a modern bindery in 1967. In organization it consisted chiefly of four complete inline bindery lines, one of which, with a 48-pocket Sheridan gatherer and other Sheridan equipment, makes 6000 books per hour, perfect-bound, soft- or hard-covered. Another line, with Smyth sewing, turns out 4800 per hour. American Book-Stratford Press today is one of the largest book-manufacturing firms in the world.[14]

Recent presswork developments, however, cast a shadow on all present binderies—and yet illuminate our thinking about books of the future. Among the last graphic arts areas to entertain automation, the bindery, as we have seen, has often been handicapped by the book's many presswork and bindery operations. Approaches to the problem were multiple, and confused. Just where book automation ought to begin varied considerably with the parties involved: computer manufacturers would start with the manuscript; bindery equipment manufacturers were content to start with sheets. Press builders, ever conscious of the appreciable plant investment—letterpress or offset—for customers always loath to buy machines usable only for limited purposes, simply sought shorter makeready times and greater cylinder speeds. We have already seen, however, that with folder and stitcher attachments, the printer himself was doing more and more of the binder's work.

To bookseller Basil Blackwell printing and binding was all the same: in 1932 he had already condemned the complicated case binding as "least satisfactory process" in bookmaking, and voiced an uncanny dream:

"One has nightmare visions of books offset-printed on rolls far longer than the old papyrus volumina, concertinaed as they leave the cylinder, and trimmed and punched for the loose-leaf binder, or sprayed with rubber solution and delivered, with top, tail, and fore-edge neatly gouged, at the rate of two thousand an hour. . . ."[15]

Surprisingly, such absurdities were—three decades later—on (or close to) the drawing board.

Daniel Melcher in 1948 restated the unorthodox scheme of continuous accordion-folded sheets, a departure from the imposition of press sheets into conventional signatures on which the structure of the book has for centuries depended. "Couldn't we somehow just drop 320 plates into a hopper," he wrote, "make a few simple adjustments and have complete books start coming out, with no need to handle each 32-page signature separately?" Melcher had proposed a not-so-naive accordion-fold plan especially for short-run technical and scholarly work, but press manufacturers totally committed to the signature system for bookwork were not interested in the "nightmarish mechanics" necessary.

As one of the largest commercial plants in the United States, Kingsport Press has often been called upon to describe the state of the industry—a chore which Colonel Palmer had performed repeatedly. In 1956 Vice President Edward J. Triebe (now retired after 44 years at Kingsport) had forecast the book of a decade later—he was instrumental in its creation—with a coy warning against hope for hasty automation: "I believe . . . that the binding of a book will [not] be in the nature of a continuous form of accordion folded sheets, held together by some instantaneous heat seal, backed, forwarded, and encased in a plastic cover—all in one operation." But in describing such a concept so clearly, Triebe in fact divulged that Kingsport was not only aware of, but indeed doing something about obtaining the facilities to make such a book.

In the Spring of 1968 the Cameron Machine Company, Dover, New Jersey (today a subsidiary of Midland Ross Corporation, Cleveland, Ohio), announced it was constructing just such a press as Melcher and Triebe visualized. As Eugene Sitterley charged, Cameron was the "outsider" bindery supplier. Long manufacturers of cloth and paper web-handling machinery, the company had been toying with its "belt" press for several years, but the concept had become more feasible only by the recent improvements of rubber plates (in paperback applications) and by duPont's new Mylar plastic sheeting, exceptionally tough under pressure, temperature, and tension variations—and yet fully flexible under the same conditions. An endless belt system, varying in length according to the number of pages in a book, permitted a press to deliver printed sheets in new, non-standard impositions; this, however, was not extraordinary. Such a press had been manufactured in 1962 (and is still at work), developed by William and Edward Stroud of the Stroud-Bridgeman Company, Toronto, Canada. Like Bredenberg and Juengst, Cameron engineers wanted more than a partial solution; they wanted to handle—automatically—the web or sheets coming off such a press. Thus folding and gathering were as much a part of the project as presswork itself. For a beginning Cameron obtained the Stroud patents.

Taking two years to evolve, the Cameron "Book Production System" began with conventional roll feeding paper (good book grades) 38 inches wide at a constant web speed of 1000 feet per minute; passing through the first printing unit all pages on one side of the web were printed by rubber plates (one for each page) mounted on the endless Mylar belt. The plates are imposed to use the full width of the web. Rollers then turn the web over so that the second printing unit prints the reverse side from a similar belt. A 4⅜ x 6-inch book of 160 pages could be printed at a rate of 200 books per minute; 320 pages at 100 per minute, 640 at 50 per minute. Between perfecting units, of course— as between printing and folding units as well—register was controlled throughout. From the introduction of raw paper to release as a finished book, alignment of web and position of printed areas remained constant with almost no handling.

Printing consultant Victor Strauss felt the variable length of the endless belt to be "beyond doubt the most novel feature of this press," although the folding and gathering, with limitless capacity, are equally ingenious. Accordion folding in several variations is done on the press so that it becomes impossible (once set up properly) for pages or "sections" to get lost, out of sequence, backwards, or upside down. The press can turn out a 5000 printing (320 pages) in two hours, performing presswork, slitting, folding, collating, and gathering, furnishing completely assembled books ready for cover application. The product can either be cased-in or paper covered with conventional adhesive-binding techniques. Ironically, this most Procrustean of all bindery machines is offered by its creators as an *alternative* to standardization.

The Cameron Machine Company announced at the same time that Kingsport Press would be the first to install the new machine. The Tennessee plant had grown considerably since the 1920's. By 1950 it covered 10 acres, with railroad sidings, docks, and post office, in addition to the plant itself, whose 300 original employees now numbered 1200. The sought-after variety and volume were obtained: bibles, texts, annuals, technical and trade books, all together estimated to be almost 10 percent of the total annual US bookmaking output. (For Kingsport Press Andor Braun, working there as book designer from 1938–1959, developed the sumptuous three-volume boxed set of type specimens and copyfitting tables unsurpassed anywhere.) By 1962 its 3000 employees were producing 30 million books yearly. Part of a one-floor shop fully a block square, the Kingsport bindery has numerous conventional machines connected everywhere by elaborate conveyor systems to obviate stacking and excess handling. Much of the materials-handling equipment, and many glueing and other devices, were designed by Kingsport engineers, and much commercial

Belt containing plates of one printing unit may be seen at center. Belts may vary from 60 to 378 inches in length to accommodate books of varying numbers of pages. [Cameron Machine Company]

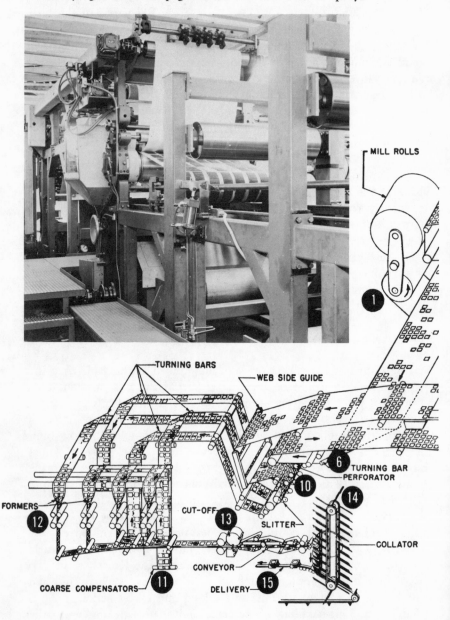

The Cameron Book Production System. Mill roll paper (1) goes through an "omega" wrap (2) for tension control before entering first printing unit (3) of flexible letterpress plates on endless belt (4). After passing through first dryer (5) the web is reversed on turning bars (6) for printing of second side (7) by a companion unit (8) and similarly dried (9). The web is then slit and perforated into one- or two-page ribbons (10) as coarse compensators (11) adjust ribbon travel length; ribbons are folded on four former folders (12), cut into pages by a three-blade rotary cutoff cylinder (13), and collected in a vertical collator (14). Books ready for binding emerge on delivery conveyor (15). [Courtesy *Graphic Arts Monthly*, September 1968]

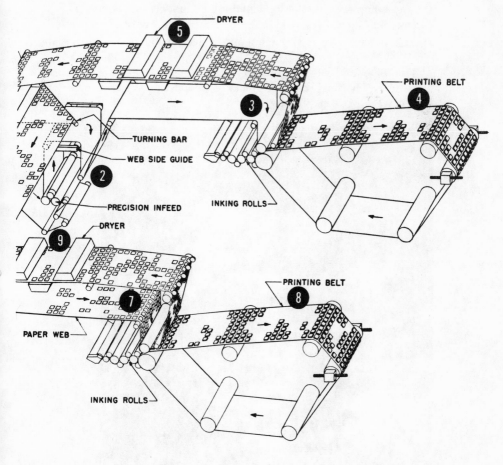

machinery has also been permanently modified for special operations.

The revolutionary Cameron equipment was installed in the Summer of 1968. Victor Strauss witnessed its initial operation and reported: "The Cameron Book Production System and the Kingsport Press installation are milestones in the history of book manufacturing. . . ." Kingsport selected the Martini adhesive binder to be coupled to what employees have named the "monster." Books emerge from the press vertically, remaining in their clamps with binding edge down; the adhesive binder takes them in that position and jogs them level, trims and roughens the spine, and glues and applies covers (printed separately). The Kingsport Martini also has a stretch-cloth applicator when hard-cover binding is wanted.

The complete installation, including binder, at about $750,000, covers 7000 square feet and weighs 75 tons; a crew of eight, including some women, is necessary. The press will manufacture books from

Two-page and one-page (*center*) ribbons being folded on triangular formers. The final one-page ribbon is chopped by a cutoff cylinder. [Cameron Machine Company]

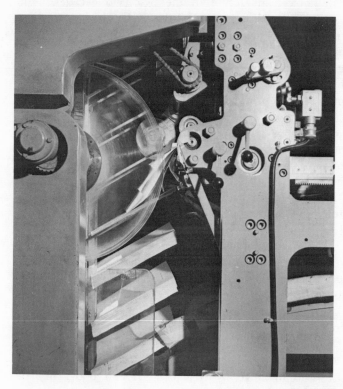

Assembly of a book on the vertical collator as cut pages emerge from rotary cutter. Each collator compartment (moving vertically) is timed to collect one complete book. [Cameron Machine Company]

4⅜ x 6 inches to 8¾ x 10 inches, and was designed for runs from 5000 to 25,000. Jobs as small as 2000 have proved practical. "Never before has the book manufacturing industry been presented with such an advance in the state of the book manufacturing art," says Cameron. "By converting book manufacture from a handling-and-rehandling batch operation to a self-contained in-line process with a 1:1 press to bindery speed ratio, considerable improvement can be made in production and delivery schedules as well as in inventory control." Kingsport (purchased in 1969 by the Arcata National Corporation) agreed wholeheartedly: with three fewer operators it discovered a 30 percent saving over conventional equipment, and was subsequently contemplating a companion Cameron press.

In 1970 The Book Press acquired Cameron's second press: instead of rubber plates it uses W. R. Grace & Company's "Letterflex" photopolymer plastic letterpress plates. The Cameron was suddenly "the biggest news in book manufacture in the past two decades," said *Printing* magazine. "A publisher would have to be dead not to get excited. . . ." Dozens of binderies and printers also took notice. But—as suggested by Triebe's reference to casing into plastic covers—additional innovations will keep all technologically interested people intrigued with possibilities.

What is done with the printed pages of a Cameron-produced book in paper covers is almost anti-climactic, if they are conventionally adhesive-bound in paper covers or adhesive-bound and cased into traditional cloth or paper covers made by conventional case-makers. But such need not happen. With many detractors usually agreeing with Dwiggins, as we have seen, the traditional machine-made case has also been reexamined for greater simplification.

Louis Margolis in 1932 reorganized a New York pamphlet bindery (located on Charlton Street), the F. M. Charlton Company, into a high-volume periodical manufactory, bringing Fay (F.) and Morris (M.), his son and daughter, into the business. Charlton was probably the first bindery—about 1939—to convert a perfect binder (made for periodicals) to do bookwork—for which accomplishment even Sheridan officials came to visit. Morris soon developed several bindery devices and, in particular, concentrated on an innovation in one-piece flexible hard covers, a product he named "Plus-Perfect." In 1947 the hard cover, thanks to PVA adhesives, could be fed to Charlton's perfect binder—again modified by Margolis—so that books in hard or soft covers—50,000 a day—could be turned out on the one machine by three operators and one foreman.

Continued development on manufacturing one-piece covers and automatically dropping them onto hopper-fed books led Margolis, father and daughter, to the creation of a separate machine. With the patented "Charlton casemaker," a machine 34 feet long affectionately named "Matilda," the one-piece case can now be produced out of card stock, scored and folded, and then, with crash and headbands, glued directly to adhesive-bound books. The Charlton type of binding is the logical cover for today's belt-printed, adhesive-bound books for the millions who want something somewhat more durable than plain paper covers. (The company was acquired in 1969 by P&F Industries, Inc.)

Many other binders and manufacturers have developed simplified or one-piece covers or cases, both in Europe and the United States. The Continental Can Company offers a unitized board case ready to be covered with woven or nonwoven material. (Nonwoven covering products—pyroxylin-impregnated papers, plastic sheeting, etc.—are inevitable successors to cloth; as highly special products, however, the unwoven materials are still troublesome—common adhesives do not always bond to plastic surfaces—and often more expensive than cloth.)

Similarly envisioned are methods of heat-sealing signatures of books, possibly joining the spine at the same time to a one-piece cover. A strip of plastic applied to gutter margins, perhaps during presswork, might after folding be fused by heat and pressure. Press sheets made entirely out of plasticized paper could also be chemically bonded along the spine. This chemical approach culminates in the one-piece cover containing a pre-coated spine adhesive which might be bonded to a similarly sophisticated book: a flexible, solid "fused-on" vinyl cover with contiguous hinge, a product of electronic case-making, was realistically described as early as 1959:

> "Perhaps the most important change in the binding process occurs in the case-making department. Out of the line of new plastics currently in the development stage are those which combine both flexible and rigid properties in a single sheet. Covering material may be extruded and formed with rigid sides and rounded, flexible backbone from a single press, transferred to electronically operated decorating equipment, and then to an automatic covering unit on the main track of the production line.
>
> "A combination casing-in and building-in machine, with high-frequency platens, would complete the operation. No wet adhesive would be needed as the case will be sealed dielectrically to the adhesive on the endsheet and spine, thus producing an exceptionally strong, tight back which will keep its shape with repeated usage. Automated shipping procedures would follow. . . ."[16]

Eliminated are glueing, warping, and drying time. The possibilities for electronically fabricated "heat sealable" cheap books are as yet unrealized, although obstacles are already noticeable. A few manufacturers now produce machinery to fabricate one-piece vinyl cases: an unskilled worker can make them in seconds. There is, however, no method at present to paste or glue book papers to the vinyl. A binder with a partial or temporary solution to this problem who issues books for the millions with vinyl covers disposed to fall off upon the slightest abuse will find himself, as we have seen, the target of hostile letters from librarians, bibliophiles, and readers alike. But the adhesive chemists again are making that bombardment unlikely.

In 1969 a "Third Generation" family of hot melts was newly announced to offer performance qualities superior to earlier adhesives and "fully comparable" with the traditional sewn binding which, said Paul E. Chamberlain, of Illinois Adhesive Products Company, Chicago, "for too long has broken the bindery production chain and reduced output speeds by its 35 books per minute capacity." The avenues and prospects opened up by the original PVA's had truly become critical and essential to the bindery of the future, and the "TG" hot melts would provide the way.

The "first generation" PVA's with primer had problems, as we have seen. Next, the one-shot hot melts provided quicker, reduced-trouble service, and although many adhesives manufacturers offered a variety of formulas, they all had too many limitations to be considered of general use. Some of them required stacking of books for 8-12 hours before they were sufficiently set for trimming. But worse were their longer ranged disadvantages—not unlike the flexible animal glues. Whether simply water soluble or emulsion-forming, the early PVA adhesives contained a solvent or wetting agent—often water—to carry the adhesive itself into the fibers. As with animal glues, even the PVA's and hot melts gradually yielded their water content through evaporation; the spine lost its flexibility as the adhesive dried, and the book "caved in," gradually disintegrating.

The TG hot melts are completely "moistureless." They are plastic-based solids at normal temperatures; at 300–400°F they melt, and within seconds as their temperature drops, they will set and regain their solidity. There is no loss due to evaporation or warping due to moisture. Because of their 8–16 second setting time they permit any bindery operation—especially trimming—to furnish instantaneous in-line production. The TG's utilize a polymer for adhesive strength, diluted with a mixture of wax and flux resins as a vehicle to lower viscosity. The result is increased fiber penetration, tackiness range, and adhesive strength. Plasticizers are added to provide flexibility against both atmospheric stress and handling abuse. Cold crack and cold flow are minimal. Despite their 7 or 8 components the TG hot melts are simple compounds.

The TG's are expected to be fully suitable for cased-in work, because of their superior flexibility, durability, and permanence, although a molecular memory problem exists with them. This can be solved by using only a small amount of TG adhesive to permit immediate trimming, and—in alternate "patches" on the spine—conventional glues to retain the rounding. A better solution would be the reheating of a full TG spine after rounding (using quartz lamps or infrared treatment) in which case the TG will melt and reset in rounded form. For the cased-in adhesive-bound book endpapers can be simply attached to boards with conventional adhesives. A production speed of 150 books per minute is possible.

Interesting side applications emerge. A film of TG hot melt, for example, could be applied to the back of cloth for conventional cases; as the fabric comes into position against the board (in the presence of heating elements which melt the adhesive) bonding takes place almost instantly. Without glue pot and glue application and drying systems, case-making could be done much faster. Since the adhesive is non-aqueous, warping is eliminated.

For these sophisticated adhesives, however, cost may be a problem; they market between 45 and 60 cents per pound, compared to animal glue (thus still doing 95 percent of perfect-bound catalog and telephone directory work) at about one-third of those prices. Although they are not dispersible, the hot melts easily convert old animal glue machines and have become the fastest growing adhesive on the market.

Long an enthusiastic champion of perfect binding, Chamberlain concluded: "Hot melt bound books have the same basic structure as Smyth sewn books, both in terms of appearance and opening characteristics." Smyth sewing, despite its new increased speeds and automation, can not compete with adhesive binding with regard to cost; and if the latter were every bit as functional and lasting as the former, who would pay more? The age of future books had received its most important green light.

Further adhesive developments are still in the laboratory stage. Microencapsulation (a procedure for trapping liquids—like the dye in carbonless copy paper—in microscopic pods which are crushed to release their contents) can carry an adhesive, deposited on finished cases or paper covers, to the book in process. Advantages are described by Charles Potter of Illinois Adhesive Products:

"A microencapsulated adhesive could be instant-acting—it would set the instant the capsules were broken. This means that encapsulated adhesive could be carried in a non-critical solution and applied to the book independently of temperature and other considerations. The cover and book would then be positioned and a plate pressed against the cover to break the capsules, adhering the cover instantly."[17]

This scheme would solve the critical "timing" problem in most present-day machines, where the glue—at correct temperature and viscosity—must reach its application area—in correct film thickness—a moment after the work receives accurate positioning and yet before machine pressure is applied—a combination of circumstances very difficult to keep in adjustment. Tremendously high binding speeds would become feasible. Furthermore, common two-part epoxy resin adhesives, the strongest bonding agents commercially available, might be used; one part could be encapsulated and the other could be the vehicle in which the capsules are deposited.

"The adhesives industry is traditionally very secretive," said Potter in 1966, suggesting that other adhesive firms are not asleep in this and similar research areas. The National Starch & Chemical Corporation, for example, in 1970 announced elimination of memory in its "Flexback 34-1034" hot melt and at the same time (working with McGraw-Hill, Westinghouse, and the Hellerbond Company, Columbus, Ohio) it revealed a thermoplastic adhesive, "Hellerbond," for reinforcing the hinges of a book: bonding is activated by passage of the book through a magnetic field which melts the adhesive but does not heat the paper. It is apparent, in the long run, that the book industry will owe much of its future to the success of chemists instead of engineers.

James B. Blaine (recently retired from the John F. Cuneo Company, Chicago), addressing the 1969 annual meeting of the Book Manufacturers Institute, admitted that changes of the last quarter century have been nothing short of radical. As an old binder himself, he knew (like the venerable French binder Gruel 75 years before) other old-timers might stumble over the new technology: "We must now contend with such words as synthetic, emulsions, hot melts, alkali dispersible resins, compatability, stability, viscosity. . . . You need a chemist or two on your staff to guide you. . . ." Bookbinding, he added, should more properly be called "book manufacturing" (purists had never been happy calling case work "binding," which they reserved for hand work where covers are built up layer by layer in the individual book). The adhesive-bound book was certainly a fully modern product in all respects bearing very little resemblance to traditional binding; "book manufacturing" as an indication of the greater scope of a new industry was a fitting title.

"The complete bindery of the future is, of course, already here," said Blaine. "No folding machines, a minimum of Smyth sewers and one huge patent binder, which takes the signatures from the adjoining web press room and, with the miracle of hot melt, delivers a complete book and pops it into a shipping carton." With only one principal machine, even the hard-won concept of straight-through conveyorization of materials is rendered obsolete along with a large number of ancillary machines so painstakingly developed in the last hundred years. The product of this simplified manufactory, however, will be stronger and more attractively decorated than ever before; it will be economically produced in whatever quantities wanted; it will be flexible, durable, easy to open and read; and it can even be available in tidy paperback or classic hard-cover—well rounded backbone, carefully squared—either edition standing proudly on home or library shelf.

But more important, the book of the future bindery will be manufactured quickly, for when time is critical tomorrow's book can be ready at the end of the month, if necessary, to discuss the month's news. And it will not be a restricted edition for a select few; it will be a book for the edification and entertainment of millions. It stands ready at the service of both large and small publishers who want to shape the future of publishing.

The hectic years following World War II had suddenly and decisively placed the United States foremost in publishing (and binding) matters. But the nagging problem of leadership and direction in bookwork had not yet been solved. American designers had frequently questioned traditional procedures, as American binders had also—through constant invention—seen no obligation to retain classic (manual) bookmaking techniques. Both unconsciously sought to shake loose from the conventions of European and British bookwork; neither realized that the humble paperback had any lasting pretensions to the future of book construction—that it was, in fact, the bridge to that future.

The PVA adhesives, of course, had been instrumental; they were the final modification which makes the adhesive-bound book, whether paperback or hard-cover, a uniquely American product—without inferiority complex. The paperback publishers had laboriously found their new mass markets quite independently of the traditional bookstore, and learned to serve them well. Their dogged dedication had created an industry almost apart from old conventional methods. Their product, furthermore, by its unassuming size, its cheapness, its mass production and its mass acceptance, was the solution for America's future—or at least the preponderant portion of it. The remainder, the adhesive-bound hard-covered book, literally manufactured almost completely on the same equipment as the paperback, offers simultaneous paperback and hard-cover publishing where both markets exist for a book. The result, to almost everyone's satisfaction, will be a new breed of books by the millions, both cheap and good. It spelled the end to America's design and bookbinding apprehensions.

Considering its form of construction, the gamut of illustrations and color work now possible, and the speed with which it may be produced, the adhesive-bound book meets new standards of publishing which further reinforce its usefulness. Consider the changing publishing scene:

(1) Television, with its immediacy and convenience, has taken a heavy toll on both magazines and newspapers which formerly presented topical materials. Its coverage, of course, is highly perishable.

(2) The transmission of pictures around the world by satellite, television networks, etc., and the production of book composition by computer and other speedy processes, gives book publishers a po-

sition in handling current affairs as high in priority as any other medium.

(3) The many areas of public interest serviced by television—news, sports, feature materials, contemporary biography, current historical and political events, etc.—are also the proper subject of books (and nonbooks). Fully illustrated paperbacks as picture books will have an important market.

(4) Along with up-to-the-minute photographs and text, future manufacturing processes will make it economical and feasible to incorporate into books by the millions cheaply pressed sound recordings, slides for projection, three-dimensional effects, and, where applicable, construction materials, specimens or samples, making multi-dimensional instruction and entertainment packages out of a simple book.

Thus the varieties of editorial approach for the future book publisher are almost endless. More than one publisher has already experimented with a novel "instant book" series on topical events. NAL offers a wire-stitched format called "Broadsides," slightly larger than the usual paperback; Dow Jones & Company has a similar product called "Newsbook"; Yale University Press issues "Yale Fastbacks." Another publisher, New American Review, has found surprising paperback sales of 120,000 for material formerly associated with "little" literary reviews; still others are thinking about presenting an hour's television between soft covers, just as more than one nonbook has been based on stills from popular movies. But distributing these books by the millions must also be taken into consideration.

New techniques in book distribution have already been well founded by paperback publishers. For a long time they were prisoners of the magazine distributors who, for national coverage, consisted of a network of 600 local, independent wholesalers servicing some 90,000 stands, stores, and sales racks. But handling books like periodicals (issuing new titles monthly, rebating in full for unsold copies) was ruinous and unnecessary, and most publishers large enough soon organized their own distributorships. Today they employ market research firms, they carefully control inventory and returns, they disperse salesmen for exploiting new areas, they furnish book training to drivers who stock today's 110,000–120,000 retail outlets, and offer bonuses for exceeding quotas. They utilize educational sales specialists for the school and college market (the most promising of all), they exploit foreign markets wherever they are permitted to do so, and —thanks to new jet flights—they ship bulk quantities around the country fast by air. Few publishers of hardbound books and few bookstores, even in concert, show anywhere near such aggressive marketing. The net effect can be amazing service (although quite unsuspected by the browser): "Our own standard," says Bantam Books, "is that within 48 hours we'd like to have every [new] book delivered everywhere in the country." There is no question that such paperback distribution methods will succeed even for greater quantities to come.

Lest future Morrises or Armitages rail against the publishers of mass paperbacks for perpetuating an abomination on fine bookmaking, Maurice Temple Smith, director of Martin Secker & Warburg, has, despite his own firm's proud allegiance to hard-cover publishing, carried the thread of history forward (beyond Morris) so that paperback publishers would not be strangers to earlier movements:

> "In the eighteenth century authors lived on patronage and publishers produced books for the libraries of gentlemen. In the nineteenth century the arrival of the steam-driven press made it possible for the first time to produce enormous quantities of badly printed books, and that is what the hardcover publishers immediately proceeded to do. In the twentieth century this aspect has been taken over by the paperback publishers, who are doing it far more cheaply than it could be done in hardcovers, and also, incidentally, often working to a far higher standard of design than their Victorian and Edwardian predecessors. . . ."[18]

Although British bookmen have been most perceptive of the trends in publishing, they do not apparently care to accept tomorrow's challenges. The snobbish 1964 Penguin statement preferring a small select readership, and recurring British fears that American paperback publishers—with greater resources—might swamp England, indicate that the British are somewhat uncomfortable with Sir Allen's brainchild. (Lane, 67, died in 1970; S. Pearson & Son, London, acquired Penguin Books that same year.) Although Penguins average over 75,000 copies per title, quantities—over 50 percent—are exported around the world; avaricious British readers themselves generally have tastes too varied, too discriminating, to encourage mass British paperbacks. In 1969 England published 23,000 new titles, most in hard cover in fairly small editions. Hans Schmoller, Penguin's director of production, in 1968 nevertheless recognized apprehensively that the vitality of paperbacks spelled an exciting future:

> "Not long ago one spoke of books—and also paperbacks. In recent years people have taken more and more to speaking of hardbacks and paperbacks, or hardbacks and softbacks. Will the day come, whether we like it or not, when we think of books—and also hardbacks? Herein lies the revolution that may yet come. . . ."[19]

British publisher Clive Bingley has also commented on new publishing directions:

"There are grounds for suggesting that books are at present under-going a profound change of identity. . . . [Paperbacks] are slowly changing the form and content and therefore the nature of books. As paperbacks move closer towards magazine functions, so the traditional book form may prove to be the one common medium of communication which is in fact shrinking instead of growing."[20]

Both Schmoller and Bingley may have suspected that America would have no reluctance bringing this revolution about.

In the United States tremendous growth still looms ahead for a burgeoning reading public increasingly inviting lower-class and under-privileged groups—who have not been great readers (or book buyers) —to participate. Too, over 40 million students in the near future will need books. With bookstore distribution still woefully incomplete and (again) fairly forbidding to poorer readers, the success of the paper-back will prove to be more an American phenomenon than any other country's. Despite its British (or continental) origins, the mass-market paperback—like Walt Whitman's Immortal Muse—has been coaxed to the new world; she's here, installed, with palpable intent to stay.

Marshall McLuhan associated the peculiar American success of the paperback with stupefying incursions of television in the United States:

"The phenomenon of the paperback, the book in 'cool' version [the traditional hard-cover book with its "confessional" author-reader rela-tionship is normally 'hot'—demanding rapt reader attention but no participation], can head the list of TV mandates, because the TV transformation of book culture into something else is manifested at that point. Europeans have had paperbacks from the first. . . . The paper-back, especially in its highbrow form, was tried in America in the 1920s and thirties and forties. It was not, however, until 1953 that it suddenly became acceptable. No publisher really knows why. . . ."

McLuhan suggests that the public's difficulty with old paperback spines disintegrating and new ones snapping shut, and the bewildering variety of titles (the two paperback features most condemned, profes-sionally), may curiously have been advantageous factors in this suc-cess:

"Not only is the paperback a tactile, rather than a visual, package; it can be as readily concerned with profound matters as with froth. . . . The paperback reader has discovered that he can enjoy Aristotle or Confucius by simply slowing down. The old literate habit of racing ahead on uniform lines of print yielded suddenly to depth reading. Reading in depth is, of course, not proper to the printed word as such. Depth probing of words and language is a normal feature of oral and manuscript cultures, rather than of print. . . . The paperback itself has become a vast mosaic world in depth. . . ."[21]

Thus the electronic media become more than simple rivals of the book. They exert new pressures on reading and learning that bicycle, radio, and motion picture never attempted. And new pressures have repeatedly been the major force at work shaping book construction.

In 1968 the Battelle Memorial Institute prepared a confidential report for MGD Graphic Systems, projecting printing conditions up to 1990. Revealed in 1970 as the source for a "Comprint 90" conference, the Battelle Report predicted no great standardization over the next 20 years, although it expects, by 1978, that bindery functions will increasingly be combined into fewer automated machines, culminating by 1990 in a "closed-loop" system consisting of a single inline operation for printing, binding, shipping. The report is comforting about books: "Books are an established graphic arts product form which, despite many threats, pressures and forecasts to the contrary, will continue to exist in about the same physical configuration well into the 21st Century." But this concession to tradition overlooks evolutionary developments already at work in the United States.

The making of a characteristically American book will not simply be a matter of updating European styles; the cased-in book (physically and typographically), as we have seen, is a British product fundamentally unchanged since the 1820's. A new book comes into existence when new, distinct pressures come to bear on contemporary publishing problems. Such was the effect when Bradel and Lesné developed temporary bindings; such was the result when Archibald Leighton created cloth cases. Such was the situation when paperbacks and cheap literature emerged in the mid-1800's. So also was the climate when Allen Lane produced Penguins and Robert de Graff produced Pocket Books, although with these twin experiments distribution innovations had been as important as construction changes.

For the future a new ingredient will be present in world-wide publishing—self confidence that American book manufacturers and publishers know what they want and know how to get it done. They will no longer strive to imitate French quality, British craftsmanship, or German sturdiness. All those instrumental in creating a new package for the printed word will do so without a moment's hesitation over European preferences and traditions. Book designer Marshall Lee's 1964 description of a modern book—"a series of rectangular leaves joined at one edge and covered with a protective material"— no longer bears any technical relation to Arnett's classical definition of the fashioning of that product; gone altogether are necessary references to thread, glue, paste, board, and leather. Tomorrow's bookmen with new techniques and better equipment will continue to package the printed word for the millions, and more.[22]

*"I raise a voice for far superber themes for poets and for Art,*
*To exalt the present and the real,*
*To teach the average man the glory of his daily walk and trade,*
*To sing, in songs, how exercise and chemical life are never to be baffled;*
*Boldly to thee, America, to-day! and thee, Immortal Muse!*
*Our freedom all in thee! Our very lives in thee!"*

—Walt Whitman

["He was applauded as he advanced to read, besides several times throughout, and at the close. He did not respond in the usual way by bowing. All the directors and officers of the Institute crowded around him and heartily thanked him. He extricated himself, regained his old Panama hat and stick, and without waiting for the rest of the exercises, made a quiet exit by the steps at the back of the stand."]

—From a New York correspondent to the
*Washington Chronicle,* 11 Sept. 1871

# REFERENCES

For complete description of sources appearing only by surname in the text and below, refer to the Bibliography, which contains all heavily utilized materials, usually of interest in their entirety. Under topical sections below are collected additional references, journal articles, and unpublished sources of peripheral or specific value. Foreign or obscure periodicals (often defunct) are identified by city of origin; the following abbreviations are used for those frequently cited:

| | | | |
|---|---|---|---|
| *APC* | *American Publishers' Circular* | *BPI* | *Book Production Industry* |
| *BBR* | *Bookbinder* | *INP* | *Inland Printer* |
| *BKB* | *Bookbinding* | *PW* | *Publishers' Weekly* |
| *BI* | *Book Industry* | *SA* | *Scientific American* |
| *BP* | *Book Production* | *TAB* | *The American Bookmaker* |

Also abbreviated here are *Dictionary of American Biography* (*DAB*) and *National Cyclopedia of American Biography* (*NCAB*).

## INTRODUCTION: THE BOOKS OF OLD

1. *APC*, 15 April 1867, 350, quoting *The Round Table*, 30 March 1867.
2. From *Bookbinding*, Rev. Ed., by John Pleger, 421, used with permission of The Inland Printer.
3. Brander Matthews, 172.
4. Francis Meynell, *Typography: Type Specimens*. London: Pelican Press, 1926, 38.
5. *Arts et Metiers Graphiques* [Paris], 15 Sept. 1927, quoting poet Paul Valéry.
6. From *The Evolution of Publishers' Binding Styles, 1770–1900*, by Michael Sadleir, 6, used with permission of Constable & Company.
7. Rogers (Lehmann-Haupt), 184.
8. From *Modern Book Design*, by Ruari McLean, 36, used with permission of Longmans, Green & Company.
9. AIGA "50 Books of the Year" Catalogs, 1950–1970.
10. "Official Tally of Bindery Equipment," *BKB*, Sept. 1961.
11. F. C. Gould, "The Mechanization of Book Binding." *Sixteenth Series of Printing Craft Lectures Delivered at Stationers' Hall . . . 1937–1938.* London: School of Printing and Kindred Trades, 1938.
12. James Shand, "The Significance of American Periodicals," *Penrose Annual*, 1939, 64.

13. C. H. Duell, *Annual Report of the Commissioner of Patents for the Year 1900*. US GPO, 1901, xii.

14. INTRODUCTION: Henry B. Wheatley, "On Binding in Cloth," *BBR*, Oct. 1888, 52; "The Bibliography of Bookbinding and Binding Patents," *The Library* [Oxford], Vol. 4 (1892), 228–229; Duell, op. cit., xi; Thomas W. Herringshaw, *National Library of American Biography*, Vol. 5, 273, "Smyth"; Meynell, *Typography*, op. cit., 38, 43; Paul Beaujon [Beatrice Warde], "Art of the Book," in Warren E. Cox, Ed., *Graphic Arts*. Garden City: Garden City Pub. Co., 1936, 107; Edward J. Triebe, "Binding: The Cinderella of the Graphic Arts." *Graphic Arts Monthly*, March 1958, 28; Correspondence, Joseph W. Rogers, March 1969.


## 1. FRANCE: LA RELIURE BELLE

1. Lesné, 308, from "Epitre à Thouvenin."

2. Bosquet, 172, quoting Lesné.

3. HAND BINDING: *La Grande Encyclopedie* (c. 1900), Vol. 28, 373, "Reliure"; William Y. Fletcher, *English Book Collectors*. London: Kegan Paul, Trench, Trübner, 1902, 263; Douglas Leighton, "Canvas and Bookcloth: An Essay on Beginnings," *The Library* [Oxford], June 1948, 39.

WORKMAN: *Paper and Press* [Philadelphia], Oct. 1892, 230; *TAB*, June 1893, 216; *BKB*, Sept. 1941, 36; Sept. 1943, 47.

4. Williamson; Harrison; *Paper and Press*, Sept. 1894, 321; Lockwood.

5. Hachette & Co., *An Historical Notice upon the Establishment of Messrs. Hachette & Co.* Paris: 1876, introduction.

6. Paris letter dated Dec. 1863, *APC*, 1 Feb. 1864.

7. AWAKENING OF INDUSTRIALIZATION: "Alfred Mâme," *TAB*, June 1893, 224; *La Grande Encyclopedie*, op. cit.; P. J. Angoulvent, "The Development of the Book," *Fleuron* [London], No. 3 (1924), 69; Nicolas Rauch, "Les Livres de l'Epoque Romantique," *Formes et Couleurs* [Paris], Nos. 3/4 (1945); G. Baudry and R. Marange, *Comment on Imprime*. Paris: Circle de la Librairie, 1955; Daniel B. Updike, *Printing Types: Their History, Forms, and Use*. Cambridge: Harvard U. Press, 1962, Vol. II, 160; Reynolds Stone, "The Albion Press," *Journal of the Printing Historical Society*, No. 2 (1966), 63.

MASSIQUOT: *L'Imprimerie* [Paris], May 1866, 353; July 1871, 1085.

PUBLISHER-BINDERS: *BBR*, May 1892, 39; Jan. 1893, 154; May 1893, 256.

BINDERY MACHINES: *L'Imprimerie*, Dec. 1864, 151; Sept. 1865, 235; March 1874, 426.

8. "Paris Société des Amis des Livres," *BBR*, Vol. 3 (1889–1890), xxvi.

9. Bosquet, 26 ftnt.

10. FRENCH BIBLIOPHILIA: W. H. Edmunds, "Artizan's Visit to the Paris Exhibition," *BBR*, Nov. 1889, 75; "A French Binder's Visit to London," *BBR*, Dec. 1892; "Bosquet's New Work on Binding," *Paper and Press*, March 1894, 172; Polly Lada-Mocarski, "French Fifty Books of the Year: 1966 Exhibition," *AIGA Journal*, Vol. 5 (1966).

HAND BINDERS: *BBR*, April 1887, 154; August 1888, 19; Jan. 1891, 5; July 1892, 12; *TAB*, March 1891, 76–77; June 1892, 205; June 1896, 165.

## 2. ENGLAND: THE BOOK BEAUTIFUL

1. Ellic Howe, "London Bookbinders: Masters and Men, 1780–1840," *The Library* [Oxford], June 1946, 33.

2. Hannett, 127.

3. *Official Catalogue of the Great Exhibition of the Works of Industry of All Nations, 1851*. London: Spicer, 1851, 93.

4. Darley, 40–41; also The Times "Printing Number" (1912), 33.

5. Knight (1865), II, 162.

6. LIMITED PRODUCTION: Bernard Quaritch, "A Short History of Book-binding," *BBR*, May 1887, 171; "Archibald Leighton," *BBR*, Jan. 1888, 99–101; "A Glance at the Bindings in the Paris Exposition," *BBR*, Sept. 1888, 35; "German Bookbinding Seen through English Spectacles," *BBR*, Jan., 1893; William L. Andrews, *Gossip about Book Collecting*, 2 Vols. New York: Dodd, Mead & Co., 1900, II, 89–90; Howe, "London Bookbinders," op. cit., 28, 35; Leighton, "Canvas and Bookcloth," op. cit., 39, 43, 46; Terence Ulrick, "Lewis Kitcat," *Book Design and Production* [London], Autumn 1958, 57–58; Stone, "The Albion Press," op. cit., 58, 68–69.

HAND/MACHINE BINDERS: *BBR*, Oct. 1887, 55–56; Oct. 1892, 77; April 1893, 233; *TAB*, April 1888, 104.

7. *Sketches of London*, Vol. II. Philadelphia: Carey & Hart, 1839, 52.

8. George H. Putnam, II, 234–235.

9. Bernard Quaritch, *A Catalog of Fifteen Hundred Books Remarkable for the Beauty or the Age of their Bindings. . . .* London: Quaritch, 1889, iii.

10. ENTREPRENEURAL PUBLISHING: *Sketches of London*, op. cit., 55–63; The Times, *The Literature of the Rail*. London: Murray, 1851, reprinted from *The Times*, 9 August 1851; Fletcher, op. cit., 261; Austin Dobson, *Thomas Bewick and His Pupils*. London: Chatto & Windus, 1884, 173; "The Railway Book-Stall," Chambers' Journal [Edinburgh], Vol. 8 (1904–1905), 375; "Rudolf Ackermann—Nature's Nobleman," *INP*, Feb. 1917, 634–635; Beaujon (Cox), op. cit., 114; Janet A. Smith, *Children's Illustrated Books*. London: Collins, 1948, 18–22; David Keir, *The House of Collins: The Story of a Scottish Family of Publishers from 1789 to the Present Day*. London: Collins, 1952; Hans Schmoller, "Reprints: Aldine and After," *Penrose Annual*, 1953, 35–36; Edward Liveing, *Adventure in Publishing: The House of Ward Lock, 1854–1954*. London: Ward, Lock, 1954; Updike, op. cit., II, 198–199; Ervine Metzl, *The Poster: Its History and Its Art*. New York: Watson Guptill, 1963, 34.

11. Cobden-Sanderson (1922), 100.

12. "Cloth-Binding as a Trade," *BBR*, June 1890, 185.

13. The Studio, *Modern Book-Bindings and Their Designers*, 6.

14. CRAFTSMANSHIP REVIVAL: Quaritch, Catalog, op. cit., xiv; E. Lenore Casford, *The Magazines of the 1890's [Albemarle, Yellow Book*, and

*Savoy*]. Eugene: U. of Oregon, 1929, 12–13, 33; Francis Meynell, "Modern English and Continental Books," in Cox, op. cit., 118; Viola Meynell, Ed., *Friends of a Lifetime: Letters to Sydney Carlyle Cockerell*. London: Jonathan Cape, 1940, 215; Joseph Thorp, *B. H. Newdigate: Scholar-Printer, 1869–1944*. Oxford: Basil Blackwell, 1950, 25; Noel Rooke, "Sir Emery Walker, 1851–1933," *Penrose Annual*, 1954, 40–43; Walter Kubilius, "Mechanization Slowly Gaining Ground in European Binderies," *BP*, Sept, 1957, 60; Updike, op. cit., II, 201–218, 272; S. Tschudi Madsen, *Art Nouveau*. New York: McGraw-Hill, 1967, 79.

COBDEN-SANDERSON: *BBR*, Nov. 1890, 4; March 1893, 214; *TAB*, Jan. 1890, 3; Feb. 1902, 480; March 1902, 55; *PW*, 14 Sept. 1895, 335; *INP*, Jan. 1917, 488.

## 3. GERMANY: DIE SCHONE BORSE

1. GERMAN BOOK TRADE: "The Bookseller's Fair at Leipsic," *APC*, 16 May 1857, 306; "Leipsic as a Book-Mart," *TAB*, Jan. 1888, 17; "Publishing in Germany," *TAB*, Nov. 1889, 123; "Jubilee of the Firm of Karl Krause, Leipzig," *INP*, Nov. 1905, 274–275; Kubilius, "Mechanization Slowly Gaining Ground," op. cit., 59–60; Paul Standard, "Jan Tschichold: Proponent of Asymmetry and Tradition," *PW*, 1 May 1967, 88.

BÖRSENVEREIN: *APC*, 26 June 1858, 307; 2 Feb. 1863, 3; 1 July 1863, 198; 1 Jan. 1864, 176; 15 June 1865, 72.

KRAUSE-BIAGOSCH: *BBR*, March 1890, 136–137; July 1891, 14; *BKB*, Oct. 1926, 28; June 1955, 46.

2. CONTINENTAL BOOKWORK: "Leipzig as a Home of Wholesale Bookbinding," *BBR*, April 1889, 158; Otto Zahn, "Incised Leather (Lederschnitt)," *TAB*, Jan. 1892, 2; Temple Scott, "Modern Book-Making in Germany," *The Graphic Arts* [Boston], April 1911, 289–295; *A General Guide to the International Exhibition for the Book Industry and the Graphic Arts at Leipzig, 1914* [Bugra '14 Catalog]; Fritz Homeyer, "Germany," *The Dolphin* [New York], 1933, 281; Meynell (Cox), op. cit., 121, 122; "Carl Ernst Poeschel," *Print*, Vol. VI, No. 4 (1950–1951), 12–13, 20; Earnest Elmo Calkins and Blanche Decker, "History of the AIGA," *AIGA Journal*, Vol. IV, No. 5 (1952); Rooke, "Sir Emery Walker," op. cit., 40–43; Updike, op. cit., II, 219–220; John Dreyfus, "Count Kessler and the Cranach Press," *PW*, 2 Dec. 1968, 60.

LEIPZIG: *BBR*, July 1889, 13; August 1889, 29.

ZAHN: *BBR*, Sept. 1892, 53; *PW*, 5 Oct. 1895, 335.

3. Crane, 246.

4. Frederic G. Melcher, Editorial, 2157. Reprinted by permission of R. R. Bowker Company, a Xerox Company, from *Publishers' Weekly*, December 11, 1943. Copyright © 1943 by R. R. Bowker Company.

5. Tauchnitz, 70.

6. BAUHAUS ERA: *DAB*, Vol. 9, 323, "Elbert Hubbard"; Hugo Steiner-Prag, "European Books and Designs," *The Dolphin*, 1933, 216; 248; Meynell (Cox), op. cit., 115, 120, 123; Herbert Bayer, Walter Gropius, and Ise

Gropius, Eds., *Bauhaus 1919–1928*. New York: Museum of Modern Art, 1938, 148; Bertram Evans, "Design in Continental Magazines," *Penrose Annual*, 1940, 42; *Updike: American Printer and His Merrymount Press*. New York: AIGA, 1947; Roger Fourney, *Manuel de Reliure: Reliure à la main; reliure industrielle; dorure sur cuir; dorure sur tranches*. Paris: Béranger, 1952, 131, 156–157, 170–171; US GPO-PIA Joint Research Bulletin B-1, *The Process of Marbling Paper*. US GPO, 1953; Paul Angoulvent, *L'Edition français au pied du mur*. Paris: Presses Universitaires de France, 1960; L. Hirschfeld-Mack, *The Bauhaus*. Victoria, Australia: Longmans, Green, 1963, 2; Walther Scheidig, *Crafts of the Weimar Bauhaus, 1919–1924*. London: Studio Vista, 1966, 6, 27; Herbert R. Lottman, "Italy: Il Boom in Paperbacks Slows Down," *PW*, 17 April 1967, 31–33.

CHARPENTIER: *L'Imprimerie* [Paris], May 1871, 1099; *PW*, 20 Oct. 1877, 472.

GERMAN PUBLISHING: *Paper Box Maker* [New York], March 1899, 5; *PW*, 18 April 1925, 1375; *BKB*, Dec. 1945, 55.

BRODART-TAUPIN: *BKB*, Feb. 1954, 51; *PW*, 30 March 1970, 30.

BAUHAUS: *BKB*, July 1929, 30; May 1937, 34; Feb. 1939, 22; May 1942, 53; Sept. 1945, 75.

WOMEN BINDERS: *Paper and Press* [Philadelphia], Feb. 1894, 108; *Paper Box Maker*, Nov. 1896, 16; Jan. 1897, 17; Nov. 1898, 2; April 1899, 8; *BKB*, March 1947, 39; Dec. 1949, 57, 59; June 1953, 51.

## 4. PUBLISHING HERITAGE AND THE WIRE STITCHER

1. Brainard, 43–44.
2. *APC*, 23 April 1859, quoting *The Boston Transcript*.
3. Altemus advt, *APC*, 24 April 1858, 203.
4. Nicholson, 170.
5. EARLY AMERICAN PUBLISHING: "The Average Quality of American Book-Manufacture," *APC*, 15 Nov. 1864, 34; "Mammoth Book Manufactories," *APC*, 15 April 1868, 313; "An Afternoon in Harper's Book-Bindery," *Typographic Messenger* [New York], March 1869; "J. B. Lippincott Company," *Paper and Press* [Philadelphia], April 1887, 114; S. Hunt, *Centennial of the Methodist Book Concern*. New York: 1889; *A Brief Description of The Riverside Press, Cambridge*. Cambridge: 1899; "The Riverside Press at Cambridge," *TAB*, Sept. 1903, 36–40; Arthur L. Ralston, "Changes in the Methods of Bookbinding," *TAB*, July 1910, 641–642; "The Story of Gold Leaf," *BKB*, July 1925, 8; Downing P. O'Harra, "Book Publishing in the United States to 1901," *PW*, 16 March 1929, 1391; 18 May 1929, 2345; Dorothea L. Mann, "Cornhill and the Booksellers," *PW*, 11 May 1929, 2229; E. W. Palmer, "Whither Book Publishing and Manufacturing?" *BKB*, March 1948, 34, 77; Robert E. Spiller, Willard Thorp, Thomas H. Johnson, Henry S. Canby, et al., *Literary History of the United States*, Rev. Ed. New York: Macmillan, 1953, 806, 860–864; Gerald Gross, Ed., *Publishers on Publishing*. New York: Grosset & Dunlap,

1961, 16, quoting J. B. Lippincott; J. B. Lippincott Co., *The Author and His Audience*. Philadelphia: 1967.

HARPER'S: *APC*, 15 Oct. 1868, 290–291; 1 April 1869, 265.

RIVERSIDE PRESS: *APC*, 1 May 1868, 6; *TAB*, Sept. 1895, 93; *BKB*, April 1931, 30; *PW*, 6 May 1968, 84.

RUTTER-TAPLEY: *TAB*, June 1910, 504; Sept. 1915, 96; *BKB*, June 1935, 16; April 1938, 26; Dec. 1951, 53.

6. *APC*, 1 June 1863.

7. US GPO (1950), 87.

8. L. E. Chittenden, "The Value of Instruction in the Mechanic Arts." Address to the American Institute of the City of New York, 1889.

9. Austin, Catalog, with Sheridan tip-in dated 17 Oct. 1861.

10. Sheridan advt, *BKB*, Sept. 1927, 7.

11. Editorial, *Paper Box Maker* [New York], June 1899, 10; bookwork costs, July 1899, 3.

12. BINDERY ORGANIZATION: "Purchase of the Adams Press Concern by R. Hoe & Company," *The Printer* [New York], May 1859, 4; "An Afternoon in Harper's Book-Bindery," op. cit.; *DAB*, Vol. 4, 575, "Luther C. Crowell"; Vol. 9, 104, "Richard M. Hoe"; Vol. 9, 105, "Robert Hoe"; Vol. 19, 40, "Stephen D. Tucker"; *NCAB*, Vol. 27, 14, "Cyrus Chambers, Jr."; *Memoir of Hayward Augustus Harvey*. New York, 1900; John F. McCabe, "Plant of the Famous Harper Brothers," *Printing Trade News* [New York], April 1909, 25; Ralph W. Polk, *Elementary Platen Presswork*. Peoria, Ill.: Manual Arts Press, 1931, 5; Spiller et al., op. cit., 958–959; Walter Kubilius, "Automation Comes to the Book Industry," *BKB*, Nov. 1956, 49; "Viewpoints on Bindery Automation," *BP*, March 1964, 65–67; Correspondence, Marian Lawson, Sept., Oct. 1969.

SANBORN-STANDARD: *Typographic Messenger*, Oct. 1872, 73; Sept. 1888, 75, 96.

SHERIDAN: *TAB*, Dec. 1888, 189; Jan. 1895, 29; May 1914, 390; *INP*, May 1914, 292; *Paper and Press*, Nov. 1893, 278–280; *BKB*, July 1931, 36; March 1933, 44.

PAPER CUTTERS: *TAB*, Dec. 1888, 189; Jan. 1889, 16; May 1889, 125; June 1889, 152.

FOLDERS: *TAB*, Nov. 1886, 160; Nov. 1887, 179; Dec. 1887, 216; March 1896, 88; June 1906, 560; *Paper and Press*, March 1894, 174; *INP*, June 1903, 428, 430; August 1905, 38; Dec. 1906, 420; June 1907, 423; *BKB*, June 1927, 34; July 1940, 26; Jan. 1942, 35; March 1942, 25; June 1954, 36.

13. "The Cheap Libraries," *PW*, 6 Oct. 1877, 396–397.

14. *American Newspaper Reporter* [New York], 11 Dec. 1876, 910.

15. "Books in Summer Suits," *TAB*, July 1887, 6.

16. *Memorandums in Regard to International Copyright Treaty between Great Britain and the United States*. New York: Harper, 1879, 12.

17. Letter to editor, *PW*, 2 Feb. 1884, 151.

18. Editorial, *PW*, 8 July 1876, 130.

19. CHEAP PUBLISHING: George H. Putnam, "International Copyright: Considered in Some of its Relations to Ethics and Political Economy."

Address delivered 29 Jan. 1878. New York: Putnam's Sons, 1879, 51; *Biographical Sketch of Norman L. Munro*. New York: Atlantic Publishing & Engraving Co., 1885; *DAB*, Vol. 4, 303, "Peter F. Collier"; Vol. 13, 331, "George Munro"; John F. McCabe, "The Late Peter Fenelon Collier, Publisher," *Printing Trade News*, May 1909, 25–26; P. P. Howe, *Malthus and the Publishing Trade*. New York: Kennerley, 1913; Spiller et al., op. cit., 234; Donald L. Steinhauer, "Golden Days," *Dime Novel Roundup*, Supplement 1, 1957, 38; P. B. G. Upton, "A Technologist Looks at Books," *Printing Technology* [London], Vol. III, No. 2 (1958–1959), 100; Gross, op. cit., 414, quoting Charles Scribner, Jr.

   LOVELL: *TAB*, Dec. 1895, 188; *PW*, 30 Jan. 1873, 107; 25 March 1876, 409; 19 April 1879, 470–471; 29 March 1890, 460; 24 May 1890, 703; 14 June 1890, 799; *American Newspaper Reporter*, 2 Oct. 1876, 751; 23 Oct. 1876, 799.

 20. Lockwood, 55.

 21. Hector Orr, "Heyl's Machine for Making Paper Boxes," *Franklin Institute Journal*, Oct. 1873, 217–219.

 22. American Paper Bottle Company literature, Henry R. Heyl memoirs.

 23. *Heyl's System, Wire Book Sewing* [pamphlet].

 24. *PW*, 29 Sept. 1877, 373.

 25. Letter from Carl Louis Lasch, Henry R. Heyl memoirs.

 26. Letter to editor, *PW*, 29 May 1875, 567.

 27. *PW*, 8 Nov. 1879, 563.

 28. *PW*, 25 Sept. 1880, 408.

 29. *PW*, 25 Sept. 1880, 406.

 30. *BBR*, April 1890, xl.

 31. MECHANICAL JOINING OF SHEETS: Henry R. Stiles, Ed., *The Civil, Political, Professional and Ecclesiastical History and Commercial and Industrial Record of the County of Kings and the City of Brooklyn, N.Y., from 1683 to 1884*, 2 Vols. New York: Munsell & Co., 1884, Vol. 2, 740, 878; *NCAB*, Vol. 13, 77, "Louis Goddu"; Henry R. Heyl memoirs; Meynell, *Typography*, op. cit., 43; "The 1876 Exposition Needed Catalogs—and the Wire Stitcher was Born," *BKB*, August 1935, 20; Spiller et al., op. cit., 20, 234, 803–805, 955, 1124; Baudry and Marange, op. cit., 520; "Librarians Ask for Better Papers, Bindings, Standardization of Sizes," *BP*, Dec. 1959, 49; Ford Foundation, *Scholars' Work and Works*. New York: 1963.

   WIRE STITCHER: *Paper and Printing Trades Journal* [London], March 1878, 10; *PW*, 20 July 1878, 65, 85; 12 May 1883, 541; 29 Sept. 1883, 462; 1 May 1886, 574; 13 Nov. 1886, 690; *TAB*, March 1886, 48; June 1886, 204; March 1888, 70, 74; June 1888, 157; July 1888, 18–19; *BBR*, 1888, xxxiv; March 1888, 139–140; Nov. 1888, 169; Nov. 1890, 5; May 1891, 15; *BKB*, Sept. 1927, 20; Sept. 1935, 46; June 1937, 44.

## 5. BINDERY MECHANIZATION AND THE BOOK SEWER

 1. Butterworth, 133.

 2. *SA*, 18 March 1848, 204.

3. *SA,* Supplement, 15 Oct. 1881, 4812.

4. "Mammoth Book Manufactories," op. cit., 312.

5. "William Matthews, Brooklyn, New York," *BBR,* June 1892, 276.

6. SMYTH: New York State Adjutant General's Office, *A Record of the Commissioned Officers, Non-Commissioned Officers, and Privates of the Regiments. . . .* Vol. 6. Albany: 1866; "Mammoth Book Manufactories," op. cit., 312; "William Matthews, Brooklyn, New York," op. cit., 275–276; Stiles, op. cit., 740; *DAB,* Vol. 7, 323, "David McC. Smyth"; Vol. 12, 420, "William Matthews"; *Harvey Memoir,* op. cit.; Edward W. Byrn, *The Progress of Invention in the Nineteenth Century.* New York: Munn & Co., 1900, 385; "David M. Smyth," *INP,* Dec. 1907, 431–432; Thomas C. Cochran and William Miller, *The Age of Enterprise: A Social History of Industrial America.* New York: Macmillan, 1942, 113.

APPLETON: *PW,* 18 Oct. 1873, 407; 15 Nov. 1890, 705; *TAB,* May 1896, 144; June 1896, 165, 167; *BKB,* April 1929, 60.

7. Thompson and Parkhurst Patent No. 150,495, 5 May 1874.

8. "Technical Bookbinding," *BBR,* March 1888, 140.

9. *SA,* 9 August 1879, 84.

10. *SA,* 25 Oct. 1879, 256.

11. The Smyth Manufacturing Company, records.

12. The Smyth Manufacturing Company, records.

13. [Hartford] *Evening Post,* Dec. 1879; also *BKB,* Dec. 1949, 37.

14. SMYTH MANUFACTURING COMPANY: American Institute of the City of New York, Prospectus, 1876, Exposition Catalogs, 1869, 1879; *NCAB,* Vol. 7, 323, "David McC. Smyth"; Vol. 16, 41, "Arthur I. Jacobs"; Vol. 19, 255, "James E. A. Gibbs"; "David M. Smyth," op. cit.: Henry O. Dwight, *The Centennial History of the American Bible Society.* New York: Macmillan, 1916, 365, 441; "N.Y. Bookbinders Guild Holds Interesting Meeting [I.D. Mackenzie on Smyth]," *BKB,* Feb. 1926, 24, 34b; Gould, "The Mechanization of Book Binding," op. cit., 66–67; James P. Blaine, "Sewing on Tapes," *BKB,* July 1940, 16; Correspondence, Charles E. Brainard, July 1969.

SMYTH SEWER: *SA,* 7 Feb. 1880, 92; *TAB,* April 1888, 95; June 1888, 158; Nov. 1907, 338; *BBR,* Jan. 1889, 101–102; *BKB,* Sept. 1928, 46; June 1929, 30; April 1930, 25; Sept. 1937, 64; April 1938, 34; May 1941, 36; March 1942, 39; Dec. 1946, 31; Dec. 1954, 34; Feb. 1958, 51.

15. From *Seventy Years of Textbook Publishing,* by Thomas Bonaventure Lawler, copyright, 1938, by Ginn and Company, © Copyright renewed, 1966, by T. Newman Lawler, used with permission.

16. Oversewing Machine Co. advt, *BKB,* June 1928, 11, quoting definition in the E.B.A. Bookbinding Manual.

17. *BBR,* May 1888, 167.

18. *BBR,* May 1890, 171–172.

19. Van Kleeck, 47.

20. Stephen (1908), 33.

21. *PW,* 7 April 1900, 718.

22. SMYTH AND COMPETITORS: "The New Book-Sewing Machine [Mar-

tini-National]," *INP*, Dec. 1903, 443; George H. Putnam and John B. Putnam, *Authors and Publishers: A Manual of Suggestions for Beginners in Literature*, 7th Ed. New York: Putnam's Sons, 1904, 266; R.R.K. Horne, "American Machinery Bolsters European Book Market," *BKB*, May 1953, 47; "Sewing Equipment—Side and Saddle, *BP*, Oct. 1959, 58–59, 71; *E. C. Fuller Facts* [New York], April 1965; Frank B. Myrick, "Some New Advances in Bindery Technology," *PW*, 1 Jan. 1968, 59; Correspondence, Martini Bookbinding Machinery Company, Oct. 1969.

PLIMPTON: *TAB*, Feb. 1905, 475; *BKB*, June 1939, 50; Oct. 1941, 35; May 1942, 38; June 1945, 37; May 1948, 63; Nov. 1960, 91; *BPI*, Feb. 1965, 46, 49; *PW*, 13 April 1970, 60.

BREHMER: *TAB*, June 1886, 204; May 1888, 126–127; *BKB:* August 1925, 12, 16; August 1937, 32; Feb. 1948, 5; August 1950, 51; *BP*, August 1959, 11.

FULLER-HORNE: *TAB*, Nov. 1894, 152; April 1895, vii; May 1896, i; *BKB*, April 1931, 58; May 1937, 76; April 1938, 34; May 1943, 35; Jan. 1945, 71; March 1950, inside front cover; July 1955, 44; April 1961, 62.

MCCAIN: *Printing Trade News* [New York], July 1910, 64; *BKB*, Oct. 1934, 52; Nov. 1934, 4; Dec. 1934, 8; Jan. 1937, 32; Nov. 1940, 41; *PW*, 25 Dec. 1967, 35; *BPI*, April 1967, 12, 37; March 1968, 15; June 1969, 88.

J. SMYTH-NATIONAL: *TAB*, Dec. 1887, 216; May 1906, 327; June 1914, 529; *INP*, Feb. 1903, 774; Dec. 1903, 331; May 1906, 274; April 1907, 39; Oct. 1908, 116; April 1913, 289; April 1916, 100; *BKB*, April 1925, 24; May 1925, 35; Feb. 1960, 17; August 1961, 13.

## 6. PERIODICAL PRODUCTION AND ADHESIVE BINDING

1. Automatic Machinery Company advt, *American Printer*, Jan. 1905, 287.

2. Van Kleeck, 50.

3. FINAL MECHANIZATION: Trow Directory, Printing and Bookbinding Company, *Minutes of the Annual Meeting of Stockholders . . . July 17, 1894; DAB*, Vol. 3, 375, "Ebenezer Butterick"; Vol. 13, 334, "Frank A. Munsey"; *NCAB*, Vol. 13, 231, "Ebenezer Butterick"; Vol. 20, 47, "Frank A. Munsey"; Vol. 22, 43, "George W. Wilder"; Edward Larney, "Binding 16 Million Magazines a Month," *Curtis Folks* [Philadelphia], March 1924, 3; Erman J. Ridgway, *This for Remembrance* [Munsey]. Chula Vista, Cal.: 1926; Alfred Bredenberg memoirs.

MUNSEY: *TAB*, August 1902, 526; Oct. 1908, 238; *INP*, Nov. 1906, 268; *Printing Trade News* [New York], Nov. 1908, 24.

BUTTERICK: *TAB*, August 1905, 571–572; *Printing Trade News*, July 1910, 51.

J. LOVELL-US BOOK: *Paper and Press* [Philadelphia], July 1890, 28; *TAB*, Feb. 1893, 80; *PW*, 15 Feb. 1890, 274–275; 29 March 1890, 460; 5 April 1890, 495; 30 April 1932, 1888; Lockwood, "John Lovell."

C. LOVELL-BREDENBERG: *TAB*, August 1892, 48; April 1906, 168; May 1909, 328; *Paper and Press*, May 1893, 390.

SMYTH GATHERER: *TAB*, Oct. 1896, 124; Nov. 1896, 154; Jan. 1901, 287, 370; May 1901, 227; *INP*, April 1900, 94; Oct. 1900, 8, 162; Sept. 1901, 854; Oct. 1901, 54; Nov. 1901, 379; August 1902, 775.

COMBINATION MACHINES: *INP*, Dec. 1906, 420; July 1913, 601; Feb. 1914, 651; *TAB*, Feb. 1907, 618; July 1913, 649; *BKB*, June 1944, 49.

4. John F. McCabe, "The Trow Printing Company's Enormous Plant," *Printing Trade News*, Oct. 1909, 43.

5. George Juengst & Sons [catalog].

6. Juengst Patent No. 1,244,861, 30 Oct. 1917.

7. "Some Glue Dont's," *BKB*, August 1925, 6, attributed to Gane Brothers & Lane.

8. The Times "Printing Number" (1912), 33.

9. INLINE CONCEPT: Trow Directory, Printing and Bookbinding Company, op. cit.; *DAB*, Supplement I, 212, "Cyrus H.K. Curtis"; Larney, op. cit., 2–3; Ridgway, op. cit.; H. A. Upton, "Handling Glue in the Bindery," *BKB*, Jan. 1932, 39; Cochran and Miller, op. cit., 269; McGraw-Hill Book Company, *The Story of Forty Years of Growth*. New York: 1949; Fred C. Warner, "German Immigrant [Juengst] Founded Industrial Dynasty in Somers," *Patent Trader* [Mt. Kisco], 11 June 1959; Fred C. Warner, "George Juengst," *Westchester Historian* [Tuckahoe], April–June 1960, 31–34; W.O. Faxon and Robert E. Fogg, "Adhesive Binding," *BI*, first issue 1963, 75.

GLUE: *BBR*, August 1889, 30; July 1890, 12–13, 19; *TAB*, Jan. 1895, 13; *BKB*, Sept. 1926, 36; Jan. 1931, 21; Jan. 1942, 27; Dec. 1945, 33.

JUENGST-AAMCO: *Printing Trade News*, August 1908, 28; August 1909, 39; Oct. 1909, 43–44; Nov. 1909, 19; July 1910, 87; *INP*, Sept. 1907, 919; Oct. 1907, 95; Feb. 1910, 758; Jan. 1913, 508; Feb. 1913, 657; Oct. 1916, 9, 116; *TAB*, Oct. 1907, 216; Jan. 1908, 526; July 1908, 580; Oct. 1910, 237; *BKB*, March 1926, 14; Sept. 1927, 13 suppl.

SHERIDAN: *TAB*, Sept. 1908, 3; March 1911, 100, 108; Oct. 1911, 234; *INP*, Sept. 1908, 838; April 1912, 16; *BKB*, March 1933, 3, 44; Oct. 1935, 40; July 1940, 30; *BP*, March 1964, 19; July 1966, 16.

10. Correspondence, Marian Lawson, Sept., Oct. 1969.

11. Sheridan advt, *INP*, April 1913, 45.

12. Sheridan advt, *BKB*, Jan. 1938, 3.

13. Alan Dutscher, "The Book Business in America." Bernard Rosenberg and David M. White, Eds., *Mass Culture: The Popular Arts in America*. New York: Free Press, 1957, 128.

14. Robert de Graff, Letter to Editor, 1499. Reprinted by permission of R.R. Bowker Company, a Xerox Company, from *Publishers' Weekly*, April 22, 1939. Copyright © 1939 by R.R. Bowker Company.

15. MODERN PAPERBACK PUBLISHING: "The Twenty-first Birthday of 'The Strand Magazine,'" *The Strand* [London], Dec. 1911, 615; "Dollar Books are Still Just a Noble Experiment," *Business Week*, 31 Dec. 1930, 10; Allen Lane, "Penguins and Pelicans," *Penrose Annual*, 1938, 41; Ben Ziven, "A Publisher Looks at the Bindery," *BKB*, Sept. 1948, 53, 79; P.K. Thomajan, "Pocket Book Publishing," *American Printer*, Sept. 1950, 25; H. Strehler,

"Pocket-Books on the Continent," *Penrose Annual*, 1954, 32–33; William E. Williams, *The Penguin Story, 1935–1956*. Harmondsworth: Penguin Books, 1956, 10; "Paperbacks—Menace or Manna?" *BP*, July 1959, 47; Reginald Pound, *The Strand Magazine, 1891–1950*. London: Heinemann, 1966; Correspondence, Marian Lawson, Sept., Oct. 1969; Clarence Petersen, *The Bantam Story: Twenty-five Years of Paperback Publishing*. New York: Bantam Books, 1970.

PENGUIN: *BKB*, Sept. 1939, 100; July 1944, 53; *PW*, 1 May 1967, 91.

POCKET BOOKS: *PW*, 30 April 1932, 1888; 16 Sept. 1968, 52; *BKB*, July 1929, 22; August 1939, 15; April 1940, 51; May 1945, 41; Nov. 1952, 70; *BP*, July 1962, 44.

16. From *Paperbacks in the Schools*, Alexander Butman, Donald Reis, and David Sohn, editors. Copyright © 1963 by Bantam Books, Inc.

17. Schick, 119, 120.

18. MODERN PAPERBACK BINDING: "Hot Melts Build a Market," *Chemical Week*, 18 July 1953, 68, 70; "Resinous Adhesives for Bookbinding," *Chemical Age*, 12 Sept. 1953, 547; J. W. Clement Co., *A Printer's Measure*. Buffalo: 1954; Walter Kubilius, "Automation Seen in Bindery Display, *BP*, August 1957, 30; James Milliken and Winthrop H. Lee, "A Year's Experience with Flexibound," *BP*, August 1957, 36–38; R.J. Nadasky and L.A. Clement, "Dielectric Drying for Perfect Binding," *BP*, Oct. 1958, 39; "High-Speed Bookbinding," *Adhesives Age*, July 1959, 39; W.O. Faxon and Robert E. Fogg, "Mechanical Aspects of Adhesive Binding," *BP*, Dec. 1963, 36–39; Faxon and Fogg, "Adhesive Binding," op. cit., 75, 78; part II, Feb. 1964, 50; Louis Dudek, *Literature and the Press: A History of Printing, Printed Media, and Their Relation to Literature*. Toronto: Ryerson, 1960; Ford Foundation, op. cit., 11, 14, 26; *Reader's Digest*, July 1967, 15–16; Hans Schmoller, "The Paperback Revolution." Raymond Astbury, Ed., *Libraries & The Book Trade*. London: Clive Bingley, 1968, 35; Correspondence, Martini Bookbinding Machinery Company, Oct. 1969.

FLEXIBLE ADHESIVES: *BKB*, Dec. 1937, 42; Jan. 1940, 30; April 1946, 35, 54; August 1947, 49; Oct. 1953, 61; August 1956, 68; Sept. 1961, 69; *BP*, June 1957, 46; Jan. 1959, 41; Feb. 1959, 45; Nov. 1959, 45; Dec. 1959, 36; *BPI*, Feb. 1966, 35; April 1966, 54; July 1966, 55; May 1967, 7; June 1967, 42–43; Nov. 1969, 53.

ADHESIVE BINDERS: *BKB*, August 1952, 35–36; *BP*, March 1959, 34; Nov. 1959, 50; Dec. 1963, 46; May 1964, 43; Sept. 1964, 13; *BI*, first issue 1963, 88; Feb. 1964, 46, 74; August 1964, 15; *BPI*, Oct. 1966, 46; July 1967, 61; Sept. 1967, 67; Nov. 1968, 66; Nov. 1969, 53.

## 7. AMERICA: THE AUTOMATED LINE

1. From *Fifty Books Exhibited by the Institute, 1926*, 1, used with permission of The American Institute of Graphic Arts.

2. From *Fifty Books Exhibited by the Institute, 1926*, 9, used with permission of The American Institute of Graphic Arts.

3. From *Economic Survey of the Book Industry: Final Report*, by O.H.

Cheney, used with permission of the Association of American Publishers. Inc., and R.R. Bowker Company.

4. Otto L. Bettmann, "A Selection of Fifty Books in Germany," 80, quoting Arthur J. Symons. From *Penrose Annual*, 1933, used with permission of Lund, Humphries & Company.

5. From *A Rendezvous with the Book*, by Merle Armitage, used with permission of The Book Press, Inc.

6. Arthur W. Rushmore, "Book Planning, Design and Illustration," *BKB*, Jan. 1945, 59.

7. W. A. Dwiggins, "Trade Book Design," 26. From *Graphic Forms*, by Gyorgy Kepes et al., used with permission of Harvard U. Press.

8. MODERN BOOK DESIGN: Putnam and Putnam, *Authors and Publishers*, op. cit., 16; J.F. Tapley Company, *Why the Present High Costs in Bookbinding*. New York: 1920, 21; Rushmore, op. cit., 59; Book Jacket Designers Guild, Annual Exhibition Catalogs, 1948, 1949, 1952; Thorp, op. cit., 23; "Jackets," *AIGA Journal*, Vol. 3 No. 5 (1951), 8–9; Metzl, op. cit., 37, 55, 60, 64; Madsen, op. cit., 97.

9. The Times "Printing Number" (1912), 2.

10. *"Nelsons" of Edinburgh: A Short History of the Firm.* Reprinted c. 1915 from *The British Printer.*

11. Sheridan advt, *TAB*, July 1909, 605.

12. *BKB*, July 1926, 18, 22.

13. Blaylock, 4–5.

14. Palmer, "Whither Book Publishing and Manufacturing?" op. cit., 75.

15. Dutscher, op. cit., 129.

16. Peter de Florez, "The Coming Revolution in the Bindery," *BP*, June 1964, 67.

17. "System Design," *BPI*, April 1969, 44, quoting Donald J. Maloney.

18. INLINE BOOKWORK: "Warping of Glued Covers," *Paper Box Maker* [New York], Feb. 1897, 18; *"Nelsons" of Edinburgh*, op. cit.; John J. Pleger, "Bookbinding and Printing Establishments," *INP*, June 1916, 369; Palmer, "Whither Book Publishing and Manufacturing?" op. cit., 75, 77; Kubilius, "Automation Comes to the Book Industry," op. cit., 49–50; Lewis Kitcat, "Some Practical Aspects of Book Production: III. The Bookbinder and the Finished Product," *Journal of the Royal Society of Arts* [London], March 1958, 262; Upton, "A Technologist Looks at Books," op. cit., 101, 103–104; "High-Speed Bookbinding," op. cit., 39; Peter de Florez, "Automation's Impact on the Bindery," *BP*, Oct. 1959, 53–54; Gross, op. cit., 285, quoting John Farrar; 108–109, quoting Frank N. Doubleday; de Florez, "The Coming Revolution in the Bindery," op. cit., 67; Peter de Florez, "Binding: Turning Point in Systems Development," *BPI*, Oct. 1967, 66; Myrick, "Some New Advances in Bindery Technology," op. cit., 51; Victor Strauss, "Stop-and-Go or Flow Production," *PW*, 7 Oct. 1968, 74; "The Fully Integrated Bindery," *BPI*, Sept. 1969, 51, 53.

MURRAY-NELSON: *BKB*, Jan. 1949, inside back cover; March 1949, 51; July 1949, 44; *BP*, August 1962, 5.

STEINMANN-WOLFF: *BKB*, Dec. 1937, 32; Sept. 1943, 28–29; *PW*, 2 Oct. 1943, 1355–1356.

MCKIBBIN-BOOK PRESS: *BKB*, May 1940, 20, 67; May 1946, 31; July 1951, 51; Oct. 1953, 40; June 1955, 55; April 1956, 38.

CRAWLEY: *BKB*, August 1947, 13; Feb. 1954, 53; *BP*, March 1964, 17, 65, 67; *BPI*, Feb. 1965, 10; April 1965, 64; Jan. 1969, 71.

SMYTH: *BKB*, Dec. 1944, 25; Feb. 1953, 39–40; April 1953, 41; April 1958, 2–3; Sept. 1958, 6–7; *BPI*, April 1964, 7; June 1965, 70; July 1967, 70.

DE FLOREZ-HANOVER: *BKB*, July 1946, 31; May 1949; Dec. 1949, 61; Sept. 1953, 55; July 1956, 49; *BPI*, Dec. 1965, 46; Feb. 1966, 10; Nov. 1968, 66; March 1969, 72.

19. Brehmer-Hepp literature (Geliot-Hurner-Ewen, Ltd., London).

20. *BPI*, Nov. 1970, 60.

21. AUTOMATED SEWING: Peter de Florez, "Automation's Impact on the Bindery, Part II," *BP*, Nov. 1959, 57; Peter de Florez, "Supplies for Bookmaking: A Look into the Future," *PW*, 6 March 1967, 86–87; Victor Strauss, "Stop-and-Go or Flow Production, Part II," *PW*, 2 Sept. 1968, 66.

SMYTH: *BKB*, Feb. 1944, 30; Dec. 1944, 25; July 1949, 43; Dec. 1954; April 1958, 58; *PW*, 1 Jan. 1968, 59; *BPI*, Jan. 1967, 8; Feb. 1967, 40; Oct. 1967, 69; Feb. 1968, 62–63; Nov. 1968, 67; March 1969, 69; April 1970, 55; August 1970, 50.

OTHER SEWERS: *BKB*, Jan. 1949, 44; *BP*, May 1964, 61; *PW*, 5 Jan. 1970, 65; *BPI*, April 1967, 63; June 1967, 11; April 1968, 31.

## 8. BOOKS FOR THE MILLIONS

1. AIGA, *The Fifty Books*. New York: 1969, quoting Frederick B. Adams, Jr.

2. "The Moving Image," *BPI*, Oct. 1965, 54.

3. From *Most Notorious Victory: Man in an Age of Automation*, by Ben B. Seligman, 106–107, 113, used with permission of The Macmillan Company.

4. C. Peter McColough, "Xerox—and Some New Dimensions." Address to The Investment Analysts Society of Chicago, 25 April 1967.

5. Editorial, *BPI*, Jan. 1969, 67.

6. Hermann Zapf, "Typography for the Future: Applying the New Technology not Refusing it," 54. Reprinted from November 3, 1969, issue of *Publishers' Weekly*, published by R.R. Bowker Company, a Xerox Company. Copyright © by Xerox Corporation.

7. From *Most Notorious Victory: Man in an Age of Automation*, by Ben B. Seligman, 108, used with permission of The Macmillan Company.

8. "GPO Maps Expansion, Improvement Plans," *BP*, Sept. 1962, 66–67, quoting James L. Harrison.

9. Eugene Sitterley, "What Has Happened to Bindery Equipment Research?" *INP*, June 1970, 40.

10. NONBOOK WORK: Bernard Berelson, "Who Reads What Books and

Why?" Rosenberg and White, op. cit., 120–122; "Electronic Reading Machine," *BP* March 1960, 45; Ford Foundation, op. cit., 17–18, 20, 26, 31–32; "Publishing and its Problems," *BPI*, Nov. 1965, 31; "Education," *Time*, 3 Sept. 1965, 52; *Electronic Composing System.* US GPO, 1966; "Microfiche Comes of Age as a Publishing Medium," *BPI*, Dec. 1966, 46; Lawrence Sandek, "Man's World of Facts," *Data Processor* [IBM Corp.], Nov. 1967, 21–22; Maurice T. Smith, "The General Publisher," Astbury, op. cit., 63; Joel A. Roth, "Computer Assisted Instruction," *BPI*, Jan. 1969, 40–45; Joel A. Roth, "To-Order Publishing Comes of Age," *BPI*, April 1969, 39; Curtis G. Benjamin, "Book Publishing's Hidden Bonanza [nonbooks]," *Saturday Review of Literature*, 18 April 1970, 19; Petersen, op. cit., 24.

11. Annual BMI Meeting, *BPI*, Dec. 1966, paraphrasing Dexter Robinson.

12. Comstock & Westcott literature, c. 1969.

13. From *Wide Margins*, by George Palmer Putnam II, used with permission of Harcourt, Brace, Jovanovich, Inc.

14. ADHESIVE-BOUND HARD-COVER BOOKS: George H. Doran, *Chronicles of Barabbas, 1884–1934.* New York: Harcourt, Brace & Co., 1935, 84; "A Summary of 'Adhesive' Binding Techniques," *BKB*, August 1952, 35; Kubilius, "Automation Comes to the Book Industry," op. cit., 60; Milliken and Lee, "A Year's Experience with Flexibound," op. cit., 36–37; Kitcat, "Some Practical Aspects of Book Production," op. cit., 258–267; "High-Speed Bookbinding," op. cit., 39; Blair Hawkes, "Viewpoints on Bindery Automation," *BP*, March 1964, 65–66; "Backbone Preparation for Adhesive Binding," *BPI*, April 1966, 54; Nathan B. Leitner, "Significant Advances Seen for Adhesive Binding Technology," *BPI*, May 1967, 7; Arthur Mayer, "A Look Ahead in Bookbinding Adhesives," *BPI*, June 1967, 42.

LITTLE & IVES: *TAB*, Oct. 1907, 192; March 1908, 86; March 1913, 103; *PW*, 3 Oct. 1936, 1414; *BKB*, June 1933, 44; Sept. 1937, 32; Feb. 1937, 61; March 1946, 24; March 1950, 58–60.

CAHEN-WORLD: *Printing Trade News* [New York], Nov. 1910, 68; *BKB*, March 1926, 14; May 1926, 26; Sept. 1948, 41; Dec. 1961, 36; *BP*, Dec. 1962, 51; Oct. 1963, 119; *PW*, 16 Sept. 1963, 89; 6 July 1964, 122–123; 1 Feb. 1971, 45.

SEARS-KINGSPORT: *PW*, 27 Jan. 1923, 251–252; 14 Feb. 1925, 494–495; 23 May 1925, 1770; 11 July 1925, 99–102; 2 Sept. 1963, 42, 44; 13 July 1964, 151–152; 9 August 1965, 32–33; *BKB*, May 1926, 24; June 1926, 34; June 1950, 36–38; Dec. 1953, 34.

KITCAT-FLEXIBACK: *BKB*, August 1945, 27; Dec. 1946, 33; Jan. 1956, 51.

SATENSTEIN/AB-SP: *BKB*, June 1947, 55; April 1950, 57; July 1950, 29; March 1961, 39; *PW*, 14 Oct. 1963, 86–87; 7 August 1967, 78.

15. From *The World of Books*, by Basil Blackwell, 31, used with permission of J. M. Dent & Sons.

16. "The Automated Book Plant of 1975," *BP*, Sept. 1959, 85.

17. Charles Potter, "Adhesives," *BPI*, July 1966, 57.

18. Smith, "The General Publisher," 69. From *Libraries & The Book Trade*, Raymond Astbury, Ed., used with permission of Clive Bingley, Ltd.

19. Schmoller, "The Paperback Revolution," 39. From *Libraries & The*

*Book Trade*, Raymond Astbury, Ed., used with permission of Clive Bingley, Ltd.

20. Edward H. Roberts, "The Book Trade and the Role of the Library," 183–184, quoting Clive Bingley. From *Libraries & The Book Trade*, Raymond Astbury, Ed., used with permission of Clive Bingley, Ltd.

21. From *Understanding Media*, by Marshall McLuhan, 283 (Signet Ed.). Copyright © 1964 by Marshall McLuhan. Used with permission of McGraw-Hill Book Company.

22. FUTURE BOOKS: "Methods and Materials for Electronic Casemaking and Binding," *BKB*, June 1953, 32; "Electronic Casing-in Method Now in Production," *BKB*, Oct. 1954, 34; "The Automated Book Plant of 1975," op. cit., 83, 85; "Adhesive Suppliers and Edition Binders Dispute 'Antiquated Practices,' Perfect Binding Progress," *BP*, Dec. 1959, 36; Ford Foundation, op. cit., 28; Marshall Lee, "Function and Format in Book Design," *BP*, Feb. 1964, 49; "The Unseen Revolution in Bookbinding [simplified cases]," *BPI*, Oct. 1967; Paul E. Chamberlain, "A Breakthrough in Adhesive Binding," *BPI*, Feb. 1969, 48–51; Dwight Yellen, "A Look at Mass Marketing in the 1970's," *PW*, 24 August 1970, 31–32; "A Roundable Hot-Melt for Hardcover Adhesive Binding," *BPI*, Nov. 1970, 39–41; Leonard Shatzkin, "Stronger Books, Possible Savings [Hellerbond]," *PW*, 16 Nov. 1970, 66–68; Victor Strauss, "Long-Range Prospects in Book Production," *PW*, 14 Dec. 1970, 28–30; "New Technologies [Comprint 90]," *BPI*, Dec. 1970, 44.

MARGOLIS-CHARLTON: *BKB*, April 1942, 37; Sept. 1947, 41; May 1960, 68; *BP*, August 1963, 97; *PW*, 12 June 1967, 101; *BPI*, July 1969, 8.

CAMERON: "The Vanishing Signature," *BPI*, May 1968, 2–5; Paul J. Hartsuch, "New Book Production System," *Graphic Arts Monthly*, Sept. 1968, 54–61; *PW*, 2 Dec. 1968, 56–57; Victor Strauss, "Cameron's New Belt Press," *PW*, 6 Jan. 1969, 58–66; *Business Week*, 5 April 1969, 54; *BPI*, July 1969, 12; *INP*, March 1970, 27; Jeremiah E. Flynn, "Inline Book Production at 2000 Pieces per Minute," *Printing*, Sept. 1970, 41–43; Thomas B. Cosden and Paul D. Doebler, "Taking the Gamble Out of the Book Business," *BPI*, Oct. 1970.

## PART DIVISIONS

Walt Whitman's "After All, Not to Create Only," recited on invitation of the Managers of the American Institute of the City of New York on the opening of their 40th Annual Exhibition, New York, 7 Sept. 1871, of which only portions appear here, was revised by the poet and appears in his *Leaves of Grass* as "Song of the Exposition."

# BIBLIOGRAPHY

ABBOTT, JACOB, *Harper's Story Books: The Harper Establishment, or, How the Story Books are Made*. New York: Harper & Brothers, 1855, 160 pp.

ADAM, PAUL, *Der Bucheinband Seine Technik and Seine Geschichte*. Leipzig: Seemann, 1890, 268 pp, plates.

ADAMS, JOHN, *The House of Kitcat: A Story of Bookbinding, 1798–1948*. London: G. & J. Kitcat, 1948, 64 pp.

ALTICK, RICHARD D., *The English Common Reader: A Social History of the Mass Reading Public, 1800–1900*. Chicago: U. of Chicago Press, 1957, 430 pp.

*The American Bookmaker* [New York], 1885; *The Printer and Bookmaker*, 1897; *The American Printer*, 1900ff.

AMERICAN INSTITUTE OF GRAPHIC ARTS, *Fifty Books Exhibited by the Institute, 1926, with Introduction by W. A. Dwiggins and Frederic G. Melcher*. New York: The John Day Company, 1927, unfolioed.

—, *The Look of the Book*. New York: 1960, 110 pp.

*American Publishers' Circular and Literary Gazette* [New York], 1855; superseded by *Publishers' Weekly*, 1872.

ANDREWS, WILLIAM L., *Bibliopegy in the United States and Kindred Subjects*. New York: Dodd, Mead & Company, 1902, 130 pp.

APPLETON-CENTURY COMPANY, *The House of Appleton-Century*. New York: 1936, 48 pp.

ARMITAGE, MERLE, *Notes on Modern Printing*. New York: William E. Rudge's Sons, 1945, 74 pp.

—, *A Rendezvous with the Book*. New York: George McKibbin & Son, 1949, 30 pp.

ARNETT, JOHN, *An Inquiry into the Nature and Form of the Books of the Ancients: with a History of the Art of Bookbinding. . . .* London: Richard Groombridge, 1837, 212 pp.

AUSTIN, FREDERICK J., *Press Maker, and Manufacturer of Stationers,' Printers,' Bookbinders' and Other Machinery . . .* [catalog]. New York: 1861, 32 pp.

BAIN, JAMES S., *A Bookseller Looks Back*. London: The Macmillan Company, 1940, 304 pp.

BALLOU, ELLEN B., *The Building of the House: Houghton Mifflin's Formative Years*. Boston: Houghton Mifflin, 1970, 695 pp.

BARROW RESEARCH LABORATORY, *Permanence/Durability of the Book: A Two-Year Research Program*. Richmond: W.J. Barrow, 1963.

BERALDI, HENRI, *La Reliure du XIX Siècle*, 4 vols. Paris: L. Conquet, 1895–1897.

BERRY, W. TURNER, and H. EDMUND POOLE, *Annals of Printing: A Chronological Encyclopedia from the Earliest Times to 1950*. London: Blandford Press, 1966, 316 pp.

BETTENDORF, HARRY J., *Paperboard and Paperboard Containers: A History*, Rev. Ed. Chicago: Board Products Publishing Company, 1946, 136 pp.

BLACK, ROBERT K., *The Sadleir-Black Gothic Collection: An Address before the Bibliographical Society of the U. of Virginia*. Charlottesville: U. of Virginia Library, 1949, 15 pp.

BLACKWELL, BASIL, *The World of Books: A Panorama, Foreword by Hugh R. Dent* [Dent Memorial Lecture]. New York: Oxford U. Press, 1932, 52 pp.

BLAYLOCK, FREDERICK R., *Adhesives for the Graphic Arts Industries*. US GPO, 1941, 24 pp.

*Bookbinder* [London], 1887; *The British Bookmaker*, 1890; *The British Printer*, 1894ff.

*Bookbinding* [New York], 1925; *Bookbinding and Book Production*, 1936; superseded by *Book Industry*, 1962.

*Book Industry* [New York], 1963–1964.

*Book Production Industry*, 1964–present.

BOSQUET, EMILE, *La Reliure*. Paris: Lahure, 1894.

BOUCHOT, HENRI, *The Book: Its Printers, Illustrators, and Binders, from Gutenberg to the Present Time*. . . . London: H. Grevel & Company, 1890, 384 pp.

BOUND, CHARLES F., *A Banker Looks at Book Publishing*. New York: R.R. Bowker Company, 1950, 130 pp.

BOWKER, R.R., "Great American Industries: A Printed Book," *Harper's New Monthly Magazine*, July 1887, 165–188.

BRAINARD, NEWTON C., Ed., *The Andrus Bindery: A History of the Shop, 1831–1838*. Hartford: Case, Lockwood & Brainard, 1940, 46 pp.

BRASSINGTON, W. SALT, *A History of the Art of Bookbinding with Some Account of the Books of the Ancients*. New York: The Macmillan Company, 1893, 278 pp.

THE BRITISH MUSEUM, *Bookbindings from the Library of Jean Grolier: A Loan Exhibition*. London: The Trustees of the British Museum, 1965, 78 pp, plates.

BROPHY, JOHN, *Britain Needs Books*. London: National Book Council, 1942, 72 pp.

BUTMAN, ALEXANDER, DONALD REIS, and DAVID SOHN, Eds., *Paperbacks in the Schools*. New York: Bantam Books, 1963, 152 pp.

BUTTERWORTH, BENJAMIN, Ed., *The Growth of Industrial Art*. US GPO, 1892.

CARTER, JOHN, *Binding Variants in English Publishing, 1820–1900*. London: Constable & Company, 1932, 172 pp.

—, *Publisher's Cloth: An Outline History of Publisher's Binding in England, 1820–1900*. New York: R.R. Bowker Company, 1935, 48 pp.

THE CASE, LOCKWOOD & BRAINARD COMPANY, *A Sketch Descriptive of the Printing-Office and Book-Bindery of The Case, Lockwood & Brainard Company*. Hartford: 1877, 40 pp, plates.

CHARVAT, WILLIAM, *Literary Publishing in America, 1790–1850*. Philadelphia: U. of Pennsylvania Press, 1959, 94 pp.

CHENEY, O.H., *Economic Survey of the Book Industry: Final Report*. New York: National Association of Book Publishers, 1931, 338 pp.

—, *Supplementary Report of the Economic Survey of the Book Industry for Bookbinding Executives*. New York: Employing Bookbinders of America, 1932, 70 pp.

CHEW, SAMUEL C., Ed., *Fruit Among the Leaves: An Anniversary Anthology*. New York: Appleton-Century-Crofts, 1950, 535 pp.

CHIVERS, CEDRIC, *Books in Duro-Flexile Binding* [catalog]. Portway, Bath: 1900.

CLAIR, COLIN, *A History of Printing in Britain*. London: Cassell & Company, 1965, 314 pp.

COBDEN-SANDERSON, THOMAS J., *Cosmic Vision*. London: Richard Cobden-Sanderson, 1922, 134 pp, bibliography.

—, *Ecce Mundus: Industrial Ideals and the Book Beautiful*. Hammersmith: Hammersmith Publishing Society, 1902.

—, *The Journals of Thomas James Cobden-Sanderson, 1879–1922*, 2 vols. New York: The Macmillan Company, 1926, 400, 438 pp.

COCKERELL, DOUGLAS, *Some Notes on Bookbinding*. London: Oxford U. Press, 1929, 106 pp.

COLBY, ROBERT A., " 'The Librarian Rules the Roost': The Career of Charles Edward Mudie (1818–1890)." *Wilson Library Bulletin*, April 1952, 623–625.

COOPER, GRACE ROGERS, *The Invention of the Sewing Machine*. Washington, DC: Smithsonian Institution, 1968, 156 pp.

*The Country Life Press, Garden City, New York: Its Garden, its Home, its Sundial*. Garden City: Doubleday, Page & Company, 1913, 56 pp.

CRANE, WALTER, *William Morris to Whistler: Papers and Addresses on Art and Craft and the Commonweal*. London: G. Bell & Sons, 1911, 278 pp.

CROCKETT, A.J., "George Munro, 'The Publisher.' " *The Dalhousie Review*, Spring–Autumn, 1956.

*Crowell, Thomas Young, 1836–1915: A Biographical Sketch*. New York: T.Y. Crowell, 1926, 96 pp.

CUNDALL, JOSEPH, *On Bookbindings Ancient and Modern*. London: G. Bell & Sons, 1881, 132 pp.

DARLEY, LIONEL S., *Bookbinding Then and Now: A Survey of the First Hundred and Seventy-Eight Years of James Burn & Company*. London: Faber & Faber, 1959, 126 pp.

DAVENPORT, CYRIL, *The Book: Its History and Development*. London: Archibald Constable & Company, 1907, 258 pp.

—, *Byways Among English Books*. London: Methuen & Company, 1927, 190 pp.

—, *Roger Payne: English Bookbinder of the Eighteenth Century*. Chicago: The Caxton Club, 1929, 82 pp, plates.

DAWSON, CHARLES E., "Modern Book Covers." *Penrose's Pictorial Annual*, 1908–1909.

DAY, KENNETH, Ed., *Book Typography, 1815–1965: In Europe and the United States of America*. Chicago: U. of Chicago Press, 1965, 402 pp.

DENT, J.M., *The Memoirs of J.M. Dent, 1849–1926, with additions by Hugh R. Dent*. London: J.M. Dent & Sons, 1928, 258 pp.

DERBY, J.C., *Fifty Years among Authors, Books, and Publishers*. New York: Carleton, 1884, 739 pp.

DEUBNER, L., "The Art of the Book in Germany." Charles Holme, Ed., *The Art of the Book*. London: The Studio, 1914.

DEVILLE, ETIENNE, *La Reliure Francaise*, 2 vols. Paris: G. Van Oest, 1930.

DIEHL, EDITH, *Bookbinding: Its Background and Technique*, 2 vols. New York: Rinehart & Company, 1946, 252, 406 pp.

DODD, EDWARD H., JR., *The First Hundred Years: A History of the House of Dodd, Mead, 1839–1939*. New York: 1939, 64 pp.

DODD, GEORGE, *The Curiosities of Industry: Paper, Its Applications and its Novelties*. London: George Routledge & Company, 1853, 24 pp.

—, *Days at the Factories; or, The Manufacturing Industry of Great Britain Described*. . . . London: Charles Knight & Company, 1843, 548 pp.

DONNELLEY, R.R, & SONS COMPANY, *Extra Binding at the Lakeside Press, Chicago*. Chicago: 1925, 20 pp, plates.

—, *A Rod for the Back of the Binder: Some Considerations of Binding with Reference to the Ideals of the Lakeside Press.* Chicago: 1928, 32 pp.

DUFFUS, ROBERT L., *Books: Their Place in a Democracy*. Boston: Houghton Mifflin, 1930, 226 pp.

DUNLAP, GEORGE T., *The Fleeting Years: A Memoir*. New York: 1937.

DUPONT, PAUL, *Une Imprimerie en 1867*. Paris: Paul Dupont [company], 1867, 320 pp.

DWIGGINS, W.A. and L.B. SIEGFRIED, *Extracts from an Investigation into the Physical Properties of Books as They are at Present Published*. Boston: Society of Calligraphers, 1919, 18 pp.

ECKERSTROM, RALPH E., *Contemporary Book Design*. Urbana, Ill.: Beta Phi Mu, 1953, 26 pp.

EDE, CHARLES, Ed., *The Art of the Book*. London: The Studio, 1951, 214 pp.

ENOCH, KURT, "The Paper-Bound Book: Twentieth-Century Publishing Phenomenon." *The Library Quarterly*, July 1954, 211–225.

ESCARPIT, ROBERT, *The Book Revolution*. London: George G. Harrap, 1966, 160 pp.

EXMAN, EUGENE, *The Brothers Harper: A Unique Publishing Partnership and its Impact upon the Cultural Life of America from 1817 to 1853*. New York: Harper & Row, 1965, 416 pp.

—, *The House of Harper: One Hundred and Fifty Years of Publishing*. New York: Harper & Row, 1967, 326 pp.

GARVEY, ELEANOR M. and PETER A. WICK, *The Arts of the French Book, 1900–1965: Illustrated Books of the School of Paris*. Dallas: Southern Methodist U. Press, 1967, 120 pp.

GETTMANN, ROYAL A., *A Victorian Publisher: A Study of the Bentley Papers*. Cambridge: Cambridge U. Press, 1960, 272 pp.

GILLISS, WALTER, *Recollections of the Gilliss Press and its Work during Fifty Years, 1869–1919.* New York: The Grolier Club, 1926, 134 pp.

THE GROLIER CLUB, *Commercial Bookbindings: An Historical Sketch, with Some Mention of an Exhibition of Drawings, Covers, and Books, at The Grolier Club.* New York: The Grolier Club, 1906, 48 pp.

—, *An Exhibition of Some of the Latest Artistic Bindings done at The Club Bindery.* New York: The Grolier Club, 1906, 48 pp.

GROVE, LEE E., "Adhesive Bookbinding: A Practice Reviewed." *Library Resources & Technical Services,* Spring 1962, 143–160.

GUINZBURG, HAROLD K., ROBERT W. FRASE, and THEODORE WALLER, *Books and the Mass Market.* Urbana, Ill.: U. of Illinois Press, 1953, 66 pp.

HALDEMAN-JULIUS, E., *The First Hundred Million.* New York: Simon & Schuster, 1928, 340 pp.

HANNETT, JOHN, *Bibliopegia; or, The Art of Bookbinding,* 4th Ed. London: Simpkin, Marshall & Company and Mozley & Son, 1848, 166 pp.

HARPER, J. HENRY, *The House of Harper: A Century of Publishing in Franklin Square.* New York: 1912, 690 pp.

HARRISON, THOMAS, *The Bookbinding Craft and Industry: An Outline of its History, Development, and Technique.* London: Isaac Pitman & Sons, c. 1925, 128 pp.

HEATH, D.C., & COMPANY, *Forty Years of Service.* Boston: 1925, 62 pp.

HITCHCOCK, FREDERICK H., Ed., *The Building of a Book: A Series of Practical Articles written by Experts in the Various Departments of Book Making and Distributing.* New York: The Grafton Press, 1906, 376 pp.

HOE, ROBERT, *A Lecture on Bookbinding as a Fine Art, Delivered before The Grolier Club.* New York: The Grolier Club, 1886, 36 pp, plates.

*Hoe, R., & Company, Manufacturers of Type, Revolving and Single and Double Cylinder Printing Machines,* . . . [catalog]. New York: 1867, 138 pp.

HOWE, ELLIC, *The London Bookbinders, 1780–1806.* London: Dropmore Press, 1950, 182 pp.

HUSTON, J.A., *Historical Sketch of the Government Printing Office, 1861–1961.* Washington, DC: The Fortson Press, 1916, 100 pp.

HOUGHTON, MIFFLIN & COMPANY, *The Firm of Houghton, Mifflin & Company, Publishers, Boston, New York, Chicago, and London.* Cambridge: Riverside Press, 1889, 48 pp.

HUBBARD, ELBERT, and ELBERT HUBBARD II, *The Book of the Roycrofters: Being a History and Some Comments.* East Aurora: Roycrofters, 1921, 40 pp.

HUXLEY, LEONARD, *The House of Smith Elder.* London: Smith Elder, 1923, 250 pp.

*Inland Printer* [Chicago], 1883–present.

JACKSON, HOLBROOK, *The Printing of Books.* London: Cassell & Company, 1938, 286 pp.

—, *Of the Uses of Books.* New York: Limited Editions Club, 1937, 30 pp.

JAMES, PHILIP, *English Book Illustration, 1800–1900.* London: Penguin Books, 1947, 72 pp, plates.

JENNETT, SEAN, *The Making of Books.* London: Faber & Faber, 1951, 474 pp.

JOHANNSEN, ALBERT, *The House of Beadle and Adams and Its Dime and Nickel Novels: The Story of a Vanished Literature,* 2 vols. Norman: U. of Oklahoma Press, 1950, 476, 444 pp.

JUENGST, GEORGE, & SONS, *The Juengst Gatherer-Collator, Jogger-Stitcher, Wireless-Binder* [catalog]. Croton Falls: c. 1915, 12 pp.

KEPES, GYORGY, et al., *Graphic Forms: The Arts as Related to the Book.* Cambridge: Harvard U. Press, 1949, 128 pp, plates.

KEYNES, GEOFFREY, "William Pickering, Publisher: A Memoir and a Hand-List of his Editions." *The Fleuron,* 1924.

KILGOUR, RAYMOND L., *Estes and Lauriat: A History, 1872–1898. With a Brief Account of Dana Estes & Company, 1898–1914.* Ann Arbor: The U. of Michigan Press, 1957, 238 pp.

KINDER, LOUIS H., *Formulas for Bookbinders.* East Aurora: The Roycrofters, 1905, 115 pp.

KINGMAN, JOHN E., Ed., *Charles A. Juengst, Inventor.* c. 1921.

KNIGHT, CHARLES, *The Old Printer and the Modern Press.* London: John Murray, 1854, 314 pp.

—, *Passages of a Working Life during Half a Century: With a Prelude of Early Reminiscences,* 3 vols. London: Bradbury & Evans, 1865.

—, *The Struggles of a Book against Excessive Taxation.* London: 1850, 16 pp.

KRAMER, SIDNEY, *A History of Stone & Kimball and Herbert S. Stone & Company with a Bibliography of their Publications.* Chicago: Norman W. Forgue, 1940, 380 pp.

LAWLER, THOMAS B., *Seventy Years of Textbook Publishing: A History of Ginn and Company.* Boston: Ginn & Company, 1938, 306 pp.

LEE, MARSHALL, *Bookmaking: The Illustrated Guide to Design & Production.* New York: R.R. Bowker Company, 1965, 400 pp.

LEHMANN-HAUPT, HELLMUT, *The Book in America: A History of the Making and Selling of Books in the United States,* 2nd Ed. New York: R.R. Bowker Company, 1951, 494 pp.

—, Ed., *Bookbinding in America: Three Essays,* Rev. Ed. Hannah D. French, "Early American Bookbinding by Hand"; Joseph W. Rogers, "The Rise of American Edition Binding"; Hellmut Lehmann-Haupt, "On the Rebinding of Old Books." New York; R.R. Bowker Company, 1967, 293 pp.

LEIGHTON, DOUGLAS, *Modern Bookbinding: A Survey and a Prospect.* London: J.M. Dent & Sons, 1935, 64 pp.

LEJARD, ANDRÉ, *The Art of the French Book, from Early Manuscripts to the Present Time.* Paris: Les Editions du Chene, 1947, 166 pp.

LESNÉ, FRANÇOIS A.D., *La Reliure, poème didactique en six chants,* 2nd Ed. Paris: 1827, 382 pp.

LEWIS, FREEMAN, *The Future of Paper-bound Books.* New York: New York Public Library, 1953, 12 pp.

LOCKWOOD, HOWARD, Ed., *American Dictionary of Printing and Bookmaking.* New York: H. Lockwood & Company, 1894, 592 pp.

LYLE, PAUL, "Conventional Binding Operations Paced to Today's Needs." *Printing Progress: A Mid-Century Report.* Cincinnati: The International Association of Printing House Craftsmen, 1959, 323–339.

MCGEHEE, RAMIEL, Ed., *Designed Books: Books and Typography Designed by Merle Armitage.* New York: E. Weyhe, 1938, 128 pp.

MCLEAN, RUARI, *Modern Book Design.* London: Longmans, Green & Company, 1951, 48 pp.

—, *Victorian Book Design & Colour Printing.* New York: Oxford U. Press, 1963, 182 pp.

MCLUHAN, MARSHALL, *Understanding Media: The Extensions of Man.* New York: New American Library, 1964, 311 pp.

MCMURTRIE, DOUGLAS C., *Design in Bookbinding, as Represented in Exhibits at the Sixth Triennial Exposition of Graphic Arts at Milan, Italy. . . .* Chicago: 1938, 24 pp.

—, *The Golden Book: The Story of Fine Books and Bookmaking—Past & Present.* Chicago: Pascal Covici, 1927, 406 pp.

MADISON, CHARLES A., *Book Publishing in America.* New York: McGraw-Hill Book Company, 1966, 628 pp.

MANSFIELD, EDGAR, *Modern Design in Bookbinding: The Work of Edgar Mansfield.* London: Peter Owen, 1966, 120 pp.

MARIUS-MICHEL [company], *La Reliure Francais, Commerciale et Industrielle: Depuis l'invention de l'imprimerie jusqu'à nos jours.* Paris: Morgand & Fatout, 1881, 138 pp.

MARTIN, HENRY, et al., *Le Livre Francais.* Paris: Librairie Nationale d'art et d'histoire, 1924.

MATHEWS, CORNELIUS, *An Appeal to American Authors and the American Press, in behalf of International Copyright.* New York: Wiley & Putnam, 1842, 16 pp.

MATTHEWS, BRANDER, *Bookbindings Old and New: Notes of a Book-Lover, with an Account of The Grolier Club of New York.* New York: The Macmillan Company, 1895, 342 pp.

MATTHEWS, WILLIAM, *Modern Bookbinding Practically Considered: A Lecture.* New York: The Grolier Club, 1889, 96 pp.

MEYNELL, FRANCIS, *English Printed Books.* London: Collins, 1948, 48 pp.

MIDDLETON, BERNARD C., *A History of English Craft Bookbinding Technique.* London: Hafner Publishing Company, 1963, 308 pp, plates.

MISTLER, JEAN, *La Librairie Hachette de 1826 à nos jours.* Paris: Hachette, 1964, 408 pp.

MONTAGUE & FULLER, *A Catalogue of the Latest Improved Bookbinders' and Printers' Machinery. . . .* New York: 1892, 44 pp.

MORRIS, WILLIAM, *The Ideal Book. An Address to the Bibliographical Society of London, 1893.*

MOTT, FRANK L., *A History of American Magazines,* 5 vols. New York: Appleton, 1930–1938; Cambridge: Harvard U. Press, 1957–1968.

MUMBY, FRANK A., *The House of Routledge, 1834–1934: With a History of Kegan Paul, Trench, Trübner and Other Associated Firms.* London: George Routledge & Sons, 1934, 232 pp.

—, *Publishing and Bookselling: A History from the Earliest Times to the Present Day*. New York: R. R. Bowker Company, 1931, 480 pp.

MUNSEY, FRANK A., *The Founding of the Munsey Publishing House*. New York: 1907, 56 pp.

NEWDIGATE, BERNARD, *The Art of the Book*. London: The Studio, 1938.

NEWTON, A. EDWARD, *This Book-Collecting Game*. Boston: Little, Brown & Company, 1928, 410 pp.

NICHOLSON, JAMES B., *A Manual of the Art of Bookbinding: Containing Full Instructions in the Different Branches of Forwarding, Gilding, and Finishing. . . .* Philadelphia: Henry C. Baird, 1856, 318 pp.

NORDHOFF, EVELYN HUNTER, "The Dove's Bindery." *The Chap-Book*, March 1, 1896, 353–370.

OSWALD, JOHN CLYDE, *Printing in the Americas*. New York: Gregg Publishing Company, 1937, 566 pp.

OVERTON, GRANT, *Portrait of a Publisher, and the First Hundred Years of The House of Appleton, 1825–1925*. New York: D. Appleton & Company, 1925, 96 pp.

PALMER, E.W., *A Course in Bookbinding for Vocational Training*. New York: Employing Bookbinders of America, 1927, 452 pp.

*The Paper Box Maker and American Bookbinder* [New York], 1892?

PARTON, JAMES, *History of the Sewing Machine*. Jamestown, N.Y.: The Howe Machine Company, 1872.

*Penguins: A Retrospect, 1931-1951*. Harmondsworth: Penguin Books, 1951, 18 pp.

*Penrose['s Pictorial] Annual*, 1894–present. London: Lund, Humphries & Company.

PETERSON, THEODORE, *Magazines in the Twentieth Century*, 2nd Ed. Urbana, Ill.: U. of Illinois Press, 1964, 484 pp.

PLANT, MARJORIE, *The English Book Trade: An Economic History of the Making and Sale of Books*, 2nd Ed. London: George Allen & Unwin, 1965, 500 pp.

PLEGER, JOHN J., *Bookbinding*, Rev. Ed. Chicago: Inland Printer Company, 1924, 426 pp.

PRIDEAUX, SARAH T., *Bookbinders and their Craft*. New York: Charles Scribner's Sons, 1903, 300 pp.

—, *Modern Bookbindings: Their Design and Decoration*. London: Archibald Constable & Company, 1906, 132 pp.

*Printing and the Mind of Man: An Exhibition of Fine Printing in the King's Library of the British Museum (July–September 1962)*. London: The British Museum.

*Publishers' Weekly* [New York], 1872–present.

PUTNAM, GEORGE HAVEN, *A Memoir of George Palmer Putnam*, 2 vols. New York: G.P. Putnam's Sons, 1903.

PUTNAM, GEORGE PALMER, II, *Wide Margins: A Publisher's Autobiography*. New York: Harcourt, Brace & Company, 1942, 352 pp.

RAMSDEN, CHARLES, *French Bookbinders, 1789–1848*. London: C. Ramsden, 1950, 228 pp.

RANSOM, WILL, *Private Presses and Their Books*. New York: R.R. Bowker Company, 1929, 494 pp.

RINGWALT, J. LUTHER, Ed., *American Encyclopedia of Printing*. Philadelphia: Menamin & Ringwalt, 1871, 512 pp.

RIVIÈRE, ROBERT, & SON [company], *Examples of Bookbinding Executed by Robert Rivière & Son Exhibited at the Leipzig Exhibition in 1914....* London: 1920, 36 pp.

ROGERS, JOSEPH W., *The Industrialization of American Bookbinding*. Master of Science Thesis, School of Library Service, Columbia U., 1937. [abridged in Lehmann-Haupt, Ed.]

ROMER, FRANK, *100 Years of Books*. Jersey City: The Davey Company, 1942.

ROSNER, CHARLES, *The Growth of the Book-Jacket*. Cambridge: Harvard U. Press, 1954, 74 pp.

—, *Printer's Progress: A Comparative Survey of the Craft of Printing, 1851–1951*. Cambridge: Harvard U. Press, 1951, 124 pp.

SADLEIR, MICHAEL, *The Evolution of Publishers' Binding Styles, 1770–1900*. London: Constable & Company, 1930, 96 pp.

SARGENT, GEORGE H., *Lauriat's 1872–1922. Being a Sketch of Early Boston Booksellers with Some Account of Charles E. Lauriat Company. . . .* Boston: 1922, 60 pp.

SCHICK, FRANK L., *The Paperbound Book in America: The History of Paper-Backs and their European Background*. New York: R.R. Bowker Company, 1958, 262 pp.

SCHMIDT-KÜNSEMÜLLER, F.A., *T.J. Cobden-Sanderson as Bookbinder*. Esher, England: The Tabard Press, 1966, 32 pp.

SCUDDER, HORACE E., *Henry Oscar Houghton, A Biographical Outline*. Cambridge: The Riverside Press, 1897, 160 pp.

SHEEHAN, DONALD, *This Was Publishing: A Chronicle of the Book Trade in the Gilded Age*. Bloomington: Indiana U. Press, 1952, 288 pp.

*T.W. & C.B. Sheridan, Manufacturers of Papercutters,' Bookbinders,' Printers,' and Paper-Boxmakers' Machinery* [catalog]. New York: c. 1915, 78 pp.

SHOVE, RAYMOND H., *Cheap Book Production in the United States, 1870 to 1891*. Urbana, Ill.: U. of Illinois Library, 1937, 156 pp.

STEINBERG, S.H., *500 Years of Printing*. Harmondsworth: Penguin Books, 1955, 278 pp.

STEPHEN, GEORGE A., *Commercial Bookbinding: A Description of the Processes and the Various Machines Used*. London: W. John Stonhill & Company, 1910, 76 pp.

—, "Decorative Book Covers." *Penrose's Pictorial Annual*, 1910–1911.

—, *Machine Book-Sewing, with Remarks on Publishers' Bindings*. Aberdeen: The Aberdeen U. Press, 1908, 26 pp.

STERN, MADELEINE B., *Imprints on History: Book Publishers and American Frontiers*. Bloomington: Indiana U. Press, 1956, 492 pp.

STRAUSS, VICTOR, *The Printing Industry: An Introduction to Its Many Branches, Processes and Products*. Washington, DC: Printing Industries of America, 1967, 814 pp.

THE STUDIO, *Modern Book-Bindings & Their Designers*. London: The Studio, Winter 1899–1900, 82 pp.

SWINNERTON, FRANK, *The Bookman's London*. Garden City: Doubleday & Company, 1952, 162 pp.

TAUCHNITZ, BERNHARD [company], *The Harvest: Being the Record of One Hundred Years of Publishing, 1837–1937*. Leipzig: 1937, 76 pp.

THOMPSON, ELBERT A., and LAWRENCE S. THOMPSON, *Fine Binding in America: The Story of The Club Bindery*. Urbana, Ill.: Beta Phi Mu, 1956, 44 pp, plates.

The [London] Times Literary Supplement, "Printing Number." October 13, 1927, 64 pp.

—, "Printing Number." September 10, 1912.

US GOVERNMENT PRINTING OFFICE, *100 GPO Years: 1861–1961. A History of United States Public Printing*. US GPO, 1961, 164 pp.

—, *Theory and Practice of Bookbinding: Apprentice Training Series*. US GPO, 1950, 246 pp.

UNWIN, STANLEY, *The Truth about a Publisher*. New York: The Macmillan Company, 1960, 455 pp.

—, *The Truth about Publishing*. Boston: Houghton Mifflin Company, 1927, 312 pp.

VAN KLEECK, MARY, *Women in the Bookbinding Trade*. New York: Survey Associates, 1913, 270 pp.

VAUGHAN, ALEX J., *Modern Bookbinding: A Treatise Covering Both Letterpress and Stationery Branches of the Trade, with a Section on Finishing and Design*. London: Charles Skilton, 1960, 240 pp.

WALKER, EDWARD, *The Art of Book-Binding, Its Rise and Progress; Including a Descriptive Account of the New York Book Bindery*. New York: Walker, 1850, 64 pp.

WAUGH, ARTHUR, *A Hundred Years of Publishing: Being the Story of Chapman & Hall, Ltd*. London: Chapman & Hall, 1930, 326 pp.

WHEATLEY, HENRY B., *Bookbinding Considered as a Fine Art, Mechanical Art, and Manufacture*. London: William Trounce, 1880, 27 pp.

WIEMELER, IGNATZ, "Bookbinding, Old and New." *The Dolphin*, No. 1, 1933.

—, *Ignatz Wiemeler, Modern Bookbinder*. New York: Museum of Modern Art, 1935, unfolioed.

WILEY, JOHN & SONS, *The First One Hundred and Fifty Years: A History of John Wiley & Sons, Incorporated, 1807–1957*. New York: 1957, 242 pp.

WILLIAMSON, HUGH, *Methods of Book Design: The Practice of an Industrial Craft*, 2nd Ed. London: Oxford U. Press, 1966, 433 pp.

WINTERICH, JOHN T., *The Grolier Club, 1884–1950: An Informal History*. New York: The Grolier Club, 1950, 38 pp.

ZAEHNSDORF, JOSEPH W., *The Art of Bookbinding*. London: G. Bell & Sons, 1890, 190 pp.

—, *A Short History of Bookbinding and a Glossary of Styles and Terms Used in Bookbinding*. . . . London: Zaehnsdorf, 1895, 32 pp.

# INDEX

# Date Due

| | | | |
|---|---|---|---|
| RETURNED 1973 | | | |
| APR 1 7 1995 | | | |
| | | | |
| | | | |
| | | | |
| | | | |
| | | | |
| | | | |
| | | | |
| | | | |
| | | | |
| | | | |
| | | | |
| | | | |
| | | | |